Creating Stores on the Web

2nd Edition

BEN SAWYER

DAVE GREELY

JOE CATAUDELLA

PEACHPIT PRESS

Creating Stores On the Web

Ben Sawyer, Dave Greely, and Joe Cataudella

Peachpit Press
1249 Eighth Street ◦ Berkeley, CA 94710
510/524-2178 ◦ 800/283-9444 ◦ 510/524-2221 (fax)

Find us on the World Wide Web at:
http://www.peachpit.com

Peachpit Press is a division of Addison Wesley Longman

Editor ◦ Corbin Collins
Production Coordinator ◦ Kate Reber
Compositor ◦ Maureen Forys, Happenstance Type-O-Rama
Interior design ◦ Mimi Heft
Cover design ◦ Gee+Chung Design
Cover illustration ◦ Joseph Kelter/BadCat Design, Inc.
Indexer ◦ Rebecca Plunkett

Colophon
This book was created with Quark XPress 4.04 on a Power Computing PowerTower Pro 250. The fonts used were Meta Plus (FontShop), NIMX Quirks (ImageClub), and Missive (T-26). Final output was at Edwards Brothers in Ann Arbor, MI, and it was printed on 50# Arbor Smooth.

ISBN 0-201-70005-0

9 8 7 6 5 4 3 2 1

Printed and bound in the United States of America

To my mother-in-law Sue and my father-in-law Dana for welcoming me into their family eight years ago and not throwing me out yet.

—Dave Greely

To my friend Adam Mattessich, who has helped me through a lot of thick and thin stuff over the years.

—Ben Sawyer

To the Cataudella and Bruno families.

—Joe Cataudella

Acknowledgments

In the spring of 1998, Peachpit Press published the first edition of *Creating Stores on the Web.* Now here we are, approaching the year 2000, and the second edition is hot off the press. Although the first edition received outstanding reviews and helped many people make successful ventures into the world of Web retailing, we think this edition is far better. We have a lot of people to thank for that:

Corbin Collins, our editor and San Francisco tour guide, carried us through the first edition. The lessons we learned from him back then hopefully made this edition a less painful process for him. He definitely made it an enjoyable piece of work for us. His attention to detail never ceases to amaze us. He even amazed us with the information that *w* is sometimes a vowel.

Peachpit Publisher Nancy Aldrich-Ruenzel, for giving us the opportunity to do it the first time, and do it better this time.

Production Coordinator Kate Reber and compositor Maureen Forys for making it all look so attractive.

The entire marketing department, who have really helped sell the first edition and seem extremely excited about this new version—especially Gary-Paul Prince who did more to promote the first book than any PR staff at any of our previous publishers ever did.

And everyone else at Peachpit who contributed to both editions of the book and will help this one be even more successful.

David Rogelberg and Sherry Rogelberg at Studio B, our book agency.

Justine Clegg, a valuable former employee of Digitalmill who is already missed. We wish her luck with her business, **www.art-connections.com**.

Sarah DeMarchi of TRUSTe, for allowing us to use some of her organization's documentation.

Krista Lee at Open Site for helping us understand their myriad of market-leading auction servers and services.

Warren Ashton and Molly Shapiro at iCat for keeping us in the loop and on the site.

The folks at Smartplanet.com who are helping launch a course using *Creating Stores on the Web*. We also want to thank all the professors, teachers, and trainers who have found this book useful for their classrooms as well.

Alan Sawyer, who helped us understand better than ever the nature of interactive shopping, and Leon Schiffman, who helped us understand more about marketing than most would care to know.

All of the people who contributed to the outstanding stores that are featured in the book.

Ben and Dave would like to thank Joe Cataudella for adding a voice of experience.

Joe would also like to acknowledge the help of David A. Bango and Dominick Bruno for their help in building Tronix and, of course, all of Tronix's customers.

Finally, we would all like to thank the many readers of the first edition, especially those who wrote to us, and those who visited www.storebuilder.com or posted recommendations and reviews on their own Web sites. Thanks for making the first edition (even with its faults) a great success.

Table of Contents

PART I

Introduction

Before you learn how to build and manage an online store, it is important to know why you should do so. Part I answers that question and also shows you how Tronix and other Web retailers have survived and thrived. You'll also learn why people shop online and why they don't, how many are doing so now and how many are expected to do so in the future. Part I also introduces some proven Web store business models.

Part I Table of Contents

CHAPTER ONE

Frequently Asked Questions

Let's cut to the chase. If you're like most people, you have questions, and it's likely that some of them are answered right here.

What kind of person does it take to run an online store?

An aggressive one! Running an online store takes the same kind of personal traits that are necessary to run any business. You have to be committed, a bit of a risk taker, willing to work long and late hours, and driven to succeed. Being a little crazy doesn't hurt either. Online stores are a new frontier.

You also have to be organized and able to deal with setbacks without flipping out. You have be committed to providing better customer service than your competitors. And if you ever want to grow past a one- or two-person operation, you need to have vision and a clearly defined plan.

It also takes someone who is willing to learn and change. Internet commerce is a growing field that will mature over the next few years. Be prepared to grow with it.

How much will it cost to get my store up and running?

There are so many variables, it's tough to put an exact figure on it. Will you hire a lawyer and an accountant, or will you try to deal with incorporation and tax issues on your own? Do you plan to work out of an office or your home? Will you have any employees? Do you plan to start with a large inventory of products or will you order as demand warrants? Can you build your own Web site or will you hire someone to do it for you? All of these factors will determine how much money you will spend to get your store launched.

Tronix's entire initial investment was about $12,000. Of course, we didn't have much of a cushion for inventory, but in our case we stocked only what had already been ordered. Today it is easy for large companies to spend an average of $1 million to build an initial e-commerce site. A medium-sized company can expect to spend thousands of dollars to enable an e-commerce store. However, small companies can avoid high costs by keeping things simple, using the various store-hosting services, and being frugal. You should expect to continuously spend money as you build out from humble beginnings.

What equipment and software do I need?

A computer!

OK, there's a bit more to it than that. You'll need to download and install the top two Web browsers—Netscape Communicator (or Navigator) and Microsoft Internet Explorer. You'll have to choose email and newsgroup-reading software, a File Transfer Protocol (FTP) program to upload files to your site, a visual Web authoring tool and an HTML code editor, image editing software, a point-of-sale program, shipping and tracking software (available from the various shipping companies), a scanner, and possibly a digital camera.

You might also purchase accounts on America Online and CompuServe if you want to converse in their private bulletin boards and chat rooms as part of your store's community-building strategy.

Most small-sized store creators will want to choose a hosted store solution (many are profiled in this book) or a Web hosting solution that includes some e-commerce additions. If you intend to run your own server (as opposed to using a store-hosting service) you'll need to acquire a dedicated server (you can lease them) and choose which e-commerce server software to use. Do-it-yourselfers will also need to consider what credit card processing technology to use, as well as optional tax-calculating software, traffic-reporting software, and more.

To find out what some of your options are, check out Chapter 6.

You'll also need a good deal of equipment for shipping purposes. Packing materials, boxes, a shipping table on which to pack boxes, a scale to keep shipping charges accurate, etc. For more about shipping-related needs, see Chapter 17.

Can I run my store out of my house or apartment or should I find an office?

That largely depends on the volume of business you're doing and, of course, the size of your home. If you're just getting started, don't have an overwhelming inventory, and don't have the money yet to spend on an office, working out of your home may be your best—or only—option.

If you have an empty basement or garage in which you have absolute privacy and which is capable of being wired for phones and perhaps a cable modem or ISDN connection, using such a space to limit your overhead might be a good idea. However, as your business grows, you'll probably need an office for a number of reasons.

One reason is to separate your work from the rest of your life. No matter how hard you try, you'll never be able to escape work if it's just a few steps away. Although starting any small business requires a strong commitment of both time and effort, you do need to be able to get away from it or you'll eventually grow tired of your so-called life and bag the whole thing. And no matter how many times you tell your kids to stay away while you're working, eventually one of them will skin his or her knee and coming running for your help. Or they'll just decide they're bored and want to play.

Another consideration is where you'll warehouse your goods. Sometimes you'll store them in your own office, other times you'll want a separate warehouse (preferably located near overnight-shipping facilities). Many larger Web retailers warehouse items separately from their offices, and some even set up multiple warehouses around the world to facilitate fast and inexpensive shipping to their customers. For smaller-sized stores, there are also pick 'n' pack operations that will rent you a piece of a warehouse, and will also process and ship your orders for a fee. One thing to consider when choosing an office location is whether you'll locate the goods you sell on or off your office premises.

As your business grows, you just won't have the space to run your store out of your home. You also have to be aware of local zoning laws. Some residential neighborhoods don't allow business to be conducted in them, although a small operation in a basement will likely be acceptable. And your city or town may be willing to make exceptions to existing codes, assuming your business is not detrimental to the quality of life of your neighboors and doesn't affect property values in the area.

So, to answer your two-part question, yes and yes.

How many employees do I need? Can I do it myself?

That's the beauty of running an online store. You *can* do it yourself. Tronix started that way and is still a one-person operation (with a friend occasionally helping out). Sure you'll need some help getting started—a lawyer, an accountant, and someone to design your site if you decide you can afford it or realize you don't have the ability to do it yourself.

Other than that, you can go it alone and add employees as growth warrants. You'll work long and hard, but that's a given for any small business owner. And no matter how big your business gets, you'll never need to hire someone to staff the cash register and lock up on Saturday night.

Remember also that you can outsource many chores like shipping and warehousing. The downside to that is not having direct control over those people and what they do. As you'll see with Tronix, small stores on the Web thrive through very close personal attention to every detail. If you can outsource labor-intensive work, that's great. Just be sure it doesn't jeopardize your ability to closely maintain impeccable and specialized service.

How much money can I make?

That depends on what you sell, how organized you are, how well you publicize your store, and so on. As with a traditional store, your future is in your hands. Some people start a small community restaurant and they're happy to remain at that level. And some become McDonald's.

The opportunity to make money on the Web is expected to grow dramatically as the public becomes more aware of its advantages and less concerned about placing credit card orders. According to a study by Boston Consulting Group, the online retailing revenue for 1999 was expected to be more than $36 billion in North America—a 145 percent increase over 1998. However, the top 50 sites accounted for almost 75 percent of the market in 1998. For more figures and analysis, see Chapter 4.

The opportunity to make a lot of money is there and is only expected to increase.

What are some advantages and disadvantages to running an online store?

There are plenty of both. First the bad news:

When you run an online store, you're at the mercy of your Internet Service Provider. If the ISP goes down, you go down. Also, since it's easy for competitors to get started, this is a very competitive field. Since e-commerce is still relatively new, your pool of customers can be small, and you have to really reach out to those potential customers. Since you don't have a storefront on Main Street, people aren't going to just walk by, poke their heads in, and buy something. If you don't make yourself known to potential customers, they may never find you. And if you treat one of those customers poorly, word can spread very rapidly on Usenet.

You can also fall prey to stores that have the ability to stock larger inventory, provide better customer service, and do more extensive marketing, but that is true as well of traditional stores. You either need some technical ability or, if you don't have those skills, the money to pay someone who does. There are security and fraud issues, and running an online store can be extremely time-consuming.

Now the good news:

Your startup costs are potentially much lower than those of a traditional store-owner. Operating on the Web allows you to have an immediate international sales presence from wherever you decide to set up shop. Speaking of which, you can set up shop anywhere in the world provided you have good Internet access. There is no need to relocate.

You can also create a personalized shopping experience. Depending on your budget, there are a number of high-end software products that help guide shoppers to the items they want. You have the option of providing electronically distributed goods for immediate fulfillment. Small operations with slim inventories can more effectively compete with larger companies. As long as your ISP doesn't go down, you can be open 24 hours a day, 365 days a year without hiring anyone.

If that isn't enough, there's a book of more reasons to follow.

How much content do I need to generate?

You can either generate your own product descriptions or rely on the manufacturers' literature, assuming you don't make the products you sell. Your company will need to provide and update the content for pages dealing with company policy, common questions, what's new, shipping information, and so on. News and reviews of products can be culled from other sources.

You'll also have to type in prices and product descriptions, even if they've been provided for you. Although you'll have to generate a large percentage of your site's content, it won't account for the majority of your total workload.

Content will always be a costly proposition. It takes time to develop good written content, scan photos, collect reviews, and more. However, good content can be great for sales, especially if you provide better information than your competitors.

The key is finding the right balance between the time needed to create content, how good the content is, and how much it helps your sales. Some of the high-end Web stores such as Amazon.com use sophisticated bulletin boards and review features to generate content from their customers. That isn't too hard to do, and the more creative you can be about generating good e-commerce content without spending time and money, the better.

Are there any specific laws and regulations covering online stores?

In short, yes. In medium, get a lawyer. In a long-winded answer, there is a plethora of laws governing both the online and retail universes that will affect your business.

A lot of Internet law has yet to be developed—cases either haven't come up or are still pending. As a store-owner, you need to stay on top of the news and have a lawyer who can keep you apprised of the shifting legal winds. Some good online legal sources are FindLaw (www.findlaw.com), the Cyberspace Law Center (www.cybersquirrel.com/clc/), the Cyber

Law Encyclopedia (gahtan.com/techlaw/home.htm) by Alan M. Gahtan, CyberSpace Law (www.ll.georgetown.edu/lr/rs/cyber.html) by the Georgetown University Law School, and the Web Law FAQ (www.patents.com/weblaw.sht).

Many of the legal issues are the same as those traditional stores deal with: advertising regulations, export laws, customs, guidelines for shipping perishables, and so on. Interstate commerce as it pertains to the Web remains an unresolved issue.

The only legal advice we're qualified to give is this: Consult an expert. You should never assume you are sure about anything. If you have even an inkling that you might be misinterpreting or overlooking a law, talk to your lawyer. There's nothing like a temporary shutdown and a fine to kill your cash flow. For more legal information, see Chapter 21.

How do I find a good lawyer?

There are plenty of lawyers out there. Some would say there are too many. It's important to find a good business lawyer who is sensitive to your needs as a new business owner, if you're just starting out. You should be able to find a good lawyer without dragging your business down with legal expenses.

There are some lawyers currently specializing in Internet-related law, but since much of the law concerning the Internet is undeveloped, there isn't a huge need to retain a lawyer with an Internet specialty. A good business attorney can quickly get up to speed on any Internet-specific law.

If you don't know a lawyer, ask around. Someone you know will almost surely be able to point you in the right direction. If not, ask the owners of similar-sized businesses to recommend a lawyer.

What sells best on the Web? What should I sell?

As the Internet has grown in recent years, companies of all sizes are selling nearly everything online. What has worked among the early entrants have been small commodity-oriented items such as books, CDs, video games, software, and so on. These items are easy to ship, are bought in high frequency all over the world, have extremely large selections, and are relatively low in cost. But don't limit your options to these. What you decide to sell is up to you.

Something to think about is a computer-related product, since by definition nearly everyone shopping online is a computer owner. Tronix has been successful in selling computer games in part because the people who buy them are likely to be online.

In more recent years, non-commodity items have become all the rage as sites like eBay enable huge online flea-markets that attract would-be and professional collectors from all over the world to shop for antiques, rare goods, and simple used items.The best advice, though, is to sell something you are enthusiastic and knowledgeable about. If you think roughing it is not having a cable modem for your Internet connection, don't sell hiking gear. And if you think punk is the only music worth listening to, don't sell violins. For more on auctions, see Chapter 25.

Of course, you may be just taking your traditional store online, in which case you'll know which of your products sell best.

Once I've started selling things, how do I get the products to the customers?

You have a number of shipping options that you can make available to your customers. Depending on how quickly your customers want their products, and how much they want to pay in shipping charges, you can ship using everything from standard first class mail to FedEx First Overnight.

The key to making the shipping process easy is spending the time to research the various options and decide which shipping company or companies best suit your needs. You'll probably patch together a quilt of shipping coverage that meets all the needs and demands of your customers. To learn more about this, ship yourself to Chapter 17.

Can I make my store virtual?

Your marketing and sales are virtual. Fulfillment companies make it possible to run a completely virtual store in which you never see a product or pack a box. Expect to see an increase in these large warehouses, which store your inventory for you. Web merchants pay a storage fee and when orders come in, the merchants simply tell the warehouse what to send and where to send it. Passing along the risk of holding inventory is the difference between being very virtual and being totally virtual.

Is there anything I can sell and distribute directly over the Web?

The Web isn't just a place to sell goods, it can also be an excellent distribution medium for certain items, provided they are electronically transferable. (Please email us if you have figured out how to download milk and eggs.)

While most stores sell goods that have to be shipped to users, a number of stores don't. For example, music stores eventually will transfer your new CD to you electronically. Many software stores are already using ESD (Electronic Software Distribution) instead of shipping their products to the user on disk or CD. The software is downloaded directly over the Internet.

Electronic distribution is not limited to music or software. Expedia (**expedia.msn.com**), Microsoft's airline tickets and travel services "store," sells airline tickets that are nothing more than a password to be given at the gate. This same type of password sale will eventually be used for all sorts of things, like car rentals, hotel rooms, movie tickets, concert tickets, and more. Eventually these items could even be transferred to so-called *smart cards,* which you just slide through a scanner as you walk through the terminal gate or into your favorite theater.

Three keys to electronically distributed sales are security, bandwidth, and record keeping. Security is needed to protect items like distributed music and software from being easily replicated by end users. Also, since the product itself is stored on a server, no one wants to have a virtual break-in where a hacker can copy all the wares and distribute them for free. Bandwidth is crucial because end users need fast access such as that provided by a T-1, ISDN, or cable modem to receive a full-length CD, movie, or video game. Finally, record keeping is critical because it's harder to count how many copies have been properly sold through electronic distribution. That is why companies have created sophisticated and secure systems that will tell companies how many downloads of a top software package have been properly handled by a particular merchant.

The technology is still catching up, but it won't be long before a number of major products will be bought and distributed directly over the Web.

Should I consider combining my traditional store with an online store?

Yes. Well, maybe. Let it be said that not everyone has to be on the Web. A store that's doing well might not do any better if taken to the Web. And a struggling store won't necessarily be saved by the Web. Sometimes building a site can even be a mess, sucking out the money and time you have and creating headaches you don't want.

However, existing traditional stores have a number of compelling reasons to get online and compete for sales. The most obvious reasons to get online are to expand sales and avoid losing sales to competitors who are online. However, why take the "scared stiff" approach? Existing stores should be compelled to go online by the inherent advantages they have over cyber-only competitors.

An existing store already has a lot of the infrastructure set up for such an operation. It will already have stock, distribution relationships, shipping accounts, product knowledge, a name, and a customer base. The trick is transferring your store's ambience, reputation, and operational style—your "brand"—so that it shines through on the Web. Let your traditional customers know you're on the Web by posting your URL in your store and on all of your mailings, stationery, business cards, and so on.

Maine-based mail-order and retail behemoth L.L. Bean (**www.llbean.com**) is a great example. The company thrives on its reputation for excellent customer service, product knowledge, and outdoors expertise. When L.L. Bean launched its carefully created Web site, all this was apparent. L.L. Bean didn't immediately accept orders on its site, explaining that it would wait until it could guarantee its customers' transactions would be safe. L.L. Bean also warned that color representation of items shown on the Web was not an exact match to reality. These were classic reinforcements of L.L. Bean's reputation for customer service and also smart public relations moves.

L.L. Bean also launched with an extensive database of park and camping site information. Not only was this interesting content to offer as a draw to the site, but it also reinforced L.L. Bean's image as an expert in camping and outdoor activities.

As L.L. Bean shows, traditional retailers can benefit from having a Web presence. But you don't have to rush and stumble. Instead, create a true cyberspace equivalent to your existing store. The best online stores with real-world components are the ones that are able to operate as a totally integrated entity and together are able to attract, retain, and service happy customers.

A study commissioned by Shop.org and conducted by the Boston Consulting Group found that online retailers spend about $42 to acquire each new customer, while retailers who have a presence offline *and* online spend about $22 per customer. And although those offline retailers spend more to keep their customers, the study also found that retailers who sell online and offline pull in 62 percent of online revenues.

What are some of the most successful online stores?

The most successful online stores have been pioneers that launched interesting new ways to shop online but didn't forget that online stores, like traditional stores, have to be focused, have to provide outstanding customer service, and must create an interesting shopping experience.

However, *successful* is a relative term. Some operations that are considered successful haven't actually turned a profit yet. These stores, such as Amazon.com, are considered successful because they are projected to earn a profit once a critical mass of accustomed online shoppers is available.

Then there are stores like Tronix Multimedia—smaller operations that are run profitably on shoestring budgets by aggressive proprietors who have combined a good store choice with a readily available market and built a loyal clientele. Though most of these stores will never reach millions of dollars in sales, they don't have to in order to be profitable and provide excellent returns for their owners.

Some traditional retailers have also done well building a Web presence. Although not every store has successfully managed to add online sales to its repertoire, some stores and catalogs such as L.L. Bean.com, Insight.com, and Walmart.com have taken early leads.

What are online auctions?

Most online auctions deal with computer-related items, while some have gone into other areas of merchandise. Online auctions are a newer phenomenon than online stores, but there is an increasing number of players. The big difference between stores and auctions, besides the way you procure goods, is the entertainment value involved in auction sites. Online auctions are also able to generate large profit margins by purchasing excess goods at well below retail price, starting the bidding at less than that, and riding a bidding process that drives the final price well past what the auctioneer paid but still well below the retail price. Everyone goes home happy.

Onsale, Inc. (www.onsale.com) was the early leader in the online auction battle. Onsale requires participants to bid upward in $25 increments to help guarantee lucrative profit margins. But although Onsale, which recently merged with software/computer online retailing store Egghead, may have been the early leader, mention Internet auctions today and most people will think, "eBay!" (www.ebay.com). eBay enables people to sell goods online in an auction style and has become the leader in online auctions and personal selling. Amazon.com, Lycos, and others have also jumped into the personal auction fray, but it is eBay that pioneered the concept and remains the leader.

If you want to set up an auction for a few goods, eBay and Amazon.com are great services to use. But you can also set up an auction-based store of your own using specialized auction packages such as OpenSite Auction, which is used by many major auction sites on the Web. In Chapter 25, you will find more information on developing an auction-oriented store.

What's the difference between simply selling something online and running an online store?

It's the same difference between setting up a lemonade stand in front of your house and opening a store that happens to sell lemonade.

The online equivalent of a lemonade stand would be to simply go online and inform people that you have a particular item that you'd like to sell, and anyone who is interested can contact you via email, regular mail, or phone.

Building an online store is much more involved. You'll probably be selling a variety of related products through a virtual inventory. You'll have to make your store known to potential customers and work to get them and keep them. In short, selling something online takes no time, little effort, and will likely provide minimal income. Opening an online store requires long hours of work, tireless effort, and will hopefully provide you with a living. Selling online might be a hobby or a means of selling one specific service or product. Running an online store is about selling an entire array of services and products. It is also about selling the store itself.

Isn't online retailing really competitive? Will I be able to succeed?

Online selling is extremely competitive; so is selling cars, insurance, or anything else. As an online store owner, you must find out exactly who your competition is. Make sure you can answer the following questions.

- How many online companies are selling similar products?
- What are their prices and shipping options?
- How fast are they getting their products to their customers?

- What is the word of mouth on Usenet newsgroups about your competition?
- How slick/functional are their Web sites?
- Where does your competition advertise (e.g., links, major magazines)?

Will you be able to succeed? Of course you will be able to succeed. That doesn't mean you will. A little luck never hurts, but success, as Boston Celtics coach Rick Pitino says, is a choice. Cliche alert: You'll get out of it what you put into it.

Can I just open my store and let the orders roll in?

That would be nice, wouldn't it? Unfortunately you can no more do that than you could open a store on a rural road, never advertise, and stay in business for more than a couple of months. In other words, NO!

There are a number of things you should do to increase your visibility—so many in fact that we have an entire section devoted to promoting your store. Chapter 10 will show you how to find customers through Usenet, online forums, and referrals. Chapter 11 discusses promoting your store on the Internet: submitting to search engines, where to get your store listed, how to do link exchanges, how to set up leads and bounty programs, and more. Chapter 12 will show you how to advertise on a shoestring budget. And Chapter 13 focuses on international sales. These chapters will show you not only what to do, but also what not to do.

What is spam? Is it a good thing?

Spam is unsolicited email sent out in bulk without any regard to the recipients' interest in the subject. This type of spam, unlike the canned meat of the same name, is not so good. If you decide to use spam as a way to promote your store, be prepared to incur the wrath of a large number of people. You will probably lose more customers than you gain. If you happen to annoy a hacker, you might end up with a trashed Web site. There are plenty of ways to promote your store without spam.

I don't know much about computers, let alone HTML code. What should I learn before opening my online store?

If you're the management type, you might just outsource the entire project, set the goals, pay the experts to build you a killer store, and watch the cash roll in. If you're in the real world, you'll want to learn some fundamentals and dig in a little so that you can keep your costs low and stay on top of the ever-changing Internet. The best management comes from being able to do the work but choosing, for other compelling reasons, not to. That way, no one will pull a fast one on you and you can step in when something goes wrong.

You should be familiar with how to use a computer and you should pick up some Internet experience. After you know your way around, you'll want to learn some HTML and how to use a basic HTML code editor. You don't need to be an expert but some basics will help. To gain this knowledge, you can start with this book. You should also look into some other books and check out some of the major online resources and guides listed throughout this book. There is a lot of learning to do, but there are some very good aides available—especially the ones listed in this book.

For those of you more versed in the Web, we recommend that you get intimately familiar with a top-rate email package. As you'll learn later, your ability to command an email program is paramount. Brush up on the ability to quickly edit Web pages and learn the ins and outs of uploading and downloading from your site. It will be critical to know how to make minor edits and changes throughout the life of your store. You might also want to learn how to operate a scanner and/or digital camera and subsequently fix up the images in a good image editing program.

For those of you who are computer experts but not well-versed in the retailing trade, stop thinking you're ready to go. Running a store on the Web is a lot more than just hacking out some cool HTML code and uploading JPEGs. You need to provide top-notch customer service, make correct orders, maintain stock, deal with the local UPS driver, and collect and maintain all the taxes and money. This stuff is enough to make even the most knowledgeable Java programmer curl into the fetal position. We're here to help.

Should I hire someone to develop my site, or should I do it myself?

That depends on your knowledge, your willingness to learn, and your cash flow. If you don't know HTML, don't care to know HTML, and have enough money, you can have someone do the work for you. If you're an established retailer like L.L. Bean or Eddie Bauer looking to build a Web presence, of course you'll want to hire someone to do the work. But if you're a small startup, learning HTML will allow you to do your own site maintenance while keeping your costs low.

Designing your own site is also a creative, if grueling, process. It can be satisfying to put together your own site from scratch, much like creating a piece of art. Anyone can buy a painting and hang it in the living room. Few people can create that painting themselves.

Are there any "Shop in a Box" products available?

Yes. An example is Yahoo Store (**store.yahoo.com**), which is a combination authoring tool and hosting service. You can build your store on their browser and then the company serves your finished site.

You don't have to know any HTML (although you can take advantage of your HTML skills if you have them); you just enter the information you want to provide, such as names, prices, and descriptions. You can update your site as often as you want and all you need for software is an ordinary browser: Netscape Navigator or Microsoft Internet Explorer.

Chapter 23 covers iCat Commerce Online.

What are Net.Commerce, Open Market Transact, and Microsoft Site Server?

Net.Commerce is IBM's main e-commerce Web server. Open Market's Transact is another major e-commerce server, and Site Server (formerly Merchant Server) is Microsoft's e-commerce package. All of these programs are high-end Web servers devoted to building Internet storefronts and e-commerce sites. While they are major programs for creating a shopping environment, tracking orders and users, obtaining demographic information, and securing payments, these programs would be overkill for most smaller store sites. And as good as they are, they do leave a lot of store building work for you. Plus their costs almost certainly place them outside the budget of a start-up business owner. However, if you're building a major e-commerce site (one that might receive thousands of orders a day), you might check into these packages and others, such as Broadvision.

What are online malls and how do they work?

The idea behind online malls is similar to that of traditional shopping malls. A developer will launch a site on the Web that offers entrances and integrated shopping experiences across a multitude of product lines and vendors. Everyone is under the same roof; that roof could be the same URL or a similar-looking interface with different vendors.

Behind the scenes, many of the stores run on the same server, taking advantage of a unified shopping infrastructure, including credit card checking, digital cash acceptance, personalization tools, and so on. The mall operator charges vendors a rental fee for space on the system or takes a percentage of every transaction. As a small operator, launching a store as part of an online mall allows you to reside on a server that has been specifically created for online selling. The mall operator may also offer other services, such as promotions help and design assistance. The downside is that you might not have as much control over your site.

The first malls were on the specialized online services like America Online and CompuServe. However, several groups—including IBM—have experimented with Web-based malls. There is still a question about how well the mall concept will translate to the Web. Since any site is as close as any other site on the Web, how important it is to have a store located on the cyberspace equivalent of the local mega-mall?

Instead, what may arise are closer affiliations and seamless linking and purchasing ability between vendors selling complementary goods. It won't exactly be a mall, but the concept of pulling a variety of stores together for a unified online shopping experience could be powerful. For example, if you sell specialty food goods you might put your store on an online mall that hosts hundreds of other specialty food vendors.

By attracting traffic to this one-stop URL, every individual vendor can potentially benefit. And being affiliated with a mall doesn't mean you can't have your own separate store on the Web. Many sites are affiliated with different malls and other "vendor grouping" initiatives to build traffic.

I hear there is a risk involved in accepting credit card orders. Should I accept them?

Purchasing goods over the Internet using a credit card is becoming a more secure process, although it is not yet perfect. As the industry moves closer to a secure transaction standard, credit card purchases will continue to become less worrisome.

Whether or not you accept credit cards is up to you. Most Web stores, including Tronix, accept them. The main risk is to the shoppers; as long as they understand that no transaction can be guaranteed secure, it's up to them to decide whether or not they want to send their credit card number off into cyberspace.

In a purely business sense, the more payment options your store offers, the better your sales will be. In the end, it's tough to run a successful cyberstore without accepting credit cards.

What other kinds of security risks do I have to worry about?

The biggest risk is fraudulent credit card usage and the proper handling of customers' personal email information. You also need to make sure your provider is secure enough to block break-ins. To learn more about eliminating these risks, see Chapter 16.

What are SET, SSL, e-cash, and TRUSTe?

SET (Secure Electronic Transaction) is an open industry standard detailing the use of payment cards over open networks like the Internet. SET uses digital certificates to authenticate parties involved in a transaction. Introduced by Visa and MasterCard, with assistance from technology partners IBM, Terisa Systems, GTE, VeriSign, RSA, Netscape, Microsoft and SAIC, the SET specification was completed in May 1997. The SET consortium is working on creating a SET software compliance process; a structure to manage and issue the SET digital certificates to the payment brands; validation of vendor software against the 1.0 spec and the deployment into the global market; roll-out of programs through financial institutions, merchants, and cardholders.

SSL (Secure Sockets Layer) was introduced on Netscape 2.0 as a technology to protect credit card numbers. Users are often advised if they are using an older browser without built-in SSL to phone in their order.

E-cash systems such as Digicash and NetCash allow the customer to deposit money into an account and then use that account to purchase items off the Internet. E-cash is untraceable, which improves privacy. You can lose only as much cash as is in your electronic wallet, as opposed to someone stealing your credit card number and maxing it out. However, e-cash is uninsured. If your hard drive crashes or your e-bank goes under, there is no way to retrieve the lost cash.

IBM is also launching a payment server called eTill, which will allow Web merchants to accept a variety of forms of payment.

TRUSTe is a coalition that has been formed to limit the amount of junk email you get. If a store has a TRUSTe tag, that store agrees not to release any of its customers' information to other businesses or to mailing list companies.

I've heard a lot about VeriSign. Who are they?

VeriSign, Inc. (**www.verisign.com**) provides digital authentication services and products for electronic commerce and other forms of secure communications. Digital IDs are crucial to establishing confidence in the security of electronic transactions. A Digital ID binds a person's or company's identity to a digital key that can be used to conduct secure communications or transactions. The Digital ID is intended to give the parties involved in a transaction confidence in its origin and can then be attached to electronic transactions and communications as the critical authentication component.

VeriSign was selected by Visa in July 1997 to operate an Internet-based authentication service for electronic commerce solutions based on SET. VeriSign will operate the Digital ID service for Visa which, in turn, will make it available for Visa member financial institutions wanting to roll out secure electronic commerce services.

Don't confuse VeriSign with VeriFone, the company that was purchased by Hewlett-Packard and which manufactures and provides services for credit card transaction equipment.

Are there any good references to help online store proprietors?

Some of the best information will come from simply checking out other established Web sites. There are also a number of good books out there, including *Getting Hits: The Definitive Guide to Promoting Your Website* by Don Sellers (Peachpit Press) and *How to Grow Your Business on the Internet* by Vince Emery (Coriolis Group Books).

There are also some Usenet spots such as alt.business.misc, comp.internet.net-happenings, and alt.internet.commerce where online merchants can share ideas. To search for more Usenet spots, try searching with Deja.com (www.deja.com).

Of course we're partial to this book. You can also search this book's companion Web site, www.storebuilder.com, which has links to more information and tools to help you build your online store.

All right, I'm going to start an online store. Where do I start?

That's easy. Read this book.

CHAPTER TWO

The Story of Tronix

Since launching Tronix in late 1993, Joe Cataudella, a long-time video game devotee, has seen the World Wide Web—and online retailing—change dramatically as the technology has allowed for snappier graphics and more secure transactions and as consumers have grown more comfortable shopping online. Tronix has gone from a struggling start-up selling five or six games a day to an established online presence handling dozens of orders daily.

Since co-authoring the first edition of *Creating Stores on the Web*, Cataudella has seen business grow substantially. In addition to being profiled in numerous laudatory magazine articles, Tronix has become more adept in preparing orders in advance. Cataudella has also worked hard to automate more functions on the Tronix Web site and in the office. While the competition has increased dramatically, so has Tronix's efficiency.

Through it all, Cataudella's philosophy of honest customer service, a user-friendly Web site, and the ability to fulfill orders while maintaining a relatively small inventory has kept Tronix near the front of the pack of online video game retailers. Like most start-ups, Tronix had to be innovative and flexible while learning from early mistakes. For anyone hoping to dive into online retailing, Tronix is an example of success that shows what is possible with a little sweat, a lot of creativity, and the willingness to change with the ever-shifting Internet.

This chapter focuses on what Tronix has done to become a solid, profitable business. You can apply most of the lessons here to your own philosophies as you move toward the reality of running an online store.

A Beginning in Retail

Cataudella's retailing roots were laid in New York City as a jack-of-all-trades at Leigh Computers.

"I've been a game player all my life," Cataudella says. "That inspired me to get involved in the business. I started with an Apple computer and took the game-playing route rather than programming. I had studied graphic design before it was done on computers, and that aspect of games intrigued me. When I first got a computer, I did a few freelance projects. I did graphic development for a game that, because of a lack of planning, eventually fell through."

Shortly after graduating from high school, Cataudella, went to work at a computer center in New York. The company folded about a year later, but when Leigh Goldstein, a co-worker, opened Leigh Computers, Cataudella joined him. Initially Leigh's only employee, Cataudella worked as a manager and a salesperson, learning all aspects of retailing along the way.

"I did a bit of everything and became pretty successful at it," he remembers. "But I didn't always want to do things Leigh's way. I had a lot of suggestions—in fact, I set him up with his first Nintendo account before it was a big name. If he was still in business he could be a Nintendo dealer and a lot of other things, but he was afraid to take any risks."

Cataudella was more of a risk-taker. Although his customer service ideas weren't perfectly tailored to retail, they helped him gain the trust and admiration of the store's customers. Rather than push product out the door, Cataudella offered his honest opinions. If a product wasn't good for a customer, he says so.

"At some of the big retail outlets, the salespeople will tell the customer everything's great," he says. "The idea of retail is to get rid of inventory. Telling a customer that a product isn't great doesn't fit in with retail. I was always honest. I didn't feel right about telling a customer a certain product was great if I hadn't looked at it or if I didn't believe it myself."

Cataudella's approach helped build a loyal customer base.

"People believed my advice and kept coming back, but Leigh didn't really agree with the way I was doing things," Cataudella says. "He didn't think it was helping business if I wasn't pushing stuff out the door. Customers became friends. They'd come in and we'd have conversations and it was a real family atmosphere. It was someplace people wanted to shop."

But Goldstein eventually lost his enthusiasm for the business and in 1993, after nine years, Leigh Computers folded.

The Birth of Tronix

With Leigh Computers out of business, Cataudella went the entrepreneurial route, with his nephew serving as the primary investor. A few months after Leigh Computers folded, Cataudella began the arduous task of starting his own business—an online video game store, www.tronixweb.com.

"My nephew and I had talked about starting our own business," Cataudella says. "We never thought it would happen but we had to follow that dream."

Starting a small business requires more than just dreams of fame and fortune. Simply getting Tronix off the ground was Cataudella's biggest challenge. While his nephew took care of the financial end of the start-up, Cataudella did the legwork, scouting out office space in New York City and setting up merchant accounts with credit card companies.

"Looking for office space in New York wasn't easy, and that's probably the case everywhere," Cataudella says. "I looked at a lot of spaces that weren't great. That was probably the most frustrating part. My nephew was the investor and he already had a lawyer, so that gave us a head start. He took care of all the paperwork with the lawyer."

Even more difficult than finding a suitable space, which Cataudella eventually settled into on Seventh Avenue, was convincing the credit card companies to give him the merchant accounts necessary to allow credit card orders. Credit card companies are hesitant to deal with strictly mail-order businesses. Cataudella had to convince the companies that he would be doing some retail sales as well. A lot of former customers from Leigh Computers made the trip to Cataudella's office, but his business quickly became primarily mail order.

Another hurdle—one faced by all but the most fortunate start-ups—was money. Tronix was launched in late 1993 with an investment of about $12,000.

"At the beginning it was hard to see how much money you needed," Cataudella remembers. "We weren't thinking about profits, we were just thinking about paying the rent and surviving. I paid the rent and security deposit and all the start-up costs, which didn't leave much money for inventory. We had a very, very small inventory and started out basically doing special orders. Not everybody will be able to work with such small inventory, but we're within walking distance of our distributors. That was a big advantage."

By the summer of 1994, things were starting to fall into place for Tronix. But success didn't come without some early struggles.

Learning on the Fly

When Tronix was launched, customers didn't exactly flock to the Web site and spend hundreds of dollars. Not only was Tronix new, the idea of shopping on the Web was also in the embryonic stage. For about the first five months of existence, Tronix filled five or six orders a day as Cataudella learned some important lessons about mail-order sales and operating on the Web.

"We used to have periods when the orders would really come in," he says. "We just barely survived in the summer and then the holidays would come and we'd make enough money to get caught up. It was a survival thing. Little by little, I stumbled on things that made us more efficient. Even now we're picking things up to help us get orders out faster. Anything to save a minute."

Cataudella says one of his early mistakes was making himself too vulnerable in accepting credit card orders. "I had a few charge-backs at the beginning," he remembers.

Cataudella has a strictly enforced policy of shipping to the billing address but says, "You can use your judgement when it comes to shipping to a person's place of employment for a new customer. Generally, shipping to a (business) establishment is usually safe, as potential frauds would not want to place an order and have it shipped to where they work. You just have to make sure to get both the billing and shipping addresses."

Cataudella also says that, depending on the kind of products you sell, you will get an idea of the kind of customer who frequents your store, and this knowledge can help limit credit card hassles, as it has for Tronix.

"In our case, being an electronic game dealer, the majority of our buyers are male, ranging from pre-teens to middle age," he says. "A fairly common order form for Tronix will come in with a woman's first name. While not trying to generalize, it's a fair bet that games like Mortal Kombat or Dragonball Z will not be being played by an adult female. There are exceptions, but it's best to go the extra mile with card verification. Even if the full address checks out clean with the verification process, it's best to call the office or home and speak to the cardholder.

"In many cases, it is simply a woman buying a gift for her husband or a mother purchasing a product for her son or daughter. But kids can also gain access to their working mom's credit card. If we do call, we always ask for the cardholder by full name and talk only to them."

Cataudella also says he wasted a lot of time addressing envelopes and packing boxes. But as the number of orders grew, Tronix became more efficient out of necessity. Envelopes are now self-addressed ahead of time and boxes are pre-padded during down times.

"I have a lot better process now," Cataudella says. "I'm obsessed with everything being perfect, as any business owner would be. We've had to become a lot more efficient as the number of orders has grown."

Keys to Success

As Cataudella continued to learn, Tronix's chances of surviving grew. By 1995, Cataudella was confident Tronix would survive and thrive. He credits his commitment to honest customer service, his ability to stay ahead of the competition in terms of his Web site, and his belief and interest in what he's selling as keys to Tronix's success.

Honest Customer Service

"Customer service is the reason we've been successful," Cataudella says. "At Leigh's, I learned a lot about customer service—how to treat people and how not to treat people. Now, with a lot of orders coming through email, it's a bit different because there isn't that face-to-face contact. But you still have an opportunity to make shopping at your site an enjoyable experience. If your site is easy to use, and you get the products to your customers on time, people will want to come back. If they have to spend a lot of time navigating your site, or if it takes forever to load, or if you promise two-day delivery and it takes a week, you're going to lose customers, and before long you'll be out of business."

For Cataudella, honesty is the best policy. As a store operator, the obvious goal is to sell things to people who want or need them. But, Cataudella insists, that doesn't mean pushing inferior products on unsuspecting customers.

"You can avoid selling bad products by not stocking many of them," he says. "That way you never have to tell somebody something's fantastic if it's not, and you won't be stuck with lousy products. It also keeps your inventory from getting too big."

In the world of online sales, speed is of the essence. The Web provides immediate gratification and, in the case of Tronix, a young clientele that wants its orders immediately.

"Everyone wants it yesterday," Cataudella says. "When we get something in, it's like bees to honey. A lot of people call because their local store hasn't gotten a particular game yet. They want new releases as soon as they're available."

And if an online store can't provide a compelling reason to shop there rather than walking down to the corner, what's the point?

"You have to provide a reason for them to shop online," Cataudella says. "If you can get them an item faster than anyone else or if you can give them a good price, they'll shop online."

A Clean Web Site

In the beginning, there were limited options for Web site construction, but Cataudella spent a lot of time monitoring the competition.

"I had many sleepless nights," he says. "I'd see a site that was better than mine and it would drive me crazy. The competition was the most overwhelming thing. You see something and immediately have to counteract it. For the first two years I spent about 30 minutes a day just checking Web sites. Now I'm comfortable checking them once a week."

And the more he saw, the more he realized he was near the front of the pack.

"For the most part I was able to beat people to the punch and make them react to what I was doing," Cataudella says. "The more time I spent in front, the more I realized that's the way it was going to be. I always seemed to be a step ahead of them in terms of balancing my Web site and being innovative."

Cataudella says he was the first video game merchant to include reviews on his site. He wrote the reviews and stuck to his credo of honesty.

Great games got great reviews. Mediocre games got mediocre reviews. “Not everyone reads the reviews, so you can be honest and it’s not going to cost you a lot of sales. In the long run, it’s better to lose one sale because of a fair review. If you write how great a product is, and people buy it and find out it’s not so hot, you might lose them as a customer. That could end up costing you dozens of sales in the long run.”

As the technology to create snazzy Web sites grew, Cataudella admits to getting carried away with the possibilities. As soon as a particular technology became available, up it went.

“I felt like I had to use everything that was available, but I soon realized that wasn’t the case,” he says. “A clean Web site without all the whip cream works best. It makes things faster because you don’t have to wait for the animation to load. A lot of other sites have scrolling marquees, but I don’t think they’re worth it. Eventually you fall back to the basics. The way the Tronix Web site is laid out, you can tell we didn’t mess around.”

The Tronix site has evolved and continues to do so. Rather than enticing customers with fancy graphics, the site is simple, easy to read, easy to navigate, and quick to load. The customers are there to shop, not to “ooh” and “ahh” over the graphics.

For a while the site’s background color was black, but Cataudella has recently done a 180-degree turn, going back to the white background the site had previously.

“I noticed more and more shops—no matter what type of business they are—are sticking with white backgrounds,” Cataudella says. “Black was fine for Tronix for a while, but I felt white gave me the flexibility to use natural shadow effects, which always gives your site a look of class.

“Our UPS driver—a computer aficionado himself—visited the former layout and commented that he liked it a lot, but also added that it had this dark, ‘gothic’ look. That was the single comment that drove me to reverse the color. Having a gothic theme is fine for pushing Batman paraphernalia, but not for a professional retail site dedicated to the electronic entertainment industry.

“After playing with white backgrounds, I realized my entire format would have to be completely revamped as the foreground objects clashed horribly. I gave my site a complete facelift over a three-day weekend. Since all of my Web's departments were already intact, all I needed to do was change the theme. I removed my graphics-based, navigational panel and decided to go back to basics. Using standard fonts and good old hyperlinks, I played with various colors and came with a simple, yet attractive navigation panel. I also changed our logo and added a nice border that surrounds one side of the page. The final result was a cleaner look, and a speed increase of about 20 percent to 40 percent depending on the page."

Cataudella says he received primarily positive response from customers who liked the look and the quicker load time. After some minor problems were pointed out by a handful of customers, Cataudella enlisted his loyal customers for help and found out that a simple browser upgrade by those customers solved the problem.

"When designing a site, I realized it's impossible to please every user," Cataudella says. "It is one thing to make sure your site sits well with both Netscape and Internet Explorer, but you shouldn't have to water it down to include older browsers. It's best to ask those customer to upgrade."

A Love for Games

For all his customer service experience and sound Web site philosophy, Cataudella says Tronix wouldn't be as successful as it is if he didn't love what he was doing. He shares his customers' enthusiasm for video games, which makes it easy to put the necessary extra thought and effort into his business.

"It's essential that you have an interest in what you're selling," he says. "If you don't care about it, eventually the competition is going to beat you into the ground. You see people who are purely in it to make a buck and have no idea about what they're selling. Of course you want to make money, but you see a lot of store owners just checking the top 10 lists and selling those products. They usually fail because there is no connection with the customer."

If you sell what you know—and what you love—you'll have a better chance of making it through the tough times. Besides making your job more fun, it's just good business. If your customers can sense your enthusiasm for and knowledge of your product, they'll keep coming back. If they think you're just trying to turn a buck with no regard to their happiness, they'll go elsewhere. Let your passion set you apart.

Cataudella also has the benefit of retail experience, further easing his transition to the entrepreneurial life. He launched Tronix already knowing how to operate a credit card machine and other business hardware. His nine years at Leigh Computer also helped shape his customer service philosophy.

"If you have some retail experience, that's just another advantage," Cataudella says. "The best combination is to have some retail experience as well as a genuine enthusiasm for what you're selling. You see a lot of people trying to start online businesses who might be fanatical about (their products) but have no idea about the business end."

Why Many Web Stores Fail

While Tronix has survived, several of its competitors have come and gone. Many of the reasons for failure aren't unique to operating on the Web.

"Extensive inventory of the wrong items has led to a lot of failed companies," Cataudella says. "And you see companies trying to make extra money on shipping charges or not getting shipments to customers on time. Those things will kill you."

Choosing the right products to stock just requires a little research. In Tronix's case, a visit to the annual Electronic Entertainment Expo (E3) helps Cataudella find the hottest new products. Almost every industry will have similar trade shows.

Some online store-owners think the Internet will do all the work for them. Although the Internet provides some advantages over traditional mail order or retailing, you have to work to reap those benefits. Otherwise, it's like taking steroids and sitting on the couch with a bag of chips, a six-pack, and a remote control.

"Some people think they can just put up a Web site and ride the Internet to success, which is a mistake," Cataudella says. "A lot of them aren't even aware of the newsgroups, which are the best places to spread the word about your store."

Others jump into a supposedly hot market only to find it is already saturated, or they deliver poor customer service. With an immediate medium such as the Internet, word spreads in a few days. If you don't treat your customers right, there won't be any left.

Becoming a Workaholic out of Necessity

Cataudella says he enjoys his social life too much to be a workaholic. But running an online store requires a commitment, if not a workaholic schedule.

Cataudella's typical day includes 10 or 11 hours of Tronix-related work, although only about 7 of those hours are spent at his Seventh Avenue office. He spends at least an hour a day upgrading the Tronix Web site. "We're constantly making changes even if they're only minor changes," Cataudella says. "If I see a word spelled wrong, I change it immediately."

In the morning, Cataudella spends about two hours going through his email and separating the orders from the inquiries. He processes the orders immediately and deals with the inquiries at night at home. The rest of the day is primarily dedicated to ordering stock, packing boxes, and getting them shipped. Cataudella also spends some time answering phones, the avenue through which about 25 percent of orders are placed.

"We used to get about 90 percent of our orders through email," Cataudella says. "Most of the people who call are long-time customers who want to know about a certain game. The phone calls slow me down, but I grin and bear it."

He also spends about six hours on the Internet on weekends and the Christmas rush often means a full Saturday in the office. The heaviest Web upgrading is done at night when Cataudella gets home. It's something he wishes he had more time for.

"I'd like to spend more time on the creative end of things, like upgrading the Web site and writing reviews," he says. "Packing boxes can get old."

Tronix has improved its efficiency by investing in a high-end laptop and a newer, affordable point-of-sales program.

"The laptop makes your business mobile," Cataudella says. "Working out of an office on a desktop PC was fine, but after a relentless holiday season, I realized we had to take our work home. During our busy season, I found myself getting up earlier every morning just to catch up from the day before. Now I can look up tracking information during off-hours. If a customer claims they never received their package, I'm able to make sure their order has shipped without having to wonder what happened until I get back to my office. A high-end laptop can also eliminate some headaches if you are traveling or simply away for the weekend.

"The biggest advantage is being able to process invoices ahead of time. On days when major products accompanied by long waiting lists are about to premiere, I can process the invoices and verify addresses the night before or even days ahead. When the big day rolls around, I've already saved myself a few hours of invoice processing, and I'm ready to take on newer orders coming in by phone or email that day."

Another valuable time-saver that Cataudella has discovered is queuing up a large amount of email replies to general questions.

"In the earlier stages of your business, you may have the energy and newly found enthusiasm to spend nights replying to email," Cataudella says. "But when your business becomes more successful, you'll have more email then you can handle each day. The thought of spending evenings replying to continuous inquiries becomes tiresome.

"Also, customers may get used to receiving answers during off-hours. The one time you wait for normal business hours to reply, you can bet that customer will wonder why they didn't get an answer as fast as usual. If you have the spare energy, go ahead and get some of those email replies done at night. That way there is less of a build-up in the morning; you can prepare the email replies on your laptop, working offline. The next business morning, you can simply send off all of your emails at once."

The most obvious measure of Tronix's success is financial. When Cataudella launched Tronix, he hoped to make a living and he has. He has also enjoyed more subtle rewards than a growing bank account.

"When a customer comes back and says he's never dealt with a better business, that keeps you going," Cataudella says. "When you get written up in a magazine and the article says how great your store is, that makes you feel good. And when you keep seeing your name on the newsgroups and it's always in a positive light, you know you're doing things the right way. And of course there's no boss. You're in control."

Looking Ahead

Although the online retailing business has changed dramatically since Tronix's 1993 launch, the metamorphosis isn't complete. Cataudella says Tronix needs to be flexible enough to grow with the Web.

"The whole industry has changed," he says. "Secure transactions, rather than just emailing credit card numbers back and forth, have given it a more professional atmosphere and helped online retailing become more established. The Web itself has come a long way with Java and some other advances. At the beginning, the most you could do was a simple list."

Cataudella agrees with the forecasts of massive growth in online retailing. He also admits he never saw it coming back in the early days of Tronix.

"We live in such a busy society, people don't have time to run to stores," he says. "I know I don't. The Internet can take care of a lot of things and allow people to use their free time for something more enjoyable than shopping. The growth has taken me completely by surprise. At the beginning I thought the Web might be a phase that wouldn't last. Then I never thought there would be a method for secure credit card transactions. That was a big step."

"I have seen the whole thing getting more professional and more well-done as people see what works and what doesn't," Cataudella says. "Shopping carts are becoming more automated. The way credit cards are taken and approved is running more smoothly, and people are becoming more confident in the security of credit card transactions."

But for all the advancements in technology, there is one aspect of Tronix that will never change—the top priority is customer service.

"I became concerned when a major U.S. retail chain decided to add a Web-based mail order to their already successful enterprise," Cataudella says. "As time went on, I saw no decrease in sales or customers at Tronix. In fact, I even went as far as recommending this chain when we didn't have a particular item that someone requested. But most people said, 'Nah, I can't deal with them.'"

Whether they are shopping in a traditional retail store or at a Web store, people still need to be treated with care and respect; no matter how much the Web changes retail, that will never change. Tronix's commitment to customer service has helped it stay ahead of its competitors.

CHAPTER THREE

Lessons From Other Online Retailers

Although Tronix has certainly been successful, it is just one of thousands of online stores that continue to profit as electronic commerce flourishes. This chapter focuses on a few successful stores that cover the spectrum from small to enormous. And while some of these stores have very large budgets that exceed the reach of most companies, you can still learn from them and adapt some of their features into an operation with a more limited budget.

This chapter discusses three online stores and also suggests other stores worth visiting and studying. The first is Fogdog Sports, a major sporting goods store that exists only on the Web and sells products manufactured by other companies. The second is Eddie Bauer, an established retailer and mail-order company that is taking advantage of the Web with an outstanding, feature-rich

Web store. The third is Surf Warehouse, a California-based surf shop that sells both the poducts of other manufacturers and its own surfboards and is expanding its reach through the Internet.

Fogdog Sports

www.fogdog.com

Fogdog Sports is one of the largest Web sporting goods stores, offering products such as footwear, clothing, and equipment for a wide variety of sports. Originally lauched as SportsSite.com, Fogdog says more than two million people visited its site in the first six months after its June 1998 launch. Fogdog has nearly 60,000 items in stock from manufacturers such as Adidas, Reebok, The North Face, and Nike (Nike bought a percentage of Fogdog in September 1999).

Fogdog's home page allows customers to quickly visit one of six specialty shops and shop by department, sport, and brand.

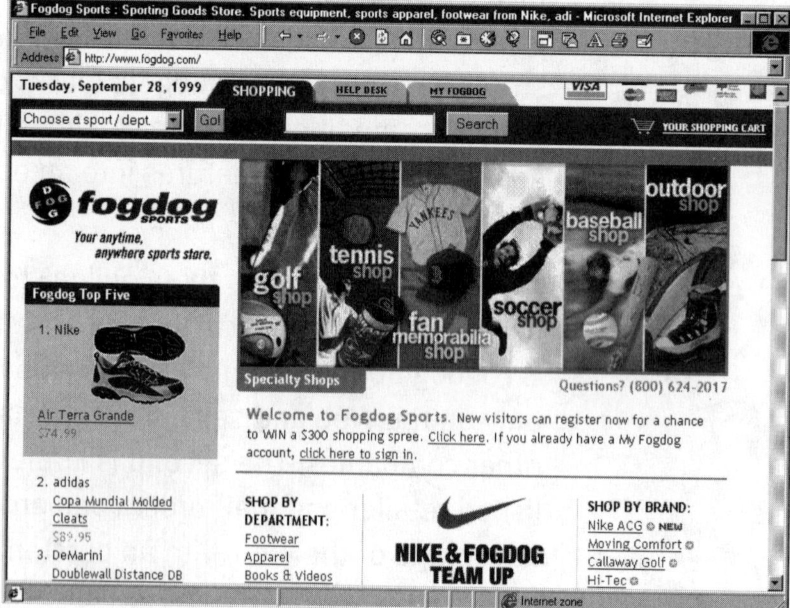

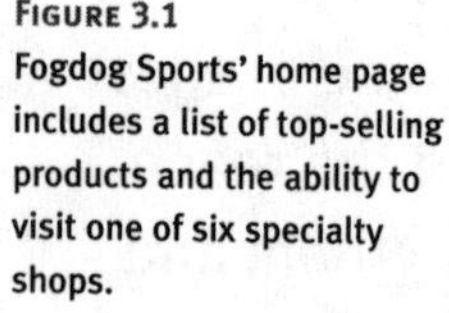

FIGURE 3.1
Fogdog Sports' home page includes a list of top-selling products and the ability to visit one of six specialty shops.

Store Features

Sports is obviously an event-driven market, and Fogdog takes advantage of that by featuring items related to current major sporting events such as U.S. Open, the women's soccer World Cup, the major league baseball home run race between Sammy Sosa and Mark McGwire, and golf's Ryder Cup. If your store deals in an event- or release-driven market that leads to widespread media coverage, this is a good example to follow. Customers are naturally drawn to those events and are often more inclined to buy items surrounding those events. Other examples are toy stores selling *Star Wars* action figures, bookstores featuring books related to hot movies such as *The Blair Witch Project,* and video game dealers selling games for the new Sega Dreamcast.

Leading up to the Ryder Cup, Fogdog not only featured a new driver, but also listed the different golf balls used by members of the European and American teams (Figure 3.2). That way, people wanting to buy the same ball used by Tiger Woods, Sergio Garcia, and the others knew which kind to buy.

FIGURE 3.2
Fogdog's Golf shop took advantage of interest in the Ryder Cup by featuring the golf balls of choice of the players for the American and European teams and also featuring a new driver.

Fogdog Top Five

Customers are very interested in best-seller lists, which are used to sell trackable items like books, music, software, video games, and more. An extension of this is Amazon.com's new Purchase Circles, which allow people to see what the hot-selling items are in certain geographical regions and even within companies and branches of the government. Fogdog highlights its five top-selling items, whether they are Nike running shoes or Wilson footballs, on its home page.

Product Pages

Not suprisingly, Fogdog's product pages (Figure 3.3) feature color photos and the ability to add the product to a shopping cart. The product descriptions appear to be written by the manufacturer, but Fogdog also allows for customer reviews. This is a good way to get customers involved and also offers an opinion that is unbiased. However, you can never count on glowing reviews. One golf club received glowing, five-star reviews from six of the seven customers and a terrible, one-star review from the seventh (making us wonder whether the problem was the club or the golfer!). Most customers will be intelligent enough to understand and discount rare bad reviews of otherwise positively reviewed products.

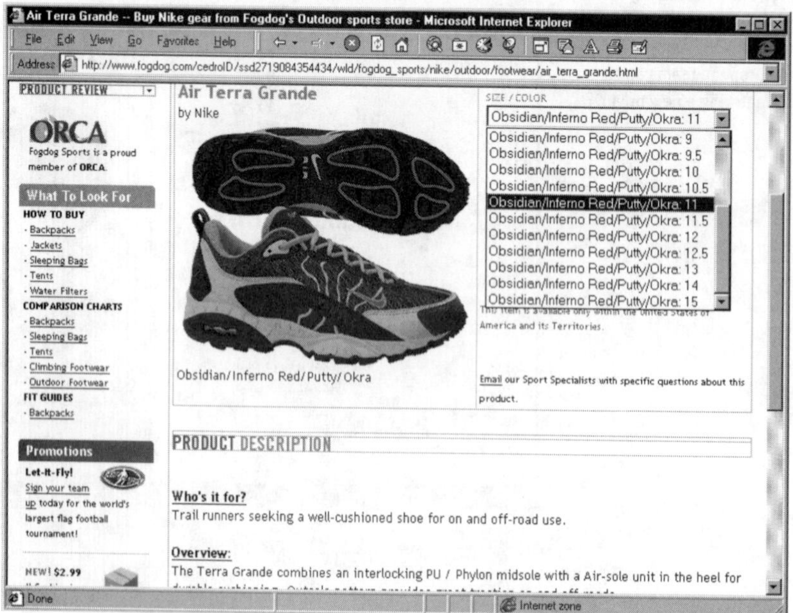

FIGURE 3.3
Fogdog's product pages use a drop-down list to select color and size and include a product overview and customer reviews.

Fogdog Search Squad

With the vast amount of sporting goods on the market, local sporting goods stores usually don't have every pair of sneakers, brand of tennis racquet, or type of hockey equipment on the planet. Fogdog doesn't either. However, in its quest to provide top-notch customer service, Fogdog offers the Fogdog Search Squad (Figure 3.4). Customers who haven't been able to find that elusive pair of Kobe Bryant sneakers can fill out the Fogdog Search Squad request form and Fogdog will go looking. Fogdog promises to respond within two to three business days whether it finds the item or not. If the Search Squad finds the item, customers will be quoted the price (including shipping and sales taxes). Customers can then complete the purchase over the phone using a credit card.

This approach can work well for stores with the manpower available to look for hard-to-find items. Before you offer a similar service, be sure you can handle the potentially increased workload. Otherwise you'll spend all of your time chasing rare items and be left with little time to tend to the daily tasks of running your store. Also, don't promise what you can't deliver. There's no sense offering to look for items only to disappoint your customers when you fail to come through for them.

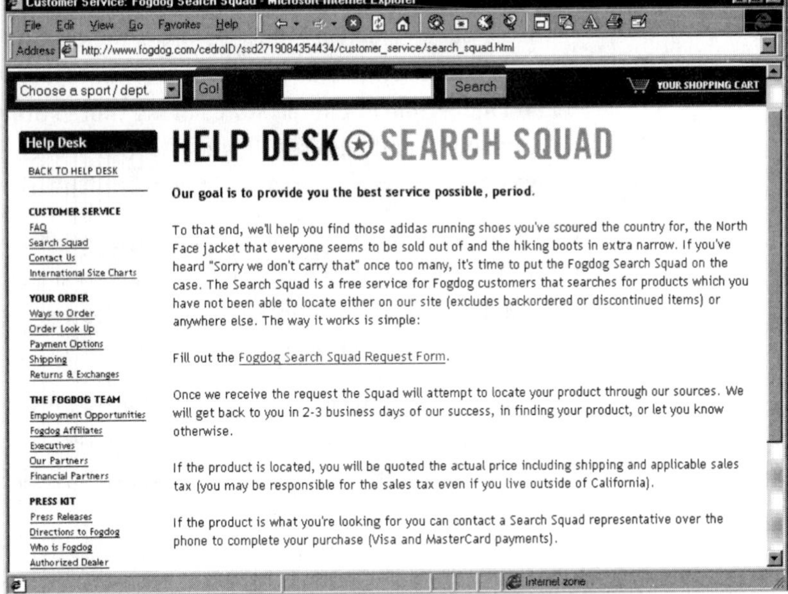

FIGURE 3.4
If Fogdog doesn't have a hard-to-find item, the Fogdog Search Squad will go looking for it.

Other Features

Fogdog also offers gift certificates, the ability for customers to sign up for personalized service (which forces the member to give his or her email address), and an affiliate program.

Similar Stores

Some other top stores that exist only on the Web like Fogdog Sports are:

- Amazon.com (www.amazon.com).
- CDnow (www.cdnow.com).
- Beyond.com (www.beyond.com).
- Rumpus Toys (www.rumpustoys.com).

Eddie Bauer

www.eddiebauer.com

Eddie Bauer's fastest growing store is the one that resides at www.eddiebauer.com. Eddie Bauer—with traditional mail order catalogs and more than 600 retail stores in the United States, Canada, Japan, Germany, and the United Kingdom—sells sportswear and casual wear for men and women, and home furnishings.

Eddie Bauer has been online since 1996 and in 1998 launched its Virtual Dressing Room, which allows customers to select clothes and then click and drag to match shirts with shorts, sweaters with skirts, and so on. All the customer needs is a Java-compliant browser.

Though most smaller stores will not have the time, money, or need for such a tool, it is an example of how a store can use a unique feature that enhances the customers' experience and therefore can keep them coming back.

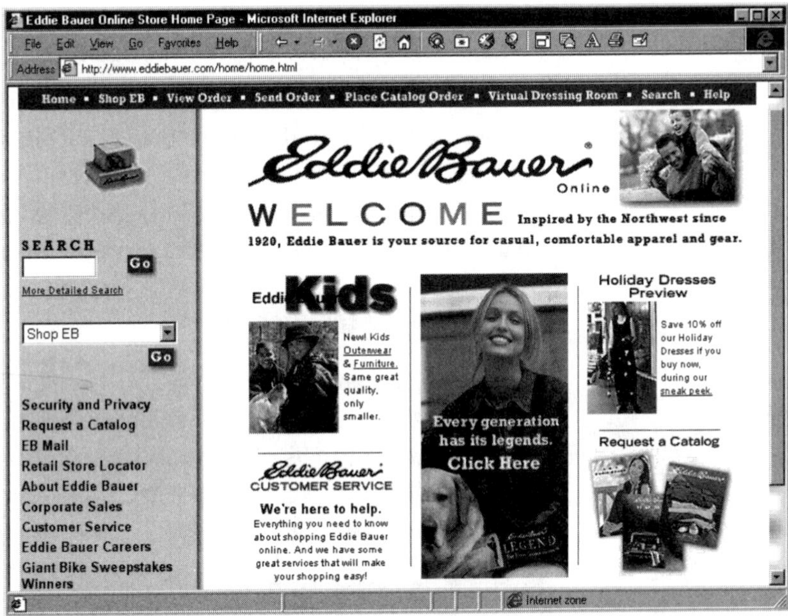

FIGURE 3.5
The Eddie Bauer home page at www.eddiebauer.com uses a clean design and smart use of graphics to offer an attractive introduction to the site.

Home Page

Eddie Bauer's home page is an outstanding example of efficient design, tasteful color selection, effective use of graphics, and product highlights. The bar across the top of the page includes shopping-related links: Shop EB, View Order, Send Order, Place Catalog Order, Virtual Dressing Room, Search, and Help.

The left side of the page also allows you to search the site or to use a drop-down menu to begin shopping for specific items. But these links are more informational in nature, allowing visitors to find out about Security and Privacy, use the Retail Store Locator, learn more about the company, scan job listings, or use features such as the Reminder Service and Wish Lists (more on these last two later).

There are more shopping links across the bottom of the page that lead to departments such as Footwear, Luggage and Gear, Weekly Specials, Clearance, and E.B. Home.

The body of the home page naturally includes the corporate logo. When we checked out Eddie Bauer's Web site, the fall fashion season had begun, and that was reflected by the fact that a summer shirt was on sale and the top photo and colors had an autumn theme. Also featured on the body of the home page was a bicycle sweepstakes (leave your contact information and have the opportunity to win a mountain bike), the Virtual Dressing Room, and the opportunity to sign up for an email newsletter that details special events and sales (pointing out on the home page that customers' email addresses will be kept private).

Highlights and Features

Eddie Bauer's crisp design is certainly a highlight, but like any quality retail Web site, it is the attention to detail and special offerings that set it apart from many of its competitors. Though the Virtual Dressing Room (Figure 3.6) is the slickest, most obvious highlight of the site, there is more to learn here.

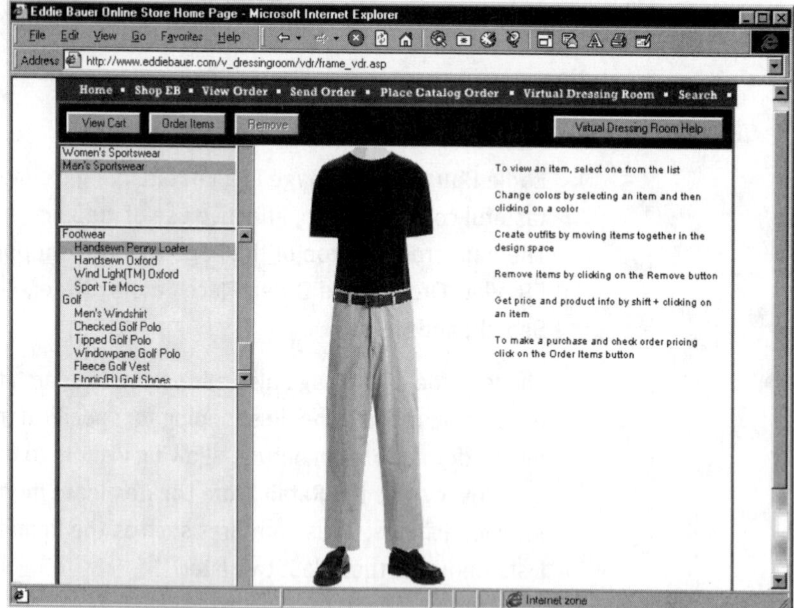

FIGURE 3.6
Eddie Bauer's Virtual Dressing Room allows shoppers to see how various combinations of clothes look when worn together.

Security and Privacy

Some Web retailers unfortunately don't make it easy to find information on security and privacy. Although the Web has become an increasingly accepted place to shop, customers—especially those shopping online for the first time—still have some trepidation when it comes to using a credit card on the Web or turning over their personal information. It doesn't matter that those same people have no trouble doing the same over the phone—Web retailers must make shoppers aware that shopping online is safe.

Eddie Bauer makes this information easy to find—and shows that it is a priority for the company—by placing Security and Privacy atop the links on the left side of the page. One click and shoppers are told plainly about SSL technology and that email is not encrypted and is not considered a secure means of transmitting credit card numbers. Then they offer their toll-free number for anyone who remains unconvinced. The page also explains that the Web site identifies customers' Internet Service Providers but not individuals and does not sell or disclose any information given out during the ordering process.

Customer Service

Eddie Bauer's Customer Service page is comprehensive and easy to follow, offering information on ordering online, shipping, international orders, special services (such as gift boxes), gift certificates, and more.

While you might not offer the amount of services that a major company like Eddie Bauer does, you definitely should provide instructions and information related to ordering, shipping, international orders (if you accept them), and so on. Remove the element of surprise. Your customers need to know how your store works without guessing or searching your site far and wide for buried information.

Eddie Bauer's ordering instructions (Figure 3.7) are easy to follow and include attractive graphics. A chart displaying Eddie Bauer's delivery and handling information spells out to the penny how much it will cost to ship various amounts of merchandise either Standard (five business days), Express (three business days), or Express Plus (two business days).

Eddie Bauer, with hundreds of retail stores, has a customer-friendly return policy that allows customers to return merchandise through the mail or to a nearby retail store. If this makes sense for your business, offering the ability to return unwanted items to a retail store reinforces your commitment to customer service. The Retail Store Locator helps customers find the nearest Eddie Bauer store.

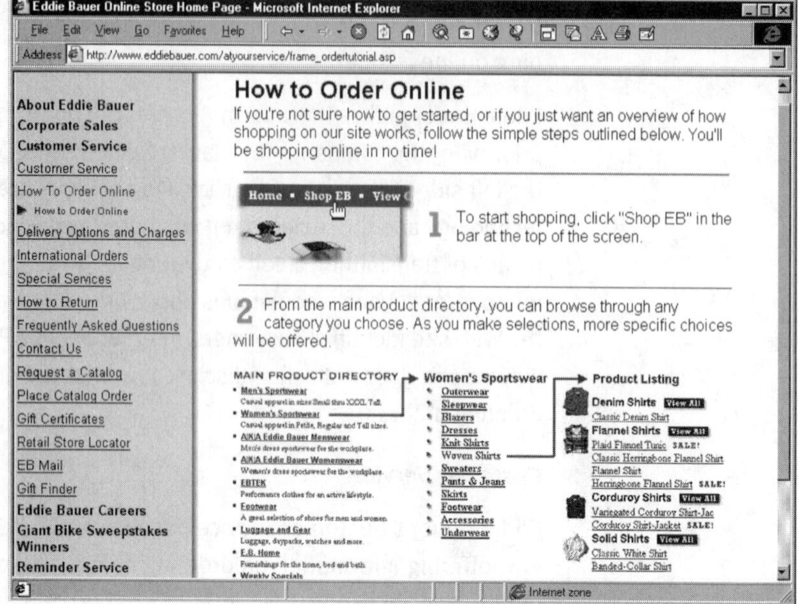

FIGURE 3.7
Eddie Bauer's online ordering instructions include simple steps and helpful graphics.

Lending a Hand

Each year, online holiday shopping grows dramatically. Why not make holiday shopping even easier for your customers? Eddie Bauer does this by offering not only gift wrapping but also a Gift Finder, Wish Lists, and a Reminder Service.

The Gift Finder (Figure 3.8) allows you to select the type of recipient (couple, man, woman, teenage boy, teenage girl), the event (anniversary, birthday, graduation, etc.), the type of gift (clothing and sleepware, home decor, etc.), and a price range. The customer is presented with a number of choices that can then be quickly ordered. This is the kind of unique offering that the Web allows.

The Wish List and Reminder Service are exactly that—allowing customers to have email reminders of important gift-buying dates sent to them or to create their own wish list that friends or family can see.

FIGURE 3.8
Eddie Bauer's Gift Finder makes holiday shopping easy.

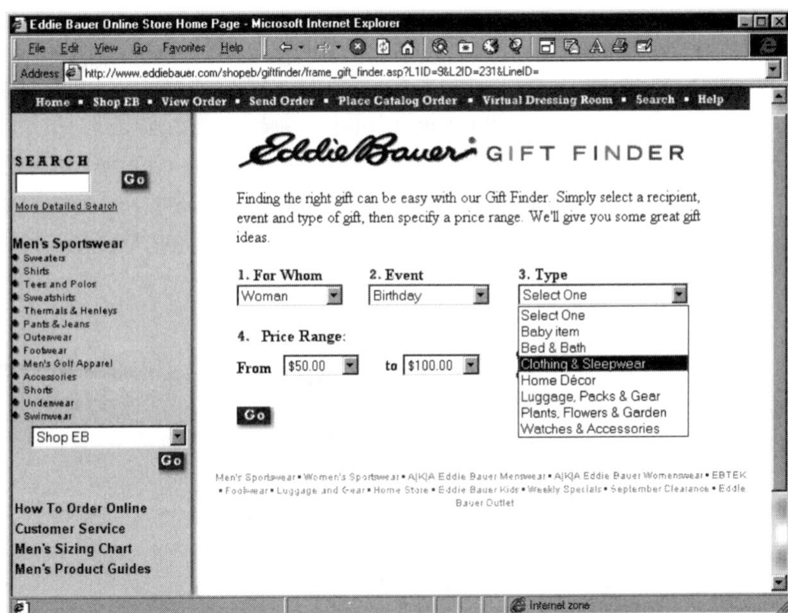

FIGURE 3.9
Never forget an important shopping date again with Eddie Bauer's Reminder Service.

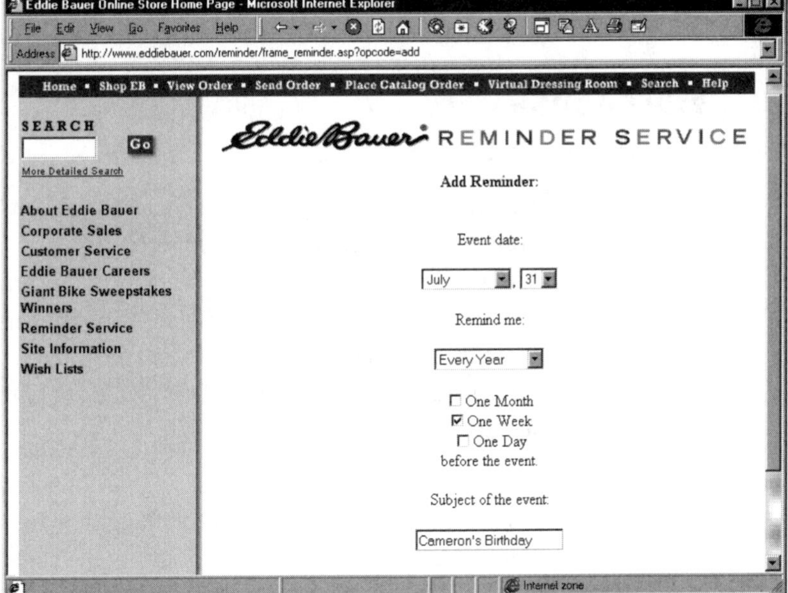

A Standout Site

Eddie Bauer's site sets a high standard with quality graphics, clean design, smart color choices, and customer-friendly navigation—all to be expected from a large, successful company with deep pockets. However, it is the attention to detail and customer service options that make Eddie Bauer worth studying.

Similar Stores

Other retail and mail order stores on the Web worth investigating are:

- L.L. Bean (**www.llbean.com**).
- J.Crew (**www.jcrew.com**).
- The Gap (**www.gap.com**).
- Eastern Mountain Sports (**www.easternmountainsports.com**).

Surf Warehouse
www.surfwarehouse.com

Surf Warehouse is a great example of a relatively small brick-and-mortar store taking advantage of the opportunities provided by the Internet. Surf Warehouse's La Jolla, California location certainly attracts plenty of area surfers, but the Web offers it the opportunity to extend its reach not only up and down the California coast, but to the East coast and beyond. Surf Warehouse can take advantage of the lack of surf shops in many areas.

Surf Warehouse offers an interesting mix of accessories such as surf wax, board bags, wetsuits, and clothing that are supplied by manufacturers. However, the real attractions are the custom, stock, and used boards from board shapers Steve Walden and Dev Gregory. Custom orders take just three to four weeks to complete.

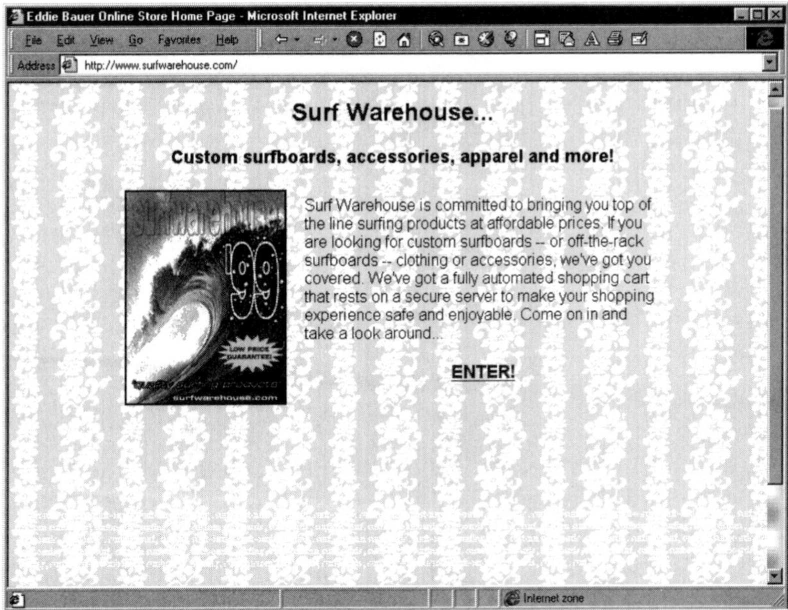

FIGURE 3.10
Surf Warehouse's welcome page.

Home Page

The body of Surf Warehouse's home page is packed with information on product types, a few small graphics, and of course a nice surfing photo. There is also a link to an art gallery of work by Surf Warehouse team rider Pat Veillon.

On the left side of the page products are listed by category, and there are also links to informational pages about ordering, store policies, and how to link to the Surf Warehouse site. Customers can also sign up for Surf Warehouse's "low volume" newsletter. Surf Warehouse also offers a product search—a simple feature that can make their customers' shopping experience easier.

Start Shopping

Clicking on the product category takes the customer to a list of products (complete with prices, photos, and product availability). One more click on the desired item, and the customer receives more information, a photo, and the ability to easily add the item to a shopping cart.

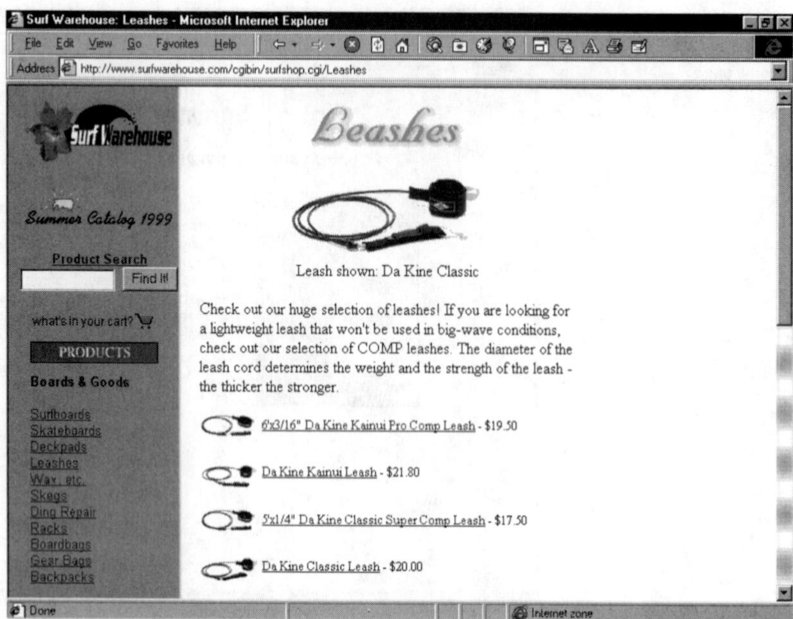

FIGURE 3.11
Products are divided into categories such as surfboards, skateboards, wetsuits, and leashes.

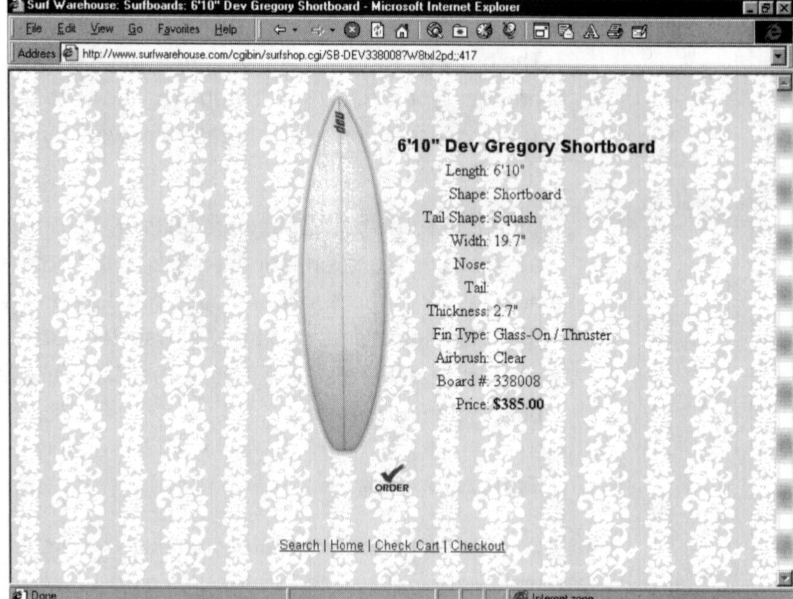

FIGURE 3.12
Surf Warehouse's product pages include all the basic information.

More Information

Many Web stores overwhelm their customers with infomation about the company. Surf Warehouse keeps it simple by offering an email address to use when help is needed, contact information, directions for shoppers, and a company policies page that spells out how to return items and what to do in the rare instance a product is damaged during shipping. Surf Warehouse also plans to offer a board-design forum soon, a feature that will surely be attractive to hardcore surfers.

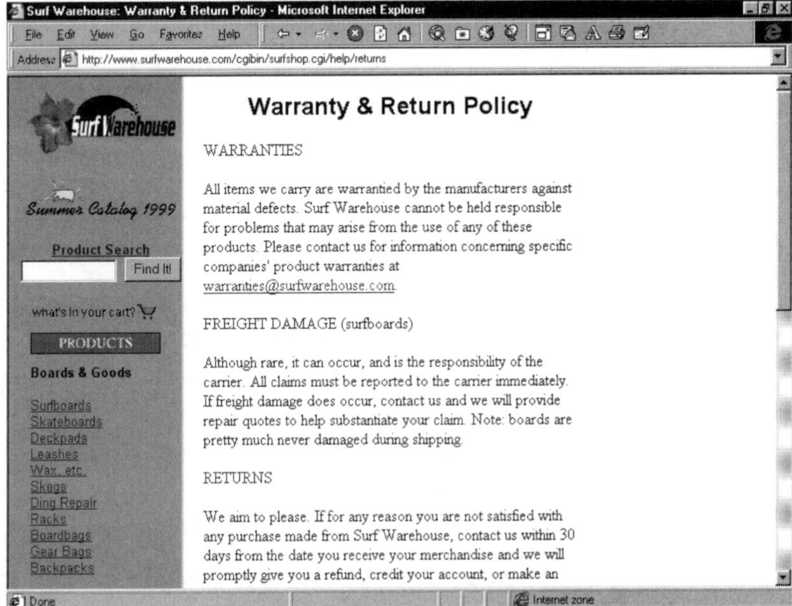

FIGURE 3.13
Surf Warehouse spells its company policies out clearly and succinctly.

Knowing the Customer

Surf Warehouse obviously knows what its customers want. As a group, surfers are passionate about one thing: surfing. The site doesn't waste time with bells and whistles but instead offers a site that is easy to use. Want a new surfboard? Just need a new leash or some cool water board wax? In only a few minutes, Surf Warehouse's customers can to do what they really want to do—shut off the computer and paddle out!

The Surf Warehouse site is a good example of a business that has expanded its reach via the Web without spending an enormous amount of money.

Similar Stores

Although the major stores on the Web get much of the attention, small stores shouldn't shy away from the growth opportunity that the Web provides. Here are some other smaller stores worth looking into.

- Cape Porpoise Lobster Co. (**www.capeporpoiselobster.com**).
- W.O. Hesperus (**www.wohesperus.com**).
- Archie McPhee (**www.archiemcphee.com**).
- Mud In Your Eye Pottery (**www.mudinyoureyepottery.com**).

Learn from Others

We could fil an entire book with Web stores worth visiting, either as a customer or as a merchant in search of ideas. Even if Web stores sell different products than you or have far larger or smaller budgets, you can still learn what to do and what not to do by visiting as many store sites as possible. When you think you know all there is to know about operating a successful Web store, that's exactly when you should begin looking around for new, fresh ideas.

Online retailing continues to grow and evolve and will continue to do so for many years. To find out where it might be headed and why, move on to Chapter 4.

CHAPTER FOUR

Understanding the Online Store Market Opportunity

The goal of this chapter is simple—to help you understand why online shopping is such a big growth market, what the traits of online shoppers are, and why they actually shop online.

This chapter is divided into three critical sections, each building on the preceding. First we will show how many people around the world are connected to the Web, because unless they are connected, it's hard for them to be customers. Then we will explain the basic makeup of people on the Web—who they are, where they are from, and what they are doing. Finally, we will look at the future of online shopping and how this all fits together to answer the most critical questions: why is online shopping actually better for people, and how do you design your store based on all of these issues?

The source of the expected success of online shopping is twofold. First, shoppers have easily identifiable reasons for people to buying online, which creates direct demand for Web-based stores. It is not just a pure demand for the goods, but also a demand for the way in which they are bought and sold. Second, merchants have a number of compelling reasons to move much of their business online. Not only can merchants take part in the Web's growth, but they can also streamline customer interaction and other operations to extract extra profits from the same sales.

At its core, the online store is a new way for people to interact and pursue commerce opportunities. Once you understand all the fundamental forces at work (and how they change how commerce works), you will be more prepared for success in the world of Web retailing.

Starting with the Fundamentals

Anyone wanting to order something from your Web store must fulfill a number of prerequisites: They must own a computer, connect it to the Internet, and begin using the Web. These are the critical building blocks for understanding the online shopping market. Therefore, before looking closely at the specifics of online shopping, it's important to examine the nature of computer owners, Internet connections, and usage of the World Wide Web.

From Computers to Devices

When people think of surfing the Web, they almost always envision the use of a standard personal computer, an image that has been etched into our minds since the first IBM PCs and Apple Macs shipped more than 15 years ago. However, in today's technological world there are a number of new computer-like devices that also offer connections to the Web. At the gut level, they are very capable computers. But on the outside, they look like very different devices—machines such as screen phones, Web TVs, and even video game consoles.

The notion of what is or isn't a computer will change over time. Even today there are cellular phones and handheld PCs (such as Palm devices) that are capable of providing Web access. This is why most market researchers count not only the number of personal computers in use, but also consider an array of Web-capable devices. We will try to do the same.

Despite the rise of alternative devices, common personal computers will remain the dominant form of Web access for some time. PC sales are booming on a worldwide level—not just in the United States, Japan, and major European countries, but also in places such as China, Brazil, Singapore, India, and Korea. Overall in 1998 and expected in 1999, worldwide PC shipments increased 15 to 20 percent according to research firm Dataquest. The sub-$1,000 PC market is growing particularly fast.

PC Market

During 1997 and especially 1998, dozens of vendors began rolling out speedy and Web-capable PCs that cost less than $1,000. This spurred aggressive home consumer demand for PCs and led to strong growth in the PC market. That segment is now growing faster than almost any other segment of the PC industry as vendors push prices down even further and pack more power into newer generation machines. Last year it was estimated that close to 12 million sub-$1,000 PCs were sold in the U.S. alone.

For a summary of key computer hardware figures, see Table 4.1

Table 4.1 Key Computer Hardware Figures

210 million computers and other devices will be linked to the Internet by the end of 2000	*—Jupiter Communications*
92 million PCs were sold worldwide in 1998. Growth is averaging more than 15 percent yearly and is even higher in some markets such as the U.S., where aggressive pricing of sub-$1,000 PCs and the Internet are driving demand for computers.	*—Dataquest*
The consumer PC industry will continue to skyrocket in 1999 as homes snap up more than 13 million new machines, 4.5 million of which will be first time computer purchases.	*—Forrester Research*
More than one million WebTV consoles have been sold since it debuted in 1997. Estimates are that some 15 million Web console devices (either WebTVs or video game consoles that can also surf the Web) will be in homes by the end of 2002–2003.	*—Various reports*
Estimates are that more than 6 million handheld PCs, like the Palm PC or Windows CE, sold in 1998 and as many or more will sell in 1999.	*—Various reports*

Game Consoles and Web Appliances

WebTV is not being as rapidly adopted in the early going as some might have predicted, but they are a growing force. The device appears destined to become an interesting platform that should grow as it matures and, most likely, combines with its video–game console cousins. As more TVs and set-top cable boxes ship with built-in capabilities, the market may even piggyback on the overall television sales and cable installation market. This is already beginning to happen.

TIP ▸ ***According to WebSideStory's Statmarket, which tracks and reports traffic statistics for more than 100,000 small- to medium-sized Web sites, WebTV already accounts for more than 1 percent of all Web traffic. This is a small number but a significant one because it is growing, and because most are being used by home consumers.***

Handheld PCs

Another potent group of devices that will surf the Web are handheld, such as those from Palm Computing or using the Windows CE system. These devices, especially the Palms, are booming right now, selling at a clip of 4 to 5 million units per year. The latest Palm model, the Palm VII, offers wireless access to special online services, and that is only a hint of what to expect from the next generation of Personal Digital Assistants (PDAs). Equipped with better, color screens, higher resolution, and wireless access, these devices will enable people to surf the Web and access email while outside the home and office. While most shopping will be done via office- and home-based systems, as PDAs become a dominant form of portable computing, no doubt they will be a key to people interacting with merchants on the Web and especially through email.

A new category in the handheld market is the so-called *smartphone*. These devices, such as the Nokia 9000, combine voice phones with small screens and keyboards, enabling them to offer some common handheld functionality to access Web-based information. Research firm IDC distributed a press release predicting shipments to reach 8.8 million units by 2001.

So between just PCs, Web TVs, and handheld devices, there will be plenty of new computer-capable hardware sold over the next few years. Almost all of it will be attached to the Web.

Research firm Jupiter Communications predicts that overall the number of devices accessing the Web will grow to more than 210 million by the end of 2000, with more than 160 million users. This includes many different devices, not just computer workstations or servers, and not just items people use at home or at work. Eventually, all sorts of devices—copiers, fax machines, ATMs, pagers, and even vending machines—could be connected in some form to the Internet, enabling a rich, worldwide e-commerce system.

The range of devices that will allow people to access the Web, or which are connected directly themselves, is an important issue. These numbers and trends indicate that many Web surfers, and therefore shoppers, will access the Internet through more than just common home computers. Stores that can appeal to buyers, whether they are on a Web-enabled TV, home computer, or portable phone, will have an advantage.

These devices will affect Web design and e-commerce because they will require Web stores (and other types of Web sites) to prepare content and technology that works with many different types of displays and devices. WebTV, for example, doesn't support Java, and many handhelds feature screens that are grayscale with resolutions well below the lowest computer resolution of 640 by 480 pixels (the Palm's screen is 160 by 160). In addition, displaying graphics on a TV set device (like a video game console or WebTV) alters their appearance, as opposed to displaying them on a crisp, high-resolution computer monitor. As shoppers begin to use more non-computer devices to interact with merchants on the Web, online stores will have to adapt. Those that do so will find even more consumers in the online universe than will their competitors.

Software

A critical aspect of Web-connected devices is the underlying access software. As many Web developers know, the software that is used to get access to the Internet dictates the capabilities of its users. Although Microsoft Internet Explorer and Netscape Communicator (or Navigator) try to be relatively compatible, both browsers implement things the other doesn't. Thus, all eyes are on browser platforms from Netscape and Microsoft so that developers (and store owners) can better discern what their sites should support.

The browser battle was initially won by Netscape, which crushed a room full of hopefuls to gain close to an 80 percent market share. However, Internet Explorer has responded and now has 75 pecent of the market.

TIP ▸ ***Watch the browser upgrades carefully, as features added to newer versions of the browser platforms have the potential to greatly transform the Web and Web-based commerce. Upcoming browser technologies like XML (eXtensible Markup Language) and electronic wallets will usher in an even more mature technology framework upon which to build Web stores.***

Web-User Demographics: From Hardware and Software to Users

The underlying hardware and connections turn traditional store customers into Web customers. Once someone acquires the necessary hardware to go online, he or she joins a fast growing populace that makes up a strong demographic mix that is quite attractive to merchants on the Web. Several companies and universities conduct demographic research of online users. One major group is the Graphics, Visualization & Usability Center (GVU) at the Georgia Institute of Technology and its WWW User Surveys (**www.cc.gatech.edu/gvu/user_surveys/survey-1998-10/**).

Web-user demographics are exceedingly important to developers creating content and Webcasts, or in general trying to build audiences for their Web sites. When the need for market research about Web-user demographics began in 1994–95, several studies raised eyebrows because of their methodology. Researching Web-user demographics isn't an exact science. By far, the most cited and well received studies are those conducted by researchers at Georgia Tech and their colleagues at Vanderbilt University, Portland State University, and the University of Michigan Business School.

This self-selected Internet use and demographic survey (as opposed to a random phone poll) brings together a wealth of information about the current demographic state of the Web. The latest survey compiled thousands of statistics, including information about gender, political affiliation and registration, usage numbers, geographic location, access speeds, and more.

General Demographics

Web users still tend to be Caucasian, male, and slightly older, much wealthier, and more educated than the general public, although the gap between Web users and the general public is closing as more people get connected. According to the latest GVU study, 47 percent are married.

The average age of Internet users is just below 38 years old. Market researcher FIND/SVP, which used a random-digit dialing poll, reported in its 1997 American Internet User Survey that the average age as 36.5 years old while the GVU survey reported that its respondents had an average age of 37.6.

Additionally, the average age has been steadily increasing as the Internet expands. Since its fourth survey, the GVU study has seen a steady rise in average age. The GVU study also found that in Europe the average age was much younger (30.8), which reveals the growth in the U.S. of older Web users while technology adoption in Europe remains more focused on younger users.

TIP ▸ ***Targeting young people may be useful for some stores. Jupiter Communications tracks the emerging children's Web market. According to Jupiter, as of 1996 about 4 million children between the ages of 2 and 17 were accessing online content. Jupiter expects that market to grow to more than 20 million by 2002 and reach almost $2 billion in revenue for developers. Forrester Research reported recently that nearly half of all people in the U.S. ages 16 to 22 have access to the Internet and that this group spends $37 billion annually and influences purchases totaling another $67 billion annually. These consumers are very apt to purchase online and aren't as beholden to brands as older consumers are. They will adopt "spontaneous trust" for a merchant or product that appears interesting (conversely this trust can erode just as quickly if the merchant or product is a disappointment). Forrester also reported that these Web-savvy consumers expect to be rewarded for providing key personal information, and that they want "deep and accurate information...available anywhere at any time."***

In terms of the gender reports, there appears to be a 60/40 split between men and women on the Internet. The earlier and previously mentioned FIND/SVP study pegged it at 60/40 and the GVU percentage of female respondents to its survey was 33.6 percent. Female Internet use has been steadily rising over the last two years. However, European respondents continue to be overwhelmingly male despite a trend upward in female respondents in the tenth survey.

In terms of ethnicity, the GVU study reported that 87 percent of its respondents classified themselves as white/Caucasian. This has remained steady over the last few surveys. It should be noted that as other countries increasingly add Web users, this percentage of Caucasian users will shrink. The GVU study tends to be biased toward North American respondents. English was also cited as being the primary language spoken by 92.2 percent of respondents, which in the overall context of international Web growth is also a high number. Still, this does speak to the fact that despite international growth, English-speaking people are the dominant population on the Web. In some ways though, these numbers are so high that the percentage it really can only go down as the Web reaches beyond its initial population origins.

Educational Attainment

Educational attainment has been steady in most of the GVU studies. In the latest survey, nearly 60 percent of respondents had completed college or had an advanced degree. This is up from the previous surveys and seems to represent a broadening of the Internet's international user base. Respondents from Europe and other countries outside the U.S. have consistently had higher levels of educational attainment than U.S. respondents. This may be because early Internet adopters in Europe and other countries are disproportionately skewed toward upper-income households with college and graduate degrees. That itself seems due to the higher costs of computers and Internet access (local phone calls are still expensive in Europe and other countries) which are more affordable by those with better education and higher incomes.

Household Income

GVU pegs the average U.S. household income of Web users at $57,000. European respondents reported a lower average household income of

$47,600. One finding was particularly interesting: people who classified themselves as expert Internet users were, as a group, earning much more than other Internet users ($62,800 for experts compared to $51,200 for novice users). This seems to support the assumption that many longtime Web users are highly educated technical people in high-paying jobs, while novice users tend to be from a much broader cross-section of households.

Based on these major statistics, Table 4.2 compares the major demographics to general U.S. population statistics.

TABLE 4.2 COMPARING U.S POPULATION WITH MAJOR WEB DEMOGRAPHICS

CATEGORY	GENERAL U.S. DEMOGRAPHICS	RELEVANT INTERNET POPULATION STATISTIC (GVU STUDY)
Average Age	All 34.6	All 37.6
	Male 33.5	Male 37.5
	Female 35.8	Female 37.6
Gender	Male 51%	Male 66%
	Female 49%	Female 33%
Household Income	$42,300	$57,300
Education	College grads 23.6%	College grads 59.3%
Race	White/caucasian 73%	White/caucasian 87%
Married	40%	47.6%

Occupation

The primary occupations of Internet users tend to be computer-related or education-related. This is logical given the computer bent of the Internet, and the fact that many academic institutions offer free access to the Net and have been connected to it for quite some time. The GVU survey reported "Trained Professional" as a general occupation choice had now emerged as the leading occupation category in its survey.

However, the computer-related category is dwindling quickly. There is much statistical research and empirical evidence supporting the fact that while the Net is the domain of millions of computer-related workers, that number has peaked while people in other occupations stampede online. Occupation type tends to be divided noticeably between younger users who are involved in education and computers and older users who tend to work in other fields or be self-employed.

Special Web Statistics

There are also a number of statistics specific to the Web and its users that are worth studying.

Community Membership

How people relate to communities of interests is an important factor in Net use. The tenth GVU survey reported that 55.6 percent of U.S. respondents feel they have become more connected to people with similar interests than before. This was nearly equal for both sexes too. While men were more likely to form Web community relationships around hobbies and professions, women respondents had increased connections to communities that focused on family and support.

TIP ▸ ***Many people who pursue communities of interest on the Internet also create on the Web. In the eighth GVU summary, there was data that supported this, reporting that 46 percent of all respondents have created a Web page. The percentage of respondents that creates Web pages of course increases with computer experience, from 19 percent among novices to 78 percent of experts. These numbers are significant when you consider that many merchants target Web pages with affiliate programs to increase store traffic and sales.***

Years on the Internet

The number of years that a user has spent on the Internet is a significant demographic to understand. In the latest GVU summary, only 5.4 percent of users had been on the Web for less than six months, while 7.6 percent had been on for 6 to 12 months. The largest two categories were people who had been on the Web 1 to 3 years (34.6 percent) or 4 to 6 years (37.1 percent). With the aging of the Web, some 15.4 percent of respondents listed themselves as being on the Web (though in this case they probably meant the Internet in general) for more than seven years.

GVU also breaks user types into four categories: novice, intermediate, experienced, and expert users. In its latest study, roughly 18 percent of people categorized themselves as experts while nearly 40 percent categorized themselves as experienced users, 28.5 percent of respondents categorized themselves as intermediate level users, and 16 percent called themselves novices. Note that the GVU summary may have a slightly disproportionate number of users who are longtime or experienced users.

New users are more evenly split between men (51.5 percent) and women (48.5 percent) than the overall Web population. GVU says that 26.8 percent of women currently online have gone online in the past year, compared to 14.2 percent for males.

Overall, the strong growth of the Internet should continue to see many first-year users for some time. At the same time, it is already apparent that the population of experienced Internet users is growing. The new users will tend to come from lower-income households in the U.S. as Internet use broadens to new demographics, and from higher-income and educated international users who are just now getting online.

Access, World Breakdown, and Language

Where people log on and in what parts of the world they live are other important factors. In the tenth survey, GVU found that nearly 80 percent of users access the Web from home and nearly a third access it from work. Researchers reported this is a dramatic shift from earlier surveys when work access dominated. This indicates that the Internet has truly broadened into the home from even a year ago. This has been helped by the number of new computer households created by the availability of PCs priced below $1,000.

Only 28 percent of users in Europe reported having their primary access from home. In Europe and internationally, the lack of home-based use is clearly tied to high phone costs that people try to avoid by logging on from their company's computers or from universities.

European growth of the Internet is slower than in the United States. The telecommunications infrastructure being what it is in Europe, coupled with a lower household rate of quality PCs, means that overall usage, while experiencing significant growth, is still lagging. The same goes for much of the rest of the world which, with the exception of Australia and Japan, face more antiquated phone networks and low penetration of PC or Web appliance devices.

In 1997 IDG developed a Web index to "measure the intensity" of the development of Internet activity in Western Europe. At the time, research indicated that Web usage in Western Europe would go from around 10.9 million users in 1997 to around 27.5 million by 2000—significant, but not overwhelming. Another study, which pegged Germany as the leading online country in Europe (a result of the presence of the online service T-Online, with more than 1.4 million users), expects the combined home and business population of Internet users there to climb to more than 35 million by 2000. As you can see, predicting Web usage in various regions of the world is an inexact science.

As the Web has grown, there have been several studies of international usage. There is now data about which countries are sending out the most Internet traffic (useful for making decisions about translation of pages and where to focus international marketing efforts). Table 4.3 shows the top ten countries (besides the U.S.) producing traffic on the Web according to WebSideStory's StatMarket (www.statmarket.com) as of August 1999. WebSideStory tracks the traffic driven to over 100,000 independent sites on the Internet and tracks nearly 32,000,000 visits per day to those sites to produce various Internet statistics.

Table 4.3 Percentages of Verified International Web Traffic Produced by Top Countries.

Japan	28.81%	France	3.51%
Germany	10.61%	Italy	3.37%
UK	6.86%	Netherlands	3.37%
Canada	4.84%	Sweden	2.87%
Australia	4.71%	Switzerland	1.08%

To predict the number of users in many major countries, we turned to Nua Internet Surveys, a service that tracks the Internet research industry. Nua compiles the latest predictions on Internet population from every major research house to provide the latest reading on the world's Internet population. We applied a growth rate to these results to predict the Internet population of many major countries as of July 1999. Our results are shown in Table 4.4.

TABLE 4.4 ESTIMATED MAJOR COUNTRY ONLINE POPULATIONS AS OF JULY '99 (+/–5%) IN MILLIONS

ASIA/PACIFIC			
Australia	4.99	Japan	16.58
China	1.82	Malaysia	0.87
Hong Kong	1.33	South Korea	5.03
India	0.65	Taiwan	3.37
EUROPE			
Austria	0.51	Netherlands	2.43
Belgium	2.01	Norway	1.66
Czech Rep.	0.34	Poland	1.09
Denmark	1.80	Russia	1.34
Finland	1.65	Spain	2.90
France	3.68	Switzerland	1.51
Germany	8.78	Sweden	3.74
Ireland	0.39	UK	13.03
Italy	5.11		
NORTH/SOUTH AMERICA			
Argentina	0.43	Mexico	0.62
Brazil	4.29	US	103.62
Canada	8.27		

SOURCE: DIGITALMILL/DFC INTELLIGENCE PROJECTIONS BASED ON NUA INTERNET SURVEYS (**www.nua.ie/surveys/**) COMPILED DATA.

Even with a growing international presence, English is the primary language of users. Among GVU's European respondents, 32.5 percent reported English as their primary language. Beyond English, European languages that were high were German (16.3 percent), Dutch (10.6 percent) and French (6 percent); all other languages were less than 5 percent.

Global Reach (www.euromktg.com), a company specializing in International Web development and business consulting, keeps an updated projection of primary used languages on the Internet. Table 4.5 shows the top ten languages by percentage as projected by their statistics.

TABLE 4.5 TOP TEN PRIMARY LANGUAGES SPOKEN ON THE WEB BY PERCENTAGE

English	59.3%	Chinese	3.2%
Japanese	9.1%	Scandinavian	2.9%
German	6.5%	Korean	2.0%
French	4.3%	Italian	1.5%
Spanish	5.1%	Portuguese	1.3%*

*BRAZIL IS THE MAJOR CONTRIBUTING COUNTRY OF PORTUGUESE SPEAKERS

SOURCE: GLOBAL REACH (WWW.EUROMKTG.COM/GLOBSTATS/INDEX.HTML)

Most Important Issues Facing the Internet

GVU asked its users what the biggest issues on the Net were. The top four were privacy, speed of the Internet, government regulation, and navigation. Among women, privacy was the most important issue. For men, privacy and regulation were the top two, with censorship a close third. This is important for store owners, who are at the center of the privacy issue. Censorship is a lesser issue unless you run Web boards and chat rooms.

Privacy seems to be the key issue of e-commerce security rather than site or credit card security (although lower on people's list, it was a measurable concern). People seem to equate protection of their privacy as an encompassing issue for site security. Anything you do to show concern about the information consumers supply to you as a merchant will make them less wary about providing that information and buying items from your store.

Poor navigation was also a major concern (ahead of e-commerce security) that merchants should be aware of and address. As we will soon explain, the ability for customers to browse, find a product, and compare it against other choices, is the critical success story of Internet shopping. This manifests itself on the Web as navigation. Poor organization of information and choices can actually hurt the sales ability of a site.

How Are People Shopping Online?

Although people are heading to the Web in droves to shop, and the number is increasing rapidly, there is still plenty of room for growth. Online retailing was expected to generate more than $36 billion (U.S.) in revenue in 1999 according to the Boston Consulting Group's study for shop.org. However, this report also said the top sites will attract a majority of this revenue. A study by the Peppers and Rogers Group/Institute says that by 2010, 29 million households in the U.S. will be heavy users of direct-to-consumer commerce. We suspect that number may be much higher as the Web rapidly matures—especially if less expensive Web appliances and gaming consoles like Sony's PlayStation II become key Web surfing machines for consumers.

Since 1997, when e-commerce really began to gel on the Web, people have been increasingly warming up to purchasing online. In the tenth GVU study of Internet usage, respondents purchased something on the Web on average less than once a month. However, the average respondent used the Web to influence overall purchasing decisions 1 to 2 times a month. In the sweet spot of Web users (ages 21 to 50) the rate of purchasing online is once per month or greater.

Planned shopping sessions on the Web also tend to be major. IDC reported in 1997 that cyber-shopping sessions are vigorous, with customers visiting an average of eight storefronts per session. Table 4.6 shows results from the latest GVU study of respondents bought.

Table 4.6 What Respondents to the Tenth GVU Web Demographic Survey Were Purchasing Online

Software	58%
Books	52.6%
Hardware	48.5%
Music	41.4%
Travel	30.2%
Electronics	30.2%
Video	15.8%
Magazines	14.9%
Apparel	13.6%
Flowers	13.3%

How Much Money People Are Spending Online

Online shopping tends to trend toward larger scale purchases. This is partially due to a lack of a good technology that supports payments of $10 or less and that little in the way of sales taxes are collected on the Internet. The GVU survey found that in the last six months prior to the survey, 38 percent of respondents had spent $500 or more online and that 33 percent had spent between $100 and $500. Meanwhile a Navidec survey reported that 53 percent of people on the Web in the U.S. have made an online purchase, spending an average of $206 per purchase.

Issues for Shopping Online

While shopping online grows, so too do people's issues regarding it. We previously mentioned concerns with the overall Internet experience such as privacy, government regulation, and navigation—but the tenth GVU Survey also focused on specific concerns about shopping online. Interestingly, quality of information, easy ordering, and reliability outranked security. Information about availability and the ability to make price comparisons also scored high on the list of user concerns. Again, we maintain that privacy is the real security concern, more so than credit card theft, although that remains an issue for the population as a whole. Once the fear of using a credit card online fades, users focus more precisely on site-specific problems they face when shopping. Many of these are information, and ease-of-use related. As you'll soon read, these go to the heart of the advantage people want from online shopping vs. shopping in the real world.

Another critical issue is customer service. Smaller online merchants who can personally get close to their customers, much like a small real-world store, can gain a critical competitive advantage. Statistics confirm this opportunity. In a recent survey, more than 52 percent of Web shoppers reported communicating (primarily through email) with merchants, yet this mail often went unanswered! This provides smaller merchants with a critical opportunity to gain sales through rigorous follow-up.

Shopping online is growing rapidly as security concerns drop, more merchants get online, and ordering through the Web becomes second nature. Yet, as the popularity of online shopping grows, merchants are quickly learning that they must address a number of key concerns to be successful. This is why it is important to understand psychologically why shopping online is so beneficial to consumers.

Understanding the Nature of Online Shoppers

It is important for online merchants to understand why people shop on the Internet. To better understand this, we turned to a range of academic-based research that attempts to explain what is so attractive about online shopping.

In one paper titled "Interactive Home Shopping: Consumer, Retailer, and Manufacturer Incentives to Participate in Electronic Marketplaces," the authors (Joseph Alba, John Lynch, Barton Weitz, Chris Janiszewski, Richard Lutz, Alan Sawyer, and Stacy Wood) explain that the biggest factors are:

- **Vast Selection.** Consumers like the access to a large number of choices, making it more likely they will find the item they want.
- **Screening.** Consumers are drawn to the ability to easily and quickly sort through choices.
- **Reliability.** The ability for stores to overcome the users' interest in physically seeing some products in order to make a buying decision is critical to online shopping's success.
- **Product Comparisons.** The true strength of online shopping is in the customer's ability to quickly compare similar products for the optimal choice (e.g. best quality, price, shipping terms, etc.).

What the paper argues is that people are most attracted to online shopping because it is much easier to view the entire universe of available choices, whittle them down to the crucial choices, and obtain the information to make a final choice.

Critical to this observation is basic knowledge of how consumers shop in general. Researchers note that shopping is a process of searching, comparing, and gathering information. However, what researchers also know is that when someone shops, he can't consider the entire universe of available choices, due to time constraints.

Instead, consumers tend to examine only a subset of all the possible choices. Researchers say this is because the time consumers save by not searching for and then comparing every available choice is worth more than the risk of overlooking the overall best choice. With this in mind, it becomes obvious that computers and online stores can greatly aid the shopping process. It is much easier for online stores to offer huge inventories. Using search engines and databases to screen those choices is easy. Finally, by offering extensive product information, Web stores can help people make the best choice after they have compiled a list of leading choices. The result is that people should feel better about the choices they make as a result of shopping online.

Another important aspect is that many consumers rely on their own memory when trying to recall alternative product choices—an imperfect process at best. By shopping online, consumers have their alternatives readily available on a computer screen. Again, this results in more efficient shopping and higher satisfaction.

Understanding the Detriments

While users are turning to the Web for efficiency in the shopping process, consumers will sometimes find traditional stores better than online stores. It is important to understand when and why.

The primary detriment to online shopping described by researchers in "Interactive Home Shopping: Consumer, Retailer, and Manufacturer Incentives to Participate in Electronic Marketplaces," are those buying decisions in which experiential information is truly needed. Experiential information comes from the ability of the consumer to smell, taste, feel, or see something. Therefore, selling items like house paint or fragrances on the Internet may be a more difficult process. This was supported by a recent Ernst & Young study that cited the inability to touch items as a key drawback of shopping online.

Experiential information is also a factor when a high level of in-store assistance is useful. As the paper points out, Home Depot is one store that doesn't translate as well to the Web as a store like Barnes & Noble, due to the highly specialized, in-person assistance you can receive at a real-world Home Depot.

Interestingly, brand experience can lessen the need for experiential analysis. Once a consumer is satisfied that a product is to her liking, she may subsequently shop online for that product because of the expectation that the brand quality and characteristics will be equal to the original purchase. This eliminates the need for repeated evaluation. For example, the first time someone buys a particular perfume, it will likely be done at a traditional store where it can be smelled. However, subsequent reorders may be done over the Web. There is also the brand of the store to consider. Clearly people buy from L.L. Bean without seeing all the merchandise in person because they expect a certain level of quality from L.L. Bean merchandise. Trust (as seen through previous experiences and brand experience) is considered a key aspect to retailing on the Web. Several studies have shown how pre-existing trust for a product or retailer can be a large strategic advantage when it comes to retailing on the Web. This is one of the reasons that pre-existing offline merchants still have an advantage on the Web over Web-only startups.

Another detriment to online shopping discussed by researchers is the application of delivery and consumers' interest in delivery. Many products do not lend themselves to delivery. Again, Home Depot is an example of a store that sells products (such as fencing or other large items) that are more easily bought in person. Additionally, some people simply don't like home delivery. They either fear the delivery people or are concerned about lost or stolen packages. This, like the credit card security issue often cited in earlier days of online retailing, may decrease as people become more comfortable with home delivery of a more diverse collection of items (such as groceries, toys, etc) rather than just clothes and books.

Finally, in most cases the need for shipping eliminates the possibility of same-day procurement of the product. While Electronic Software Delivery (ESD) promises to bring impulse immediacy to the Web for digitized items such as software and music, many products can only be transferred through physical means. That means waiting for at least a day.

In the End, Information Is Key

Researchers boil the psychology of online shopping down to the supply of information. Once consumers have created a final set of selections after studying the available universe of choices, the thing they crave is extensive information in making the final choice. In addition, the abundance of information can help eliminate the need for experiential evaluation of the merchandise. For example, Web stores such as Amazon.com that offer customer reviews provide information that can actually surpass the experience of flipping through the book.

Consumers are turning to Internet shopping because they can more rapidly assemble the best information needed to make a purchasing decision. That stems directly from one of the Web's best attributes, delivery of information, and one of the best aspects of computers, rapid processing of comparative features. This combination helps make online shopping a compelling, if not superior, choice alternative to traditional shopping.

Relating the Consumer Psychological Profile to Available Statistics

Do statistics back up consumer psychology studies? Apparently so. In an earlier GVU study, three of the top four reasons people cited for personal Web shopping were directly related to the consumer psychological profile. The reasons the GVU respondents cited for shopping online were convenience (65 percent), availability of vendor information (60 percent), the lack of pressure from salespeople (55 percent), and saving time (53 percent). An Ernst & Young survey in 1999 found that convenience and choices/variety were also quite high.

As a side note, that GVU survey also stated that personalized services are for most people not a primary reason to shop online. Researchers wrote that this "could be a result of unfamiliarity with personalized shopping services."

What Does All This Mean?

We have established three critical components of online shopping. First, there is a growing base of devices that can connect to the Web and enable people to join and interact on the Web. That base of hardware and software is growing at a rate of more than 20 percent annually and, in terms of browsers, it is splitting between market leaders Netscape (25 percent) and Microsoft (75 percent). Second, there is a healthy universe of Web users that offers more desirable characteristics for online sellers than the general U.S. or world population. Third, there is strong evidence that online shopping can have inherent advantages that will attract shoppers to the Web, even if prices are no less than those offered by traditional stores. These three factors are brewing a market that, according to Jupiter Communications, will grow to more than $35 billion in 2002.

What's a Web Merchant to Do?

How can you, as a Web merchant, take advantage of all this knowledge? First you must realize how you can use these factors to your advantage. Here are some recommendations based on what we've presented in this chapter:

Build a Customer Base and Keep It with Value-Added Services.

Stores that are able to withstand losses as they spend to grab market share will have an advantage. Audience growth is critically expensive in the start-up phase. Since advertising doesn't guarantee a sale, top sites will use cash cushions to wait out costly advertising campaigns and search engine links as audiences grow to a profitable level. This notion is based on a common Web business model in which sites deem it important to grab the audience first and keep them by offering superior content and user interaction.

Don't Assume that Stores Win on Price

Los Angeles Times technology editor Jonathan Weber summed it up best when he wrote, "Viewing the Web not as a cost-cutting tool but as a way to add unique new service helps explain a lot of what's happening—or not happening—in the online commerce arena these days." What Weber meant was that cutting costs and offering lower prices won't be at the heart of e-commerce success. Instead he, like many consumer behaviorists, argues that the bond a store develops with its customers and via its inventory scope and information will be the key. Price is a factor in a purchase decision, but its importance is often overstated in relation to the Internet. Instead, stores like Amazon.com, Virtual Vineyards, and L.L. Bean have designed online sites and consumer value that aren't focused so much on price as they are many other parts of the store equation.

Inventory Scope is Important

Consumers feel an important aspect of the Web is that it helps them analyze many choices and quickly examine nearly complete selections of the products they want to buy. Stores that offer a subset of a product type may lose out to stores that push inventory availability to the maximum. The best way to maximize inventory availability is to have partnerships streamlined to manufacturers and distributors. This way you can offer a larger selection of items that aren't necessarily in stock. Incidentally, it is situations like these that infer that middle men and distributors will not just fade away, as many predict.

Focus on Category-Killer Markets

In order to focus informational offerings and inventory, many stores simply try to solve one specific subject area of shopping while avoiding others. The reason is that users respond to the depth of a site's expertise and information, not the breadth.

Avoid Items Requiring High Experiential Exposure

Experiential buying will never be overtaken by mail order or Web-based stores because some things are just better shopped for in person. If you plan to compete in an area that has a high experiential need, you will need to increase the information available in order to offset the desire of the consumer to shop traditionally.

Navigation and "Browsability" Are Critical

As shown by concerns found in recent GVU surveys and other research, the need to have an easy-to-navigate site is a paramount concern of Web consumers. Since many consumers search heavily on the Web when making a shopping decision, anything that impedes this process forces them to go elsewhere or develop poor perceptions of the retailer. In some cases, poor navigation and site design can destroy or prevent development of the trust that merchants must achieve before a consumer will do business with them. Thus you should create easy-to-read price lists, make it easy to find items (this is more than just adding a search engine), and test your capacity to serve your site out to the public (sites might work fine initially but buckle under large groups of simultaneous users).

Numbers Can't Make Your Idea Work

Don't assume that the numbers and market survey presented here validate any specific Web store plan. Thousands of online stores are launched each month around the globe and all of them are chasing customers. Good numbers will never offset a bad idea. What they can do is help you understand which elements of your fantastic idea should be emphasized. Market research is never a stand-in, it's always about understanding. Now that you have an understanding of what's happening in the Web store market space, you have to go out and make that knowledge work.

Further Reading and Resources

Several studies, research companies, and papers will help you learn more about what has been written about here, and with new numbers and analysis in the future as the Web shopping market matures.

Academic Papers and Studies

The following studies and papers are worth looking at:

- **Interactive Home Shopping: Consumer, Retailer, and Manufacturer Incentives to Participate in Electronic Marketplaces** by Joseph Alba, John Lynch, Barton Weitz, Chris Janiszewski, Richard Lutz, Alan Sawyer and Stacy Wood. *Journal of Marketing*, July 1997

  This paper takes apart the online shopping process, and dissects exactly how it benefits consumers and how consumers specifically gain benefits from online shopping that are critical to its success. Excellent reading.

- **The Tenth GVU WWW Survey** by The GVU WWW Survey Team www.gvu.gatech.edu/user_surveys/

  The tenth version of this respected, self-selecting Web survey is now out. The survey is constantly being reissued, and its supporting writings and datasets, and all the past surveys are available on the Web.

Research Companies

Several major research companies are actively producing studies, and numbers, of interest to online store owners. They're all worth checking in on. Many times abstracts, press releases, and excerpts from their reports can be found on their Web sites.

- **JUPITER COMMUNICATIONS** (www.jup.com). Jupiter produces a number of key studies, and also produces a newsletter and conference about online shopping.

- **IDC** (www.idc.com). The research division of publishing giant IDG (including *InfoWorld*, *PC World*, and *Computer World* magazines) conducts research to determine the size and characteristics of the e-commerce markets, as well as the total worldwide installed base of computers and other technology systems.

- **FORRESTER RESEARCH** (www.forrester.com). Forrester has done a number of reports on e-commerce and has several reports on growth overall, as well as rankings of e-commerce capability by country.

Useful Internet Statistic Sites

Several major research companies are actively producing studies of interest to online store owners. They're all worth checking in on. Abstracts, press releases, and excerpts from all of their reports can be found on their Web sites.

- **NUA'S INTERNET SURVEYS** (www.nua.ie/surveys/). This large, searchable database of information from nearly every major Internet-related research study also tracks the latest worldwide Internet population growth by country.

- **STATMARKET.COM** (www.statmarket.com). Provides interesting statistics compiled from more than 100,000 small to medium–sized Web sites with a focus on the nature of their connection and computer characteristics (such as screen size, color depth, browser type, etc.) as well as country location and more.

- **CyberAtlas** (www.cyberatlas.com). Similar to Nua, this site provides a roundup of interesting research released about the nature of the Internet and related activities.

- **Global Internet Statistics (by Language)** (www.euromktg.com/globstats/). Provides a recent accounting of the primary languages used by the worldwide Internet population. Useful for understanding localization possibilities.

CHAPTER FIVE

Web Store Business Models

Despite the progress that the Web has already made and the momentum that e-commerce is gaining, much of the Web and the creating of online stores is still in its infancy. People often take for granted some of the truly unique opportunities the Web offers as a business medium. Before attempting to operate a store on the Web, having a solid understanding of the Web is essential to structuring a successful store business model.

This chapter covers the unique advantages of the Web before tackling specific business models for cyberstores.

One-to-One Relationships

One aspect of the Internet that makes it such a strong medium for business is that it offers the opportunity for people to directly interact with one another. Without the Internet, it is difficult for a company to give close, personal service to a large number of customers. Successful companies and retailers previously shied away from the idea of personal treatment and one-on-one marketing. Companies that enjoyed enormous growth and success were giants that created a common-denominator product line and treated everyone equally to create incredible efficiency both in manufacturing and sales. Some of these companies were McDonald's, General Motors, IBM, General Electric, Wal-Mart, and, later, The Gap.

Computers and the Internet provide the power and efficiency to create extremely targeted, even personal, relationships with customers. That helps smaller operations compete against major stores. Knowing your customers' sizes, favorite shipping methods, and other personal information allows you to provide better customer service.

Narrow Interest Aggregation

Although one advantage offered by the Web is the ability for large entities to "get small" and interact with customers on an individual basis, another aspect to consider is how normally narrow interests can become major markets. The Web's reach aggregates scattered groups into a single market.

For example, if one of every 25,000 people is a collector of antique bottles, would it be wise to open an antique bottle store in New York City? Considering that the New York metro area has a population of about 20 million people, there would only be 800 avid potential customers (excluding tourists) in the New York City area. However, with the population of the Internet expected to be 100 million by the year 2000, a similar store on the Web would have a potential customer base of 4,000.

These are not actual numbers but rather examples that prove a point. A quick search of the Net found more than 400 pages or sites related to bottle collecting, including Reggie's Antique Bottles (http://www.ipass.net/~rlynch/bottles/mylist.html), where bottle collector Reggie Lynch sells antique bottles (Figure 5.1).

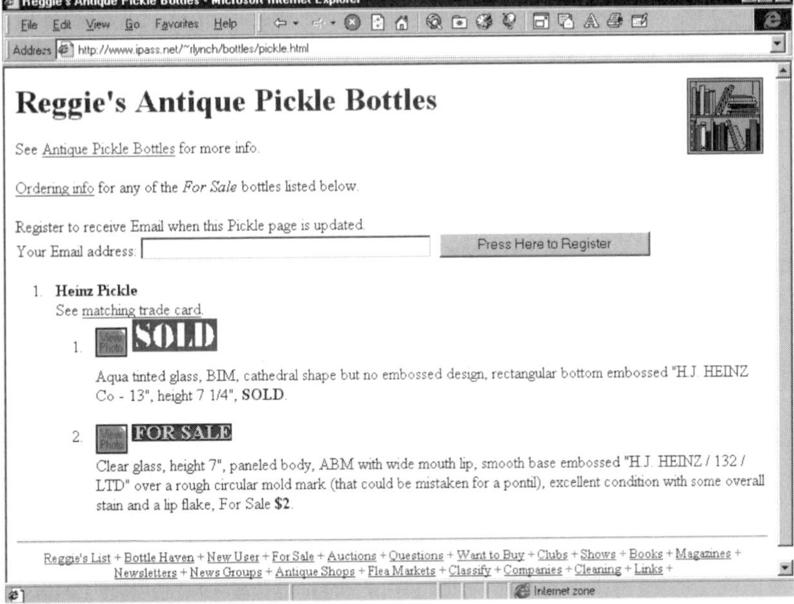

FIGURE 5.1
Reggie's Antique Bottles takes advantage of the Web's ability to sell items of narrow interest, such as pickle bottles and other antique bottles.

The ability of the Internet to help communities of interest—especially narrow ones—exist in a significant enough form to foster commerce is at least as important as its ability to support personalized customer service. Many smaller markets are served not by enormous corporations such as Wal-Mart and L.L. Bean, but rather by individuals and small companies that, in many cases, serve the passions of both customers and merchants.

Low Cost of Entry

The barrier to launching a Web store is extremely low when compared to opening up a significant traditional retail store or mail-order operation. Although major Web stores with significant site infrastructure, staffing, and content can cost millions to launch, such a cost is not always necessary for, or a guarantee of, success.

Successful sites like Tronix can be built and run for less money than almost any other type of store. Larger sites can also be interesting. Disney has poured millions into its Web site, which quickly began to generate sales equal to that of four traditional Disney Stores. Disney executives expect the Web store to grow significantly. At the low end, opening a store on the Web can cost as little as $10,000 to $20,000. But keep in mind that not only does this make the Web an enticing place to open a store, it also means that new competition may arrive at any time.

Leveraging Technology

Technology can create immense changes in the way any entity operates. The Web makes it easy to utilize and present new technology to customers in a way that is easy to use. A Web page may look very simple on the surface—click here, answer this question, fill out that form. But behind that interface could be software that automatically routes orders to manufacturing plants around the world, remembers a customer's previous presence, or checks the authenticity of a customer's credit card. This automation makes Web selling very productive. Examine the leverage that even a small store can gain by moving onto the Web—a constant, worldwide presence. Before the Web, such presence was almost impossible to achieve without a huge staff, a call center, and extensive infrastructure. Today it's an afterthought.

The Sea Is Changing

The Internet represents a new way of doing business. One-to-one relationships, narrow interest aggregation, the low-barrier to entry, and technology's leverage are the major reasons behind the growth of online stores and shopping. At every opportunity, store-owners should:

- **Build systems that create** one-to-one relationships with customers.
- **Look for narrow-interest** communities that can be aggregated and to which their stores can appeal.

- **Use the cost advantage** of the Web to compete against real-world counterparts.
- **Utilize computer technology** to become more productive while keeping things simple for users.

These are the pillar advantages of the Internet that allow store owners to utilize various business models to create a compelling shopping site.

Choosing a Business Model

Deciding on a Web business model is paramount to a store's success. Opening a Web store is more than just slapping together a nice Web site and offering products for sale. A store-owner must decide how the store will make money. As you will see, there is more than one way to operate a store on the Web.

The rest of this chapter identifies, explains, and discusses all the pure online store models. Many stores use a combination of these pure models. Although the Web is still very young, and online stores are younger still, the Internet is filled with an amazing array of stores, some of which are discussed in Chapter 3. From online auction houses like OnSale.com and eBay to import specialists like Tronix to sales-lead stores like Microsoft's Carpoint, there are a number of successful examples from which to learn.

Traditional Online Store

We should first define a traditional online store (if there is in fact such a thing): a traditional online store offers hard goods for sale. Customers browse for items that are presented on a Web site in catalog fashion and can order directly through the site or via telephone, fax, or mail. Most products are kept in stock and orders are sent out as soon as they are assembled and ready for shipping.

Auction House

The online auction model has been very well executed by sites such as OnSale. With computers running the show and processing bids, online auctions provide a great model that has proven successful in the real world. Online auctions combine the excitement of bidding with the opportunity to get a great price in real-time. Onsale.com (Figure 5.2) uses this model to sell surplus office and computer equipment. Other sites use it to sell used computer equipment.

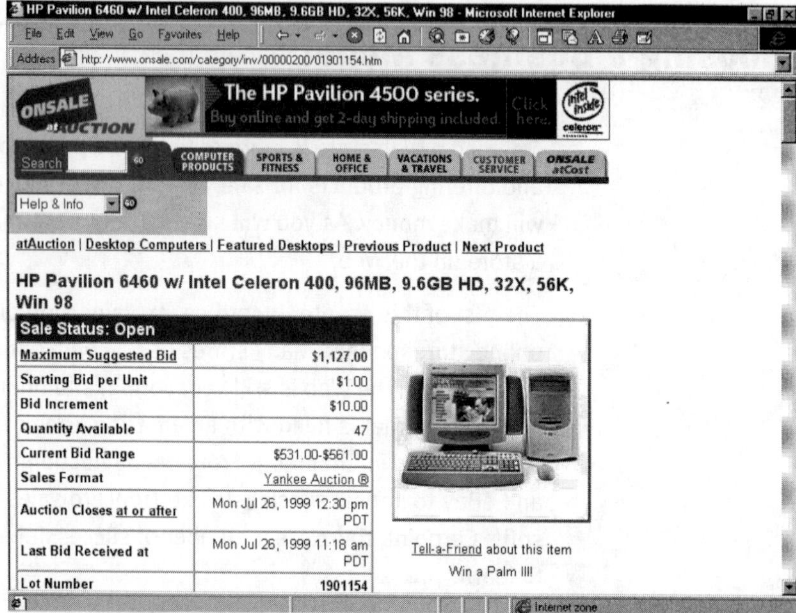

FIGURE 5.2
Onsale.com (www.onsale.com) uses an auction model to attract buyers of office equipment and other high-end merchandise.

Personal Auction Aggregator

The clear leader and best example here is eBay, but Amazon.com is also moving into this area. eBay facilitates one-to-one trading and selling in an auction format on the Web (Figure 5.3). Founder Pierre Omidyar, an early Internet enthusiast, realized that people needed someplace to meet to buy and sell unique items. As opposed to traditional auction houses that sell hundreds of items, sometimes in bulk, eBay and other personal auction aggregators let individuals buy and sell items in more than 1,600 categories. eBay makes money by collecting a percentage of each sale.

As Amazon.com has broadened its scope to become less a bookstore and more an online department store, it is offering the same service.

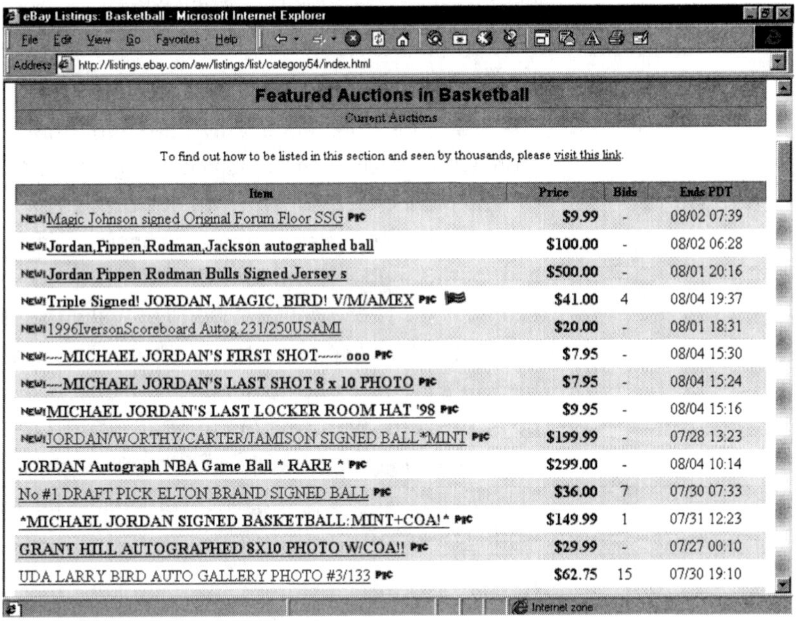

FIGURE 5.3
eBay (www.ebay.com) is the leading personal auction site.

eBay Listings: Basketball - Microsoft Internet Explorer

File Edit View Go Favorites Help

Address http://listings.ebay.com/aw/listings/list/category54/index.html

Featured Auctions in Basketball

Current Auctions

To find out how to be listed in this section and seen by thousands, please visit this link.

Item	Price	Bids	Ends PDT
NEW! Magic Johnson signed Original Forum Floor SSG PIC	$9.99	-	08/02 07:39
NEW! Jordan,Pippen,Rodman,Jackson autographed ball	$100.00	-	08/02 06:28
NEW! Jordan Pippen Rodman Bulls Signed Jersey s	$500.00	-	08/01 20:16
NEW! Triple Signed! JORDAN, MAGIC, BIRD! V/M/AMEX PIC	$41.00	4	08/04 19:37
NEW! 1996IversonScoreboard Autog.231/250USAMI	$20.00	-	08/01 18:31
NEW! ---MICHAEL JORDAN'S FIRST SHOT----- ooo PIC	$7.95	-	08/04 15:30
NEW! ---MICHAEL JORDAN'S LAST SHOT 8 x 10 PHOTO PIC	$7.95	-	08/04 15:24
NEW! MICHAEL JORDAN'S LAST LOCKER ROOM HAT '98 PIC	$9.95	-	08/04 15:16
NEW! JORDAN/WORTHY/CARTER/JAMISON SIGNED BALL*MINT PIC	$199.99	-	07/28 13:23
JORDAN Autograph NBA Game Ball * RARE * PIC	$299.00	-	08/04 10:14
No #1 DRAFT PICK ELTON BRAND SIGNED BALL PIC	$36.00	7	07/30 07:33
MICHAEL JORDAN SIGNED BASKETBALL:MINT+COA! PIC	$149.99	1	07/31 12:23
GRANT HILL AUTOGRAPHED 8X10 PHOTO W/COA!! PIC	$29.99	-	07/27 00:10
UDA LARRY BIRD AUTO GALLERY PHOTO #3/133 PIC	$62.75	15	07/30 19:10

Internet zone

Broker/Virtual Store

A broker is someone who arranges and consummates a sale, often without owning the item in question herself. Brokers may even sell items before they are in stock. This is a model that works well for online stores that want to be as virtual as possible.

The virtual store model is based on limiting stock and infrastructure costs that are generally associated with traditional stores or mail-order companies. It also relies on receiving an order before actually procuring the resulting product from a supplier. The other goal is to automate as much of the sales process at the site level as possible. Costs are kept low by limiting the amount of store-to-customer contact during the ordering process.

The key to this model's success is minimizing the time needed to fill an order. To accomplish this, a store must be close to its suppliers in order to receive products as quickly as possible. It also needs to turn those items around immediately while providing a high level of customer service. The customer service element is crucial in case the time required to deliver an item is longer than expected.

Associate Store

The associate store model draws strength from combining a real-world store with a virtual store. Many catalog outfits such as J. Crew, Eddie Bauer, and L.L. Bean operate retail stores as extensions to their mail order businesses. Web stores can consider similar opportunities. The goal of this model is two-fold. The model allows the store-owner to extend a link to the physical world to make the store more visible. The existence of a traditional store can make a virtual store appear more stable while attracting customers. Also, a successful Web store brand can be an asset to leverage into the retail world. For example, if Amazon.com continues to grow, it could decide to open physical Amazon bookstores. This would create a synergistic relationship between the virtual and real-world stores.

Of course associate stores will primarily be those that existed in traditional form prior to the growth of the Web and which added an Internet presence to take advantage of its retailing potential. Either way the associate model is arrived at allows a store to increase overall sales by combining traditional and Web-based retailing.

Electronic Distribution Store

The electronic distribution model is a new breed. Why ship a product through the mail when it can be immediately transported over the Internet? The major advantage of this model is the ability to rapidly distribute products. There is no faster way to deliver a product than directly over the same phone, cable, or T-1 line that received the order. Of course, electronic distribution is limited to certain electronically transferable products such as software and music (Figure 5.4). When someone creates a way to electronically distribute such hard items as furniture, clothes, or sporting goods, that category of item won't be limited to one part of one chapter in one book.

The success of the electronic distribution model also depends on the increase of faster distribution options and the security of electronic delivery. For more on electronic software delivery, see Chapter 16.

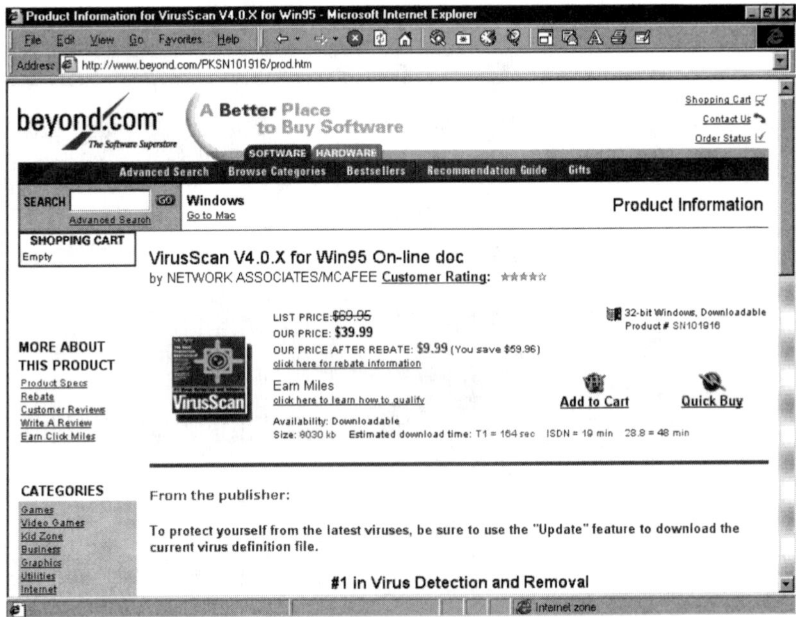

FIGURE 5.4
Software.net (www.beyond.com) utilizes electronic software delivery to sell directly over the Internet.

In-Stock Advantage

The in-stock advantage model attempts to compete against broker stores by shortening the time between the placing of an order and the receiving of the product by the customer. This model works very well against stores that work with little or no inventory and compete on price. If an in-stock store can keep its prices close to those of a broker store, it can win sales on the ability to deliver the product first.

A good example of the in-stock advantage model is Fatbrain.com (Figure 5.5). It is successfully competing against Amazon.com in one specific segment of the book market by offering a much higher availability of in-stock computer books. Anyone who has ever had an urgent need for a computer book would understand the advantage of next-day delivery. Amazon has responded to the pressure put on by Fatbrain.com and Barnesandnoble.com by building two warehouses—one on the west coast and one on the east coast—to help it fill orders more quickly.

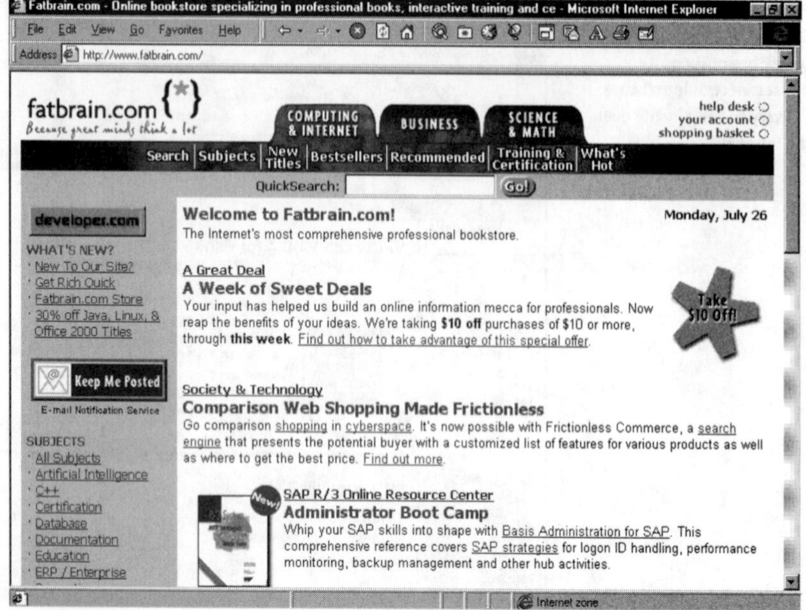

FIGURE 5.5 Fatbrain.com (www.fatbrain.com) which sells computer books, stocks more than 25,000 titles, ensuring its customers that most books can ship the day they are ordered.

Content Attraction

The content attraction model is implemented by many sites and raised to an art form by others. The theory is that compelling content will lead to more site visitors and, eventually, more sales. An example is Virtual Vineyards (www.virtualvin.com), shown in Figure 5.6.

This model is often implemented when content-focused sites create online stores as an additional revenue stream to supplement advertising and site subscription income. Sites using this model include c|net, which runs the online software storefront buydirect.com, and Online Game Review's OGR.com, which also runs an online game store.

The key to this model obviously is strong content. While many stores offer content as an appetizer, content-based stores make it their main course. Since the development of good content can be costly, so too can the deployment of this particular model.

You might also find customers who are concerned about a conflict of interest if, for example, you review a product as a publisher and sell it as a merchant. Thus it is important to make a clear disclosure of the role that your store plays in your content decisions.

FIGURE 5.6
Some major sites such as Virtual Vineyards (www.virtualvin.com) attract people with content (such its recipes or wine tasting notes) in the hopes of turning them into paying customers.

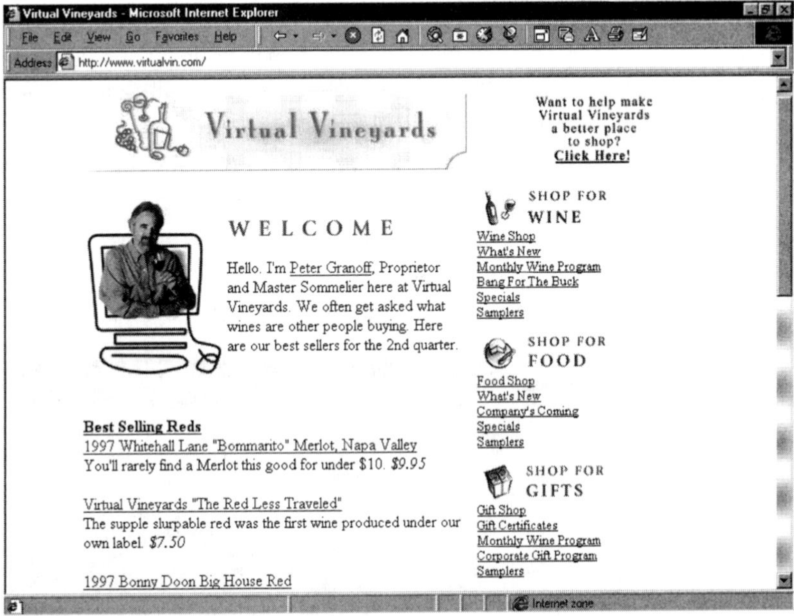

Online Associate/Affiliate

The online associate/affiliate model involves one store (the provider of the goods) that relies on a network of associated sites to find customers and lead them to the sale. The associated sites receive a royalty for the sales they help generate.

Many stores use this as a supplemental model. It is, in essence, the franchise model of cyberspace. Amazon.com, with its Amazon Associates program, is the most visible user of this model. As shown in Figure 5.7, Kilimanjaro Tours (www.kilimanjaro.com) supplements its travel business by referring visitors to books of interest on Amazon.com. Realizing that a number of Web sites referred to or recommended books, Amazon.com offered those sites an easy way to cash in on that content. By embedding a specific code in a link, an associate can link a book title to the corresponding order page at Amazon.com. If a customer follows that link and buys the book, the associate receives a percentage of the sale. The program now has more than 10,000 member sites and has instigated similar deals with a number of online bookstores.

Effectively implementing this model depends on a number of factors. A store must be able to sell products at a high enough margin to afford to offer a percentage to associate sites. It also needs the infrastructure capable of providing a high level of service (Amazon.com is able to handle thousands of requests simultaneously). Finally, the primary company must be capable of aggressively signing member sites. In short, the key to this model is a strong set of links between member sites and the store. If a more capable site were to lure away associates, the host would not only see a drop in its sales, but also an increase in its competitors' sales.

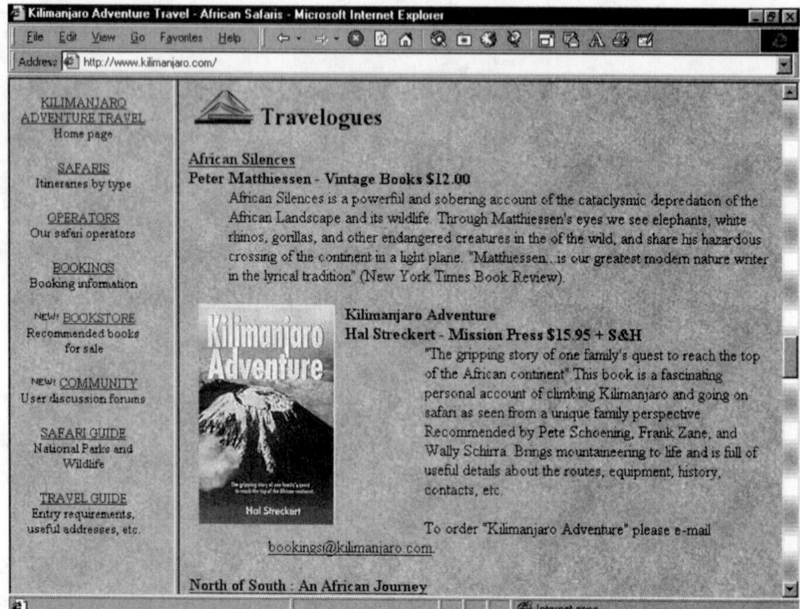

FIGURE 5.7
Kilimanjaro Tours (www.kilimanjaro.com) organizes mountaineering trips and now has a business as an Amazon.com associate store.

Price Buster

The lowest price model has existed since the dawn of time, so it is no surprise to see it being used on the Internet. Customers want low prices. What makes this model so interesting is how the Web can be used to eliminate some of the costs incurred by retailers and other companies. These savings can then be passed on to customers. For example, Tronix competes against retail stores that sell games, yet it has a fraction of the rent and much lower inventory costs. This can be used to offer lower prices and attract customers.

It is also vitally important to remember that offering the absolute lowest price is not necessarily the best model to use. A price-based business model tends to attract buyers who are looking solely for the lowest price. These customers will constantly look for the store with the lowest price, no matter how little that difference is, while ignoring all other factors. Therefore, if you compete solely on price, you stand to lose to the next low-price store that comes along. This means your margin will remain as thin as possible and you will find it difficult to implement the items that take time and money to develop such as online content or community.

Shopping Club

Shopping clubs, which also are becoming popular in traditional retailing, offer outstanding prices and other discounts in exchange for a yearly membership fee (Figure 5.8). Price clubs use the profits generated by membership fees to offset their low product margins.

Theoretically, a club with 250,000 members each paying a $40 annual membership would have $10 million to use toward lowering prices. The trick is attracting members.

The biggest problem with shopping clubs comes during their infancy. The member discounts must be substantial enough entice people to become members. However, non-member prices will not be attractive enough to lead to many non-member customers. Therefore, shopping club owners will generally have to sweat out minimal sales until there are enough members to create revenue through membership fees and membership sales.

You also have to be sure that member prices remain lower than those of non-club stores, otherwise there is no point in joining.

What some stores do is avoid creating large price differences on all items and instead offer other advantages to membership such as longer warranties or special product selection. Some stores offer deep discounts only on certain staple items while earning most of their profits in other areas, hoping that customers buy the less-discounted items in addition to the more attractively priced items.

In any case, the goal is simple: build repeat customers who return again and again because getting a return on the membership fee keeps them from considering competitors.

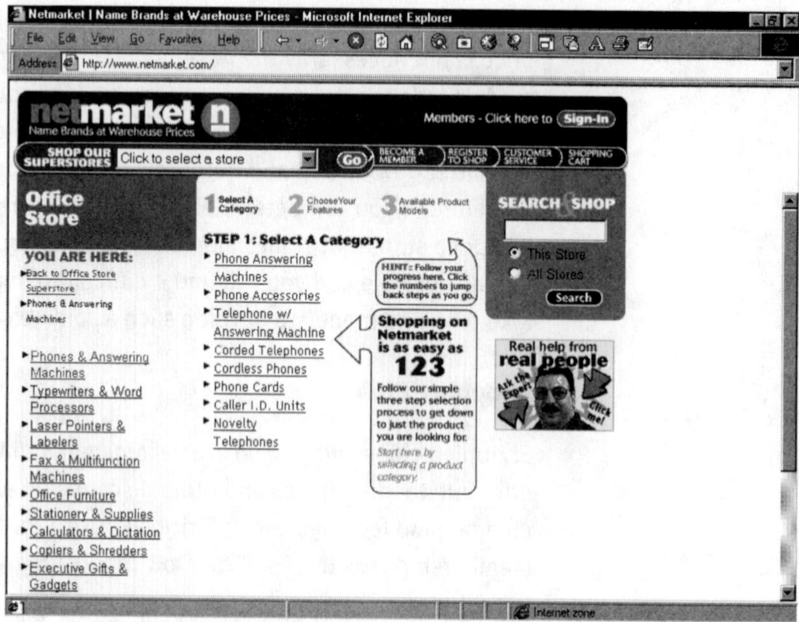

Figure 5.8
Netmarket.com (www.netmarket.com) is one of the largest online shopping member clubs.

Sales-Lead Generator

A sales lead-generating model is more about selling customers than it is about selling products. This model works best with big-ticket items such as cars. The customer asks the lead generator for information on the availability of a certain product, and the lead generator sends the customer toward the most useful supplier of the product. For example, Microsoft's Carpoint uses this model. Carpoint not only negotiates a bounty for successful automobile sales, but also charges a fee to join and belong to the service. Car dealers pay nearly $3,000 per month to belong to the site.

Sales-lead stores—like online associates—need exceptionally strong links to the dealers with which they work. The success of these networks rests primarily on having a large number of partners and users.

Community-Oriented

The success of the community-oriented model is based on developing sales through the creation of a tight-knit online community. Customers are compelled to purchase products because they want to reward the creation of a sustainable community of interest. Customers are additionally drawn to the community because of the subject matter.

For example, a comic book shop can create a viable online community that supports various discussions and online events that focus on the comic book universe. Not only do these activities generate participants who are apt to purchase comic books, but the interaction between the participants and the store creates a bond that leads to loyal, lifelong customers.

Narrow Interest

The narrow-interest store rides a small niche that is viable only on the Web to success. The only competition comes from other Web stores.

An owner of a narrow-interest store usually shares a specific interest with his customers. These stores often stock items that are custom-made or that are only available through non-traditional means such as auctions, personal buying trips, etc. Narrow-interest stores often cater to collectors or hobbyists.

Narrow-interest stores can often expand by implementing community-oriented features.

Focused Interest

The focused interest model is a relatively new online store model that has come into existence as the Web has matured. As some of the pioneers of the Web such as Amazon.com broaden their product categories, some merchants who only focus on one category are working to be the best Web store for that focused category. It is not a new business model. In traditional retailing, category-killing stores like Home Depot, Borders, and Circuit City have used this model for years.

However, as the Web matures and community, content, and service become major issues of success for Web retailers, those that choose to remain focused despite the lure of expansion into other product categories are betting on a strategy that will prove just as compelling in the online world as it has recently in traditional retailing. To be successful, the focus must be evident on the site and the extra services and content that are generated by the merchant must offer a reason for people to choose that merchant for a specific product over larger stores that offer the same product as part of a much wider product line.

Intranet Stores

This is a very low-profile store model, but one that could grow as intranets (internal company networks that are run like Internet sites) become more popular. In order to control budgets and better account for various internal product use, companies may opt to build stores directly on their intranets. The site would work like any other Web store although it would only be available to company members.

The real opportunity lies in the possibility of intranet stores that are actually specialized storefronts run by external stores for a specific corporation. For example, an online software store could offer a specialized storefront allowing Intel employees to order products through the company's intranet. The competition would be for large Web stores to become the "official" store for the company.

Custom Construction

Custom construction stores offer customized items and take advantage of the ease with which customers can order those items over the Internet.

Through an interactive process, customers can customize a particular item. The key to this system is that, by using a database, a store can remember and apply certain traits to each of a particular customer's order.

For example, Disney's online store allows customers to create personalized Disney merchandise by adding names, birth dates, and other information to items.

The future is in sites that can remember custom information for repeated use. For example, Levi's has a system with which you can walk into a retail store and be scanned for custom-sized jeans. The potential is there for people to be scanned at a local facility and then offer that information to any clothing retailer who would accept it. Dell and Gateway—two huge direct manufacturers—have been successful by offering customized computer systems ordered via the phone or the Internet.

Clicks and Mortar

"Clicks and mortar" is a term some people use to describe an e-commerce business model in which the merchant attempts to gain an advantage by having the best integration between online and real-world offerings. A seamless integration of the two—such as allowing customers to order via the Web and pick up their order on the way home—can increase the synergy between a business' offerings.

Another advantage a strong "clicks and mortar" strategy offers is the ability to order via the Web but return items locally, eliminating the hassle of shipping an item back to a company. Customers could also walk into a store or showroom to view an item and then order a specific version of it via the Web that is then delivered from a centralized warehouse. This makes it possible for retail stores to stock more items for show, since inventory might be centrally located elsewhere (in less expensive areas) rather than in the store itself.

What this strategy says is that there is a place for traditional retail stores in the electronic commerce world, but it only supplies advantage if the online and offline offerings are truly symbiotic.

Product-Specific Collective

Taking the idea of online malls one step further, these collections of stores offering similar types of products offer the economy of scale unavailable to stores working alone. These collectives can attract customers interested in special interest products such as gourmet foods, extreme sports gear, and more.

An example is Booksense.com, which brings independent booksellers together online to compete against larger store chains and online booksellers such as Amazon.com. By banding together, independent stores can collectively create the traffic and economy of scale that they couldn't do individually. Once in this online mall, customers can go to specific stores within the group and eventually find the individual owner, local merchant, or focused retailer within the product category that they desire.

Buyer Aggregation/Group Purchasing

As Accompany's Web site says, "Price goes down as volume goes up." This model allows consumers to achieve volume discounts by being part of a group of people who agree to purchase a certain product. This motivates potential customers to find other people—friends, family members, neighbors—who might be interested in buying the same product, thus driving the price down. Accompany and Paul Allen's Mercata are the early leaders here (figures 5.9 and 5.10).

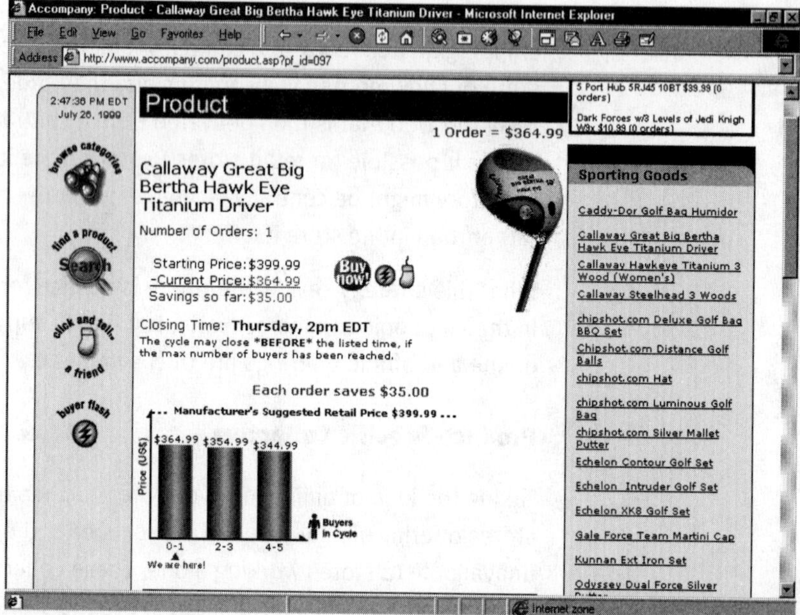

FIGURE 5.9
Accompany (www.accompany.com) says "Price goes down as volume goes up."

Accompany and Mercata work somewhat differently, though the idea is the same. And once a customer has committed to buy a certain item at a target price, the sale is final once that price is reached. There's no backing out.

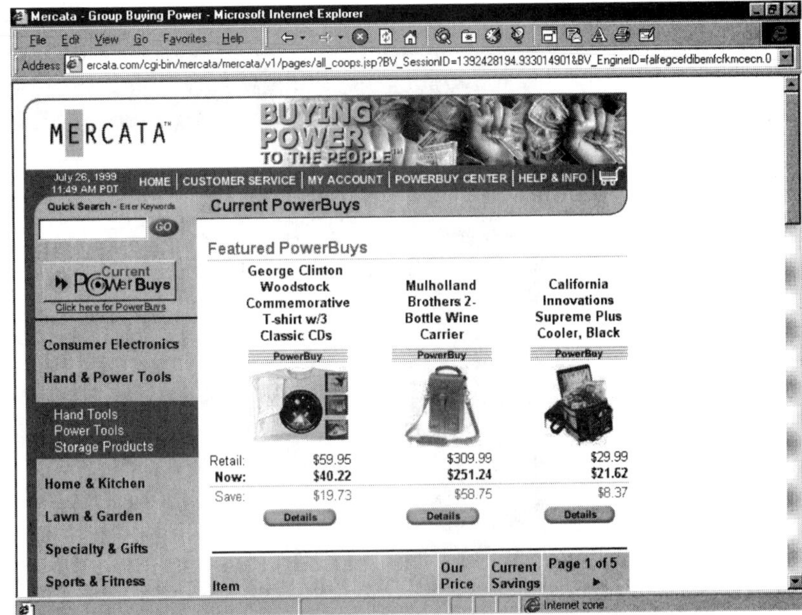

FIGURE 5.10
Mercata (www.mercata.com) also offers volume discounts to groups of individuals.

Reverse Auction

In a reverse auction, the customer sets the price for the service or product and the host searches for someone willing to fill that request. This business model has been pioneered and made popular by Priceline.com (Figure 5.11). Priceline allows customers to name the top price they would pay for an airline ticket, hotel room, new car, home mortgage, home refinancing, or home equity loan. Once the customer has named a target price, Priceline transmits this information to sellers who then accept or reject the offers made by Priceline's customers.

This model works best with big-ticket items since it is difficult to haggle over the price of inexpensive items. It also requires the products to be fairly commodity-oriented items that have a number of sellers trying to offer the same service against one another. Customers back their offer with a major credit card and must accept the charge for the item they order before knowing the exact details of who has fulfilled it.

FIGURE 5.11 Priceline (www.priceline.com) finds big-ticket items after its customers set their maximum price.

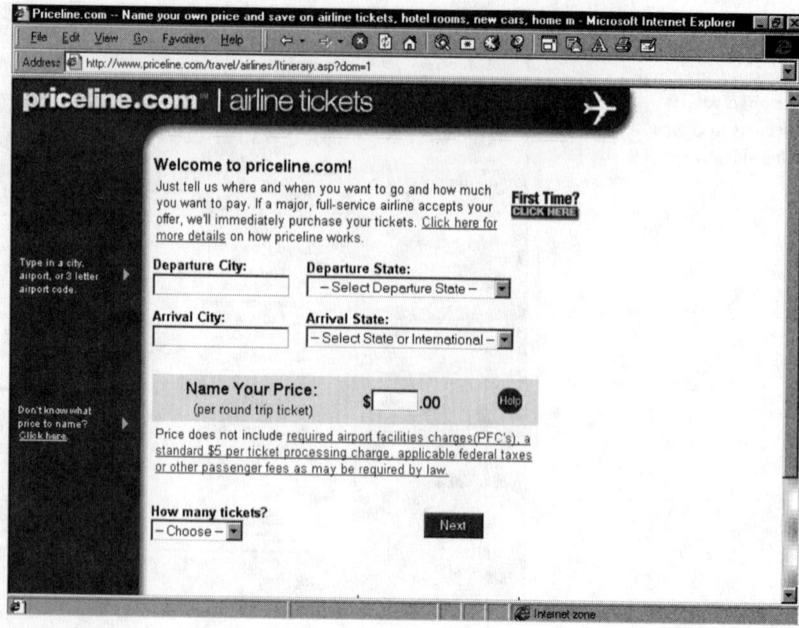

Which Model Works for You?

When deciding which model to employ, the most important thing to consider is how you intend to connect the merchandise you want to sell with the customers you want to serve. The process you choose to implement entices people to shop with you and creates the energy that moves items out the door.

After you've decided what to sell and to whom to sell it, then and only then should you search for the model that brings these two groups together. If your intended customer base requires outstanding customer service, you would be better served by choosing the community model rather than an in-stock advantage model because your customers are more interested in service options than immediate delivery. However, if you sell readily available merchandise, a low-price model might work best.

The best way to select among business models is to become familiar with them and how they are being used on the Internet. As you investigate, you will notice how the most successful stores have perfectly matched their models to their merchandise and their customer bases. Not every site can work as an auction site, and many can't operate as virtual brokers. This is not because the owners don't know how to create these stores, it's because they know that those would be unsuccessful models for their line of business.

This chapter has introduced you to several online store business models. In each case there are successful example enterprises on the Web. No single model is the best for every situation. In fact, many stores use one primary model and supplement that with certain aspects of other models. These customized models often work best.

PART II

Building Your Store

No matter what software package or process you select to build your store, there are some basics that all online merchants must understand. Part II covers fundamentals of philosophy, including launching your store, designing your store, stocking your virtual shelves, and creating compelling store content.

Part II Table of Contents

CHAPTER SIX

Launching Your Online Store

Before you sell your first video game, pair of boots, or Lear jet online, you'll have to do plenty of work that will have nothing to do with the Web, your online presence, or selling. As many business advisors will tell you, the early decisions you make concerning your business setup can be the most essential.

You have to choose a name (no kidding!), preferably find a lawyer, decide on the type of business (S-Corp., limited liability, sole proprietorship, partnership, etc.), get a tax identification number, find an office if you choose not to work out of your home, get insurance, etc. Tack a few more et ceteras on there if you'd like—you'll probably need them.

Get the point? Actually setting up the business can be more work than selling your product. And as you spend time doing it, you won't spend time doing business. However, if you simply stay organized, stay focused, and work through the long to-do list, you'll eventually reach your goal of becoming the owner and operator of an online store. You will have setbacks and you will get frustrated. Work through it.

Once you're ready to launch a store, you'll face another critical piece of work. Assuming you've done all the legal work and have your business entity set up, you will experience the hardest part of online anything—setting up the services and initial accounts you need to properly develop an online presence.

Surrounding these key tasks are several other startup items, including obtaining phone service, setting up merchant accounts with the right credit cards and banks, and forming relationships with the distributors you'll order products from. We cover it all here in a simple step-by-step process. Although you will want to go out and quiz other professionals—especially a lawyer and an accountant—we've tried to simplify the process as much as possible. The good news here is once this stuff is done, you'll never have to do it again. And if it's done properly, you'll save thousands on headache remedies later on!

That being said, let's launch.

Selecting a Name

Chances are, if you're going into business, you've been thinking about it for awhile. And if you've been thinking about it for awhile, you've mulled over some names. Although choosing a name can be one of the most fun, creative aspects of the setup, it shouldn't be taken lightly. Your name is how your business will be identified. For example, you probably don't want to call your store Overpriced Junk unless you're selling antiques to people with sharp senses of humor.

When deciding on a name for your business, think in the long term. This name will be plastered on the entrance to your Web site which, hopefully, thousands of Net travelers will visit daily. Make your business name easy to remember and short. "Rubbereyes!" (made famous by the old AT&T commercials) is better than "Ultraviolet Eye Shields Made of Flexible Material." Both names say roughly the same thing, but the first name is far easier to remember and more fun. And if your product is rubber sunglasses, fun is what you're selling. On the other hand, if you're selling surgical equipment, you might want to stay away from something like "Scalpels R Us." A serious product needs a serious name.

Before he arrived at the name Tronix, Joe played with a few other names. Once you present a name to a lawyer, he or she will do a local and national name and title search to be sure it's legally available. If there is a distinguishing appendage to the name—such as Acme Moving Co. vs. Acme, Inc.—you'll likely be able to use your desired name.

Joe's Take: *I presented my lawyer with the name Title Wave. He ran a national search to see whether Title Wave had been copyrighted. Guess what? It had. So my fabulous, witty company name was already someone else's, which brings up a somewhat obvious but important point: if someone has a company with a name you want, you can't have it. It doesn't matter if you're selling video games in New York and the other is hawking surfboards in San Diego, unless they've chosen Title Wave Board Shop as opposed to Title Wave Video Games. Back to the drawing board.*

We then opted for playing with the theme of my business—electronic entertainment—and came up with Entertronix. The lawyer searched for it, another week went by, and once again I was disappointed to hear that Entertronix was trademarked as well. Next I tried Tronix Multimedia Inc., which was available. Eventually we shortened it for the Web site, and now we're simply known as Tronix. One strong word, plain and simple, easy to remember—and fits quite nicely on our main page.

TIP ▸ ***Have a list of alternative names for your business ready in case your top choice is unavailable. You may think you have something unique, but you could be surprised how many people are thinking along the same lines. If you don't have some backup names, you may find your launch delayed.***

TIP ▸ ***Finding a lawyer is easy; finding a good lawyer is harder. Depending on where you live, you can get a good lawyer with some relevant experience for around $100 an hour. But no matter how much you can afford to spend, find a lawyer who is experienced working with small, new businesses and who can do everything you need, from conducting a name search to advising you on contractual matters. Many medium to large firms also have lawyers who specialize in Internet-related law and commerce. If your goal is to eventually grow your business past a one- or two-person operation, it's nice to have a lawyer who has helped clients do that rather than having to find a new lawyer a year or two down the road. Lawyers aren't hard to find; chances are you or a member of your family know one. But don't rely on convenience. Choose one who can provide the services you need and who will be able to answer your questions at a moment's notice.***

A lawyer with the support that is available at a mid-sized or larger firm is a plus, but be sure you won't be your lawyer's last priority. If you or someone you know doesn't know a qualified lawyer, ask some small business owners in your area if they can recommend one. A lawyer experienced in basic business and contract law will be able to catch up on most of the big Internet issues. Chapter 21 offers background on the state of e-commerce law and links to Web sites that specialize in keeping lawyers and business people up to date on the latest Internet legal and legislative happenings.

Choosing a Legal Entity

As you're chasing down a name you should also be deciding what type of business structure you will have. A number of good business manuals available in any bookstore can give you an idea of what certain structures provide and what they don't. We suggest also that you consult a lawyer, not only to advise you on what type of business best fits your needs, but also to take care of the paperwork. Most lawyers provide these services for a reasonable price (in the neighborhood of $500, possibly less) with the hope that, as your business grows, so will theirs.

Joe's Take: *A lawyer will also give you the simple paperwork needed to apply for a tax identification number. Unless you absolutely can't afford it or would rather do a pile of grinding work yourself, a lawyer is worth it. Obviously those people who can't find anything nice to say about lawyers never tried to start a business.*

TIP ▸ ***You may have seen those do-it-yourself incorporation kits. A few of these are even online. Although these kits offer a cheap way to set up a corporation or limited liability company, they rob you of the first chance to interact and set up a relationship with a lawyer and an accountant. And though it's true that you can pay 10 to 20 times more to incorporate with the help of a lawyer and an accountant, you're really getting much more than a simple incorporation. You're building relationships that will hopefully last as long as your business.***

The following is a brief rundown of the various business choices and what they provide. To avoid getting bogged down in the technicalities of the various choices, we stick to the basics. Your lawyer should be able to point you in the right direction.

Subchapter S Corporation (S Corp)

Most small companies are Subchapter S Corporations (S Corp). This type of entity gives you many of the benefits of a standard Subchapter C Corporation but is advantageous for small businesses because income passes directly through to the shareholder and is subject only to personal income tax.

An S Corp is limited to 35 shareholders—more than enough for a small business. Each shareholder must be a U.S. citizen or a resident alien and must also be a person, which rules out many foreign individuals and entities. An S Corp is not allowed to own more than 80 percent of another corporation. Certain types of businesses—insurance and financial companies, for example—can't be S Corps.

Most of the tax issues for an S Corp are the same as those of a limited liability company (LLC). If you decide an S Corp is the best method of business—which is likely for a small start-up—get some good tax advice from an accountant.

Subchapter C Corporation (C Corp)

Subchapter C Corporations (C Corps) are full-fledged corporations that can retain earnings over the course of time and are independent taxable entities. When a C Corp earns income, it must pay corporate tax. If you, as a shareholder, want to receive the remaining income after corporate taxation, you receive a dividend and must pay personal income tax on that money. In other words, the money earned by a C Corp is taxed twice—at the corporate and personal levels.

TIP ▸ ***If you plan on doing business as a sole proprietorship, you may need to file a DBA certificate (for Doing Business As) to denote the name of your business. This is a local law issue that you should check with your lawyer or accountant. The cost is pretty minimal everywhere, but look into it before you go around town promoting yourself under a company name that isn't on your bank account or checks.***

General Partnership

Being a partner in a general partnership is much like being a sole proprietor—each partner is personally liable for the obligations of the business. The partners are taxed as individuals, reporting their share of the partnership's income and their share of the partnership's expenses. Forming a partnership doesn't require the legal formalities or government filings involved in starting a corporation. The issues surrounding partnership, though, can be more complicated than doing business as a sole proprietor.

Limited Partnership

The limited partnership insulates liability of the limited partners from losses of the partnership, yet is taxed as a partnership. However, the limited partnership has some serious drawbacks. At least one of the general partners is fully liable for the losses of the partnership. To avoid this potentially devastating liability, that partner is often a corporation. This creates a problem with the IRS, which requires a corporate partner's net worth to be at least equal to 10 percent of the total contributions of the partners to the partnership. Also, a limited partner must be truly passive and is not allowed to participate in management of the partnership.

Limited Liability Company

A limited liability company insulates your personal assets from creditors or in the case your business is sued. In other words, if someone breaks his leg in a fall from a defective mountain bike you shipped and decides to sue you, you don't have to worry about the plaintiff taking your house.

The LLC gained popularity in the mid-1980s when it was ruled that an LLC could be taxed as a partnership. The popularity of the LLC comes from the fact that it offers limited liability but has the tax status of a partnership, so it is taxed only once. LLCs do not have the same restrictions as S Corps. The owners can be any type of entity—not just individuals—and there is no maximum number of members. LLCs do not restrict how the owners' rights to money or liquidation proceeds are divided. LLCs can also own subsidiaries. Unlike general partnerships, the management of the business is not restricted to owners of the business; the owner can either manage the company him or herself or appoint management. All of the members can be involved in the business without the risk of personal liability.

However, forming an LLC requires more cost and effort than other types of companies. Owners are typically required to sign an operating agreement establishing such terms as the voting rights of members and the sharing of profit and losses.

TIP ▸ ***We've given you the basic background here on what the different operating entities are. However, you should consult a lawyer and accountant before making the ultimate choice. One thing to especially educate yourself on is how to maintain the corporation or LLC in order to retain its limited liability. You must be aware of a host of paperwork and filings and stay on top of them to keep the status of your corporation.***

A Tax ID and Resale Certificate

Every business and store has to obtain at least one if not *two* key tax numbers. Your accountant and lawyer should be able to help you with this.

Tax ID Number

The federal Tax Identification Number is what identifies you to the government for all tax-related purposes. It may also be called an Employer Identification Number or EIN. If you are a one-person operation running on a very small scale, you *can* just claim income on your social security number, but we don't recommend that at all. To get a Tax ID number, just download form SS4 (Figure 6.1) from the FedWorld site at www.fedworld.gov or ask your accountant or lawyer for it, fill it out, and call the IRS number to apply. The number is constantly busy but if you keep calling during the day, it shouldn't take you more than an hour or so to get through. The operators there will step you though any questions you may have and at the end you'll be given the number. Send in the completed form when you're done.

TIP ▸ ***The Tax ID or EIN number is also the number a bank will require you to give them in order to open up a business checking account.***

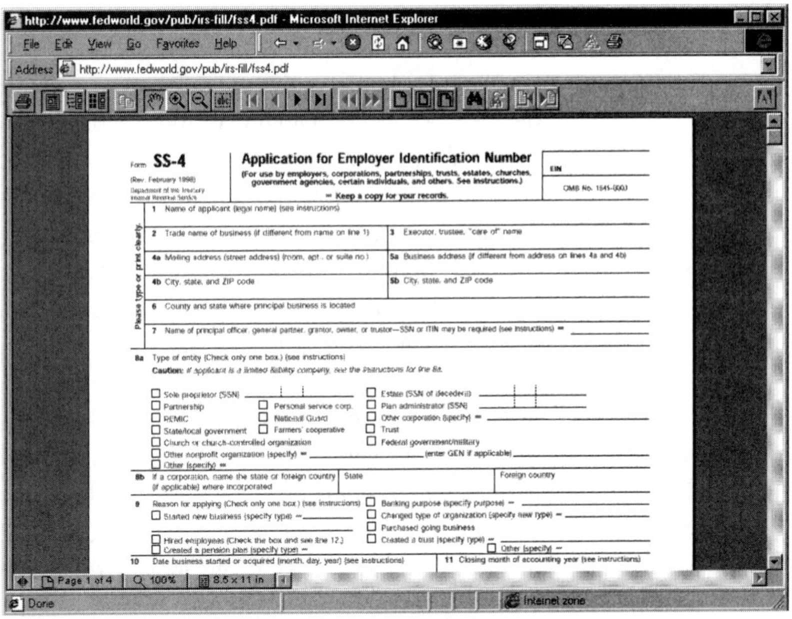

FIGURE 6.1
You can download Form SS-4 from www.fedworld.gov and fill it out to apply for a Tax Identification Number.

Resale Certificate

The second number you need is a resale certificate. This is a local tax certificate that is handled differently in every state. It can cost anywhere from $20 on up. Contact your state department of revenue for more information (many are on the Web) and they'll explain where and how to get one. The certificate, which you will need to send to distributors and have on hand for inspection, entitles you not to pay tax on any items you purchase that are either products you will resell or are components of the products you will resell. In other words, you don't have to pay tax on flour whether you are reselling it as flour or are using it to bake the cakes you're reselling. It's also the ID number you use to submit your sales tax receipts to your state tax department.

TIP ▸ ***For basic business law and self-help books for simple filings and legal documents, check out Nolo Press (www.nolo.com), a top publisher of self-help business legal books. The Nolo Web site is also a very helpful resource.***

Working Out of an Office

You've got a name. You've established your corporate entity. And you've decided to move into an office. You could run a small mail-order operation directly out of your home, but there are a number of reasons not to do that. Simply put, homes are not offices. Homes are great for people who might do light, professionally oriented work, but they're terrible for people with tons of visitors or any employees. You may be restricted by zoning laws against operating an office where your home is. It's tough to deduct home-based expenses, and it's very tough for merchants and distributors to seriously deal with a home-based operation. They'll wonder how committed you are to the business if you're constantly being interrupted by a screaming baby in the background or if your daughter's boyfriend keeps beeping through on call-waiting. Certainly you will want to work from home occasionally, but in most cases it's no way to permanently do business. That means moving to an office, and that opens another sizable, but manageable, can of worms.

Choosing an Office Space

Selecting an office involves common sense. You're working online, so you don't have to worry so much about location. You don't need foot traffic to sell your stuff, so you should be able to get a reasonable rent. But before you go looking, figure out exactly how much you can afford in monthly expenses and how high an office is on your list of priorities.

If You Just Can't Afford an Office

If you absolutely can't afford an office to start, work out of your home, but bear in mind that it's much tougher. This means setting aside a portion of your house or apartment *for work only.* Try to keep work and your personal life separate or you will soon find you have no personal life. The sooner you can get into an office, however small, the better. Working outside your home allows you to keep work at the office and your life elsewhere.

As you look for an office, think functionality. With a minimum of clients visiting you, you don't need the sweetest space in the city. You should think about air conditioning (to keep your computers and yourself from breaking down) and whether heat and electricity are included in the rent. How much will it cost for phone service and, if available, a high-speed cable modem or ISDN or T1 service? If you're on the Internet a lot, and you most likely will be, a higher speed connection can save you an hour of work a day and is worth the slightly higher cost.

Another factor to consider is how late you can get shipments out from your warehouse location (whether it is your office or separate warehouse). Some companies set up a warehouse near the airports that are used by express shipping companies in order to get shipments out as late as possible. Some airports act as hubs for warehouses and express shipping companies (many are old Air Force bases repurposed for such services). Other companies set up multiple warehouses so they can ship locally via UPS Ground or U.S. Postal Priority Mail and get items to customers quickly and inexpensively. Not every store needs this or can afford this, but your shipping needs should be a factor in your location plans.

Insurance

There's no question that you'll need insurance to cover theft, fire, and other events that could damage your equipment and inventory. If you think "It will never happen to me," it will happen to you. Would you consider not insuring your family, your car, or your home? If you decide to blow off the cost of insuring your equipment and inventory, it's like failing to insure all of those personal things. If you lose your equipment due to a fire or some other calamity, you may well lose your business. And losing your business will certainly affect your ability to pay your rent or mortgage and your car payment and, more importantly, your ability to provide for your family. Insurance really isn't an option, it's a must.

Depending on your lease, you'll probably also need limited liability insurance to cover any visitor who may be injured in the office. This can generally be provided in a package by the company with which your equipment and inventory is insured. The cost of the insurance depends upon the value of the insured property, so we'll refrain from throwing out any definite figures. A ballpark figure would be several hundred dollars a year. Remember that your ballpark might be three times as big as ours.

You also must address the health insurance needs of yourself and any employees. Again, health insurance is something you really should have. If you don't think so, go out and do something simple like break an ankle and then pay for it out of your pocket. If you are married, compare the cost and benefits of purchasing your own insurance with getting on your spouse's policy. That will depend on your spouse's policy and whether or not his or her employer provides spousal coverage.

Whether you provide health insurance to an employee is up to you during the early stages of business when any employee will likely be less than full-time. If your business continues to grow, providing a comprehensive benefits package is a way to attract quality employees.

Then there is worker's compensation insurance to cover employees injured on the job. As a corporate officer, you have the right to waive worker's compensation insurance for yourself, but you'll need to provide it for your employees. Contact an insurance company and explain your needs and they'll take care of you, but you should also comparison shop.

Phone Service

No business is a business without phone service. A number of options are available. One thing you must decide is whether your phone lines will be available for people to order merchandise or will be used only for normal business needs and some customer support. Despite the relative safety of making credit card purchases on the Internet, a significant number of people would rather place orders over the phone. Accepting orders by phone requires an assessment of how frequently the phones will ring with orders. Heavy phone orders might require sales operators and a call center (even if it is just a small two- to three-person call center).

How Many Phone Lines Do You Need?

Most small to medium-sized businesses can probably make do on between three and five lines to start. Try to figure out as closely as possible how many lines you need. Too many is a waste of money; too few will force you to soon waste time and effort upgrading your system later.

Your main line should include one number that, when busy, will roll over to the other lines until one is free to ring. You'll also need to order a separate single line for a fax machine and you may opt to order an additional voice number as a "private" line. This unlisted number is great in case you get a rush of customer calls and want to provide a separate number for distributors, critical customers, and other close associates.

If you need to handle multiple orders with sales people, you'll want to have a phone system installed. The system should have several lines that ring from the same number (known as "rollover lines"). You may also need headsets and terminals for your sales operators. Most Web stores with high phone order volume place a Web-capable machine in front of the sales operator. The operator keys the information into the terminal as if he were shopping on the on the site itself. With an authorization back from the site (as if he were a customer), the operator completes the order. You can outsource your sales operators, but this takes a certain amount of control out of your hands and can give your customers the accurate impression that they are dealing with a different company.

Joe's Take: *Actually the number of lines you need is easy to figure out if your store is small like Tronix. You need at least two lines for customers, an additional one that can be shared between the fax machine and credit card terminal, and a fourth line for Internet and email. I use that line as a private number also. When I first started, in order to save money I ran the Internet, fax, and credit card terminal off one line. As I grew, I quickly added another line to allow me to keep the Internet connection up all day rather than constantly logging on or off every time I needed to use the fax machine or get a credit card authorization.*

What Long Distance Provider Should You Choose?

Depending on how much long-distance calling you're going to do, this can be a very important decision. Even after you make it, the small business market is so cutthroat you can be sure that you'll receive repeated solicitations to change your long-distance service. Without going into the details of the dozens of plans that are offered, you should make some calls to the major providers (AT&T, MCI, Sprint, and WorldCom) and see what rates per minute they'll give you. There are so many plans you need to be proactive in your search. You should be able to get a discount plan for between 10 and 13 cents per minute. If you're going to make a lot of overseas calls, take into account how the combined rates will work out.

TIP ▸ ***Many small resellers of long-distance service exist. These companies buy minutes in huge bulk quantities and resell them to smaller companies. The biggest problem with resellers and other smaller providers of long-distance service is, well, service. As a store owner, any time someone can't reach you is lost business. It may make sense to avoid the lowest rate for the assurance that you've got top service and quality.***

JOE'S TAKE: *The problem with an 800 number is too many people may call you and waste your time. The barrier of being charged for the call is strong enough to keep kids and general inquiries down to a minimum. If I were to get a toll-free number at all, I'd only give it out to my best customers. However, if sales grow to a substantial point, a toll-free number may be a plus. International customers can reach you with a toll-free number—however it won't be toll-free for them. And remember—when you're small, every penny and every second saved counts.*

Should You Get Voicemail?

Many smaller stores will need to get a voicemail system. Using a voicemail box that is available directly from the phone company can save time and, because it's fast and digital, it sounds good and works flawlessly. A typical voicemail box addition to your main number should run about $20 to $30 a month. Call waiting works well for small office solutions with a limited amount of phone orders, but customers will not want to be interrupted by another call. Call waiting is not a good idea if it means you will constantly be interrupting customers to answer another incoming call.

Should You Invest in an 800/888 Toll-Free Number?

Due to intense competition, the ability to add an 800 or 888 toll-free number is actually fairly inexpensive. Both MCI and AT&T offer toll-free number service that you can order for $5 a month if you use them as your long-distance provider. The number actually rings through to your regular business number line, and you pay a 12 to 13 cents a minute flat rate during the call. Bills come separately. Overall, if you think the toll-free service will increase your business beyond the cost of providing toll-free service, then it's certainly a key item to have.

What Phone Hardware Will You Use?

You've got a bunch of lines ordered and coming in but nothing to use them with. You need to get phone equipment. If you only have two or three lines coming in for customers and aren't going to need more than yourself and one or two other people to answer calls, then you can just go to an office store and pick up some quality two- or three-line phones. If you've got more than three lines, you'll need to install a phone system. A phone system isn't as expensive as you might think, but if you really expect your company to grow it's best to get a solid system that can be easily upgraded to handle more lines.

You'll also need to hire a technician to install this for you. Many technicians in the phone book install and sell systems. Ask about used systems or leasing if you want to cut costs. If you have numerous phone lines (especially to accept phone orders), be sure to carefully plan the system, where the lines should be run, and how you can add lines when necessary.

TIP ▸ ***For a fax machine, get a plain paper fax or risk searching far and wide for fax paper.***

Joe's Take: *I like Hewlett-Packard's fax machines; they're priced nicely, they use plain paper, and the supplies for ink are easy to find. I also recommend getting really good phones no matter how extensive your system is—simple two-liners, like I did, or a complete system. There's nothing more frustrating than cutting corners on phone equipment and then getting a static-filled call or a broken phone a month later. Reliable Internet and phone service are your lifeblood, so don't fool around with them.*

Acquiring a Merchant Account to Accept Credit Cards

Without a merchant account to accept credit cards, you'll only be able to accept CODs (cash on delivery) or money orders and checks paid in advance. Having no merchant account, of course, is a major disadvantage, especially since most customers would not thrill to the idea of sending money to a not-yet-established, online firm. Which boils down to this: If you can't accept credit card orders, you're almost dead in the water.

CODs are fine, but your courier will charge you an additional fee, which you'll pass on to your customer. In an age of modern-day shopping, most people purchasing mail-order goods want to whip out their credit card, make their purchase, and have it delivered to them in a timely manner, especially when they have their eye on an item but don't have the cash on hand to pay for it immediately.

Getting the equipment and approval to accept credit cards will be one of your biggest startup challenges. First you'll need to convince a merchant bank to accept you. This involves a credit check and telling them a bit about your business. It's important to have done all the other paperwork and account setup before you go see these people. Everything you can do and show that proves you're going to be a credit-worthy and capable reseller is considered before they let you accept cards. In addition you'll need to acquire some equipment to communicate and get approval for cards. Finally, you may opt to find a vendor that will help you process card numbers via the Internet.

To find out more about credit cards, see Chapter 14.

TIP ▸ ***Check locally in your Yellow Pages to find a listing of merchant card service providers in your area. Card service providers vary from state to state, although a few major national players are out there. Ask your accountant, too—he or she may be really helpful. If worse comes to worst, just call or visit a few local stores until some owner or manager can help you out.***

Joe's Take: *Getting a merchant card account was one of the toughest things I had to do. The Internet was still fairly new when I applied. At the same time, these card service providers are very wary of mail-order only businesses—to say nothing of Internet-based ones. Be careful and thorough in explaining to the salesperson what you're going to do. If you're going to generate any sort of in-store traffic, let them know that immediately; emphasize it , because it's a big plus. Make sure you go to them once you've gotten a lot of your other aspects in place: an office, your business entity, phones, etc. The more bona fide you are, the better. Be prepared to get rejected at least once. Line up a few different card providers to talk to.*

Setting Up with Distributors and Vendors

If you're going to sell items over the Internet, in all likelihood you'll be reselling items rather than selling original items you produced. That means one of the biggest start-up challenges will be building a list of distributors and vendors that will provide you with the items you want to resell.

Building a list of distributors and vendors is very hard work. First, you'll have to identify the distributors and vendors. Turn to the Internet and your local library. Look for trade-oriented magazines and Web sites as well as vendors that specifically make the items you want to stock. From there you'll need to work the phones a bit and find out the names and numbers of the distributors to work with. If a vendor goes direct, you may want to deal with them that way.

Armed with some basic research, there are four key ways to find the names and numbers of distributors you can use:

- **Product contacts.** Call vendors of the products you want to stock, ask for the channel sales person, and get the names of the distributors they use and their numbers.

- **Trade publications.** Find the names of distributors in trade publications for the industry. You'd be surprised how many simple industries have one or two trade magazines.

- **Trade shows.** Attend trade shows for the particular industry, where you're bound to meet vendors and distributors.

- **Travel.** Travel abroad or in your home country to find smaller, unique manufacturers from which you can order goods.

Once you have a list of distributors and vendors (and their products), you're halfway through. You'll have to try and set up an account to order from them and perhaps submit an application. They'll want to see your reseller's certificate and get a copy of your tax ID number as well—no sense talking to them until you have those items in place.

Most distributors, regardless of industry, want to deal with stores that will provide a constant stream of large orders and that have good credit. If you're new to the business, chances are you'll have to pay up front for quite a while before a distributor will offer you terms and credit. In addition, prepare for some setbacks if you don't convince them you're going to order a decent amount (simply ask what they consider a minimum year's worth of orders).

When dealing with vendors directly, it will be the same thing. Sometimes, with very small vendors, you can get terms because of the risk that they may drop out of sight. In the end, it's a hard-work, straightforward process. Find distributors and vendors, negotiate the ability to order from them, maintain the relationships, and stay on good terms. Repeat this over and over until you have enough distributors and vendors lined up to keep you well stocked with everything you want to carry.

Joe's Take: *Having worked for a leading video game store prior to founding Tronix, I was lucky to have set up many personal relationships and reputations with top distributors in my industry. This situation made it very easy for me to avoid credit checks and applications. In some cases, with importers and foreign-based distributors, I had to work hard to get on their good side, but essentially it was a process of paying first and getting the items I wanted afterwards. As you develop a solid relationship with these distributors, the requirements will probably become less strict. All I can say is, never make a distributor mad at you, be patient when first finding and talking with distributors, and always let them know you expect to be placing big orders and moving lots of product. They're not into small-time distributors—they make money on volume.*

Choosing Your Web-Hosting Situation

Web sites of any kind (not just commerce-enabled ones) must be hosted somewhere. You can choose from one of four main types of hosting situations:

- **You do it.** Host the site locally on your own server at your specific location.
- **Lease a server** or co-locate a dedicated server from a Web-hosting service.
- **Lease space** on a Web-hosting service.
- **Use a store-hosting service** such as Yahoo Store.

Each of these has specific pros and cons. Table 6.1 covers these.

Table 6.1 Web-Hosting Choices

Choice	Description	Cost	Advantage	Disadvantage
Host site Locally	Server is located in your facility and connects to the Internet via high-speed line. Smaller stores may not need anything more than an ISDN or leased 56K line, but bigger stores will need a fractional T1 or higher. The entire server system—including security, commerce capabilities, and more—is controlled by you.	Generally the most expensive option. Can cost thousands of dollars per month.	Greatest flexibility in terms of hands on access to the equipment.	Who wants all this responsibility? Or the associated costs? Only the largest companies will want to use this approach, especially if it's in conjunction with integrating other onsite back-office systems like accounting and inventory systems.
Co-locate or lease a dedicated server from a Web-hosting service.	With co-location, you supply the hardware and software for your server, which is hosted and monitored by the Web-hosting facility. This gives you flexibility without responsibility for maintaining the connection and usually adds other features provided by the co-location facility (security, traffic monitoring, etc.). With a leased dedicated server, you don't need your own hardware, instead using standardized servers offered by the Web-hosting provider. This limits your hardware flexibility but also your upfront costs or ownership liabilities.	Most good entry-level dedicated server deals start at around $300 a month and go up from there, depending on traffic and hardware needs. They can reach into the thousands monthly, but that is usually in conjunction with store traffic, so costs rarely outpace revenues unless there is poor planning.	Excellent flexibility with less responsibility.	The biggest disadvantage is cost, which even at only $300 to $400 a month, may be out of the reach of smaller stores. Also, you still have a lot of configuration to do, and the associated support costs can run $100 to $200 an hour.

Continued on next page

Table 6.1 Web-Hosting Choices (*continued*)

Choice	Description	Cost	Advantage	Disadvantage
Lease space on a Web-hosting service	Instead of getting an entire server, you rent a portion of a server that typically includes 30 to 100 MB of hard drive space, the ability to run specific, approved scripts and commerce activities, and a maximum traffic allowance before extra fees kick in.	$30 to $100 month depending on the vendor, amount of hard drive space needed, special options activated (such as secure commerce), and traffic to your site.	Cheapest option with flexibility to design pages as you wish.	Less back-end flexibility than the first two options. Costs can climb if traffic surges.
Use a store-hosting service such as Yahoo Store	These services (see Chapter 22 for more on Yahoo Store) offer the ability to set up and manage a Web-based store using pre-built templates and services.	$100 a month or more, depending on size of store, traffic, and options used. Some charge a percentage of sales too, especially if they provide you with credit card payment ability through their systems.	Can be quickest way to get a store online, makes organizing and designing easy. Tailored to e-commerce needs.	Provides the least flexibility of all choices. Costs can be a bit higher than if you use a bare-bones commerce-hosting package tacked onto leasing your own space on a server.

There is more information about each of these approaches throughout this book. If you decide to use a developer, he might specify a hosting choice that works best with his approach to building your store.

You will also need a local Internet connection to access your site. Chances are you already have this provided by a local ISP (Internet Service Provider) or national one such as Earthlink or AT&T. There are also faster connections offered by local cable companies (using cable modems) and local phone companies (using a technology known as Digital Subscriber Line), which provide more than 20 times the speed of a local phone dial-up connection. These higher speed services (known as broadband) usually cost 2 to 4 times the price of the common $19.95 dial-up service, but the speed increase is well worth the cost. If you can get a local high-speed connection, do it. Then have a back-up dial-up service for when you are traveling or in case the local cable or DSL connection experiences trouble.

Email is such a critical application for any site or Web business that some choose to let their Web host or dedicated server company handle just the Web site and use a specific email company to handle the email. The advantage is that if the site goes down, it won't take the email with it.

If running a dedicated or in-house server, you can absolve yourself from administering your own email, which is always more difficult than running your Web site. One company worth investigating for email hosting is Critical Path (www.criticalpath.com). Email boxes hosted by Critical Path cost $5 to 7 per month, depending on how many you have.

Joe's Take: *A domain name is very important. I like Tronix because it doesn't take much effort to type in and it is easy for my customers to remember. For a while, I had a site that wasn't using a straight domain name system and when I switched over from that to tronix.com it made a huge difference in traffic. When you're thinking of a name for your store, think also of a domain name.*

Registering Your Domain Name

Chances are your Web-hosting service will help you secure a domain name for your Web site. The base cost of acquiring a domain name from the Internic service, which assigns them, is $100 for two years of registration. Expect to pay more for it to be handled by your Web-hosting service, but in some ways it's worth the extra $50 to $100 for them to do it for you.

You will want your own domain for many reasons, the biggest of which is that it will give you a more professional-looking store and a Web brand name to promote. You will be taken more seriously and your customers will find you more easily if your URL is www.greatstore.com rather than www.isp.com/`yourlogin/yourstore/.

When you register a domain name, you will be able to use it for two years, after which you can renew it for another cycle. Sometimes you'll have to use a different name than your business name, especially if it's already taken or perhaps too long. For example, if you were going to call yourself the Digital Camera Store, you might discover that www.digitalcamera.com is taken. Time to come up with a different name. Or if your store is John Smith's Outdoor Equipment you might want to choose a shorter domain name, such as www.jsmithequipment.com.

Registration of domain names is currently overseen by a special clearinghouse called the Internic (www.internic.net). Registars, of which there is currently only one, Network Solutions, provide the actual domain name registration. Domain name registration is being opened up to competition, and several test-bed registrars are just now coming online, such as Register.com.

Network Solutions (www.networksolutions.com) has a search engine that lets you check for available domain names. Many times a name will be taken, but a site using that name isn't up yet. Simply checking the Internic and finding there was no site does not guarantee the domain name is available. In the future, several companies, including AOL, will offer domain name registration, but for now, when it comes to .com and .net domains, Network Solutions is it. For foreign-based domains such as www.mystore.co.uk, you will need to check with a domain registry company in that country. There are also international domain name registry agents (the best known is www.netnames.com) that can help with international registrations.

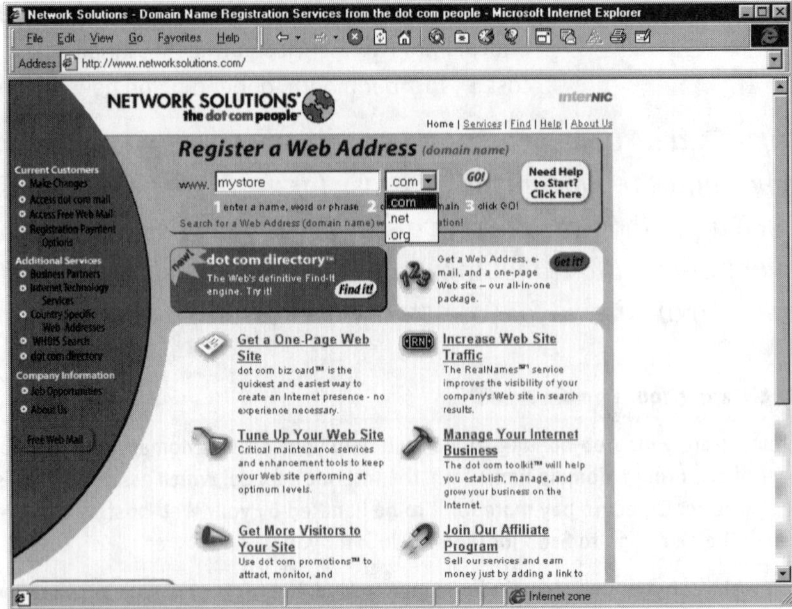

FIGURE 6.2
You can check the availability of your domain name and register it at www.networksolutions.com.

Hiring a Developer vs. Doing It Yourself

Many independent store owners decide to to do all the work themselves. Besides saving money on a developer, this also allows you to learn more about the core workings of the Internet and e-commerce. However, Web designers and developers exist to do the complicated work with the quality you need if you have neither the time nor the skills to do it youself.

We recommend that you become proficient enough at basic HTML or using a store-building service to handle minor upgrades, maintainence, and building. If you can do more than that, you increase your your flexibility. However, the more items you have and the greater your need or desire for high-end features and the use of a database system, the more likely you'll require the expertise offered by a seasoned developer.

Depending on the scope of your store, a developer should be able to do the foundation work for $500 to $5,000 (much more if you want an elaborate database-style setup with numerous bells and whistles). The expense can add up if you can't handle the maintenance on the site (such as day-to-day updates, inventory changes, etc.). In the end, this becomes largely a budgetary decision.

Throughout this book, we assume that you will do much of the work yourself. If you do decide to use a Web designer/developer, reading this book will put you in a better position to work closely with them and understand what they are doing.

Choosing the Right Software

All online stores are Web sites, and Web sites need tools to help with development. As a store owner, you might decide to hire a firm or bring in an individual to develop your Web site. But this book is also about keeping costs down and flexibility up. Even if you get a good price for site design and development, there may be times you just want to put up a shot of a new product or change a price. If you're doing it yourself, you'll need good tools as much as you'd need them for more extensive development. That being said, here's what you'll need.

Browsers

The most important piece of software any Net business needs is a Web browser. Because you are now going to deal with people viewing and using your own site, we recommend that you download the two top browsers which, as of this writing, are Netscape Communicator (or Navigator 4.51) and Microsoft Internet Explorer 5.0.

Although you may have a personal browser preference, you'll find large groups of users viewing your site using the other browser. Because each browser has some slight differences in how pages are displayed, it's important that you be able to test any site designs or changes with both browsers to make sure there aren't any problems for users of either browser.

Email and Newsgroup Reader

A crucial aspect of any online store is the email and newsgroup-reading software you use. Make sure whatever package you use can filter incoming messages, manage large email lists for newsletter mailings, and has a good address book for contact management and collecting a store mailing list that includes email and traditional mail addresses. Eudora and Claris Emailer are two excellent cross-platform email packages.

Both Internet Explorer (its email module, called Outlook Express, is shown in Figure 6.3) and Netscape Communicator also have good email products. On the PC side, there is also the popular Pegasus shareware email package that offers a lot of high-end features useful for mailing lists and filtering. Email usage is covered throughout this book. For now, your assignment is to get a good email application and learn how to use the incoming-filter features as well as how to construct contact lists in the address book segment that all of these programs have. Among the newsreaders, News Xpress and Forte's Free Agent are good products.

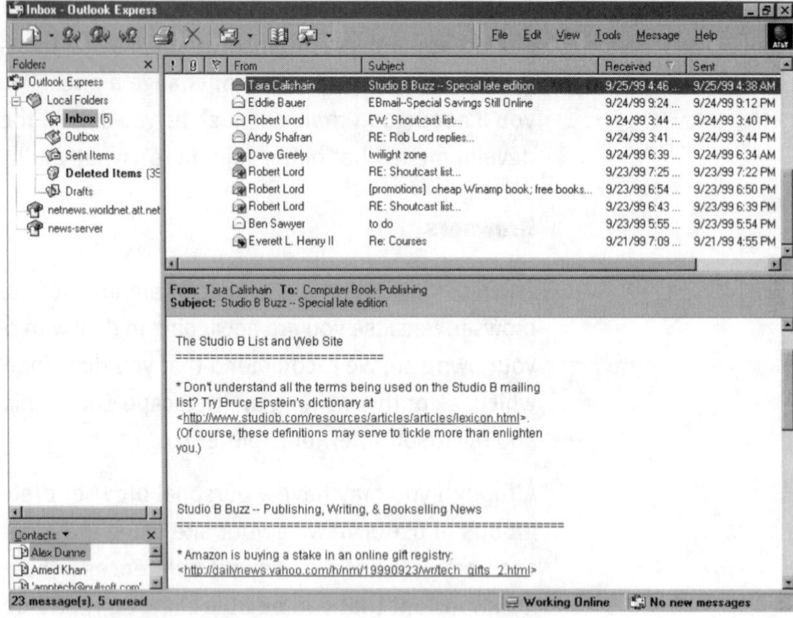

FIGURE 6.3
Microsoft's Outlook Express email program.

FTP Application

In order to upload new files to your Web site, you'll need an FTP (File Transfer Protocol) application. If you're working on a PC, CuteFTP (Figure 6.4) is the popular program. For Macs, Fetch is the most highly recommended FTP program.

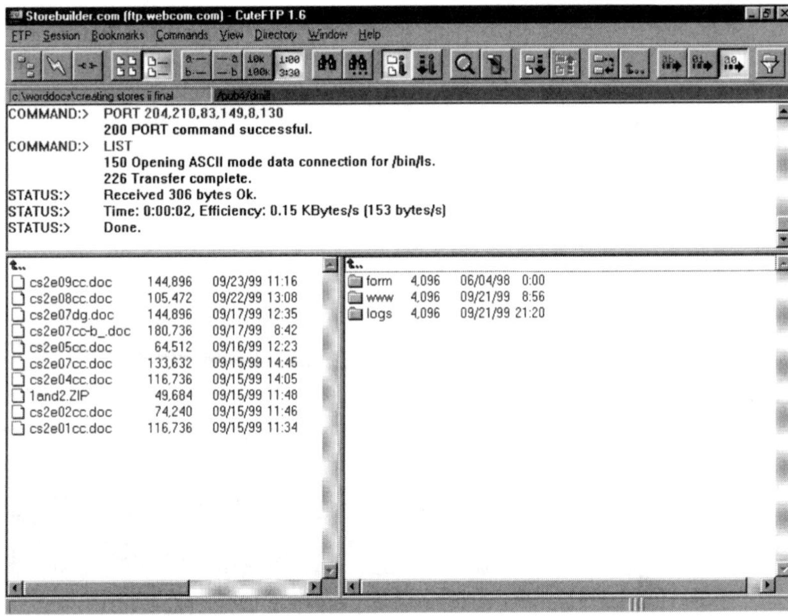

FIGURE 6.4
CuteFTP in action.

HTML Editors

There are two types of HTML editors available: those that have graphic, visual, layout-type interfaces, often called Web-authoring tools, and those that are specialized text editors. Ideally it would be great to have one super editor to recommend, but there isn't one that performs both functions undeniably well. The best solution is to get a visual editor to work with at first while you spec out the look of pages, tables, and so on. Then, when you have pages roughed out, you can switch to an HTML editor to clean up the code, add form items and scripts, plus periodically update items on your pages.

Visual Web Authoring Tools

There are a number of good visual Web-authoring tools out there. A few are both easy to use and not terribly expensive. Claris Homepage ($94 and available for Mac and Windows) is a nice, lower-end visual tool that even beginners will find excellent. Both Netscape Communicator and Microsoft Internet Explorer browser products include visual editors, which are decent, especially considering they are free.

Also worth investigating for a bit more money are the fancier, more powerful programs Macromedia Dreamweaver ($270) and Adobe GoLive ($300). Both are available for Macintosh and Windows.

HTML Code Editors

There are a number of HTML code editors available via shareware on the Web. The most highly recommended editors you can get however, are commercial products. On the Mac, the entire Web-editing community swears by BBEdit from Bare Bones Software; its advanced text-editing features make it a joy to use. On the PC side, two editors are worth mentioning. HomeSite from Allaire (Figure 6.5) is probably the best product of this type. Hot Dog Pro from Sausage Software of Australia is another popular editor.

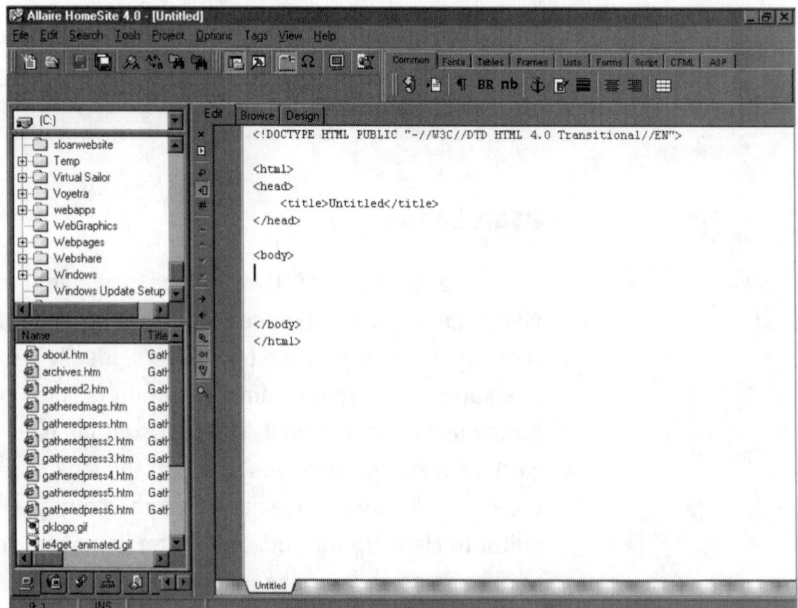

FIGURE 6.5
HomeSite in action.

Graphics Equipment and Imaging Software

Everyone needs to get some graphics onto their page. These images can be as simple as a picture of a product catalog or as complex as a full-page advertisement.

A good place to start is with a scanner—not an incredibly expensive one, but something that can scan an entire 8.5-by-11 page and that features

24-bit color depth. Hewlett-Packard, UMAX, Microtek, and Agfa are quality manufacturers with solid models priced from $300 to 1,000. Another image-acquisition tool you might want to consider is a digital camera. Depending on what your store will be selling, a digital camera can be a really handy tool to have around for producing pictures of your merchandise. If you do decide to get a camera, get one that produces pictures at a resolution higher than 640-by-480. Several cameras, all listed under $1,000, produce better than 640-by-480 resolution. They are the Kodak DC50 and DC120 cameras, Olympus 300L, and Cannon Powershot. Over time, expect many manufacturers to offer cameras that provide great resolution.

TIP ▸ ***When buying a digital camera, make sure you get the power supply the camera needs if it isn't included in the package. If you use batteries exclusively, you might end up spending a small fortune, when you could just plug it into a wall if you had the power supply. Also get a decent tripod and good editing software. A tripod will help you take immeasurably better photos, and because camera images frequently need more processing help than you can get from the free software products they typically include, you'll want to get an image editing software package like Adobe Photoshop to enhance the imagery.***

You should also acquire some decent image editing software. Chances are, something came with your scanner, that you may find useful (or not). Fortunately a number of good products, both shareware and commercial, are worth checking out.

You'll need a number of good tools for editing scanned photos and producing simple items like a nice logo, some graphical bullets, and colored backgrounds. Adobe Photoshop is available for both PCs and Macs and is the industry standard. At around $550, it's a bit expensive, so if this is out of your price range, there are a couple of shareware products to consider. Paint Shop Pro (Figure 6.6) for Windows by JASC is an excellent program and costs under $50. Matt Paint is a low-end shareware package on the Mac, but it is not nearly as comparable to Photoshop as Paint Shop Pro is. Graphic Converter from Lemke Software is now very comparable to Paint Shop Pro. Photoshop, however, is the best product out there.

Once you've got a good scanner (and perhaps a camera) and an editing package, there isn't much more you need. Yes, you could go wild and buy all the fantastic art packages in the world, but that's a personal (and financial) decision. With the products we just mentioned, you can scan in any item, crop it down, do a little processing on it, and have it up on your site in a matter of minutes.

FIGURE 6.6
Paint Shop Pro in action.

Other Software

Most of the software mentioned here relates to the tools you'll need to get online, send email, and design and post Web pages. However, since this is the launch phase, you'll want to get a few other products.

Point-of-Sale Program

You may want to take the time now to get a good point-of-sale program. Point-of-sale programs are really designed for traditional stores, but they're great for mail order or Web stores as well. These programs let you enter inventory, print out invoices, calculate sales tax and shipping, and provide sales reports at the end of the day, week, month, or year.

***JOE'S TAKE:** Fancy systems will eventually come along and combine traditional point-of-sale reports and processes with a Web-based store, but they'll be expensive and cumbersome until they're tried and tested. I continually find that by using a good point-of-sale tool offline (I use Atrex, which is available as shareware from **www.atrex.com**), I'm able to assure myself that I've got a good product. In addition, because a large portion of your store's sales will come in as straight phone, fax, or email orders, you're not going have the benefit of every order being automated through the Web site. That's reason enough to use a separate POS program to track sales information. The reports and other advanced features are quite important to analyze my store's success.*

Shipping and Tracking Software

All of the major shipping products and services are covered in Chapter 17. Be sure to check it out and get all of the services and software in place before you launch.

QuickBooks

What small business doesn't use this great program? As a store owner, you'll be writing checks for products, services, employees, and more every week. QuickBooks, from Intuit, makes it very easy to track expenses, cut checks, and compile the necessary tax records right from your computer. It's inexpensive, too. You can get a free trial version of QuickBooks 99 or QuickBooks Pro 99 at www.quickbooks.com. QuickBooks lists for $119.95, and QuickBooks Pro for $219.95.

America Online and CompuServe

Depending on your needs, you might want to consider getting accounts on America Online (AOL) and CompuServe. Although their terms of service (and common netiquette) prevent you from blatantly posting ads for your store, you may find some online forums in which you can offer your expertise, find out about new products, or join communities that can bring potential customers to your store. AOL and CompuServe have more than 10 million members worldwide. You should at least check them out to see if there are some useful areas on them for you.

Joe's Take: *When I first started my store, I was on CompuServe's gamer forums a lot (in fact I was an early sysop for them). While I didn't post obvious ads, people there eventually realized I had a video game store, and I got plenty of orders from those members without being the least bit intrusive or destructive to the forum.*

Wrap-up

We covered a lot of ground here and much of it seems to have less to do with actually building your store than you might have guessed. The next chapter will cover more, but before you head off to it, think for a moment. Right now you might be trying to launch too quickly. The moral of this chapter is to get everything set right the first time.

As the story about Tronix shows, you can have a lot of problems if you jump in without much thought. If you do not consider every detail before launching your store, you may be bitten by a shaky ISP, a weak phone system, a clueless lawyer, or other snafu. The best thing you can do during launch phase is take things slowly. Make sure you're fully ready to launch even before you upload your first pages to your site. Take the time to compare services and products and experiment with the software. Get into your office space, make sure all the phone lines work, and spend the time making sure your distributors are 100 percent behind you.

When you go on the Web, you don't have a lot of room for error. If you slip for just a second—your phones go out, your Web service goes down, your distributors won't ship you something, anything—you're going to have to do some scrambling to keep your customers.

If one customer has a bad experience or can't reach you, she might tell hundreds in a scathing post on a newsgroup. Check those newsgroups (Deja.com is a good place to visit) to find out what people think about your store, and use that information to get better. For more on newsgroups, see Chapter 10.

Taking your time helps, watching the bottom line is key (far too often Web business burn through capital for no reason), and keeping things simple is paramount. The only time you've got to make mistakes, think things through, and work out the kinks is before you broadcast your site to everyone and anyone.

Customers on the Web don't wait for you to fix things, and competitors will pounce on you faster than piranha on a drowning cow. That's why you want everything to be perfect the first time.

CHAPTER SEVEN

Joe's Template For Store Design

Now that you have the grunt work wrapped up, it's time to have some fun while moving toward the goal of having your store up, running, and taking orders. The process of creating your Web site is similar to setting up a traditional store. You'll have a chance to exercise your creative muscles and you'll also need to spend some time researching other stores. There's no need to reinvent the wheel—or the store. Hopefully you will have some unique ideas of your own, but don't be afraid to check out other Web sites to see what works and, just as importantly, what doesn't. Combine that knowledge with your own ideas to build a functional store with sizzle.

This chapter is designed to help you develop and construct your online store through simple HTML pages and some hard work, without spending a fortune. We'll point you toward some useful technical resources and give you some ideas about building a site that works for you and your customers.

Developing Your Own Web Site

HTML (for Hypertext Markup Language) is the basis for displaying text and graphics on the Web, and as a store owner, you should learn HTML basics. Learning HTML and creating Web pages is much easier than most people realize. However, some advanced HTML features and idiosyncrasies can confuse even HTML experts. Because it is easy to learn HTML's basics but difficult to master it, you should keep things simple.

This book is not a course in HTML. We will offer a few tips here for HTML and Web site production, but it's up to you to obtain basic HTML knowledge and learn how to use one of the many available HTML editors.

Get a Good HTML Tutorial and Reference Guide

A variety of Web sites offer tutorial information, and both Netscape and Microsoft maintain excellent reference guides. Table 7.1 gives information on some books and Web sites that should provide all the HTML education material you should need.

TIP ▸ ***When you're first learning HTML, don't bog yourself down trying to learn every single command. HTML has scores of codes to master, but you'll only use about 20 or 30 of them repeatedly. Table 7.2 is a list of the major HTML codes and items every store owner should know.***

TABLE 7.1 HTML RESOURCES

BOOKS	WEB SITES
HTML 4 for the World Wide Web, Fourth Edition: Visual QuickStart Guide by Elizabeth Castro (Peachpit Press, ISBN: 0-201-35493-4)	**Microsoft HTML for Beginners** http://msdn.microsoft.com/workshop/author/html/beghtml.asp Straightforward HTML instruction
Web Design in a Nutshell: A Desktop Quick Reference by Jennifer Niederst (O'Reilly & Associates, ISBN: 1-565-92515-7)	**Netscape's Documentation Site** http://developer.netscape.com/docs/manuals/index.html Netscape offers documentation on a number of technologies, including HTML
Web Style Guide: Basic Design Principles for Creating Web Sites by Patrick J. Lynch and Sarah Horton (Yale University Press, ISBN: 0-300-07675-4)	**W3C's HTML Home Page** http://www.w3.org/MarkUp/ Pointers to HTML specifications and guidelines on using HTML

TABLE 7.2 HTML CODES EVERY STORE OWNER SHOULD KNOW

Basic text formatting tags	<B>, <I>, <U>, <H1>-<H6>, <FONT>
Positioning, paragraph, and spacing tags	<CENTER>, , <NO BR>, <P>
Table tags	<TABLE>, <TR>, <TD>
List tags	<UL>, <OL>, <LI>
Form tags	<FORM>, <TEXT>, <TEXT AREA>, <SELECT>
Basic document tags	<BODY>, <TITLE>, <HTML>
Graphics and line tags	<IMAGE>, <HR>
Linking and anchor tags	<NAME>, <A HREF>, <A HREF="MAILTO:">

Learn to Write HTML at the Source Code Level

It is fairly easy to write HTML. All you need is a simple text editor such as Notepad or an HTML editor, which is a specialized text editor for HTML coding. These are discussed in Chapter 6.

Using a Web authoring tool such as Microsoft FrontPage (www.microsoft.com/frontpage/) or FileMaker Homepage (www.filemaker.com/products/homepage3.html) can help you avoid learning HTML to some extent. But although these products make creating Web pages as easy as using a word processor, they don't eliminate all need for HTML knowledge. You still will often need to modify HTML code directly rather than simply using a visual editor. For the most flexibility, it's best to learn HTML at the code level and then use an HTML text editor like HomeSite (www.allaire.com/homesite/) or BBEdit (www.bbedit.com). Then you can modify the HTML code as needed.

One big problem with visual Web page creation programs is that results can vary when you view the pages they produce in a browser. And if you reach the point that you want to add them, complex tables and frames absolutely require HTML source-level editing.

Learn the Basics of Web Graphics

As you begin building your site, you'll need to prepare graphics for the Web. Web graphics are relatively easy to deal with, once you have a graphics editor (also covered in Chapter 6). You'll be primarily concerned with three key graphics file formats: JPEG, GIF, and Animated GIF. Table 7.3 includes some good Web sites and books concerning graphics for your Web pages.

JPEG

Best used for: Digital photos or large pictures of products.

Not so good for: Graphics with text, small logos, or graphical buttons.

JPEG (Joint Photographic Experts Group) was created by a software developer consortium. This ensures that JPEG will remain a royalty-free file format.

JPEG uses what graphics experts call a "lossy" compression format, which means it does degrade the overall quality of the image to decrease the size of the file (but 99 percent of the time the loss is not noticeable). The compression feature of JPEG graphics makes them great for displaying digitized photos of products containing thousands or millions of colors. Most photographs on the Web are in the JPEG format.

JPEG files can be saved in two variants: regular JPEG and a derivative known as Progressive JPEG. When Progressive JPEG files are created, the data is arranged so that the graphics are displayed while they are downloaded. The graphics are initially very blurry but become progressively sharper as the whole file is received.

GIF

Best used for: Logos, text, graphical buttons, items that need to be irregularly shaped via transparency.

Not so good for: Photos or any graphic with more than 256 colors.

GIF (Graphics Interchange Format) was originally developed in the mid-1980s by the CompuServe online service. At the time, modem speeds of 9,600 bps or less were common. GIF provided a way to compress graphics so that they could be transported more quickly via modem. When the Web began to grow in popularity, GIF was adopted by Internet users as a standard graphics file format.

GIF's strength is that it is pixel-perfect rendering. Unlike JPEG it is not a "lossy" format, making it good for logos, text, and other graphics that aren't photographic in nature. GIF's biggest drawback is that it is limited to displaying just 8-bit graphics (256 colors). Extremely small, digitized photos don't look very good when rendered in the GIF format.

GIF also offers a format, called GIF89A, which lets you set one color of a graphic as transparent. Transparent GIFs are useful for creating graphics that let the Web page's background shine through—especially irregularly shaped graphics.

Animated GIF

Best used for: Animated logos and displaying multiple shots of the same product.

Animated GIF is a specialized graphic file format that displays multiple graphics in the same file. It comes complete with information that tells the Web browser how long to wait before showing the next frame and whether it should loop the frames repeatedly. The effect is like classic animation.

Animated GIFs are fairly easy to create with the programs mentioned in Chapter 6. They're great for adding liveliness to your page. Store owners can create an Animated GIF that cycles through different shots of the same item or cycles through various items but with different colors. Again, the drawback is the 256-color limit.

TIP ▸ ***Web sites full of free Web graphics are constantly going up and moving around. We've listed three of our favorites in Table 7.3, but you should consider regularly searching for new ones (using terms such as* Web, graphics, GIF, JPEG, animated GIF, *etc.) through search engines and indexes like Yahoo, Lycos, or Hotbot.***

TABLE 7.3 WEB GRAPHICS BOOKS AND WEB SITES

GRAPHICS RESOURCE BOOKS	GRAPHICS RESOURCE WEB SITES
Designing Web Graphics 3 by Lynda Weinman (New Riders Publishing, ISBN: 1-56205-949-1).	**Xoom's Free Clip Art Library** http://xoom.com/clips/website Bullets, backgounds, bars, icons and more—all free for the taking.
Coloring Web Graphics 2 by Lynda Weinman (New Riders Publishing, ISBN: 1-56205-818-5).	**Jelane's Free Web Graphics** www.erinet.com/jelane/families/ An excellent, well organized, and very useful collection of free Web graphics including buttons, email icons, and 256-color designs.
Web GraphicsTools & Techniques by Peter Kentie (Peachpit Press, ISBN: 0-20168-813-1).	**The FreeSite** www.thefreesite.com/freegraphics.htm As the name indicates, this site covers all sorts of free stuff—including graphics—with links to many of the best free graphics sites on the Web.

TIP ▸ ***Two great sources of commercially available Web clip art are Photodisc (www.photodisc) and Corbis (www.corbis.com). Both market a bunch of different graphics and CD-ROM collections available for sale on their Web sites. Photodisc also has several catalogs.***

Learn the Basics of FTP Transfer to Put Files up on Your Web Site

Chapter 6 lists two of the popular FTP programs. FTP programs are what you use to send your Web pages, graphics, and other items directly to your Web site. Using an FTP program such as CuteFTP or Fetch is fairly simple. If you're a novice, turn to the technical support person at your Web-hosting company for help using FTP.

Using a Database Approach

Some store owners use a database approach to create their sites. Lists of prices and products are commonly produced using database driven systems. Databases are useful because often-changed elements such as price, quantity, and new items can be quickly added by updating the underlying data in the database.

For all the benefits of the database approach, there are a number of drawbacks to consider—especially for smaller-scale stores. One drawback is that a database makes your Web site more complex and thus more expensive to set up; you have to hire someone to do your site development, and there will be some restrictions on how you can display items and design pages. However, updating items will be easier and it is much more flexible for implementing searches of catalogs, designing different sales pages, and so on.

With a database, you'll also need to create—or have a developer create—the various programs that the Web server will run to extract information from the database and then display the items in HTML on a Web page.

Another major difference with using a database approach is the need for a hosting service that will let you use the databases and the associated scripts and programs that work with the site. Not every host or hosting package offers this. In addition, those hosts and services that do let you work with a database system cost more than lower-end, static HTML hosting solutions. However, in most cases you will work with a database/Web developer who will help you choose an appropriate hosting service for your Web site.

If your site has several hundred items and numerous day-to-day price changes, then a database-driven Web site might be your best option. But if you're going to have fairly static pricing and only a hundred items or fewer, maintaining a solid set of HTML pages will keep things simpler and much less expensive.

If you want to create a database-driven Web site, you should talk with a capable Web site developer (unless you truly fit that description yourself). There are also some online solutions such as Yahoo Store (http://store.yahoo.com) that make it even easier. These services feature simple, easy-to-maintain databases. However, unlike a complete custom database service, these solutions and other similar offerings trade flexibility for ease-of-use and lower pricing.

The rest of this chapter focuses on the HTML associated with all Web sites and, more specifically, stores. In Chapter 25, you will find more discussion of database-driven Web store development. Many of the HTML tips from here on out are useful for those of you taking other approaches, such as Web-based building services like Yahoo Store, that require no HTML.

Constructing a User-Friendly Web Site

You can approach the structure of your Web site in many ways. The creativity and functionality of your site will determine, to a large extent, how well you compete in your particular market. You want your customers to be impressed the first time—and every time—they visit. You need to learn how to maintain a streamlined site that is informative, easy to navigate, and does not burden the customer with unnecessary fluff. Whatever your formula may be, make sure it gets to the point. The Tronix Web site (www.tronixweb.com), for example, is streamlined and easy to use.

Depending on your host, your hosting fees may increase with the amount of space allocated for your site. Therefore, keeping your site lean not only makes it easier to navigate and maintain, it can keep your monthly costs down. The entire Tronix site can be stored on a 3.5-inch floppy disk.

A Simple Design Philosophy for Online Stores

The chief activities of online shoppers are browsing, browsing, and browsing. It is critical that store sites respond quickly to visitors. That means creating a clean design that loads quickly rather than exquisite design that takes a long time to load.

Online shoppers are also information gatherers who like to compare items. The ability to present clear information about a product that helps customers compare or evaluate items is paramount.

Try to focus on providing fast load times and as much clear, relevant information as possible. Although this advice can apply to any Web site, it is particularly important for Web stores, where visitors might jump from place to place while comparing items and prices. Anything that makes it difficult for a customer to do this could result in losing that customer forever.

Basic Site Structure

It is essential to map out your Web store's structure. The Tronix Web site includes several departments and product type areas. Buttons for each main area appear throughout the site in the same form and in the same page area. Consistency from page to page, especially for navigation elements, is very important for any site. The Tronix Web site consists of the following pages, many of which you may be able to apply to your own site:

- **Home page.** Also considered the main page, and the entrance to your virtual store.
- **Price lists.** Individual price lists, each with its own page, categorized by product line. For stores that employ a separate page for each product (as many do), these price lists might actually links to home pages for each category of products. From there, the customer can visit the individual product pages.

- **Order Online.** Tronix's secure online order form with specific instructions about how to place an order.
- **New @ Tronix.** New products, restocks, and store-related news.
- **Coming Soon.** Customers can see what's coming and when, and place their pre-orders.
- **Shipping.** Charts for the various shipping options and pricing.
- **Company Policy.** A good online store posts company policies clearly and provides a link to them. Some might even display policies concerning returns and purchases before processing each order. This page helps keep customers from being surprised or disappointed later.
- **Tronix FAQ.** It is always a good idea to post a list of Frequently Asked Questions—and, of course, their answers.
- **Linkage.** Tronix offers links to Web pages for related sites, such as PlayStation, Dreamcast, Nintendo 64, and more. Links can be an important part of a store, providing outlets to educational information, manufacturer information, and more.

Home Page

The home page is the gateway to your business—the first page a customer views when accessing your site (the Tronix home page is shown in Figure 7.1). It's the equivalent of a window display in a traditional store. When you visit a store in the real world, the window display usually consists of various items for sale arranged in an attractive fashion, a sign with the store's hours, types of payment accepted and, in many cases, specials or closeouts. This is similar to what happens on a store's home page (without the necessary expenditures for a sign, awning, locksmith, alarm system, replacement of damaged window panes, and so on).

Your home page should show your mailing address, telephone and fax numbers, hours of operation (when you accept phone calls), and the types of payment accepted. For plastic payment, you may want to include small credit card logos, which resemble the decals adhered on the front window of any walk-in store.

FIGURE 7.1
The Tronix home page (www.tronixweb.com).

You can also include additional images or logos for some of your top items, new arrivals, specials, or sales. But don't overwhelm your customers with these. You want your customers to focus on those few items you're trying to move. You should also include dates when your business is closed (vacation, holidays) and, of course, your store's spiffy logo.

Your Logo

One of the first elements involved in creating your home page is your company logo. A number of versatile graphic design programs allow you to create a logo from a simple input of text. For the Tronix logo—and just about every other graphical item on the site—we used the powerful Adobe Photoshop and a fine shareware product called Paint Shop Pro. Both of these are great image creation programs that can easily create graphics for all the supported formats on the Web. Two other good programs are Adobe ImageReady and Macromedia Fireworks.

You should place your logo on the top half of your home page so that it is one of the first things your customers see. Integrated with the Tronix logo is contact information and our motto: "No nonsense mail-order for the serious gamer." The shape of the logo, as you can see in Figure 7.1, also allows us to attract attention to some featured items by highlighting them near the logo on the home page.

Design your logo so that it stands out but is not overly imposing; be aware of the color depth and size. The larger the logo in both size and in color count, the larger the file size. You should avoid creating a logo that loads slowly for your customers without a state-of-the art Internet connection. Try to keep your logo to 25K or less. Apply this rule to all pages involving graphical images such as icons, visual enhancements, or photo images.

TIP ▸ ***Creating your own logo can help you save money, but if you can afford a graphic designer, it is worth the cost. A good logo makes a strong, professional first impression. For a small business, a simple logo design shouldn't cost more than $1,000. If you already have a logo, you can simply scan it. However, it probably makes sense to have a designer create a perfect comp of it—especially if the scans you try don't come out straight.***

Joe's Take: *I've visited many sites where the company logo covered almost 50 percent of the home page and left me waiting ... and waiting ... and waiting for the page to load. I thought, if this is any indication of how the rest of this site is going to function, I'm not going to waste my time.*

TIP ▸ ***Take a tour of other company home pages. This will usually trigger ideas of your own and will allow you to sample the good, the bad, and the ugly. At each stop, ask yourself whether you would like to explore that company's site further or jump ship immediately. What makes you want to stay? What makes you want to leave and never come back?***

Background Color or Patterns

Choosing a background color or pattern for your Web site may not sound like a tough decision, but your site will scream "UNPROFESSIONAL!" if you use clashing colors or busy backgrounds that distract the visitor. Observe the backgrounds of other professional sites and you'll notice the classier sites tend to stay away from flashy colors or tiled backgrounds. Yes, even with all the graphic options available today, you're still better off keeping things clean and simple. Solid backgrounds in light colors work well. Dark backgrounds can also be interesting, provided you have some artistic ability. If you lack that ability, the color contrasting issues can become a problem.

Tronix's site has used both black and white at different times and is currently using white, which is easy to work with. No matter what color your foreground elements are, white will never interfere with them.

TIP ▸ ***Keep the color and theme of your site consistent. After you decide on a main page background color, think about the rest of your site. Keeping the pages all the same color is always a safe route, but varying the colors with shades can add flavor and emphasize departments or other specific sections within your store. Don't dramatically change colors from page to page—that can be jarring and distracting to the customer.***

Frames

Many Web sites use frames. Frames are independent panels that can change information or remain stationary with the same content no matter which part of a Web site you are exploring. The most common use of frames is to display a window of links to various parts of your site. This stationary panel is present on each page, so navigational links remain visible and never have to reload. While it wasn't always the case, most users are now using browsers that support frames.

If you decide to use frames, make sure you also provide a duplicate set of navigational links (either text or button-style) on every page so your "non-framed" audience can get around or offer framed and non-framed versions for the visitor to choose. If you don't design your site to accommodate everyone, you will lose potential customers.

Image Maps vs. Individual Buttons

When designing your main menu of choices, decide whether you want to use generic text links, individual buttons, or an image map. Straight text links are the easiest to lay out, but a good set of icons always looks more inviting. It's more fun clicking on visual objects such as buttons than on simple text. Navigational icons can add more flair to any Web site.

Image maps are a great alternative to independent buttons, especially if your site has numerous links. Having an image map load one sheet of choices can be faster than waiting for a number of buttons to load individually. However, image maps are more complex to develop, and if you decide later to add a new category to your inventory, you'll have to design an entirely new image map to include any new pages.

Joe's Take: *Whichever graphical approach you choose for your main navigational panel, keep the objects small, and watch your color count. You want your customers to enjoy their visit and not be waiting for a slow-loading panel of options. I've visited many sites where the Webmaster spent a lot of time developing attractive buttons, but I never stayed long enough to appreciate how talented he or she really was. A customer can't do a thing until she sees the menu. It's like going to a restaurant where the waiter doesn't arrive at your table until you've been seated for 20 minutes.*

Font Choices

Keeping your fonts similar in style and size on all pages is aesthetically pleasing and gives your site consistency. Main header information should be larger and bolder than your body text. The fonts you use should be ones that most computers have, such as Times and Helvetica (Arial on Windows). If you specify fonts, those fonts will display on every browser, no matter what kind of computer the customer is using. Some fonts look great on a word processor, but not on a Web page. The same rule applies for different browsers. For example: copyright text on the bottom of a page running under Netscape Navigator that looks small may be unreadable in Microsoft Internet Explorer. Text that is too large could scare away customers.

TIP ▸ ***If you want fancy font headers for your site but want to avoid specifying rare fonts that users may not have, try rendering the headers as GIF graphics. The downside is that whenever you want to change the text or add a header, you'll have to use your graphics program.***

Specifying Resolutions and Compatible Browsers

People cruising the Web use different computer configurations, from low-end to high-end, from PCs to Macs to Linux/UNIX boxes and WebTV. A site that is flexible enough to display well from lowest to highest resolutions will get great response from users. Design your site so that it works well with all screen resolutions (640 by 480, 800 by 600, 1024 by 768, 1152 by 864 up to 1280 by 1040).

Large text or graphics in high resolution will be enormous in the lower resolutions. Small text in low resolutions could become illegible in high resolution, and screen shots can become too small to appreciate. You can add a note to your main page specifying which resolution you modeled your site around (most that do this are designed for 800 by 600 resolution)—but that forces customers to conform to your personal preference when, in fact, you should be catering to them. On the other hand, you can't be expected to be compatible with long out-of-date browsers. Tronix has a message at the bottom of its home page that states, "The Tronix Web site is designed for Internet Explorer but also works fine with later versions of Netscape Communicator. If you cannot see our departments listed on the right column (blue background/white text), then it's time to catch up with the rest of the world and update your browser."

TIP ▸ ***The best way to tackle the Web site resolution problem is to do all your modeling in a medium resolution (800 by 600). After you get some text and images on a sample page, save your work. Then fire up a browser, load your sample page, and flip between all of your computer's resolutions to see the results. From there you can tweak the HTML design so it works well for all the major resolutions. Some programs like HomeSite actually let you test your site's look at various resolutions within the program.***

In addition to using different resolutions, your Web customers use different browsers and different versions of the those browsers. Although these browsers try to maintain the same look, there are differences in the way they display information—most noticeable in the rendering of tables and spacing. Netscape Communicator is pickier than Microsoft Internet Explorer in terms of how tables are rendered. Have both browsers available on your machine to test pages. Ask regular customers or friends with different versions of browsers to periodically check out your site and let you know if something isn't working right.

TIP ▸ ***As HTML progresses, make sure you don't get too far in front of your customer base. Although new tags and features may seem useful to adopt because of their functionality, many customers may not have downloaded the browsers that can render those new tags. When Netscape first added frames as a feature, many sites jumped to use them, only to hear the screams of users who couldn't use the site as a result.***

Accessible, Consistent Links

Your main page is the hub of your store. Every major link involved with a customer's visit should be immediately accessible from the home page. Have you ever walked into a department store looking for a simple item and found one of those obscure maps or had to deal with a frightened information booth clerk surrounded by a gang of rabid customers? Don't let your home page resemble that scenario.

Your major home page links should take your customers to price lists, shipping information, company policy, a "what's new" page, your online order form, and anywhere else they need to go. Other important links may include any specials or sales (if you decide to keep them separate from your price lists), a page for any news or reviews related to your business, and a page for common questions and answers about your company. It's also important to include your email address, so that customers can email inquiries, general comments, or advice.

Once you decide where and how your links will appear on your home page, carry this layout over to every page on your Web site. This consistency will make it easy for your customers to navigate your site.

TIP ▸ ***Customer feedback is very important. Read and reply to your customers' comments and suggestions, as it can have a great impact on the way your site turns out. You'll get valuable Web site tips from customers, some of whom will be experts in fields such as graphics and Web design. You needn't make changes to your Web site in response to every negative comment or good idea. But if several customers make similar suggestions—positive or negative—it's probably worth looking into.***

Price Lists

It is imperative to keep your price list page(s) clear, uncluttered, and fully functional (Figure 7.2). This is an informational page with one purpose—showing your customers how much everything costs. Customers need to be able to find the product they want and immediately get the price without any further effort.

One issue that might arise—and sometimes does for Tronix—is whether you should list an item without a price. Depending on what you're selling, you may not know the price of an item until you get it in stock. When Tronix first opened, it used to post TBD (to be determined) for unpriced items. However, customers want a price, and the absence of one might lead customers to believe you're either out of the item or the price is so high you don't want to list it. In the end, a solid price is best.

Joe's Take: *At first I used TBD as an excuse to list upcoming items and bulk up my stocking lists. It was pure filler and made it look like there were titles in stock that actually weren't—especially when the Nintendo 64 had just shipped and there were only two or three games available. Later, people got confused about TBD and I got so many calls and criticism I dropped TBD as a policy. Eventually I got better at setting prices.*

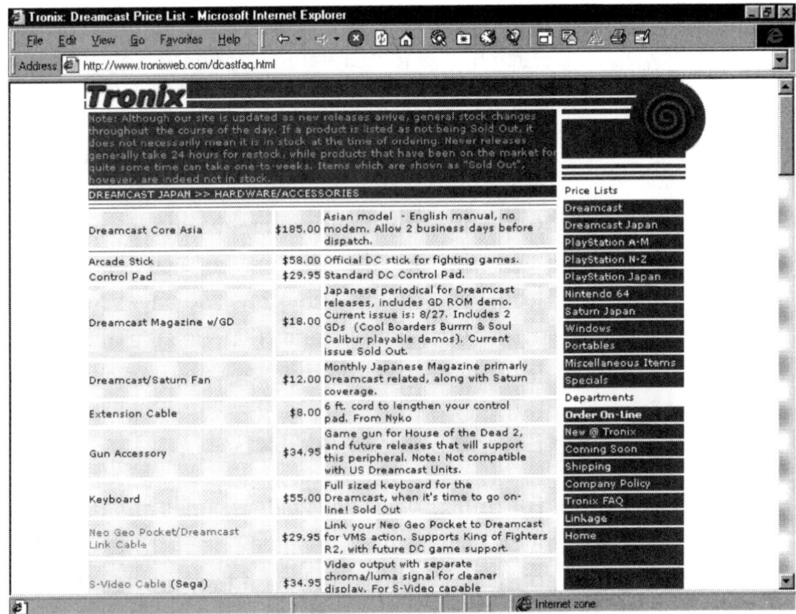

Figure 7.2
One of Tronix's price lists.

Using Tables

Price lists work best when they are organized in clear columns using tables. The versatility of tables allows you to add or delete rows as your inventory changes. A good layout to use—and the one Tronix uses—is a three-column setup. The first column contains the name of the item, the second the price (properly justified to the right so all decimal points are vertically aligned), and the third a very brief description of the product.

You can add columns depending on your line of business. You may want to list an item's color, style, dimension, and whether it's in or out of stock. You can even include a small icon that is linked to a photo of the item. Although tables keep price lists organized, they're a bit of a hassle to update. A graphical Web authoring tool, also called a WYSIWYG (What You See Is What You Get) HTML editor, is best suited for quick table updating. Once you become familiar with HTML, you can easily load the page into any HTML text editor and do it manually.

If you study the HTML layout of your price list pages, you can see where each item and its related information starts and ends by the accompanying table-related tags.

Tables take a bit longer to load than straight bodies of text do, so don't make your tables too large. If a particular line of products that you sell contains many items, you may want to consider splitting the tables onto a few pages, rather than having a customer wait for a huge price list to load. For example, Tronix has two pages for PlayStation products, divided alphabetically (A–M and N–Z). Be sure to make it obvious that the split list continues onto other pages by adding additional links as needed.

Beyond Simple Price Lists

For Tronix, which sells video games about which most of its customers are well informed, a simple price list works well. But in many cases, price lists often work best if they provide the basic information and link to a specific page with more detailed information about the product.

When creating a separate page for each item, consider the following key things:

- **Keep to a standard.** Each product page should be presented in a standard format. Obviously different types of products might require some deviation, but the more consistent the better.
- **Cross-sell.** Use product pages to cross-sell by providing links to items that go with that product. You can also up-sell by linking to better (and more expensive) items of a similar type.
- **Provide navigation.** Provide a simple icon or link to click forward or backward to the next or previous item in that category.
- **Be concise yet complete.** Provide as much information as possible, although graphics should still load quickly.
- **Make it easy.** Make sure it's easy for the user to backtrack to the price list for the product's category.

Organizing Various Categories

Categories should be separated logically. How many types of individual products will you sell? How many product lines do you have? Will they all be similar but from different manufacturers? Ultimately, you want your customers to find what they are looking for without having to bounce from page to page. Before you lay your tables out online, plan them out on paper. If your inventory consists of jewelry, for example, you might want to separate it by types—earrings, brooches, necklaces, rings, bracelets, and so on. Or you can have separate price lists for different manufacturers or designers. If your inventory is small, you could separate it more simply—gold on one page, silver on the other.

TIP ▸ ***You can link Web sites relating to your products—such as the company that produces them—right on your price lists. Customers may want to learn more about the product before making a purchase. Keeping some handy links off on a sidebar will provide access to further information. The only potential problem is that the person buys the product directly from the manufacturer, costing you a sale.***

Highlighting Your Newest Items

It is a good idea for stores with extensive repeat business and lots of new products that arrive regularly (e.g. books, CDs, games) to highlight the latest products and releases. It's easy—and a good idea—to make them immediately distinguishable from your previous stock. After you enter the new items into your store, you can place a simple change in a price list row or add an icon that says "New" to the left of the item listing.

Some of the free sites mentioned earlier in this chapter contain common types of icons, such as pointing arrows and animated "New" symbols. If you don't like what's out there, design one yourself. You can even develop your own fancy icon for indicating new stock; just be sure to address its meaning by adding a legend to the top of your price list.

Using JPEGs with Your Price List

Adding digitized shots of products to your site gives the customer an idea of what the product looks like. Depending on the size of your inventory and what you sell, you can add photos for every item you sell, or just for selected items you feel customers would enjoy viewing. For example, if you sell clothing or something that people will have to see before they buy, you should definitely include photos of all items. However, Tronix can show a mere handful of game box covers with no repurcussions.

With a good scanner or digital camera and an image-processing program such as Adobe Photoshop, you can save your images in JPEG format and link them to your items in a number of ways. You can have a page specifically dedicated to items that have digitized shots or you can turn the item into a link directly from the price list.

JPEG images shouldn't be too large or you will try your customer's patience. Tronix processes all of its images through Adobe Photoshop using an 800 by 600 resolution. Finished graphics are reduced to a maximum of 250 by 250 pixels. At this size, you can have about four images on one screen at the lowest customer resolution without bogging down the transmission. The ease with which an item can be scanned depends on its size and shape. CDs or computer games work fine, but your business may be dealing with much larger or unscannable items. Scanning a Tiffany lamp or fly rod would be quite a feat. This is where a camera or a digital camera can come into play. See the sidebar on digital cameras for more information.

TIP ▸ ***There's always a way to get a scanned image of an item on a Web site, no matter the size. Start by looking at the packaging. Does it contain a picture of the item that can be scanned? Ask your supplier if they have any promotional materials or empty packages you can use. Of course, if you have a camera, you can simply take a sharp photo of the actual product.***

Top Sellers

Hot-selling items can have their own spot on your price list or even your home page. You can create a "Top 10" list that changes on a weekly or monthly basis as popular items change. You can post this right on your home page or add it as a link above your price lists.

Digital Cameras

Store owners with products that can't be scanned are increasingly turning to digital cameras to create product shots. Digital cameras are especially popular with real estate agents. The great thing about digital cameras is that they reduce the time between taking a photo and placing it on your Web site. With a conventional camera, you've got to get the film developed and then scan the resulting photos. A digital image can be transferred immediately into your computer. A digital camera also gives you immediate feedback about the photo. Here are some tips on using digital cameras to create product shots for your store:

Get a camera with 640 by 480 or better resolution

Most of today's cameras create pictures of 640 by 480 or better resolution. Several manufacturers have created cameras that sell for less than $1,000 and provide 1024 by 768 or better resolution. The higher the resolution you can afford, the better. Although you'll reduce it to a 250 by 250 or smaller resolution, your goal is to reduce from the highest quality photo possible. The standard resolution for graphics on the Web is 72 dots per inch (dpi).

Use a power supply for the camera

Digital cameras eat batteries for lunch. If your desired camera doesn't come with a power supply, get one. The more you're able to draw power out of an outlet instead of from batteries, the more money you'll save.

Shoot in front of a backdrop

Most product shots will display best and be easiest to edit if they're photographed with a plain background such as a white foam board. Once you've shot the item you'll be able to cut away all the shadows and other background and improve the image and its sharpness. However, if your product is white or has a white label that extends to the edge of the package, use a darker background.

Get lots of light—daylight works best

Digital cameras love light. Low-light conditions are terrible and even artificial light isn't great. If you can, shoot in natural daylight conditions.

Fill the viewfinder with the item you're shooting

Since you have a finite number of pixels per photograph, make the most of them. Don't bother framing the background around the object since you'll eventually cut the background out in a paint program anyway.

For lots more information on digital photography, a book worth reading is *Real World Digital Photography* by Deke McClelland and Katrin Eismann, published by Peachpit Press.

Shipping

Your shipping page should contain all the necessary information so customers can get an idea of what fees they will be paying in addition to their purchase. You should include a list of available couriers, your shipping cut-off times, and any email and phone order deadlines you might have.

The main part of the shipping page should be your sample rate chart. Tronix's shipping page is shown in Figure 7.3. For a far more detailed discussion of your shipping page—and the issue of shipping in general—see Chapter 17.

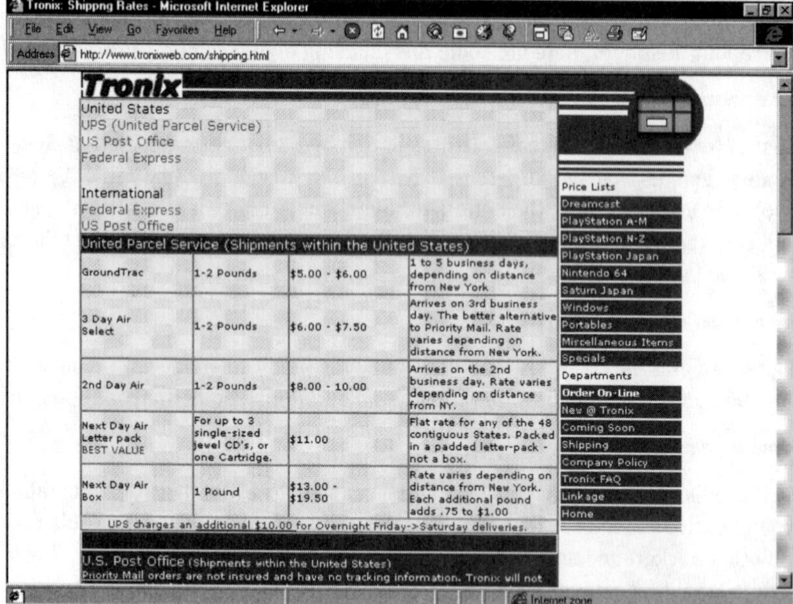

FIGURE 7.3
Tronix's shipping page.

Specials

Sales and specials are great ways to unload older stock. Many times your own distributors will be facing the same situation and will offer you a reduced price to get rid of stock. You don't necessarily have to buy their slow-moving titles, but you can combine them with your own sale items and bring them into stock when a customer places an order. You can also have holiday-themed sales, such as a Fourth of July sale or After Christmas specials. The specials should be presented in the same format as your regular price lists. You can highlight your newly reduced items as you did your new releases. If you have any specific rules about your sale items, such as "all sales final," display this information above your price list. Another way to advertise specials is on your standard price list. You can simply add a sale icon next to the reduced title, highlight the entire row with an alternate color, change the color of the typeface to red, etc. Another option is using a font strike-through that displays a slash across the original price with your lower price added underneath. Offering periodic sales can easily expand your customer base.

News and Reviews

You can also set up a page with news and/or reviews related to your products. Major Web retailers such as Amazon and CDNow include staff and user reviews. Depending on the nature of your business, you can post your own personal reviews of particular products and even devise your own rating system. Articles of interest might be press releases or general industry news. If you find information about your products on other Web sites, you can add small articles with embedded links that lead to those sites. This page is also be a good place for inside information you have heard through the grapevine about upcoming products. However, be careful what you post in such "scoops" and always consider the source.

Having a page of news or reviews is a bonus for your customers. It separates your business from the many generic cyberstores and shows that you care about your customers and the products you're selling. This area of your Web site will also complement your store by giving it an informative atmosphere. People will turn to your site as a resource and many of them will become customers. In Tronix's case, it's not uncommon to see newsgroup postings referring to the informational aspects of the site. (For more on using newsgroups to build your customer base, see Chapter 10.)

Review Honestly

If you do post your own product reviews, be honest with your audience. If you give a 5-star rating to a loser item that's been sitting in your inventory for ages, you'll lose your credibility. And if you hand out fawning reviews for all of your products, customers won't be able to differentiate between the truly outstanding and the hype. After buying a couple of mediocre products because of top-notch reviews, people will stop believing what you say. Instead, tell your audience it's not the greatest product and put it on sale. You can always discount the product, rather than having a customer purchase it after reading glowing (and embellished) reviews on your Web site. It's better to lose a few short-term bucks than your long-term reputation.

TIP ▸ ***Keep reviews short. Lengthy content on the Web gets tuned out. Short paragraphs that get to the point quickly work better.***

Order Form

When Tronix first came into existence, credit card transactions on the Internet could be frightening. Many customers either called by phone or took the risk of sending all their information through standard email. Tronix has never encountered any hacker-related problems, but the chance of someone breaking into the service provider was always something to worry about. Customers were warned that sending their credit card information through email was not safe, but many of them continued to use this method. International customers were the most common users of this method of payment because of the time difference or the fact that they simply didn't want to make an expensive overseas phone call.

As the Internet matured, online stores and shopping malls premiered at a startling pace and the Internet became a viable tool for commerce. (For details on secure transactions, see Chapter 14.) New customers inquired about safely sending credit card information to Tronix. They didn't want to call or fax long distance, and they weren't comfortable sending their credit card information through email.

As customers became more interested in placing credit card orders, it became necessary to build an online order form, which can be one of the most difficult additions to your Web site. Tronix's Web-hosting service supported Secure Sockets Layer (SSL) and offered simple template forms for its clients to download and experiment with. There are three parts to this kind of form:

- **THE FORM ITSELF**, which contains all the fields to be filled out by your customer.

- **A simple ASCII text page**, which contains all the customer information that is extracted from the form and immediately sent to your email address.
- **The "Success" page**, which is invoked after your customer submits the form. It's basically a follow-up page with final notes to the customer and, of course, a courteous thank-you comment.

A secure online order form (Figure 7.4) should be accessible and easily identifiable on every page of your site. You can have a small icon separate from your other links, or you can keep it uniform along with your order categories. Whether you prefer a button, icon, or straight text link, it makes sense to give it a color that stands out from your other links. This is the one link that will present your customer with an order form, which should ultimately produce a sale.

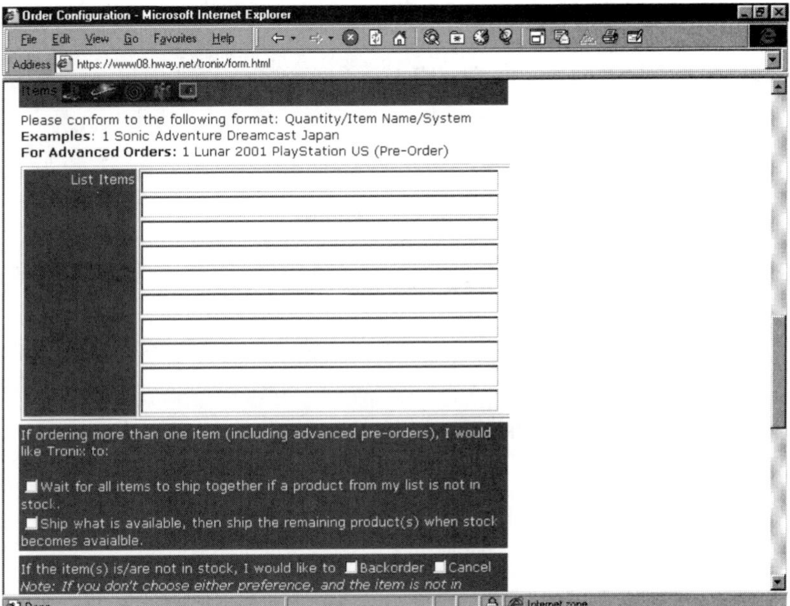

Figure 7.4
Tronix's order form.

Required Fields

The order form should be carefully designed and must include all the required fields needed to process your customer's order. It's essential for a solid online form to include the following fields:

Personal Information

- First Name.
- Last Name.
- Middle Initial.
- Home Address or Business Address.
- Home/Business Phone Number.
- Email Return Address.
- Credit Card Type.
- Credit Card Number.
- Expiration Date.
- Name of the Issuing Bank of the Credit Card (for Visa and MasterCard).

Order Information

- Item(s).
- Quantity.
- Color/Size/Style (if applicable).
- Shipping Choice.
- Submit and Reset Buttons.

Optional

- Fax.
- Phone number of credit card issuing bank (for Visa and MasterCard).
- COD.
- Pre-Order.

Field Construction

Fields should have enough space to fit all the necessary information. For instance, an expiration date usually consists of five characters: the month, a slash, and the year (05/02 for example). The credit card number field should provide enough room for all the spaces in between the groups of digits. Spaces count as characters, so if you only leave your customer enough room for the credit card digits, you'll find the process of entering the credit card number into your point of sale program much slower and with more chance of error. Look at the difference:

No spacing:	4121444455552222
Proper spacing:	4121 4444 5555 2222

Also, leave plenty of extra room in the name fields. You need to accommodate Patricia Wojechowski as well as Ed Ott.

TIP ▸ ***What about Y2K and credit card expiration dates? Unless your credit card provider requires you to collect the entire four character version of the expiration date, there is no need to require this. Check with the company that helps you process credit cards to deal with this issue.***

Provide Specific Instructions

Emphasize the importance of filling out every field carefully and correctly. If a name or address is incorrectly entered, it could lead to a customer's order sitting in a shipper's warehouse until the mistake is corrected. If a customer incorrectly types his or her credit card number, your authorization terminal will simply throw it back at you and you'll have to contact the customer for the correct information. This will slow down the order and will be especially frustrating if the customer chose an overnight service and was expecting to receive a package the next morning.

TIP ▸ ***If you notice a customer is using a Visa or MasterCard and neglected to include the name of the issuing bank, immediately contact the customer and obtain that information. Failing to include the bank name might simply be an accident or it might mean the customer only had a stolen number but no card.***

Optional Fields

There are various optional fields to consider. If you honor CODs, you can add this as a check-off box after your credit card fields. Some customers will ask whether they can pre-order an upcoming item that hasn't been released by the manufacturer. You can add a check-off box for pre-orders, or have the customer type "Pre-Order" next to the item in that field.

Some mail order companies will only ship to the card holder address that is on file with the issuing bank. Following this rule will limit fraud. After you establish a good relationship with a customer, you can consider shipping products to alternative addresses, such as a business or a relative's house.

Define Policies Clearly

Before your customer clicks the "Submit" button, you should clarify how the order will be handled. For example:

- When and how the customer will be contacted (during business hours, before a certain time, in the evening, the following day, by phone or email).
- Additional fees (such as shipping, handling, taxes).
- Options for out of stock orders.
- The deadline for orders.
- When the customer will be billed.

Whatever rules your company has established, make sure they are posted clearly so the customer is aware of them before placing an order. You can have this information explained directly above your order form, or provide a separate page for your company policies. Encourage your customers to read this information.

Success!

After a customer submits an order, he or she should be presented with a "success" page. The success page is simply a final note that shows the order was submitted correctly. You can post your thank you and perhaps reiterate a few important factors (like when they'll be contacted). You can finish this page with your address, phone number and hours of operation within your time zone. This is a good final reminder, because there are plenty of international customers who don't realize they're submitting an order early in the day while you're in bed dreaming about being a rich and famous online retailer.

Updates

An "Updates" or "What's New" page is a must-have, especially for sites that are constantly under construction or adding or changing new items. For retailing, it's essential to keep your customers up to date on any new happenings in your business. As new products are brought into stock, you'll want your customers to know what they are and when they arrived. Updates for special announcements such as a sale, a price change, a highly requested restock, or any key cosmetic changes to your Web site can be easily found on one page, separated by the date the event occurred. Rather than having separate pages for new items and Web-related updates, it might be more convenient to combine the pages and minimize the need for page hopping.

How important is an update page? You have an active group of customers who check out your site every day, yet without an update page those customers can't tell whether anything new is going on unless they hunt through the various pages of your store and fall upon a new release. If they aren't the kind of person to hang around long, they'll never know whether you just received something they've been looking for. It would be a mistake to make dramatic Web modifications without letting your regulars know about it. It would be like walking into your office one morning and finding that the night maid reorganized your desk without telling you where your calculator ended up.

Date Your Updates

After you complete the day's updates, add a notice to your home page telling people when the site was last updated. There's no need to post uneventful updates, such as a background color change on your price tables or a new font you decided to use.

Tronix has confined all updates to one page labeled "New @ Tronix." Interestingly enough, this page has the highest hit-count on the Tronix site. The page includes a list of expected new releases, news, and recent releases listed by date, beginning with the most recent.

TIP ▸ ***Link each announcement to its respective page. Customers should be able to jump right to the page or specific area of a page to get more information on the newly announced item or update. Remove all outdated information. Customers are more interested in what's new, not what arrived in stock or changes you made six months ago. The three most recent months are plenty.***

Company Policy

Every retail business has a company policy or set of rules governing transactions, and your cyberstore should be no different. It is extremely important to list all of your policies to avoid misunderstandings between you and your customers. Think about what your customers need to know before purchasing an item and present it clearly. It will save you a lot of headaches and even a possible lawsuit.

What you include on your company policy page will vary depending on your type of business. Here is some of the information you should include:

- Return policy and refunds.
- Warranty details.
- Payment.

- Credit card issues (theft or unauthorized use).
- Bad checks.
- Refused CODs.
- Rules on special orders.
- Cancelled orders.

If you're unsure about what to include in your company policy statement, check out some other mail-order sites, such as L.L. Bean (www.llbean.com) or Eddie Bauer (www.eddiebauer.com), to get an idea of how they present their policies.

FAQ

As your store grows, you'll answer more email than you can imagine. Some of it will turn into sales. Customers may ask simple questions that you don't have time to answer. A good FAQ (Frequently Asked Questions) page can help weed out some of the repetitive inquiries. A simple question and answer layout works best. For example:

- **Question:** Why are your DaVinci wine glasses so much more expensive than the other brands?
- **Answer:** Because they are imported from Italy, and the rest of our wine glasses are made in the United States.
- **Question:** What is the best time of day to place an order to ensure it will be processed and shipped that same day?
- **Answer:** If placing an order by email, it's best to send us your order the previous night, or before 3 P.M. that day. For further information, please visit our Shipping Page.

TIP ▸ ***A good idea for an optional page is one that includes customer compliments. If your customers, especially first-time visitors, can see how happy your other customers are, they will have more confidence in your service and feel better about making a purchase.***

Linkage

Whether you link to outside sites will depend on what type of business you run and what types of products you sell. If you sell products that your your company makes, there is no need to send customers elsewhere. However, since Tronix sells products created by other companies, we link to relevant pages on the Web sites of those companies (Figure 7.5). This allows customers to get even more information about a particular product if they so desire.

TIP ▸ ***Want to link to a site so the user doesn't leave your site to get there? Force the browser to open a new windows by adding the TARGET="_blank" attribute to an <A HREF> tag as shown in this example: <A HREF="www.cnet.com/reviews/" TARGET="_blank>Reviews</A>***

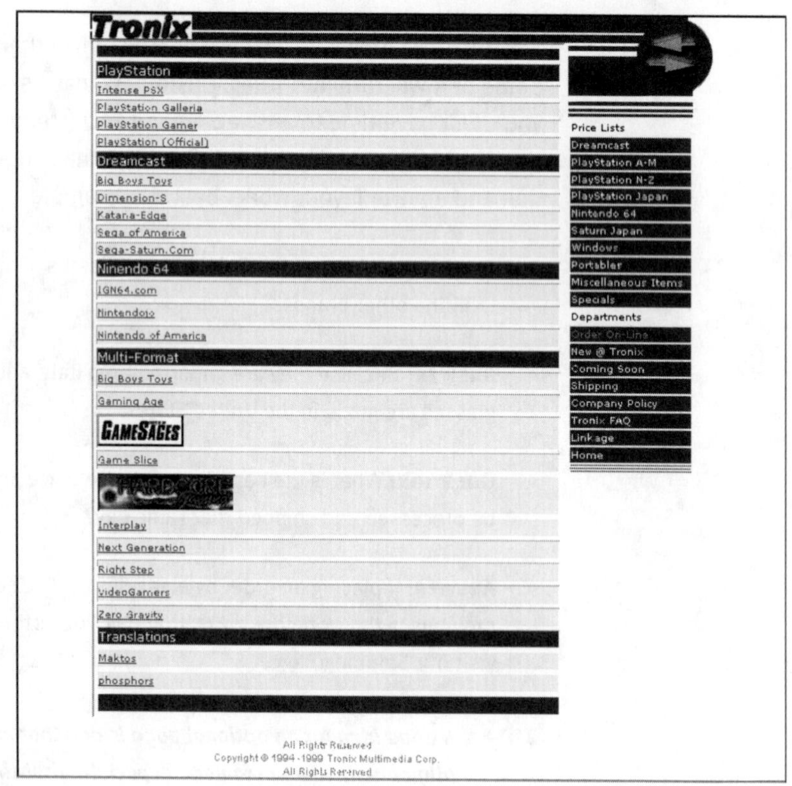

FIGURE 7.5
Tronix's link page.

Content for All Pages

There are a few things you should include on every page, including a copyright notice to discourage competitors or users from stealing graphics or review content. You can also include your phone number, address, and store hours on every page. Not everyone will come in the front door. If you have this information at the bottom of every page, you'll never have a customer searching in frustration.

Another thing to have is a small email link to you or your Webmaster with a message on the bottom of the screen in small type, something like: "Site problems or comments ‹email›." If someone notices a dead link or a problem with your page or site, you'll quickly get feedback. The easier you make it to give feedback, the more of it you'll get.

On to Inventory

Absorb as much useful information as you can as you build your Web site. Refer to this chapter and the resources we have suggested and also study as many Web sites and stores as possible. You never know where you'll find a neat design idea or a new wrinkle to keep customers surfing back to your store.

The key to building a strong store site is balancing flair and functionality. While you want to keep your site simple, quick to load, and easy to navigate, you don't want to make it dull. The more you learn by reading and studying other sites, the easier it will be for you to find this balance.

Now that you know how to get your site up and running, it's on to Chapter 8. We'll show you how to stock your shelves and keep product moving while maintaining a reasonably small inventory.

CHAPTER EIGHT

Stocking Your Store

One of the great things about owning a Web store is that no one needs to see how, where, or what you actually stock. On the other hand, initially it can be difficult to find cooperative distributors and/or producers to work with. As the Web has grown this has become easier, but the size of your business, its financial stability, your cash flow, and your confidence in the salability of your products are among the factors that determine the size of your inventory. To top it off, the idea of a Web store can be a bit frightening to distributors who aren't as impressed by or as educated about Web retailing as you are.

Many Web merchants have successfully minimized their risk by keeping inventory as small as possible. They rely on speedy distributor turnaround or patient customers. As customers place orders, the store receives the required products from the distributor or manufacturer and ships them. Although the store appears to have a large stock, in fact it is primarily paying for pre-sold items. This can backfire if the order is for a hot item and it is impossible to get the item in the customer's hands when he wants it. Usually a next-day order needs to be in stock to satisfy customer demand. In most cases, Web stores follow the 80/20 rule: They stock the 20 percent of available products that they expect 80 percent of the customers to regularly order. Remaining products are special orders. In this model, knowing which products are worth stocking and which ones aren't is crucial to your store's success. Until you have a good handle on that, the smaller the stock you can carry, the better.

TIP ▸ ***Superior knowledge of which products will sell and the ability to soothe a customer while you await the products' arrival will help you as a Web retailer. Losing sales due to inventory misses draws the ire of any retailer. As customer inquiries begin to roll in, keep track of what people are asking about. Keep a small stock of the most popular items.***

Getting Product

The first stage of stocking your store is acquiring items. Some retailers will be selling products that they make, but most will exclusively or at least partially sell items made by other companies, which requires winning support from these companies or individuals.

Building Relationships with Manufacturers, Distributors, or Yourself

Unless you are building the products yourself, you'll need to build comfortable relationships with manufacturers and distributors. It is not always easy to win their confidence. A lot of work goes into establishing the type of successful relationship that will benefit your business.

First you must decide where and how you will obtain your merchandise. Will you work directly with the manufacturer or go through a distributor? Depending on the type of merchandise you're selling, you may be able to use both. Either way, you'll find advantages and disadvantages.

Working Directly with a Manufacturer

Working directly with the manufacturer usually means paying less because you eliminate the distribution middleman. You should also be able to get new products on the same day a distributor would, instead of waiting for the distributor to receive the items from the manufacturer and then re-ship the items to you.

However, many manufacturers require a minimum order, which works against the goal of minimizing your inventory. As you grow and become more financially solid, a manufacturer's minimum order might not be a problem. But early in the life of your business, a minimum order might be enough to dissuade you from working directly with a manufacturer. Look closely at the numbers. Does a manufacturer's less expensive price outweigh the drawbacks of having to order more of a product than you would like?

Joe's Take: *I would like to work directly with Sony or Nintendo and acquire a discount level close to what my distributors have. Although that sounds like an ideal situation, if I tried to order a dozen or so pieces of a product, I might get laughed off the phone. Large corporations like Sony, Nintendo, and Sega have sizeable minimum requirements—we're talking triple digits. The companies that order such large quantities are generally distributors. Not every manufacturer will impose a steep requirement on an order. If you are considering working directly with a manufacturer, your best bet is to call and talk to someone in the new accounts department.*

The other reason to work directly with a manufacturer is that it may be the only way to get the product. Many small artisans or companies create products that only are available directly from them. They have their own way of approving vendors and may also require money up front more often. Typically the smaller the direct company, the less formal the vendor program will be. It will take a bit more work to set up a proper supply system with them.

TIP ▸ ***Maximizing availability is sometimes more critical than ensuring the best price. That is why you should open as many channels to a product as possible and use the best option when you need it. For example, just because you can get a product from a distributor more quickly, that doesn't mean you shouldn't consider opening up a direct line to the manufacturer as well. If you have a crucial sale to make, you may find working directly with a manufacturer when a distributor is out of stock can be a sale-saving option.***

Working with a Distributor

Finding the right distributors may be more suitable than working directly with a manufacturer. An established distributor can sometimes offer a better deal than the manufacturer. Distributors are generally able to order large quantities directly from the manufacturer, which leads to an unbeatable discount. An even bigger advantage to working with distributors is that you don't have to deal with large quantities. Most distributors allow any size order. There's no need to worry about keeping a large inventory, and non-moving products will be the distributor's headache, not yours.

TIP ▸ ***When first working with distributors, let them know that you're serious about your business and put together a decent-sized order for your initial purchase (unless you are ordering very expensive merchandise). If you can afford it, ordering a dozen units of a $20 item will make a better impression on a distributor than ordering two or three.***

Defective Items and Stock Balancing

When establishing an account with a distributor (or a manufacturer) make sure you ask about stock balancing and defective items.

Stock balancing allows you to return slow-moving stock toward the purchase of newer stock, as long as it is done within a reasonable amount of time. Returning defective items should be no problem, but as with your own store, distributors and manufacturers will grant this exchange only through a certain number of days. This can be critical to your business.

Even small businesses use a point-of-sale and inventory program to keep track of in-stock merchandise that needs to be sent back for stock balancing. Stock balancing is a great, no-risk policy, but very few distributors offer it. You're more likely to find stock balancing offered by the manufacturer. However, as you build strong relationships with your distributors, they may occasionally allow you to return some slow-moving stock, especially if it is something they can use in their inventory.

TIP ▸ ***Be careful when ordering the same product from multiple distributors. Make sure your don't return three pieces of a product to a distributor from whom you initially only ordered one.***

JOE'S TAKE: *Like traditional stores, you can run specials on your Web site to move dead stock. I post specials on my home page to move those last remaining titles. Remember to make specials stand out like they would in a retail store display. Some stores send out weekly specials via email to registered subscribers. You can also bundle items together, offering a chance to get a slower moving item for a deep discount when a customer orders another item.*

Is Web Selling Allowed?

You should be aware that some manufacturers will not allow their products to be sold on the Web. Because the Web helps small merchants become national and/or global, it contributes to the breakdown of sales territories that may be a closely watched aspect of a manufacturer's distribution strategy. Tupperware, for example, has cracked down on people selling its wares online. Since its sales strategy involves thousands of independent sales agents working worldwide to evangelize and sell its products, Tupperware can't afford to have these efforts undermined by a few enterprising sellers using the Web to reach beyond their usual sales area.

This is uncommon, but there are some large-scale retailer networks that could get in an uproar if independent agents and retailers were to undercut their services and sales by launching Web stores. Expect resistance to Web retailing by those people until they figure out how to reconcile their real-world sales territory with virtual stores.

Overseas exporting is also an area of possible concern. Although local selling of the product via the Web might be allowed, you may not be allowed to export the products to other countries. This may be the case in order to avoid sales encroachment by Web-based stores on local country partners, or because your government doesn't allow the wares you're selling to be exported. For example, some computer systems and software are not allowed to be sold to customers outside of the United States.

For the most part, you have little to worry about as Web retailing continues to be more accepted and popular, but be sure to check with your manufacturer, distributor, and maybe even your lawyer.

Setting Up an Account

To set up an account with a distributor or manufacturer, you will have to submit your Tax Identification Number and possibly a retail certificate, and to fill out an application. On the application, you'll have to provide information on how long you've been in business and about your business bank account. You'll also be asked to provide a list of current or previous business relationships. If you're just starting out, your list of business contacts will either be short or non-existent. Don't panic. The primary reason for the list of business references is to help the dealer decide whether or not you qualify for special *net terms.*

Net terms are like credit cards without the finance charge. For instance, a Net 30 account means you have 30 days from the invoice date to pay for the goods you ordered. In a perfect world, you have time to sell the goods, repay the distributor, and pocket the profit before the 30 days are up. Every distributor or manufacturer has its own set of rules. Some may have Net 15 accounts, and others may not offer any net terms. Unless your new distributor is related to you, it's highly unlikely you'll immediately be granted net terms, especially if your reference list is short.

Working without Net Terms: C.O.D.

So how does a new owner of a mail-order business get product without net terms? Meet your savior: C.O.D.

C.O.D (cash on delivery) means just that—whether your orders are delivered or picked up, you pay for your goods immediately. Early on, you'll need to get used to having cash, a money order, or a certified check ready to pay for your inventory purchases. Once you have established a steady relationship with your sources, you'll probably be allowed to pay with a standard company check, eliminating the annoyance of running to the bank for a certified check before your orders arrive. Paying by a company check is a pleasure because the amount is not immediately deducted from your account. Depending on your distributor's bank, how close he is to your business, and how quickly the check is deposited, you could have anywhere from two days to more than a week before the check clears, giving you a bit of time to turn over stock.

TIP ▸ ***If you have a low budget, be careful how much you order versus how much you sell. Ordering a few thousand dollars worth of inventory when you are only certain of a few hundred dollars worth of sales can be a disaster. Always leave yourself room for checks to clear with additional funds to cover overlapping purchases.***

TIP ▸ ***If you are the sole operator of your business, it's best to spend the $5 charge on C.O.D.s and pay for your goods immediately. This eliminates any bills hanging over your head (which can be overlooked during busy periods) and gives you a more realistic picture of your financial situation.***

Dell Computer's Virtual Inventory

Dell Computer is the master of the virtual inventory. The company, which is selling more than $3 million worth of items daily on its Web site, practices a very strict form of virtual inventory that not only lets it build customized computers but keeps its supply of parts and products razor thin. Orders come into Dell's store system, and items are sent on to manufacturing. The data on what parts are needed is fed into another system that automatically notifies nearby suppliers (suppliers must maintain warehouses of their own near Dell's manufacturing facility). The suppliers ship directly to Dell.

Dell rarely pays for parts that aren't going into a computer almost immediately upon coming through the door. For example, monitors aren't even on hand and instead are drop-shipped directly from the manufacturer (more on drop-shipping later in this chapter). Dell sends an email notification to a freight company, which picks the package up from the distributor and brings it straight to the customer. Products no longer have to be shipped anywhere else first, which saves Dell money. Dell saves more than $30 per monitor order by having the monitor shipped directly to the customer.

Minimizing Your Inventory Risk

In the early stages of your business, you certainly don't want to be stuck with excess stock. Stock is basically money on hold, and unless you are starting out with a hefty, regular cash flow, excess stock simply eats up money. Instead of the money going in your pocket, it sits on the floor in a big box marked "Loser." It takes time to get a feel for what types of products will move fast and which ones will collect dust. When you're starting out, carrying the smallest inventory possible makes the most sense.

Almost every business starts slowly. You may not want to stock anything until you actually have orders coming in, especially if you're selling expensive merchandise. Minimizing your stock helps you pay your business bills and hopefully even pay yourself.

The Advantages of Being Physically Close to Your Suppliers

Having your suppliers (distributors or manufacturers) located near your business is a nice bonus. It's also something you have no control over unless you want to relocate. If you work with three distributors, and one happens to be nearby, consider yourself lucky. Having your source for stock nearby allows you to physically zip over and pick up whatever you need. This allows you to eliminate shipping charges and pick up products the same day they are ordered, and customers don't have to wait for you to special order their item(s). It also gives the impression that you have the items in stock, when in fact it's down the street at the distributor. The distributor's stock room becomes your own risk-free storage spot.

Setting up Pre-Orders with Longtime Customers

Pre-orders are the best way to get an overall picture of what sells, what doesn't, and how many units to order at the time of release. You should announce available pre-orders on your site. You can include your pre-order chart in your "What's New" section, above all the current releases, or above related price lists. If you have an exact release date, include it. If not, you can label it "Coming Soon" and list the month or week of expected release. Make sure your customers are aware if a release date is not exact.

Depending on the price range of your merchandise, you can take pre-orders in various ways:

- **Online form.** Have the customer fill out your online order form and notify him when the product arrives. If the customer is paying by credit card, let him know the card will not be charged until the merchandise ships.

- **Deposit.** Take a deposit for the soon-to-be released products, especially if the item is one that might sell out quickly. However, bear in mind that some customers are a understandably leery of having money deducted from a charge card before they even see what they're getting. This method makes more sense if you are dealing with expensive items.

- **Email.** Set up an email folder for customers who don't want to commit to an order yet but who are very interested in ordering the product at the time of release. When a customer is interested in a future release, you can simply add her name to the folder that is set up specifically for that product. When the product arrives, open your folder and send each customer an announcement along with the price. Using a simple cut-and-paste method, you can send the same information to each customer, without having to type up the same email for each inquiry.

TIP ▸ ***Customers who make a commitment by filling out your online order form should receive their products before those who simply express an interest in the product. Make this policy clear to your customers by posting it on your site.***

Drop-Shipping

A drop-shipment is sent directly from the distributor to your customer's door, eliminating the extra step of having it shipped to you first. Many distributors don't offer drop-shipping, but it's worth your while to ask. As the Web grows more popular, we expect to see integrated drop-shipping offered more often by distributors and manufacturers as they adjust to the need for Web merchants to avoid carrying extensive inventory.

Advantages of Drop-Shipping

Time. That's what drop-shipping provides.

Your customers don't have to wait for their orders to go from the distributor to you, and then from you to them. This not only means your customers get their orders more quickly, but it also decreases the time you have to spend packing orders and getting them shipped. If your distributors happen to be just around the corner, drop-shipping is somewhat of a luxury. But if your distributors are far away, as will be the case in many situations, drop-shipping can be a time-saving option.

Disadvantages of Drop-Shipping

While drop-shipping sounds like a comfortable process, it isn't perfect. Drop-shipping places the responsibility on your distributor, which isn't necessarily a good thing.

Your distributor could process the wrong address, ship the wrong item, or commit any number of mistakes that will become your responsibility to fix. If you prefer to have a hand in every aspect of your business, as most small business owners do, you'll probably want to limit the amount of drop-shipping you do. That way you won't have to fumble for answers or make excuses for someone else's mistake.

Also, with drop-shipping you are at the mercy of your distributor in terms of shipping method. You may prefer to offer one option, but your distributor may only offer another.

JOE'S TAKE: *With my distributors close by, I haven't needed to drop-ship on a regular basis. Even if you don't plan to use drop-shipping, you should know whether your distributors offer it in case of emergency. If a distributor forgets to include an item in a shipment, I can simply have it drop-shipped from the warehouse.*

Keeping a Sale When You're Out of Stock

You will receive orders on almost a daily basis that you can't immediately fill. When you receive an order, check the availability of the item. If you don't have it in stock, contact your distributors or other business sources. If none of your sources has the item, find out when it will be in.

Then contact your customer as quickly as possible. By following up on an order in a timely manner, you are letting the customer know she is dealing with an organized, caring company. Give the customer the option to wait for the order or cancel.

Here's an example of an email Tronix sends in this case:

"Thank you for submitting your order with Tronix. Currently, we are out of stock on the item(s) you requested, but we should have restock by the end of this week. If you would like to wait for our restock, let us know and we will fulfill your order when the shipment arrives. If you prefer not to wait, then feel free to cancel this order by letting us know."

Virtual Product Fulfillment and Inventory Management

One way to create an even simpler stocking system is to outsource as much of the stock-to-fulfillment process as possible. To do this you can find a fulfillment company that warehouses inventory, accepts your orders, packs the boxes, and arranges the shipping as ordered. You pay fees or percentages of the order. This is a great option for stores that want to keep their focus on the Web site development and not the daily grind of product inventory.

However, this approach may be more expensive in actual dollars than if you did it yourself—you gain efficiency for a price. Product fulfillment companies are available now, but expect to see even more as e-commerce grows.

Some companies run fulfillment operations that are industry-specific, while others are cross-industry. You won't have direct control over any of your warehouse operations, so if customer service and fulfillment isn't of the quality you expect, you'll have to work with the company to develop a solution.

Another aspect of outsourced fulfillment is tight coordination with a shipping company. For example, FedEx offers a service called FedEx VirtualOrder. Customers visit your online catalog, which resides on a FedEx secure server, search for the products they need, and submit orders. FedEx then automatically assigns order-confirmation numbers and transmits orders to a FedEx Merchant Access Unit housed on your site.

Once the order is confirmed, a shipping label can be generated, and the product is tendered to FedEx for express delivery. Inventory control is automated by a warehouse that does the picking and packing. FedEx, via virtual order, is automatically on hand to pick up the package and ship it. A high level of coordination with this set-up could leave you without any inventory management to deal with other than a few spreadsheets.

If you are interested in checking out fulfillment companies, a search on the Web using keywords like **product fulfillment** can get you started in the right direction.

Most customers (especially regulars) are willing to wait for restock. During the interim, you can update them on the status off the order. This gives the whole process a personal touch and makes it less frustrating for the customer. The key to keeping a customer's order active is good communication and honesty.

TIP ▸ ***When a distributor tells you the restock of an item will occur on a given day, it is not always wise to pass this information back to your customer. If your distributor's order is late, you'll find yourself once again emailing the customer with additional bad news. It's best to give your customer a general time frame, rather than a solid date.***

TIP ▸ ***Many online merchants such as Dell are learning that they can help shape demand on the Web through a variety of tricks, like home-page placement or suggestions to interested callers. This way you can steer people away from out-of-stock items. People won't know something is out of stock if they never order it.***

Knowing Which Items Are Hot

You should know better than anyone which items are going to sell and which aren't. If you don't, you probably won't be in business very long. There are a number of ways to stay on top of industry trends. You can read trade and non-trade magazines, stay on top of the relevant newsgroups, and do your best to attend consumer and trade shows. You should also visit the Web sites of the company whose products you are selling. Calling a company that has a product you want to sell and asking for names of distributors is the easiest and fastest way to get hooked into the network of distributors serving a particular store type.

Magazines

You would be hard-pressed to find an industry that doesn't have a trade magazine. You would also be hard-pressed to find a successful merchant who didn't at least scan that industry's trade magazine. If you aren't sure what your industry's trade magazine is, go to a search engine on the Web and look for information on your industry's trade association.

Trade magazines will not only keep you up to date on particular products but also on issues affecting your business.

Newsgroups

Usenet newsgroups are a great way to spread the word about your store, as we discuss in more detail in Chapter 10. They are also useful for learning more about your customers, their tastes, buying habits, and preferences.

The more active you are in posting to newsgroups, the better. But even if you aren't constantly involved in newsgroup discussions, it's a good idea to poke your head in and see what people are talking about. For example, if you sell ski equipment there's a good chance a skiing-related newsgroup will have a number of posts and responses about the latest technology. If everyone is raving about a particular new binding, you should expect high demand.

Trade Shows

Trade shows, if they are good ones, can be your best source of product information. The only drawback is that there is a very good chance that attending one will require some travel. So, on top of the cost of attending the show, you'll also have to pay for a hotel, meals, and possibly even airfare. You'll also wind up spending at least a couple of days away from work. Although most of your expenses can be used as tax write-offs, the lost work time is not recoverable.

That said, attending a good trade show is still usually worth the time, effort, and money required. Besides the fact that they provide networking opportunities, trade shows also allow you to check out the latest products. You'll almost certainly be able to gauge the popularity of new products simply through your own judgment and through the buzz among the show attendees.

Travel and Research

For many small to medium-sized stores, one of the best ways to find unique items is to travel and look for items carried by small, lesser-known manufacturers, artisans, or distributors. Depending on the types of goods you sell, trips to other cities, states, and countries can help you find many new products to sell on your site. Local chambers of commerce, retailing organizations, and local government economic development offices can help make buying trips worthwhile by pointing you toward their local companies. After a successful buying trip, you might be able to set up direct, long-term relationships and import goods as needed.

Web Sites

Checking out a company's Web site (assuming it has one) should provide you with all the information you need about a product, how the company is marketing it, and how important it is to them. If a particular item receives minimal attention from its own company, you can expect the public's interest will be similar. On the other hand, if the company is promoting a new product all over its Web site, you can bet the company is very serious about getting that product out to the public.

Your Site

It should go without saying that popular items will also be identified by the traffic and sales provided by your store. However, remember that sales aren't the only determining factor of hot items. Look at what pages are most popular on your site—especially if you have a separate page for each item in your inventory. People may be looking at an item but not buying, indicating an interesting item that might not be selling due to a high price or some other factor. This is one of the advantages of Web retailing—you can measure not only how much a product sells (just like any retailer), but how many times a customer looks at a particular item!

Importing

Because of the vast amounts of information available on the Internet, importing has become a growing market for Web stores. Anyone with

Internet access who wants to purchase hard-to-find items such as imported goods will likely check the Web. Selling rare items and imports can add sales and set you apart from those businesses that don't.

Importing products is not as easy as setting up an account with a domestic dealer. You must first find your source for imports; a good place to begin is right on the Web. There are many import wholesalers with their own Web sites, so using a good search engine should send you in the right direction.

Joe's Take: *You can have the party from which you import bill to your own shipping account (whether it is UPS, FedEx, or Airborne). And if you plan to use various distributors overseas on a regular basis, your shipping representative may be able to give you a special discount, depending on frequency/volume.*

Conducting business with foreign companies usually involves wire transfers of money to the company's account or, in some cases, using your own credit card. If you plan to do business with foreign wholesalers, the following are a few things to remember.

Working with Import Distributors

Much like domestic buying, when importing you can either work directly with the producer of the products you are selling or with a distributor. Most of the issues are the same as when using a domestic distributor, as we discussed earlier in this chapter. Using a distributor can eliminate some of the headaches, including the issue of returning defective items. Distributors will be in no hurry to exchange slowly moving imports.

Researching Overseas Companies

Most companies with Web sites are legitimate, but you should check out international companies by making a few phone calls to the host country. Make sure the company's address and phone numbers are listed. For extensive information on international phone calls, visit AT&T's Worldwide Traveler Web page at www.att.com/traveler/index_ship.html.

If everything appears legitimate, you can go a step further by checking around to see if any of your competitors have dealt with the company. If you can't find anyone who has, you should be cautious.

The reason to be careful when dealing with foreign companies isn't because they are any more likely to scam you than domestic companies are. But if you do get ripped off internationally, it will be much more difficult to recover your losses.

TIP ▸ ***If you just get email from a company claiming it has goods that you should be interested in selling, be cautious. If there is no legitimate contact information, Web site, or knowledge in the industry of the company, take a pass.***

Paying Customs/Duties

When you place orders overseas, you are responsible for paying any import taxes on the products. United States customs will charge you a percentage of the total cost of the imported goods.

When ordering overseas, it is actually more sensible to place large orders, since both the shipping and taxes can be absorbed into your prices. For example, if you order $1,000 worth of product, shipping costs might be $75, and customs could add another $125 in taxes—you are paying $200 above the cost of the goods. If your order contains 50 pieces of an item at $20 each for the $1,000 total, you could easily spread the shipping and tax costs over the 50 pieces for an additional charge of just $4 per piece.

Wire Transfers

Wire transfers can be made through any bank, but it is less of a hassle if it is done through your own bank from your actual account. Wire transfers require all bank information from the recipient, such as branch name, address, and routing number. Overseas companies generally require advance payment, at least early in a relationship.

Wire transfers can take anywhere from a week to two weeks depending on the countries involved. Your bank will charge you a fee (usually $15 to $20) for this service. You also need to know whether the foreign dealer accepts Untied States dollars or the currency of its country.

If you are dealing in foreign currency, you must consider the exchange rate. Obviously your bank will let you know what the exchange rate is with a particular country, but if you want to check daily exchange rates, a good resource is the Olsen and Associates Currency Converter (Figure 8.1) on the Web. The O&A Converter (www.oanda.com/cgi-bin/ncc) allows you to easily calculate exchange rates among 164 countries. The exchange rate is updated daily.

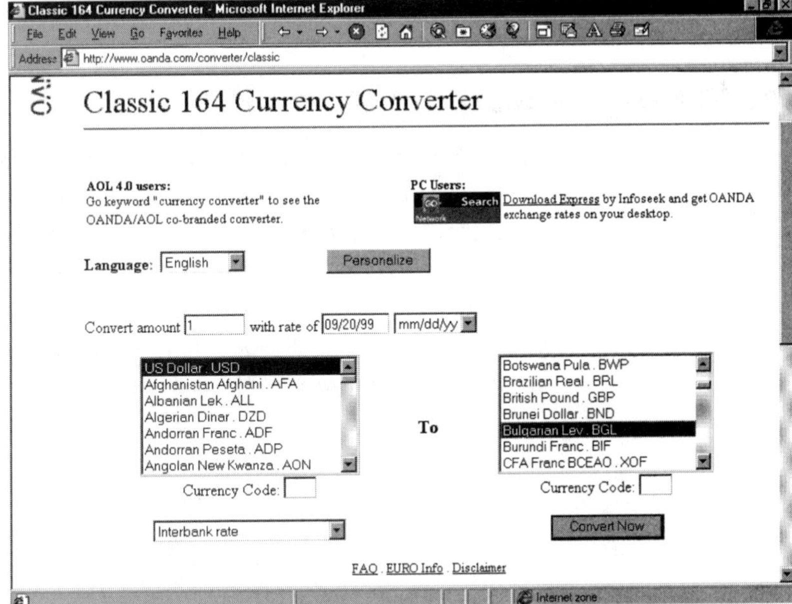

Figure 8.1
O&A Converter (www.oanda.com/converter/classic) is updated every day and allows you to easily figure out the exchange rates among 164 countries.

Build Long-Term Overseas Relationships

A good, long-term relationship with an overseas exporter can work to your advantage, especially after a continuous stream of successful business transactions. In some cases, a foreign distributor might improve the terms of your business relationship. For example, it might ship advance orders and allow you to pay later. This saves on the cost of wire transfers and cuts down on the paperwork involved.

Defective Items and Returns

Rules for returning defective items vary. Make sure you know which of your overseas suppliers accept returns and which don't. If one does accept returns, you must also be clear about shipping charges. Not only must you ship the defective item back, you also need to have a replacement shipped. Does the exporter pay for both shipping charges? Neither? Just one?

As with all other issues, know the quirks of the individual company you are dealing with.

Getting Big by Keeping It Small

The most important thing to take away from this chapter is that you should work with as little inventory as possible and as necessary. Inventory is risk. Unsold inventory is your unusable money. The more effectively you minimize your inventory, the better. And the more inventory you must stock, the more confident you need to be that it will eventually sell. Now on to Chapter 9, where we talk about how to create great Web content without spending a fortune or slaving for endless hours over your computer.

CHAPTER NINE

Creating Retail Content Without Spending a Fortune

Anyone can put price lists and order forms up on the Web and call it a store. That would be like a clothing store stacking its items on the floor and sticking someone behind the cash register to ring up orders. Neither works. Nothing to attract customers, no help for them, and before long no store.

As an online retailer, unless your prices are far lower than those of the competition, you need something to attract customers to your site and to keep them coming back. Even low prices aren't always a compelling draw. The content you provide (news, reviews, product descriptions, pictures, and so on) can be done to fit your budget. Few businesses have the revenue necessary to license and maintain the enormous state and national park database that outdoor clothing and gear giant L.L. Bean provides its customers. What good content does require is a little time and creativity, the ability to write coherently (you needn't be Ernest Hemingway), and in some cases, the help of your loyal customers.

Content is an educational service to your customers and yourself. The difference between making a sale or not often comes down to education. The customer's confidence in a product is related to the amount of knowledge the person has about that product. A site with good content leads to better-educated consumers and therefore to customer confidence. That means sales.

If you can prove you are knowledgeable about your products, your customers are more likely to keep coming back for more information and buy more products. Content must be trustworthy to be effective. And your customers will enjoy their shopping experience more than if they just pop on, order, and leave.

To provide good content, you'll have to stay on top of trends in your industry. It will take a little work, but that work will ensure you remain informed about new products and technological advances. The more you know, the better your store will be. And the better your store, the more customers it will have.

Informational Content

Tronix was among the first online video game stores to provide informational content for its customers. Tronix started with simple reviews, a news column on industry happenings, and reports on the annual E3 (Electronic Entertainment Expo) video game trade show. A review also doubled as a fairly detailed description of the particular game.

At that point, with only one or two new releases each week, it was easy to stay on top of the reviews. Now, video games are an $8 to $10 billion a year industry, and it would be impossible to review every new release without hiring people to do so. As the technology has improved, and people have come up with more content ideas, the amount of content on most Web stores has increased dramatically. How much time you spend on content will depend on your budget. If you're a one-person operation, the amount of time available for generating content will obviously be small. Don't ignore it, though. No matter how much time you spend answering the phone or packing boxes, always set aside some time to create content. A good time to do it is at night or on the weekends at home, where customer phone calls, deliveries, and daily operations won't disturb you.

Depending on what you're selling, there are a number of informational content options for you to consider.

Product Descriptions

This is the most basic content that every store needs. Obviously you can't just post price lists that say things like "Table: $100," "Chair: $75." What kind of table? A coffee table? Dining room table? Diaper changing table? A chair could be anything from a cheap wooden seat to a luxurious recliner.

The more specific the product description, the less likely you are to have customer complaints about your merchandise. Back to the wooden chair: if you provide the type of wood, the dimensions (including back height), the color, and whether or not it has arms, it's less likely a customer will call with a complaint than if the description says simply "oak chair." If your description specifically states that the chair has no arms, someone won't assume that it does.

Depending on what you're selling, you can be very creative with your descriptions. Don't overdo it where it isn't necessary. If you have an online hardware store, the only reason to describe a selection of nails as "three inches of solid, sparkling steel, flat on one end, sharp on the other, and as tough as, well, nails" would be for a laugh. Which, come to think of it, isn't a bad idea.

Some items lend themselves better to flowery descriptions than others. Decide which category your products fall into and go from there. Here is a checklist of possible items to include on your product descriptions. We do not expect you to include all or even most of these. The relevency, of course, depends heavily on the type of product:

- Description.
- Size.
- Color.
- Weight.
- Model number.
- Part number.
- Price.
- Shipping cost.
- Suggested retail price.
- Amount customer saves.
- Date released.
- Customer reviews.
- Store reviews.
- Sales rank.
- Outside links.
- Last purchase.
- In stock (yes/no).
- Availability.
- Photos.
- Virtual reality photos.
- Video.
- Audio.
- Manufacturer.
- Creator interview.
- Complimentary items.

TIP ▸ ***Before you unload the lavish prose, make sure the facts are covered. After a spectacular description of a shirt, the customer shouldn't be left wondering "Is it long-sleeved or short-sleeved?"***

Photos and Graphics

The best way to add some spark to your product descriptions or any other content area is with photos or graphics (see Figure 9.1). Just about anything can benefit from a photo, whether you're just scanning in a music CD cover, including a screen shot from a piece of software or using a digital camera to take a picture of a surfboard. However, when considering graphics, don't forget bandwidth issues.

TIP ▸ ***The more graphics on a page, the longer the page takes to load. Don't just slap up graphics and photos. Instead, take the time to optimize them and make them both attractive and quick to load. Many stores provide both thumbnails and larger photos.***

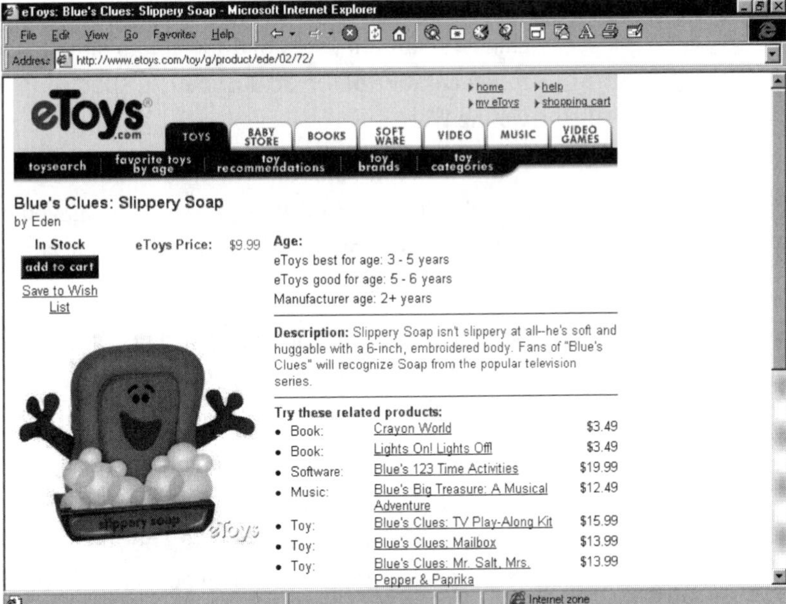

FIGURE 9.1
eToys (www.etoys.com) offers color photos so customers can see what they are getting.

If all of your products can benefit from photo representation, feel free to go wild. If none of them does, don't completely avoid it. Even a boring picture can be used to break up text here and there. However, a bunch of boring photos is a bunch of boring photos and will only clutter your page.

For more on adding photos and graphics to your site, see Chapter 7.

Joe's Take: *Pages and pages of text can get boring. A good combination of photos, graphics, and text can be very eye-catching. When Tronix first started, we didn't have photos. Once we started using them, I saw our hit ratio go up. People started saying they had seen a really great picture of something on the Tronix site, and then other people would come to check it out.*

Web Color

One key aspect of graphical content is color. It is difficult to ensure that the red you put on your Web site is the same as the red that the user sees through a browser. Differences in monitors, computers, and file formats all contribute to the fact that one color at design time might look slightly (or very) different when someone views it on the Web.

How do you eliminate this problem? It's not easy. Many sites run disclaimers that tell users that the colors on the screen may not be truly representative of the actual color. In short, don't match the house paint via the Web!

However, a few solutions can help minimize the difference between the actual color of a product and what is displayed on the Web. The first thing to do is work on optimizing graphical content for the Web as it relates to color.

Some products worth looking into are True Internet Color by E-Color (www.ecolor.com) and either ColorWeb or ColorWeb Pro by Pantone (www.pantone.com).

True Internet Color is a high-end (and expensive) solution for larger stores. To view a Web site that uses True Internet Color, consumers complete a one-time, free setup process that does not involve leaving the site, purchasing software, downloading applications, or installing plug-ins. Among sites currently using True Internet Color are J.Crew (www.jcrew.com) and Moxiegirl (www.mxgonline.com).

For smaller stores and tighter budgets, Pantone's ColorWeb ($29.95) is available for Macintosh only and provides the assurance that the color used on a Web page will not change or dither regardless of the computer platform or the user's browser. ColorWeb Pro ($69.95) is available for both Windows and Mac and offers additional features.

FAQ

A FAQ (Frequently Asked Questions—pronounced "eff ay cue" or "fack") is becoming standard on most sites. FAQs provide an easy way to answer questions about your business, how it works, how to order, how to navigate the site, and more without constantly responding to numerous similar emails. A good FAQ should reduce simple questions from your email inbox. Don't be afraid to update your FAQ if you get a good question from a customer that hasn't been answered there.

Your FAQ should include information about the products you sell, how to order, what credit cards are accepted, what secure transaction system is used, and where to find specific information on your site. You needn't give a complete answer to a question if the answer can be found elsewhere on your site. For example, if one of the questions is "What are my shipping options?" you can say what companies you use and direct the customer to your shipping page for specific information. Otherwise you'll end up with a FAQ that's as big as the rest of your site.

You can also use a FAQ to provide information about the history of the company, your guiding principles, and other more personal information if you so choose. Be sure to cover the basics first.

Table 9.1 offers 20 possible questions for your FAQ.

Some Web stores with comprehensive FAQs are:

- Eddie Bauer (**www.eddiebauer.com/siteinfo/frame_faq.asp**).
- L.L. Bean (**www.llbean.com/about/FAQ.noframes.html**).
- Amazon (**www.amazon.com/exec/obidos/subst/help/faq.html/**).
- Tronix (**www.tronixweb.com/tfaq.html**).

Table 9.1 Twenty Sample Questions for Your FAQ

What payment forms do you accept?
What shipping companies do you use?
How late can I place an order and still receive next-day delivery?
How can I contact you?
Can I visit your store's location and do my shopping in person?
How long have you been in business?
What is your sales tax policy?
Are items insured in transit?
What are your live phone operator hours?
Do you match or beat prices?
Do you have a mailing list?
Can I set up an account?
Do you accept bulk or distributor orders?
Can I special order items?
Do you have a secure Web order form?
What do you do with my personal information?
What is your return or exchange policy?
Do you accept orders by fax, phone, or traditional mail?
Do you process international orders?
Can I submit articles or reviews for your store?

News

Including news on your site (see Figure 9.2) is helpful for both you and your customers. If you're going to spend time creating content beyond product descriptions (and you should), a news section is a good place to start. A good news section contains brief, timely articles that are related to your store and of interest to your customers. You can also include product features or other features that are related to your customers' interests. You can get information from the companies you deal with, industry trade magazines and newsletters, and simply by keeping your eyes and ears open.

Obviously any good store owner will want to stay on top of the happenings within her industry. Knowing that you need to keep updating your store's news page will force you to be informed about your industry or else look like a fool. A news page is especially important in release-sensitive businesses such as music, books, movies, or, in the case of Tronix, video games. Being able to post advance word and release dates for highly anticipated products like Anne Rice's next novel or Rage Against the Machine's next record is a plus for you and a service for your customers.

If you do a thorough job collecting news, you can become a source of information—not just a store—for your customers. Your customers will consider you trustworthy if you consistently provide timely, correct information and will visit your store more often. If you prove to be the best place for information on your industry, word will spread and you'll probably find swarms of potential customers arriving at your site.

Finding news on the Web related to your business isn't difficult but depends on what you are selling. For example, there are numerous music and entertainment news sites on the Web for anyone selling music, videos, books, etc. Find the two or three sites you like best and stick to those; otherwise you might spend half of your time searching for news.

TIP ▸ ***If you link to news on other sites, be sure to check regularly for dead links. News sites often move pages to pay-per-view archives or take them down after a period of time.***

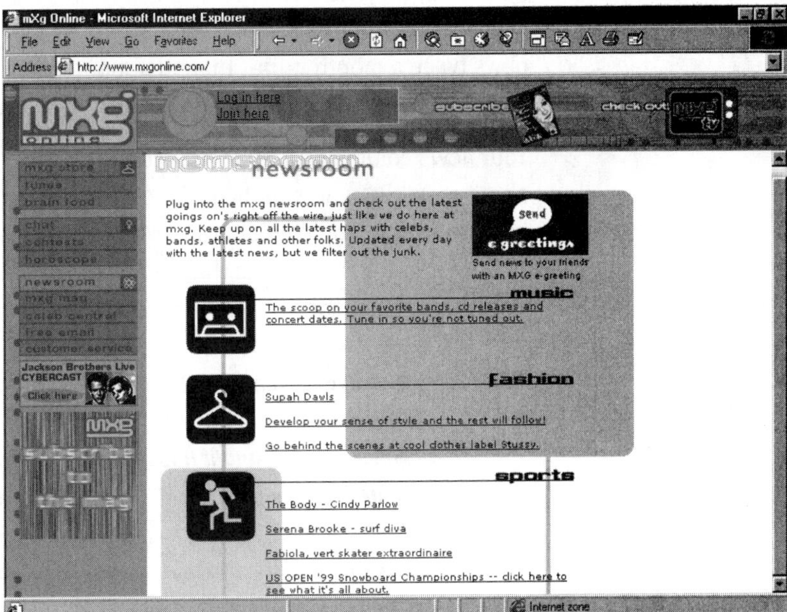

FIGURE 9.2
Moxiegirl (www.mxgonline.com) offers news on music, fashion and sports for its customers.

TIP ▸ ***If you really like to write and can find the time to do it, you can even expand your news column past the confines of what you're selling. For example, if you sell surfboards, snowboards, skateboards, and related gear, you don't have to limit your news to product information and technological advancements. Your customers will probably be interested in some of the top performers in each sport and the results of recent events. In this case, you might even want to mention when the new records by Pennywise and NOFX (two popular bands among the board crowd) are coming out.***

The amount of news available in your industry on a daily basis and the amount of time you can spend on a news column will dictate how often it is changed. If you're selling software, you could change your news column daily. Other industries may only produce enough news to warrant a monthly. It might take some time to figure out how often you should update your news column.

Don't make the mistake of promising a new column each week only to find you don't have enough time or news to support it. Cutting back from a weekly to a monthly will send a negative message to your customers. Instead, start conservatively and when it becomes apparent you have enough news and time, you can hit your customers with a message like "Due to popular demand, Pete's Pepper Pit will provide gardening news twice a month rather than just monthly!" Your customers will be pleasantly surprised and realize you really care about what you're doing.

Your news column will be a reflection of you and how much you care about your customers and your business. Assuming the prices are comparable, most people would rather buy from someone who is truly passionate about her products than someone who is just trying to make a buck. This is a chance to prove that person is you.

TIP ▸ ***Once you've decided when you're going to update your news, stick with that schedule. Your customers will hopefully be excited to read each new column, and if it isn't there when it should be, they'll be disappointed. If a major piece of news ("Gates sells Microsoft, buys fishing boat") breaks before you plan to change the news, you should update the column with that news without removing anything else. Archive the last few news columns for customers to refer back to.***

Reviews

Here's where content gets tricky. Many online store owners never have to worry about it because not every type of product is conducive to a review. But if you are planning to do reviews, our advice is to be honest. That's where reviews can be a problem. Not everything you have is going to be good, especially if you're selling entertainment media like games, books, music, and movies or products like software.

Reviews, even negative ones, are very important for many online stores. Traditional stores hand out negative reviews all the time by not stocking items. You just don't see the review. However, online stores have an incredible amount of virtual shelf-space and could list thousands of products without actually stocking them. A negative review allows you to stock a complete inventory while steering customers away from products you think they shouldn't buy.

An honest, positive review is the best thing you can hope to write. It will help sell the item, it won't upset anybody, and assuming the product really is good, it will reinforce your honest image.

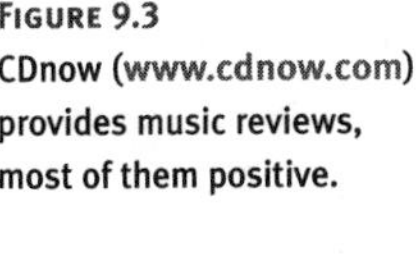
FIGURE 9.3
CDnow (www.cdnow.com) provides music reviews, most of them positive.

Joe's Take: *If you have to write a bad review, that doesn't mean you have to really rip the thing apart. In my case, I might risk offending the company or the distributor to the point of affecting my business. As an extreme and unlikely example, where would Tronix be if I completely trashed a Sony game and Sony decided it didn't want me selling its products anymore?*

Since you'll never have a reason to write a dishonest, negative review, the toughest thing you'll have to do is write an honest, negative review. Never write a dishonest, positive review. Never. Your customers will realize it, the word will spread on the newsgroups, and you'll be branded a liar and a scam artist. If you don't want to write a negative review about a product, just don't write one at all.

Sometimes you can't avoid writing a negative review. If you have been doing them all along and a much-hyped product comes out, you can't just ignore it because it fails to live up to expectations. People will notice, and it will make you look bad. In fact, you can make a negative review work for you.

Honesty is an admirable trait and not one always associated with business people. When writing a negative review, you should be able to convey the message that the product is lousy without using inflammatory language. In other words, you can say something stinks without saying "This stinks!" If there are some positive qualities to the product, mention them. You can actually gain more sales than you lose with a negative review.

Joe's Take: *In the video game industry, reviews are a good way to kill two birds with one stone. As you're reviewing a product, you're also telling people what the game is all about so it can double as an in-depth product description. Reviews were the first pieces of content we added to our site, and it really brought in a lot of customers. At the beginning it was easy to review every product because there were only one or two new releases a week. Now it's nearly impossible. Some of the products reviewed early on just weren't very good, and we had to grin and bear it by writing an honest, negative review. Those reviews were important because they were the first indication that we were honest. The customers thought we must be all right if we were willing to give a bad review to something we were selling. It's great when you hear someone say a review you wrote was right on the mark.*

Guest Columns

Guest columns are great for a number of reasons, not the least of which is that someone else writes them. They also put another face of expertise on your store. If you know someone who is capable of adding to your site's content without asking for a lot of (or any) money, you would be crazy not to use them. A lot of people will be willing to write about a topic of interest simply for the fun of it.

If you want to add a guest column to your site, run through a list of friends or business acquaintances who might be willing and qualified to help you. One or the other won't work. If they're qualified but not really enthusiastic about it, every column will involve your begging and pleading for a mediocre piece of content that arrives two weeks after you wanted it. If they're willing but not qualified, the column isn't going to add anything to your site. Instead, you'll spend a lot of time polishing garbage and finally having to break it to the columnist that you no longer need his services. However, you should be able to find at least one or two people with the time, inclination, and expertise to help you out.

Once you've found someone, you should sit down and discuss a number of potential topics that the reviewer can cover in the coming weeks or months. It's your store, so you want to have control over the content, but don't be a dictator. This person is doing you a favor. Provide a list of topics you want covered and ask for the columnist's input. She'll have plenty of ideas if she really is qualified. Before long you should have a number of potential columns.

As the columns run, bring up any potential problems so the same mistakes aren't repeated. Keep the lines of communication open and, as with product reviews, don't get nasty if a column doesn't cut it. Work together with your columnist to correct the problems. Eventually she'll get a better feel for what you want and the process will flow smoothly.

TIP ▸ ***Don't get into the situation where you're constantly scraping for ideas and your columnist is rushing to finish something at the last second. Keep a list of future column topics and the dates on which they will run. In a perfect world, the columnist will even be able to write ahead so there will never be any deadline panic for either of you. With the pressures of running a business, that's the last thing you need.***

Newsletters and Mailing Lists

Many stores and Web sites distribute an email newsletter to users who request one. A newsletter provides your customer with information without visiting your site. Receiving a newsletter might spark a customer to return to your site when he otherwise wouldn't.

A good email newsletter is generally one to two pages long and contains URLs linking people directly to the wares you are discussing. It should also include specials and other newsworthy information about your store. Avoid sending out your newsletter too often or packing it with too much information. Chances are, the customer doesn't want to spend two hours reading it. Some stores such as Amazon.com, The Gap, and eToys send their email newsletters in an HTML format. This allows them to send a much more attractive newsletter that can include graphics (such as product shots) and other Web page items. The drawback is that not everyone uses an email client that supports HTML-based email. If you do decide to offer an HTML-based email newsletter, offer it as an option alongside the basic text newsletter.

You can operate a newsletter two ways. You can simply collect email addresses and then use your email program to bulk-mail your newsletter. Some packages automate this process somewhat, but it can get a bit messy, especially as the number of customers climbs. But the more automated way to do this is to run all your bulk email through what is known as a listserver service.

A listserver is a program that can be used as a bulk emailer or as a mailing list. You can set up your own listserver, but some stores would be better off outsourcing such work, freeing up time and bandwidth. If you run your newsletter through a listserver service, you simply send it once to a special email account, and the service forwards the newsletter to every subscriber on the list.

Another way to use a listserver is to operate a discussion mailing list with it. Users subscribe to the listserver and, once on the list, they can post a message that is then replicated and sent out to other members of the list.

TIP ▸ ***One of the better listserver services is Skyweyr's Skylist, which is located on the Web at www.skylist.net.***

The key to a mailing-list discussion is to keep people talking and interacting with you as a moderator. This is very time-consuming, but it is a good way to keep in touch with very frequent customers and provide them with special content and services.

Joe's Take: *I participate on newsgroups so frequently that a mailing list would be overkill for me. Concerning newsletters, I initially liked operating one for Tronix, but it became difficult to commit the necessary time as Tronix grew. If you start a newsletter, commit to a small number of issues and work to increase the frequency. The worst thing you can do is start a newsletter and then dump it or cut back on the frequency and the content. How would it look if you produced a weekly newsletter only to cut back to monthly? Contrast that with offering a quarterly newsletter and then, as you get better or bigger, increase the frequency.*

Links

Links to other sites can provide even more information for your customers. Be clear that you are sending them to another site. You don't want to be seen as taking credit for someone else's work.

You can either group all of your links together or include them in the text of an article. Anything mentioned in an onsite article, any company you deal with, or any site you think your customers would enjoy that is somehow related to your business are good prospects for links. For more on links and links exchanges, see Chapter 11.

Don't worry about sending people off to another site never to return. Many sites worry that linking a lot to other sites is going to create a virtual siphon that will drain customers before they decide to purchase something from you. Although this may happen with a few customers, the majority of links that stores provide should be to further educate your customers. You can also force the other site to open in another browser window, keeping your site open in the original browser window, by adding an attribute to the **<A HREF>** HTML tag. For example:

```
<A HREF="http://www.peachpit.com" TARGET="_BLANK">Peachpit</A><BR>
```

Databases

One of the best types of content to offer on a site is a database. Although many sites offer an interesting database simply by listing their products with descriptions (CDnow's database of music titles is interesting in and of itself), many sites have found that offering a searchable database of information is a good draw. L.L. Bean offers a searchable database of state and national parks—something buyers of its outdoor gear and clothing would be very interested in.

The strength of database content is drawn from the ability to search for a lot of entries in a number of different ways. For example, the Internet Movie Database (**www.imdb.com**) lets you search movies by actors, title, director, crew, date, rating, and more. The database also has thousands of entries, which is what makes it so appealing. The online video store Reel.com uses this database.

Constructing a database and displaying it on the Web requires more work than just putting up pages. Your site-hosting company or an independent consultant should be able to guide you through it. Before you can display it, you need to construct it. Start by seeing if there are any pre-existing databases that you can license. Licensing will probably be less expensive than keying it in yourself.

TIP ▸ ***Some of the best uses of database content on the Web are ones that let users add to it. While you will have to edit and validate these customer entries, it can be a good way to build up the database while offering a piece of interactive content on your site. For example, the Amazon.com database catalogs book reviews submitted by patrons.***

TIP ▸ ***If you decide to provide your own information for a database, you should still hire a database consultant to develop it. If you want to save money by keying in the data yourself, that's great. Unless you have experience building actual databases, you should meet with the database consultant who will help you spec out the field lists and other features of the database.***

Database content can be a big draw to your site. Most stores will have a product database people will enjoy, but others are finding that databases of content related to the product line can actually draw people to the site and keep them coming back.

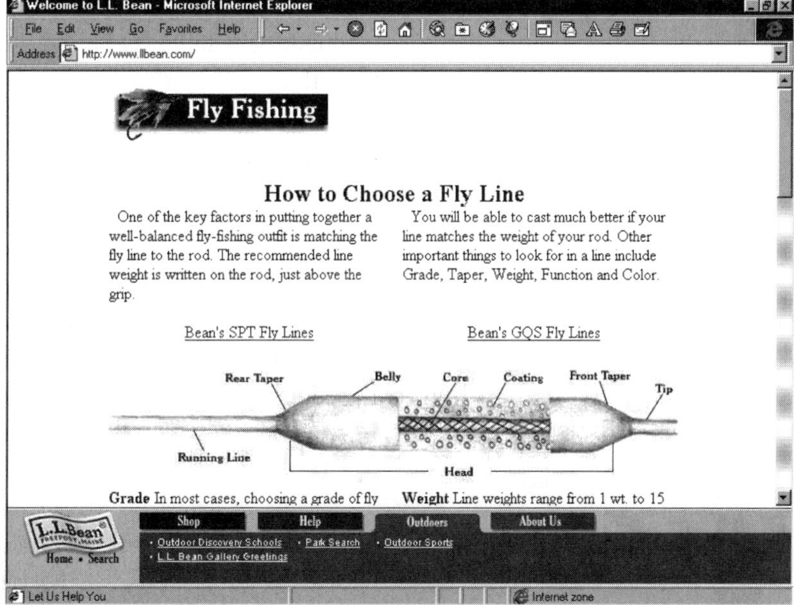

FIGURE 9.4
L.L. Bean not only offers an extensive database of information on national parks, but also provides instruction on a number of outdoor activities, such as how to choose a fly line.

Testimonials

You know your store is fantastic and so do your customers. But not everyone who visits your site for the first time will be immediately aware of your outstanding customer service, honesty, and all-around greatness. So tell them. Better yet, let your customers tell them.

A page of customer testimonials can be far more effective than your bragging. If you do your job, you will almost certainly receive email from satisfied customers. They may write to tell you how great your prices are or how their shipment arrived exactly when it was supposed to. If you receive a particularly complimentary letter, ask the writer if you can post it on your site for other customers to see. If the writer is that enthusiastic about your store, he'll probably be happy to help.

When posting testimonials, try to cover a wide range of issues. Five letters about your incredibly low prices will have a customer thinking, "I get the point!" Instead, include letters that show your store in a positive light in all areas. You needn't post every positive letter. Hopefully you'll receive so many that you would need a separate Web site to do so.

Not all the testimonials have to be fawning reviews of your store. For example, a good testimonial might come from a person who was originally shipped a defective product or received it a day late. A quick, hassle-free credit might draw a positive letter. Posting a letter like this lets your customers know that you are human and occasionally things go wrong (though not often!). When that happens, they can count on the problem being rectified in a timely fashion.

Assuming you have enough to choose from, keep the testimonials fresh by replacing them every few months. If people keep seeing the same testimonials for a couple of years, they might start wondering if anyone is still sending them in.

TIP ▸ ***A good testimonial doesn't have to come directly to you. You might see a newsgroup post that you'd like to include. Try emailing the person a message like, "Thanks a lot for the kind words about my store. Would you mind if I put it on my testimonials page?" You'll probably get an affirmative response.***

Customer-Generated Articles and Reviews

The more you involve your customers, the better. If you let it be known that customer input is encouraged on your site, you probably won't have any problem getting some content from the most loyal of them. Once you've gotten to know a customer reasonably well through email and phone conversations, you can ask her if she'd like to contribute to the site. You can offer a free item or to pay the person in exchange for her services, but she'll probably help out for free.

Remember that all the content on your site is a reflection of you and your store, so you'll have to keep a close eye on what your customers are submitting. Unlike guest columnists, who should have an amount of expertise and some writing experience, your customer contributors will probably just be fans of your particular product. Therefore, you'll probably do a lot of editing and might even decide not to use some submissions. If you decide not to use something a customer has submitted, break it to them gently and give them some constructive criticism. Nobody likes to be rejected. Don't compound the problem (and lose a customer) by being mean.

Interactive Content

Providing information for your customers is the basic level of content. It keeps your store from being nothing more than a big price list and gives people a reason to visit your site other than simply to buy something. Interactive content goes a step further, giving your customers something to do on your site.

Contests

Contests are a nice sporadic feature for your store. Not only are contests a great way to attract people to your site, you can have them as frequently or infrequently as you like. Some larger stores like CDnow and Amazon.com have regular contests for the simple reason that they can. Giving away merchandise or gift certificates each week is no big deal. For you it might be. That doesn't mean you should avoid contests altogether. You'll probably find giving away a small amount of merchandise or gift certificates to be worth it. If you find you can afford a regular contest, you can schedule them around holidays, monthly, or even weekly.

Contests are easily done via email. You can post a question or questions on your home page with an email link for answers. Depending on how much you want to give away, you can either hand out a prize to the person who submits the first correct answer or to the first five or so people with the correct answer. Once you have a winner or winners, post the answer and a congratulatory message on the home page for the winners.

If you have enough in your budget to run ten contests a year, you might consider having a couple of "Contest Weeks" each year. When the word gets out through the newsgroups, you could have people flocking to your site every day for a week in hopes of winning. Some of these people will certainly be new visitors who won't stop at answering the question. They'll probably browse your store and, if they like what they see, you'll end up with a group of new customers.

Questions

Obviously the question should be easy enough for someone to answer but difficult enough to make it challenging. If the answer is available somewhere else on your site, let people know that to encourage them to look around, just don't tell them exactly where it is. Ask questions that are related to what you're selling or to news related to your business. For example, if the Rolling Stones are on a highly publicized concert tour, a music store might want to ask a question about the Stones, such as, "Who is the oldest Stone?" (A: Drummer Charlie Watts).

Prizes

Which leads to prizes. A question about the Stones should reward the winner with the new Stones record. But there are a number of things you can give out. Hot new items are sure to get people rushing to your site. You can also use contests as an alternative to specials to get rid of old stock. If you have a product that just isn't selling, why not give it away? You're not losing much, although giving away mediocre products won't be nearly as good an attraction as handing out something new and sought-after.

Probably the best prize for a store owner to give away is a gift certificate. You can give out small gift certificates in the hopes that people will use them toward more expensive products. However, if you do this you run the risk of irritating your customers. If you are concerned with building a strong relationship with your customers (and you should be), give out a gift certificate that's hefty enough to buy something without chipping in another $20 or so. If someone uses a gift certificate for a free item, he might buy something else, too.

Polls

Polls are easy to do and a good way to get your customers involved with your store. The key to a good poll is asking a timely question that likely will draw a balanced response. Provide two or three answers for respondents to check off. The answers should tell you quite a bit about your customers. For example, the online music magazine "Addicted To Noise" has a question of the day which asks readers their opinion on a timely issue related to popular music. When it was announced that the relatively young Pearl Jam would open some concerts for the older Rolling Stones, "Addicted To Noise" asked its readers which band would put on a better performance. The fact that 67 percent of respondents voted for Pearl Jam is an obvious indication of the age of the e-zine's readers.

You can even use polls to help you decide what to stock. If you're selling competing products, a poll that indicates an overwhelming amount of support for one over the other might push you toward stocking more of the favored item.

For smaller stores, OpinionPower (www.opinionpower.com) offers both free and paid survey and polling services. SurveySays (www.cgiscripts.net/scripts/?SCRIPT=surveysays) is a script worth looking into.

Chat Rooms/Message Boards

Chat rooms and message boards can get your customers communicating and visiting your site on a regular basis. Be forewarned: Depending on your customers, there can be a lot of work involved.

The key thing about chat rooms and message boards is that they exist within the Web page. Users don't have to fire up an extraneous product like NetMeeting or a Usenet reader to participate. In addition, people usually have to be at your site to participate, thus making them a good draw. Message boards and chats can also be great content builders. Host a chat with someone relevant to your store and then post a transcript later for people who missed it. You should also cull message board answers for FAQs and other areas of your site.

Chat rooms and message boards are also great for providing customer service. Many sites are installing these items to cut down the number of customer phone calls. Instead of picking up the phone, users can just go to a chat room to find an answer to their question.

The downside to this all is the amount of work chat rooms and message boards require to maintain. Message boards need to be watched for errant or even libelous posts. You also need to answer questions quickly so people can get an answer in the next 24 hours or sooner. With chat rooms, you'll need to monitor and mediate chats with guests to make sure things run smoothly.

Another concern is cost and installation. Chat rooms and message boards require the installation of some server-side components, and the cost of such programs is not cheap. Top-notch Web bulletin boards can run more than $1,000. Chat servers can cost thousands as well. While pricing should steadily drop, strongly consider the cost vs. return before you decide to offer them.

Some chat and message board packages worth investigating are:

- Emaze Forums (**www.emaze.com**).
- eShare Expressions Interaction Suite (**www.eshare.com**).
- iChat Rooms, Message Boards (**www.ichat.com**).
- Paralogic's Anexa.com, ParaChat (**www.paralogic.com**).

Joe's Take: *Chat rooms or message boards can lead to a lot of work. You might spend a lot of time editing out lousy comments and you have to make sure things don't get too nasty. Someone might post a message that really rips a product, and you're liable because it's on your site. One of my competitors, who is now out of business, had a message board and he had to deal with a lot of obscenities on it. If you're considering a message board or a chat room, keep in mind who your customers are and figure out if you're going to have to spend hours editing posts.*

Web Boards

A Web board is a Web page-based system that allows users to write and post messages to your site. This is a great way for customers to share experiences and news about your store's products. It's also a way to hook them into your site. As a moderator you can answer questions on the board and post more information that may help people decide to buy a product.

Two very popular message board packages are O'Reilly's WebBoard (www.webboard.com) and Web Crossing (www.webcrossing.com). There are also services like Message-Board.net (www.message-board.net) and Well Engaged (www.wellengaged.com). Message-Board.net also has a free advertising-supported version of its service. You might also consider using Excite's Communities or Yahoo's Club services as well. These are discussed more in Chapter 10.

Joe's Take: *I don't have a Web board on the Tronix site but I'm intimately familiar with them from my days as a CompuServe sysop. Boards are great community builders but they're difficult to manage. If I were to do one for even a minimally busy site, I would consider paying someone (or swapping merchandise) to manage it.*

Multimedia Content

Digital video, audio, and full-fledged programs are the kings of the content hill. However, although many sites want to offer more than just text or graphics, users can't always access it due to slow connections or poor implementation by the site itself.

As the Web matures, multimedia content will become more important, so you should stay on top of the technology. Store owners need to approach multimedia very carefully. While the content potential of multimedia is quite dazzling, it is easy to get tripped up and spend a lot of time and money on content that doesn't help boost sales. To get the most out of multimedia content, make sure it is integral to your store's wares (for example, using RealAudio clips of music you're selling).

When it comes to multimedia content, there are several types to know about. Table 9.2 is a summary of the four key categories.

It is important to identify how a store can use these technologies to produce interesting content for its Web site.

TABLE 9.2 MULTIMEDIA CONTENT

CONTENT TYPE	DESCRIPTION	KEY ISSUE
Dowloadable Audio/video	As opposed to streaming, these higher quality files must be dowloaded entirely before they can be listened to or watched.	Much better quality in terms of playback, but even "small" files can be 400K to 3MB in size, creating a long download.
Streaming Audio/Video	Audio or video content is sent from the Web site to the user in near real time, offering quick access to these types of files.	Almost always requires special server software and, in the case of video, is nearly unusable by users accessing via modems.
VR Photography	Specialized graphics files that render a complete 3D scene crafted from stitched-together photos.	Files can take a while to download.
Multimedia Programs	Also categorized as software content, these are full-fledged programs, Java applets, or Shockwave programs which integrate graphics, text, audio, and sometimes video into an interactive application.	Costly to produce and often requires programming knowledge.
Flash Animations	Flash files are multimedia programs that are quick to load and provide great animation capabilties.	Flash files load quickly but aren't as capable as Shockwave files and often require you to be somewhat capable at animation for best results.

Downloaded Audio or Video: QuickTime, AVI Files, AIFF, and WAV Files

QuickTime and AVI files are the main digital video formats for computers, although you will also come across MPEG files from time to time. AIFF and WAV files are two of the most often used digital audio formats. Although the quality is very high (as opposed to most streaming audio formats, which sacrifice quality for speed), these files need to be downloaded almost entirely before a user can digest them. An upside is that you need no special server software to offer these files to your users.

If you want to have streaming audio, which gives immediate feedback and doesn't require one to download the entire clip to hear the audio, you can use RealAudio. The RealAudio format is the most prevalent audio format on the Web. Visit www.real.com to find out more about RealAudio.

To create RealAudio files, you first must digitize the audio using a program like Sound Forge (a PC product from www.sfoundry.com) or SoundEdit 16 (a Mac audio package from www.macromedia.com) and then encode (convert) the files into the unique RealAudio format. Many of the popular sound recording/editing packages offer support for RealAudio, or you can get Real's Real Producer program from its Web site. Real Producer makes converting AIFF or WAV files to RealAudio a snap.

AIFF and WAV files are too large for long, speech-length applications, but can be effective in offering a 20 to 30–second preview of a song or some other audio clip. Every known audio digitization program made supports saving audio as an AIFF or WAV file.

There is also the newer MP3 format for for encoding high-quality audio in a small file size. It's great for offering snippets of high-fidelity audio, but is unnecessary for simple spoken word or narration). To create MP3 files, you must digitize the sound clip into a WAV or AIFF format, then load them into a conversion program which will turn them into the MP3 format. You can find MP3 creation tools from Xing Technologies (www.xingtech.com).

TIP ▸ ***Have a lot of audio or video to digitize and encode? Encoding.com (www.encoding.com) is a great Web-based company that helps stores and Web sites encode their audio and video. Digital video using Quick-Time, MPEG or AVI files, is great for showing items that are kinetic in nature. That includes anything from movies and video games to robotic toys and sculptures. However, video files (no matter what format) eat up server space. Additionally, a 1.5 MB video file can take a 28.8 modem as long as 15 minutes to download. Though the quality is higher than streaming video formats, the immediacy for all but the fastest surfers is nonexistent. Your use of video clips should be judicious.***

AVI is widely used by Windows users, whereas QuickTime is widely used by Mac folks (although Windows users can view QuickTime files, too). MPEG, which can be viewed by most computer users, isn't as widely used.

To create video content, you must digitize the video using any number of video digitizing programs (the most popular being Adobe Premiere). You will also need a graphic card or digitizing device to input the video through to your computer.

TIP ▸ ***For more help on digital video see* Publishing Digital Video *by Jan Ozer published by AP Professional (ISBN 0125319428) or visit the Web site for Digital Video magazine (www.dv.com).***

Video files are best used only after other content types have been used with the particular item. They are better for higher-end items where educational content is paramount and people might accept a long download if it helps them to make a more informed purchase.

And if you want to include video on your site, don't use streaming video. Currently the quality is simply unacceptable.

Streaming Audio and Video: RealAudio and NetShow

Although there are other streaming solutions such as Xing and VDO, Real Networks' RealAudio/RealVideo and Microsoft's NetShow formats are the dominant forms. In fact, NetShow is a distant second. As we mentioned, streaming video has nearly no relevance to stores because of the poor quality. However, streaming audio content is quite good and can be very useful for stores.

Music stores are a natural for RealAudio content, which streams audio over the Internet in real time. However, useful RealAudio content isn't just for music sites. For example, you can provide audio interviews with people your customers are interested in, or audio commentary for your products. Many browsers are distributed with the Real Player directly, so plenty of people have access to it. It's also fairly easy to develop content for it.

The problem with RealAudio or NetShow is that you need to be with a Web host or have your own server with RealAudio or NetShow installed. There aren't many hosting companies offering this yet, and owning your own server is expensive. The cost should eventually drop, and these two formats will become more widely used.

Virtual Reality Photography

Virtual Reality (VR) photography is becoming more popular among store sites. As of this writing there are three dominant types of VR photography. The two most common are Apple's QuickTime VR and BlackDiamond's Surround Video (see Figure 9.5). There is also a Java-based VR format from LivePicture (now a division of graphics software maker MGI) that you can use.

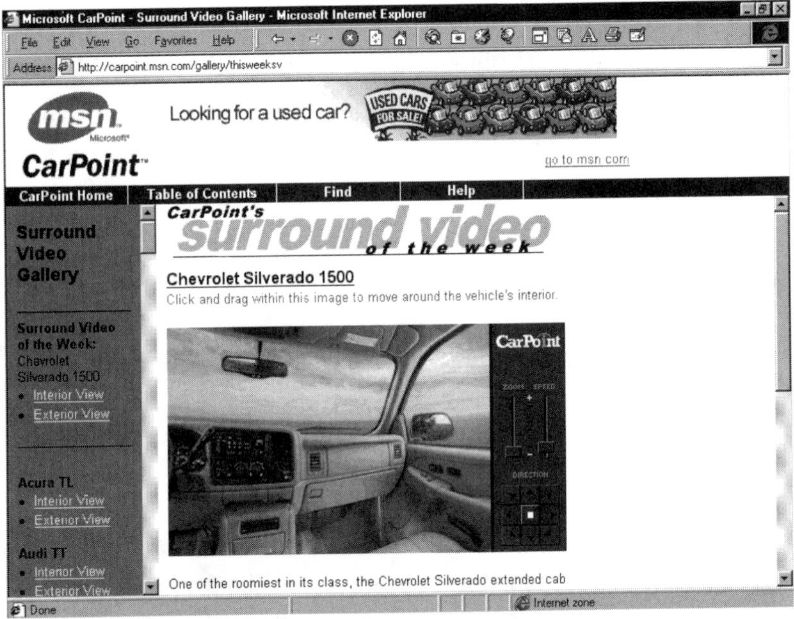

FIGURE 9.5
Surround Video helps customers explore an automobile's interior at Microsoft's CarPoint (carpoint.msn.com).

These two technologies allow you to take multiple pictures of an area and, after "stitching" them together, provide a 180 to 360 degree photo of an image. Users viewing the image can use a mouse to navigate the scene. This makes VR photography great for large spaces such as real estate or for the insides of cars (which is what Microsoft's Carpoint.com uses it for).

QuickTime VR also lets you create object movies. By photographing all around an object, you can create a 360 degree view of it. Surround Video doesn't offer this feature, which is great for all kinds of objects.

To create VR photographs you need two things—a camera (preferably digital) and a "stitcher" program, which lets you put the pictures together into the final product. PhotoVista (www.livepicture.com/products/photovista/) from LivePicture is a good stitcher. Spin Panorama by PictureWorks (www.pictureworks.com) is also very good.

For QTVR 3D object photographs, you once had to use Apple's own stitcher as well as a special "object rig," which lets you position the object and rotate the camera around it. PictureWorks has released Spin Object, a panoramic object creation program that lets you output object movies as QuickTime VR, Animated GIFs, and digital video movies.

To photograph objects, you may need an object rig. The best rigs are made by a company called Kaidan (www.kaidan.com).

Software Content

Software content on your site could be programs that you let users download. These could be more advanced, multimedia looks at products offered by the store or, in the case of stores that actually sell software, demos of the products.

Software content might also be a custom program or shareware that is of use to your customers. For example, a store catering to gardeners might offer an entire download of utilities and software that is of use to gardeners. A camera store might offer downloads of popular shareware or demo software for working with digital images.

There are several ways to offer software content to your users:

- **Build custom software.** This is an expensive route, but if you have a large base of customers and have competition it can be worthwhile. The best thing to do is to tie the software directly to the store itself. For example, the gardening store might make a custom version of garden-planning software that would enable the user to place an order with the store for the seeds and any other items needed to create the planned garden.

- **Offer access to relevant shareware or demoware.** There are literally thousands of demos and shareware programs that you can offer as free downloads. Make sure that whatever you post is directly relevant to your customer base. Don't offer a download just for the sake of offering it.

  Some shareware comes with explicit licensing agreements. Don't ever assume that it's fine to distribute shareware, check first. Then, consider the strains on bandwidth shareware downloads can cause. Keep in mind how quickly a 6MB download can eat up bandwidth if it's downloaded

200 times a month. Find out what the total transfer allowance is from your Web-hosting service. There might be a limit before you run into an extra fee.

- **Link to relevant shareware or demoware.** Simply linking your customers to the shareware or demoware site is less taxing on your own server. Find the relevant link to a page on one of the bigger shareware Web sites like Jumbo.com, Tucows.com, Shareware.com, or Download.com, and send users to it.

Getting into the software content business—especially custom software—is a very expensive proposition. While the attraction of a custom program might give you an edge over your competition, don't bother with it unless it's nearly critical to the success of your store. Shockwave/Flash and Java are are two types of software content being used by stores.

Shockwave/Flash

To add motion and interactivity to their Web sites, many designers rely on Shockwave and Flash, produced by Macromedia. Shockwave files are Director movies saved in a special format for distribution over the Web. Director files that are processed in this way are said to have been "shocked." Flash is a graphics/animation program whose files are saved in vector format (as opposed to bitmaps), allowing them to be downloaded quickly.

Shockwave's power lies in its ability to add full-fledged multimedia content to Web pages with relative ease. Unless carefully planned for online dissemination, however, Shockwave files can easily become too large for speedy distribution over regular dial-up Internet connections. Movies created in Flash, though lighter and nimbler than Shockwave files, can't draw on the full range of multimedia options available to Director programmers.

Because Shockwave movies are only as good as the Director movies from which they are created, and because Director is a monumentally complex program, most Web developers contract with outside specialists, rather than trying to produce Shockwave content. Macromedia's Web site (www.macromedia.com) even provides a searchable database of Director programmers for hire.

You can also find on the Macromedia Web site a database of Flash-skilled animators and Web designers. A great use of Flash online is RumpusToys (www.rumpustoys.com), a children's toy company that uses Flash to create animated movies starring the characters that are their stuffed animal toys. Figure 9.6 shows the RumpusToys site in action.

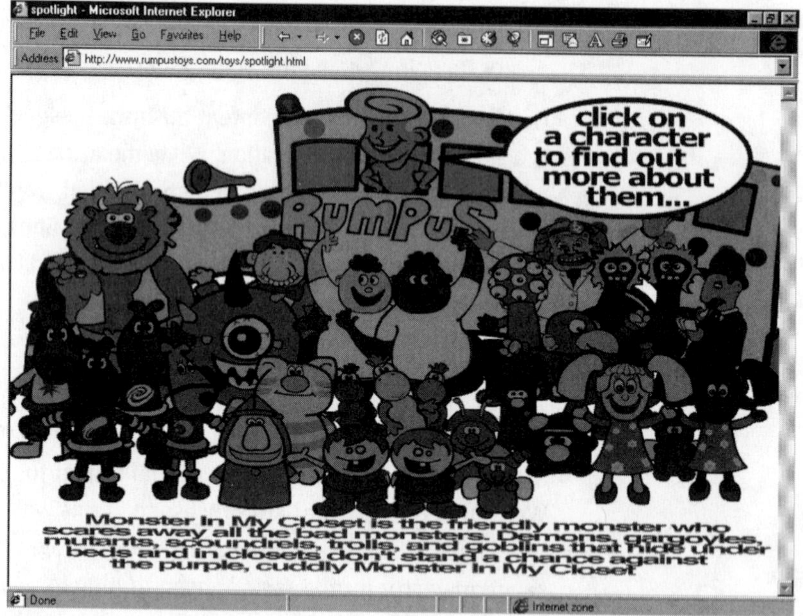

FIGURE 9.6
Rumpus Toys (www.rumpustoys.com) used Flash to create a fun site for kids.

Java

Java applets are a major way to deliver software-oriented content directly on a site. For example, instead of having that garden planning application written for download, you might have it as a Java app that runs directly off your Web site when the user loads it.

As with other forms of software content most store owners will need to work with a contract Java programmer to design and develop the custom program.

Tips for Generating Good Content

Anyone can generate content. Good content separates the wheat from the chaff, the contenders from the pretenders, and in some cases the businesses from the out-of-businesses. What is good content? To some extent it can be defined like good art—"I don't know, but I know it when I see it." Or is that obscenity? Anyway, there are a few guidelines that will keep your content strong. But remember, it will be your creativity that takes your content from the simply good to the truly great.

Be Accurate

No matter how creative you are—if you're wrong, you're wrong. Having incorrect information on your site is no way to build a community of loyal customers. While many customers will shop at your store simply for the prices or the convenience, many will choose you over your competitors because of your knowledge and passion about your industry. If you continually post incorrect information, your credibility will suffer and so will your business.

Sometimes you will simply be presented with incorrect information, which is why attribution is important. If you run an online sporting goods store, and a sneaker company tells you its new line will be out in time for Christmas, attribute the information to the company by writing, "According to XSneaks, the new Joe Shmoe basketball shoe will be out in time for Christmas." Then, if the sneakers are not available, blame for the misinformation is on XSneaks, not you. If an irate customer calls screaming, "You said the Joe Shmoe shoe was going to be available by Christmas," you can remind him it was XSneaks that said that, and hopefully give the customer an explanation for the delay.

TIP ▸ ***Of course there will be times when you are wrong. If the mistake is yours, admit it. There's nothing worse than someone trying to blame a mistake on someone else. For those rare instances, immediately remove the incorrect item and add a correction to your news page. That should keep customers from deluging you with phone calls and email to point out your mistake.***

Consider Your Customers' Needs

You'll probably have all kinds of information you want to share with your customers. Do they need it all? Probably not, just because it's important to you doesn't mean it's important to them. As a store owner, you should have little difficulty figuring out what your customers need to know and what they could care less about.

For example, feel free to provide personal information in your FAQ if it emphasizes your experience and expertise in your field or helps your customers identify with you a bit more. They will probably feel better about shopping at your site if they know there is a likable person behind all that HTML. However, you needn't burden them with a rambling tale about how the tragic death of your cat has left you emotionally scarred since childhood.

Keep news, contests, and polls related to what you sell or to topics that you know your customers will find interesting. For example, posting daily professional sports scores on a sporting goods site might not have anything to do with selling sneakers, but it will probably be of interest to your customers. Posting sports scores on other kinds of sites might cause people to wonder, "Who is the jock running this place?"

As for product descriptions, include as much technical information as needed. If you're selling computers, simply saying, "It has a bunch of memory and is really fast" won't cut it. On the other hand, unless you're selling quality craftsmanship, you needn't tell your customers how the jeans you're selling were stitched together.

Be Innovative

Our philosophy is, "Don't be afraid to fail, just don't do it too often." That could be rephrased as, "Take chances, just not stupid ones." However, since stupid is in the eye of the beholder, you may not know that an idea is a bad one until after you've tried it. Considering the very competitive nature of your business, you need to set yourself apart from the field. One way is by consistently providing content that isn't available elsewhere. It might be an entirely new content area, or it might just be a fresh way of presenting information.

How do you do this? Know your business, know your customers, know what's out there and spend time thinking about how you can be different. What would you like to see if you visited an online store in your market? More often than not, what you want to see will be what your customers want to see.

Innovation is simply thinking more and thinking better than everyone else. The more you think about your content, the better the chances you'll come up with something truly interesting and unique.

Keep it Simple, Stupid

Being innovative is the key to breaking ahead of the pack on the Web, but the other key is not biting off more than you can chew. It is very hard to dig yourself out of a hole on the Web, so don't try everything at once. Some very advanced content technologies have been covered here—but not all are recommended for people who don't have the resources or the knowledge. Most people should keep things simple.

The power of the written word is going to stay strong on the Web for some time. Some of the best store content is similar to what you find on the Tronix Web site—nice pictures, simple blurbs, and an occasional review. If you keep things well written and consistently publish interesting content, people will respect your content far more than if you set up the most amazing chat room and have all sorts of custom Java programs tied into a killer database, but no meaningful discussions or information.

Once you've mastered getting content up on a regular basis, you might go for something fancier. The key to how fast you grab at more complex content ideas is watching what your competitors do. If you feel that some other store's content is outstripping yours to the point that you're losing sales because of it, it's time to upgrade your content. Until then—or until you really have the ability to pull off something fancy—we encourage you to stick with simple articles, JPEGs, and reviews.

Beat the Competition

If you find yourself constantly checking out your competitors' sites and saying, "What a great idea!" then you're not beating the competition and you're not being innovative. When you have a great new content idea, don't sit on it. Chances are somebody else will have it up before you do.

If Appropriate, Use Humor

Take your business seriously, but don't take yourself too seriously. Some products don't lend themselves to humor, but if yours do, don't be afraid to use it. Humor and other types of asides can work well on the Web to make something that seems very "virtual," like your store, project some emotion and attitude that other physical stores try to convey.

If you plan on poking fun, direct it toward yourself rather than outward. In this era of political correctness, any joke you might tell could lead to an avalanche of email or even calls to boycott your store.

Give Honest Reviews

We've been over this, so we'll keep it brief. Don't lie. When your mom said, "Honesty is the best policy," she was right. If you refuse to print a negative review, remember something else Mom always said: "If you don't have anything good to say, don't say anything at all." Just don't lie.

Update Regularly

Keeping the same content on your site month after month is like having no content at all. Eventually, your customers will have seen it all and they're not about to re-read it just for the heck of it. This doesn't mean you have to redesign your Web site every week.

As you look at your site and the information therein, ask yourself if you are bored with it. You'll probably become bored with your site more quickly than customers will, simply because you'll have to look at it every day. However, when you can't stand to peruse your own site, it's time
to spice it up. New graphical touches or different uses of color are nice, but you should be just as concerned with keeping the information fresh. Change it as often as you can without making it impossible to keep up with everything. Here's where a "What's New" section is a big help. Your customers can immediately find out where you've made updates without searching the entire store for something new.

JOE'S TAKE: *I spend an average of one hour a day generating content. I do a redesign every six months. A major overhaul of the Tronix site takes about 30 to 40 hours. When you see the same thing every day, you get sick of it. You have to go with the times. As the technology advances, you advance your Web site.*

Essential Gravy

If the price lists, order forms, and overall functionality are the meat and potatoes of your online store, the content is the gravy. Your site will consist of pretty dry meat without at least a dollop of gravy. The key is finding the right amount so that your site is plenty tasty without giving your customer indigestion. If you have the time, pour on the content. Just don't forget about the meat and potatoes.

If you're not too hungry, move onto Part III: Promoting Your Store. This includes information on finding your customers, promoting your store on the Internet, a guide to advertising, and how to do international sales.

PART III

Promoting Your Store

Build it and they will come—assuming you promote it. Launching an online store and simply waiting for flocks of customers to arrive is a recipe for failure. Part III shows you how to find customers; how to promote your store on the Internet; where, when, and how to advertise; and how to attract the important international market.

Part III Table of Contents

CHAPTER TEN

Finding Customers Online

Your site is finished. You've got inventory. You're ready to do business. What else do you need? Well, customers. No customers, no income, no store, and you're back where you started. By now you realize that getting your store off the ground is going to take a lot of work, and that includes attracting customers; they aren't going to just show up. In fact, enticing customers to visit your Web site might be even more difficult than drawing them into a traditional store. On the other hand, there is a much larger pool of customers from which to draw, and with a little planning, effort, and diligence, you can make a large number of potential customers aware of your store.

There are two primary ways to attract customers to your site: through conventional means, such as advertising and public relations (see Chapter 11), and through the Internet. That involves finding communities of interest online, becoming an active member of those communities, and following some strict Internet etiquette

("Netiquette") to build customers by attracting online followers. There are literally thousands of interesting online communities, forums, and mailing lists that are frequented by people who are passionate about the subjects of those communities. Many of these community members are interested in purchasing items connected to that interest—whether it is Star Wars movies, sailing, wine, music, or anything else.

This chapter shows you how to find and attract people who are interested in what you are selling. We'll show you:

- How to find customers on the Usenet, mailing lists, and online forums.
- How to post messages that will make people aware of your store while not being intrusive.
- How to spread the good word about your store.
- What not to do.

Forum and Community Types

Internet forums and communities form in a number of ways. Many work on the same basic premise—people post messages or participate in discussions that relate to a particular interest or topic. These messages are usually archived for others to see, and if they want they can join the conversation. Some communities may keep conversations going for days, weeks, even years. One community of computer book authors has been going strong for nearly four years. Some may keep permanant archives. Others, such as many Usenet newsgroups, may supply only the most recent week or so of messages. In general, the idea is for a community to form around participation in a large group discussion (usually accompanied by many different conversations and side messages).

There are four identifiable types of forums or communities found on the Internet:

- Usenet newsgroups.
- Email discussion or mailing lists.
- Web-based bulletin boards or forums.
- Private online service forums (such as AOL, CompuServe).

Owners of small stores have a unique opportunity to become integral members of any of the many of these Internet communties. By acting as an informational resource and by posting intelligent messages, you can attract community members to your Web store. And in turn, they may attract other members by word-of-mouth.

Making Use of the Usenet

Usenet newsgroups are the heart and soul of many major online discussions and communities. In recent years, public newsgroups have been abused by people spamming (posting unrelated commercial offerings). This has angered some users and has pushed many away from these public forums toward more closely moderated private discussions.

Despite this, you will find some excellent forums on the Usenet. Remember that Usenet veterans are hardcore participants who react strongly and negatively to blatant advertising or commerce-related posts. You must be committed to being a member and let members seek out your store.

Newsgroups are basically bulletin boards dedicated to a particular subject and used by people interested in that subject. You can find newsgroups dedicated to almost any musical act, actor, actress, sport, hobby, or other interest on the planet. People post messages discussing, for example, the upcoming Korn tour, the latest Brad Pitt movie, or the chances of the Denver Broncos winning another Super Bowl without John Elway. You can also find newsgroups frequented by people who might be interested in shopping at your store. For example, if you sell skateboards, you could find potential customers at alt.skate-board. If you have a music store specializing in rock music, there are dozens of spots like alt.fan.pearl-jam, alt.fan.korn, or alt.fan.nin.

There is always a percentage of worthless bandwidth and inappropriate or offensive postings, but most posts are interesting, informative, and useful. You can skim through endless debates, helpful hints, product announcements, shameless plugs, and the ever-popular flame wars, in which a post instigates an avalanche of passionate, contrary opinions.

An online merchant can gain plenty of potential customers by working the newsgroups. You can also learn more about your customers and the industry in which you are working by identifying the sites that community frequents for news. The more time you can spend scanning the newsgroups, the more you are likely to learn.

There are also specific newsgroups, usually referred to as marketplaces, aimed at users who are interested in buying and trading items. This is where it's safest to post small advertisements without getting flamed. Outright ads in these groups are welcome—elsewhere they are not. In most cases, your best advertising will come from being visible and dragging along your implicit advertising as you gain a reputation for being informed and helpful. You can keep your store plugs to a minimum and still gain plenty of exposure. There is sure to be a newsgroup related to whatever you're selling. For example, if you sell a special shampoo for a horse's mane, you probably won't find any newsgroups dedicated to horse shampoos. But you will certainly find groups for horse enthusiasts. Any number of their members could be interested in your product. Many times, before you post you will want to search the entire Usenet. You can also search for any references to yourself or your products. There are several ways to do this, which are covered throughout this chapter.

Finding the Newsgroups of Your Customers

There are a number of sources to help you find relevant newsgroups. Three of the easiest and most effective are Deja.com (www.deja.com), HotBot (www.hotbot.com), and HotBot News (www.newbot.com). Deja.com (Figure 10.1) is probably the best of the three for finding newsgroups.

To search for particular newsgroups, you can start with specific keywords before branching out into more general categories as necessary. You should experiment with various words and combinations, varying the generality and specificity. If your search is too specific, you may find nothing. If it is too general, finding the most useful newsgroup among the hundreds of possibilities could be just as difficult.

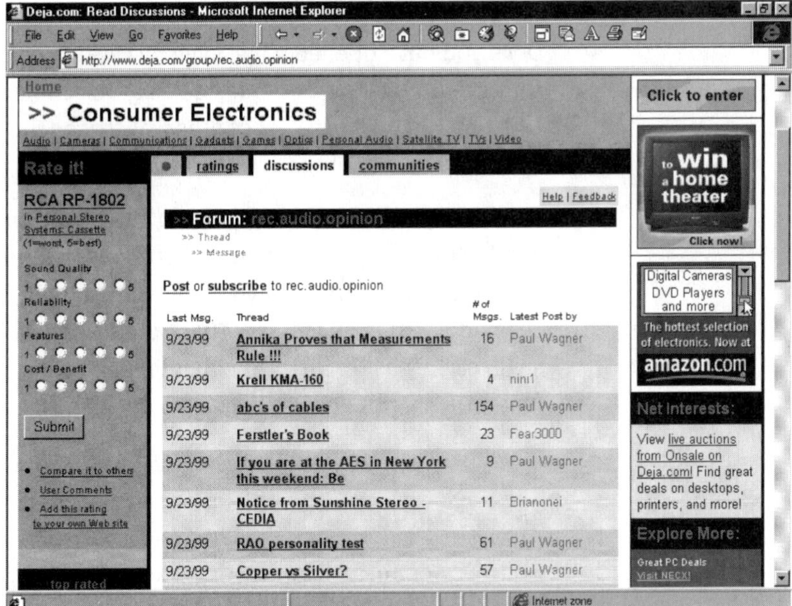

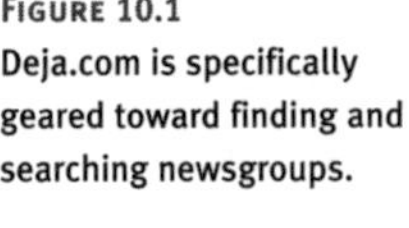
FIGURE 10.1
Deja.com is specifically geared toward finding and searching newsgroups.

Returning to the example of the horse shampoo salesman, he could do a search for **thoroughbred** or simply **horse**. He may even try **shampoo**, but could spend an entire day scrolling through all the possibilities, most of which will be geared toward human hair. How about a search for **animal shampoo**? As you tailor your search, a subject relevant to your business will show up. Subscribe to the groups you think can help you add customers or learn more about your specific industry and begin following and posting to the discussions.

Deja.com

Deja.com is a search engine specifically geared toward finding the newsgroup or discussion topic you're looking for. There are a number of ways to do searches depending on the information you have and that which you are seeking.

Quick Search

The Quick Search asks you to enter a specific question or topic and responds with a number of possible newsgroups to visit. Threaded discussion results are listed and can be organized by date, subject, newsgroup, or author.

Once you have opened a message by clicking on the subject line, you can click on the author's email address to send an email or click on "Posting History" for a list of other messages the person has posted. You can read any of the previous posts by clicking on the subject line.

With the document opened, you can move back and forth through the discussion thread by clicking either "previous in thread" or "next in thread." Or you can move through your search results by clicking "previous in search," "next in search," or "back to search results." To post a message, click "post reply" and either login if you are Deja.com member, or follow the instructions to become a member.

Members can also request that specific threads be tracked for them.

Power Search

Click "Power Search" by entering a keyword or keywords and choosing a match option of "all" or "any" and an archive seach of "complete," "standard," etc. You can limit the time frame to current discussions, discussions within the last year, or discussions since 1995 and can even choose from one of several languages. Then search by subject, forum, and/or author.

Categories

The primary categories are arts/entertainment, automotive, computing/tech, consumer electronics, health, home/family, money, people, politics/media, recreation, sports, and travel. Each category is divided into subgroups. For example, clicking on sports will result in baseball, basketball, football, and more. Choose a subgroup and search, read, or post.

HotBot

At HotBot (www.hotbot.com), you can search the Web or Usenet. Enter a keyword or phrase and search for all the words, any of the words, the exact phrase, words in the title, the person, links to this URL, and the Boolean expression (AND, NOT, etc.). You can have your results returned with full or brief descriptions, or just the URLs.

HotBot News

HotBot News (www.newbot.com)is most helpful when searching for news stories on the Web. For example, you can enter **microsoft** as a keyword and find all the stories dealing with Microsoft that have appeared on the Web in the past 6, 12, 24, or 48 hours. If that time frame isn't enough, you can go back three days, four days, seven days, or indefinitely. You can use HotBot News in the same manner to search for newsgroup postings.

Other Newsgroup Engines

Two other sites may also be of interest to you as you search for newsgroup information.

The University of North Carolina's Sunsite hosts a newsgroup searching engine that lists newsgroups based on various interest topics. It also can search and list associated FAQs and other interesting information. Check it out at http://sunsite.unc.edu/usenet-i/search.html.

Another great site is called Tile.Net and is located at www.tile.net/tile/listserv/index.html.

This site lets you search for names of newsgroups and topical mailing lists.

Usenet Software

When you apply for an Internet account, your package will usually contain a Web browser, an email client, and a newsreader. Two perfectly OK newsreaders are the ones integrated with Netscape Communicator and Microsoft Internet Explorer. Both are easy to use but not as extensive as some of the standalone products on the market. If you are already familiar with the relevant newsgroups, you can simply add them to your Netscape or Internet Explorer setup.

The more powerful, standalone newsreaders usually offer a broader range of features. There are several major newsreaders available for Mac or PC, many of them shareware (check **www.download.com**). Forte's Free Agent (Figure 10.2) is perhaps the most popular standalone newsreader. Free Agent, as the name suggests, can be dowloaded and used for free and provides multipane viewing and the ability to read online or offline. Other features include flexible article purging, database compacting, carbon copying for email and article posting, editing of all fields, and cancelling of posts.

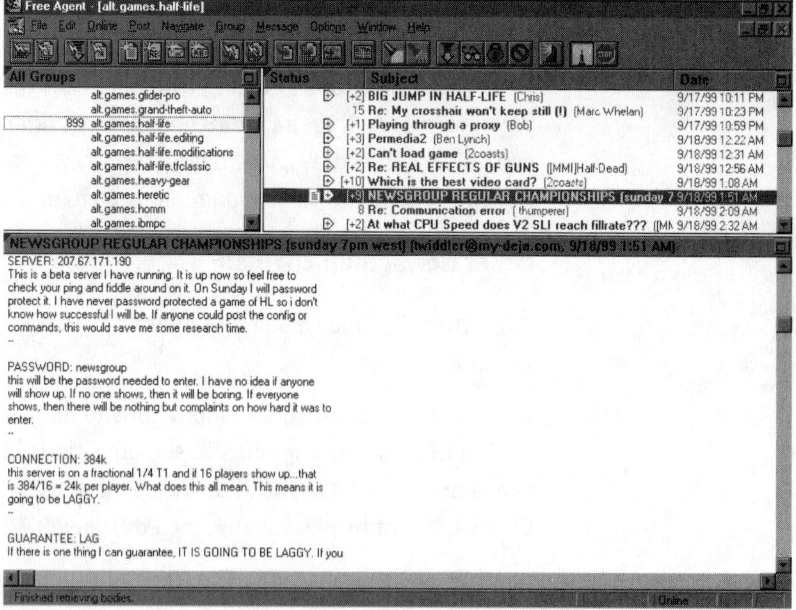

Figure 10.2
Forte's Free Agent is a popular newsgroup reader that is free for download.

Using Mailing Lists

Another great place to find customers is in mailing lists. Mailing lists are a little different from newsgroups because they foster discussion through email rather than on the Usenet. These lists require direct subscription in order for someone to participate. Users send an email message to the list and include a command (such as "subscribe") in the body or subject line that initiates the subscription. Members receive messages posted to the list by other members and join the discussion.

TIP ▸ ***There are two major search engines that provide links to many of the mailing lists that exist on the Internet. The best one is Liszt, located at www.liszt.com. It contains over 90,000 listings. There is also the List of Lists located at catalog.com/vivian/interest-group-search.html.***

The subscription and delivery method of discussion is what makes mailing lists interesting and valuable. Since list members must seek out and choose to subscribe to the lists, they tend to be more deeply involved in the subject matter.

Many mailing lists are privately moderated and unreceptive to advertising. Using the participatory approach is best. Study the instructional message you'll receive after subscribing; it will contain the rules of the newsgroup. If you think advertising is allowed, sending an email to the moderator just to be sure can help facilitate good will.

Mailing lists can generate dozens, if not hundreds of messages a day. Often the best thing to do is subscribe to the "digest" version of the list. A digest combines the day's messages into one daily message or several delivered at intervals during the day. You can also deliver private messages to other members. Be careful. There are few things more embarrassing than sending what was intended to be private message to the entire mailing list.

Since even small mailing lists can quickly lead to a large pile of email, we suggest you use a separate account or filters on your email to handle the inflow. Otherwise, you may be overwhelmed by mailing list messages commingling with direct customer emails.

You should also know how to get off a mailing list. When you subscribe, whatever you do, hang on to the instructions for "unsubscribing." If you can't figure out how to get off, you'll end up feeling like Michael Corleone—"Just when you think you're out, they pull you right back in." You'll just have to post a message to the moderator and ask how to get off.

Many mailing lists are actually sponsored by advertising, which can be a much more direct route to customers—relatively inexpensive and quite focused. When you subscribe to a list, find out if it is supported by advertising. Then, become a participant before you actually buy advertising. This will let the members know that you are helpful, knowledgeable, and open for business.

Joe's Take: *Mailing lists are great places to find customers. But keep in mind, they're moderated far more closely than newsgroups, and you should participate frequently. It takes work to produce useful information and join lively debates. Try working just one or two lists at a time. Members tend to stay on mailing lists, so you can work one for several weeks before moving on to another.*

Using Online Forums and Clubs

Online forums are similar to newsgroups except they have one or more moderators to oversee all the messages. Also known as Web boards or bulletin boards, forums also differ from newsgroups because they usually exist internally on one of the major online services like CompuServe or AOL, or on a specific Web site rather than existing as newsgroups do, as Internet entities unto themselves. Some of the larger portal Web sites also offer forums, which are known by such forum synonyms as Clubs (Yahoo, Lycos), Communities (Excite, InfoSeek) or Pods (Tripod).

Moderators watch for offensive material such as harsh language, subjects that stray from the forum's topic, and advertising. CompuServe, America Online, and Prodigy have their own forums that are formed and maintained by SysOps (System Operators), a technical term that is now being replaced by the term *moderator*. If you have a membership to any of these services and try to use a forum for advertising, your message will be deleted. Depending on the service, you will be warned not to try it again. After a couple of warnings, you may have your membership revoked.

As with newsgroups, people generally join forums because they share common interests, not to get pounded with advertisements. Suppose you joined a music forum and found a section dedicated to the Beatles. Imagine that while scanning various messages trying to find the name of a particular song from *Sgt. Pepper's Lonely Hearts Club Band*, you wound up wading through store advertisements that claim to have every Beatles album at unbeatable prices. You would be annoyed.

If you plan on "invading" one of these online services, you should contact its customer service department, which will guide you to the proper places for advertising. You can also search around yourself. Every online service has its own search engine. Perhaps you can find a forum that has a section dedicated to buying or trading items. Let the moderator know your intentions, and find out if it is acceptable to advertise there.

Initially, online forums were slow to develop on the Web itself. Now, however, with Yahoo Clubs, Excite Communities, and places like iVillage, Talk City and Tripod, Web-based forums and communities are popping up everywhere. As forum software gets better and easier for sites to deploy, you may begin to find yourself with tons of services to check in on.

Creating an Excite Community

Excite is one of the several online services that allow you to create your own community. To do so, go to www.excite.com/comm/new/ **and click on Start your own Community. You will be asked to enter a community name and description. You can choose to have your community listed in the Excite Community Directory, which involves selecting a topic and entering some keywords. Or you can keep your community private so only members can participate. Once you build your own community, you can post photos, events, links, and contact lists as well as host discussions and send community email.**

Finding the Online Forums of Your Customers

CompuServe, AOL, and Prodigy have areas where you can find forums by entering keywords.

On AOL, you simply call up the keywords function, type in a keyword, and click Search. You can also go to the Directory of Services, which is accessed through the program menus or through keyword **directory**.

You can access CompuServe's index of forums by selecting the Go function and typing in the keyword **index**.

To find an index of Prodigy's bulletin boards check out the Member Services.

Here's where to find forums on the major Web services:

- Yahoo Clubs. **clubs.yahoo.com**
- Tripod. **tripod.com/interact/**
- GeoCities. **geocities.com/chat/**
- Excite. **excite.com/communities/**
- Lycos. **boards.lycos.com/**
- InfoSeek. **go.com/Community/**
- TalkCity. **boards.talkcity.com/cgi-bin/WebX.cgi**
- Snap! **home.snap.com/main/messages/door/0,312,-0,00.html?st.sn.fdcm.0.mb**
- InsideTheWeb.com. **insidetheweb.com**

TIP ▸ ***ForumOne (www.forumone.com) has a list of over 300,000 Web-based forums. You can use it find useful forums and online communities to join. You can also subscribe to the Online Community Report (www.onlinecommunityreport.com), an email newsletter that covers online forums and communities.***

Software for AOL, CompuServe, and Prodigy

Getting the software for AOL, CompuServe, and Prodigy is easy. If you haven't already received AOL software in the mail, we have to question whether you actually exist. To get in touch with AOL call 1-800-827-6364 or visit www.aol.com.

CompuServe can be reached at 1-800-848-8990. To get the software, point your browser at world.compuserve.com/cs/csfaq.asp and click on the indicated phrase in the first question. Prodigy software is available at www.prodigy.com.

Rules and Tips for Posting

So you've figured out where you need to post messages—now what? How do you approach this group? Do you go in full-force and advertise your business name surrounded by a border of asterisks—the equivalent of a theatre marquee? Do you post your entire inventory with prices, hoping to lure people to your Web site? Those are definitely aggressive approaches, but if you're in an area that is not defined as a buying or trading group, you would be in for some nasty responses. Before you start posting the first thing that comes to mind, consider the following tips.

Stick to the Topic

When posting in the newsgroups or forums, stick with the topic. Just because you are selling hand-held electronic chess games doesn't mean you should promote them in just any video game group, such as Nintendo or Sega. Those people will certainly let you know you've entered the wrong territory. If you want to post information about your products, try to find newsgroups that are geared toward buying or selling. If you find newsgroups that are general discussion areas for the types of products you sell, pay close attention to them. Remember, though, members of these types of newsgroups are there to share information and are not fond of getting inundated with ads.

Think before you post. With a number of potential customers watching, you don't want to make a fool of yourself. If an individual makes a worthless post, the consequences are no worse than the other newsgroup members thinking the person is a dork. As the representative of an online store, an uninformed post can cost your credibility and customers. Most newsgroups have a large number of regulars, so if you make a bad first impression, you'll certainly be remembered.

Keep Promotional Posts Subtle and Simple

An accepted and effective approach is simply to become active in the newsgroups—posting your opinions and taking note of what others have to say. If you can subtly include the fact that you own an online store related to the newsgroup, you'll likely have people inquiring about your store without having to shove it down people's throats. Here's an example:

Just wanted to send a note that we have received Soul Calibur at Tronix and I played it for an hour last night. It's really very good—the reviews and previews for this title were dead on. It's one of those titles that really makes the Sega Dreamcast shine. The graphics are fluid and the controls are very intuitive. If you're not a fighting game fan, this might not be the title for you (try NFL2K or Get Bass for an alternative).

In other news, we also got Tonk-Tonk, which is just an awful game and not worth your time at all.

That's all...

Joe
joe@tronixweb.com

TRONIX http://www.tronixweb.com
PlayStation * Saturn * Nintendo 64 * PC * Imports
Hours: M–F, 10–5 EDT. 212.447.5980
No-Nonsense Mail-Order for the Serious Gamer

After you become a familiar presence you can be a bit more forward. For example, if you sell items such as baseball cards, toys, or other premiere-sensitive items, you can begin to post simple "what's new" messages. If you participate in many other discussions without trying to sell people anything, list members usually won't mind these brief, informative commercial posts. When you post information like this to a group, try to take a "journalistic" approach as in the above message. Be informative and unbiased. Don't try to sell the item, just talk about it.

If you're going to post an ad (and do this only if you think it's acceptable in the particular forum), it should be something small and simple. You can use a header like "New @ Tronix." Potential customers can see a list of what's new, and of course a date in the header will let them know when the ad was posted. You can simply list your newest arrivals with a trailing line of text, which lets people know how to get further information. Your signature can contain all the rest of the pertinent information (such as store hours, URL, phone, fax, etc.). Most newsreaders today recognize links, so your Web site's URL can simply be activated right from the message, leading readers to your site.

TIP ▸ ***A great way to get your store's name in front of people with a bit of subtlety is by including it in your signature. People will quickly connect your intelligent posts to your store and naturally feel good about visiting it.***

Here are some sample messages that we would post to two newsgroups related to Tronix customers—the Sony PlayStation newsgroups and the general video game marketplace.

To: rec.games.video.sony,rec.games.video.marketplace
NEW AT TRONIX: 4.22.98

****

Tomato Brawl
Knights from Hell (2 CDs)
Spider Mountain
For more information, visit our web site at:
http://www.tronixweb.com

TRONIX http://www.tronixweb.com
PlayStation * Saturn * Nintendo 64 * PC * Imports
Hours: M–F, 10–5 EDT. 212.447.5980
No-Nonsense Mail-Order for the Serious Gamer

The information is simple and there are no prices, which can flag your post as a flagrant advertisement. If you post pricing, you might draw responses like: "I don't think your prices are that good" or "I got that item cheaper somewhere else, so stay out." If potential customers see the prices in the newsgroups, they may not bother to see what else you carry. If you have items you want to post for a special sale, you can follow the same format as above replacing "New" with "Sale." Sales are usually more acceptable, as everyone is always looking for a good bargain. They're also a great way to bring in new customers.

Keep your signature down to about four lines of text. Large signatures tend to aggravate users.

What to Respond to and What to Avoid

Replying to the proper messages becomes a talent after a while. When you own an online store, everything you post in the newsgroups becomes an immediate reflection of your business. As you thread various topics, you might see people asking about where to find a certain product. You can join in with a reply and mention your business, as long as it's done in a way that does not look like a desperate grab for customers. For example:

[user@somewhere.net] Hey, does anyone know where I can find those new infrared Bose desktop speakers?

[you@somewhereelse.net] They should be available at most stores by now, but if you're having trouble finding them, we just received some stock a few days ago. Our web address is in our signature.

Notice the approach. Don't push your store down the user's throat. Give the person options. Another post that's ideal to respond to is a question someone may have about a product.

If the question relates to an item you carry, and you're familiar with it, you can reply with a small review. For example:

[you@somewhere.net] The translucent CD holder you are referring to unfortunately holds only 40 discs and it's not that convenient to get at your discs once it's full. I've had those in stock, but the newer model X holds a lot more and is designed with better spacing for easier identification of your discs.

With this type of response, you are helping a consumer make a better decision while simultaneously setting up a pointer to your business.

The types of postings that are best left alone are complaints about other stores or those by disgruntled users who like to go online just to whimper or find fault. Replying to someone's complaint about a purchase from a store with, "You would have had a better deal had you come to us," does not solve a person's problem. It simply makes him or her look unintelligent and makes you look arrogant. While it could grab some attention and maybe even some customers, it also sets you up as a perfectionist—which you'd better be after a post like that. It also is a blatant invitation for flames and looks incredibly self-serving.

Responding to an Attack

If a customer goes public with a complaint about your store, reply publicly and personally with concern and ask how you can remedy the problem. This will show your customer that you are interested in the problem, and others will take notice. For example:

[user@somewhere.net] I went looking for a tape of Phish's "Lemonwheel" concert in Limestone, Maine, and Phred's Phishing Hole doesn't have it. Can you believe that? I'm never visiting that site again.

[phred@somewhere.net] We have to apologize for the lack of a "Lemonwheel" tape at this point. We actually had a copy—a legal one!—, but the sound quality was so poor we didn't feel it would be fair to make it available. We're working on getting a tape we feel comfortable distributing, but until then—"We will trade no Phish before its time!" We're sorry for any inconvenience and thanks for your patience.

You can also take your disagreement into a private exchange, but always remain civil. If you privately call your nemesis a moron, there's always the chance your tirade will be made public by the recipient. Never email anything you don't want revealed publicly.

Joe's Take: *Posting in the correct newsgroups without overdoing the advertising was a great way to get the word out about Tronix. As I scanned the Net, I came across a number of newsgroups with topics that were associated with my line of business. The products I currently carried (or planned to carry) were discussed openly, so I jumped right into many of these topics, answering questions, and posting informative information (small capsule reviews of games or release dates in my case). I didn't post any ads, other than my automatic signature file which was basically four lines of store information (company name, Web site URL, office hours, phone/fax number, formats carried). After a number of postings, the email started to roll in. It ranged from simple inquiries to actual orders. Between the simple link to my site in my signature, and a hearty dose of intelligent posts, Tronix began to form a name for itself. Forums and newsgroups each* *have something to recommend them. With no monitors, anything goes on Internet newsgroups. It also means they are less organized than online forums. A topic about the best digital cameras on the market can suddenly turn into a feud about presidential candidates. For storeowners, newsgroups do have an obvious advantage over online forums. If a topic labeled "what online shop carries a good assortment of DAT movies?" is posted, you can jump right in and give them your movie store URL without worrying about the deletion of your reply by a SysOp. If you have good customers who frequent the forums or newsgroups, they'll usually jump in and recommend your service. I had the opportunity to be a SysOp for one of CompuServe's popular video game forums and had to weed out any advertising I came across myself. You can imagine what it was like, owning an online business selling games, reading questions about where to find a certain product and not being able to refer people to Tronix. If you were a regular member you couldn't get away with it, so being a SysOp and attempting to direct someone to your Web site was a big no-no.*

Other Ways to Spread the Good Word

Posting in newsgroups or online forums is a great way for you to get the word out about your store. This self-generated content can promote the image of your store and yourself. If done correctly, potential customers will soon realize that you have the products they want. Just as importantly, you can promote yourself as knowledgeable and easy to deal with. Once you have built up a base of loyal customers, they will do much of the work for you with strong word-of-mouth. Their positive posts can be used to endorse your business and, in some cases, customers might even go out of their way to help you succeed.

Monitor and Cull Posts to Promote Your Store

Reading the newsgroups should be a daily routine. Once you've decided which newsgroups will be your permanent hunting grounds, run through a quick scan every day and keep your eyes out for any topics that you think would benefit your retail business. Most newsgroup readers will allow you to mark a particular thread so you can follow its progress as people reply to the topic. Decide when it's best to join in and offer information that will benefit both the group and your store.

Getting Customers to Help Online

In the early days of your business, your primary method of advertising will be through your own periodic posts. As time goes by, individuals who are satisfied with your service will surely make reference to your store to others in the group. The great thing about the Internet is how fast information spreads. One happy customer's comment, whether it is in a newsgroup or Internet Relay Chat (IRC), can lead new customers to your Web site within minutes. Newer customers who decide to give your company praise will bring in even more.

Unfortunately, not every customer you correspond with will be active with the newsgroups, forums, or IRC, but of course the traditional word-of-mouth can be just as effective. From time to time, customers who purchase items from your store and receive shipments on time and in perfect condition will send you email comments about how they've enjoyed your service. When you feel comfortable enough with them, you might want to make a subtle suggestion that they mention your place. For example:

Customer: I really like your store. I have purchased a number of products from you and I just want to say you have a wonderful service!

You: Thanks again for your business and the much appreciated feedback. Since we're fairly small right now, it would be great to get the word around a bit so we can grow and keep providing great service. Perhaps you can mention my place if you see other people looking for similar products?

The key is to make them feel like they have a stake in your store's survival—if they love your store and service enough, they'll want to make sure you don't have to scale back your operation or go out of business.

What Not To Do

We've tried to give you an idea what to do when searching for customers online. Nearly as important is what not to do.

- **Don't knock the competition in your posts.** It makes you look unprofessional and could backfire. No one is perfect (including you), and chances are if you rip someone, they'll find a way to rip you right back.

- **Never overdo your posts.** One small post several times a week is plenty. Excessive posting will almost guarantee your writing something that can garner negative feedback.

- **Be careful when posting about new items.** Do you actually have them in stock? A lot of companies jump the gun to grab an audience on a new item not yet in stock. Think about the people who will contact you by phone, especially if you don't have an 800 number. Long-distance callers will not be happy when they find the item is not yet in.

- **Stay away from those UPPER-CASE ASSAULTS.** You can use upper-case letters here and there, but an all-upper-case advertisement on the Net is like an annoying television commercial with a screaming salesman. It also makes you look inexperienced with the Internet.

- **Don't overdo it when cross-posting.** If you want to get your message out to a number of related newsgroups, be careful when you cross-post. If you are selling baseball cards, there's no need to plug your shop through 30 different baseball-related newsgroups. People often join many similar groups, and you don't want them running into the same advertisement everywhere they look.

- **Do not plug or push anything** that is related to your business in a newsgroup that has nothing to do with your business.

- **Don't come across as biased** and don't get into feuds with anyone in the newsgroups. If you disagree with someone's opinion on a specific topic, it's best to stay out of it.

- **Don't lie.** Don't post high praise about your store while trying to keep your affiliation secret. Savvy Net users will immediately associate your email address with your Web site, and you'll look like a dishonest fool.

- **Avoid posting lengthy price lists in newsgroups,** especially those not set up for buying or trading. This is what your Web site is for, so there's no need to force-feed your inventory to other users.

- **Don't waste time chatting.** Chat rooms are generally a waste of time unless you are the guest.

An Easy, Personal Way to Reach Customers

It's extremely easy to find potential customers online. Not only are participants in newsgroups and online forums readily reachable, they are generally passionate about the subject. If someone consistently participates in a newsgroup dedicated to mountain biking, you can be sure she'll be interested in hearing a bit about xtremebike.com's selection of suspension forks. The more you participate, the more people will get to know you and your store.

Using the newsgroups and online forums is a personal way to reach customers unavailable anywhere else. To ignore the newsgroups and forums is to ignore your customers. If you find the relevant newsgroups, follow this chapter's posting tips, and remain dedicated to becoming a contributor to the online community, customers will almost certainly follow. That said, it's on to Chapter 11, where we'll show you how to promote your store on the Internet and through more traditional means.

CHAPTER ELEVEN

Promoting Your Store Online and Offline

You have the greatest online store on the Web. Your content is second to none. Your graphics sizzle. Your prices and service are unmatched. So now you sit back and wait for customers to flock to your site, spend gobs of money, and pay for your yacht, right? Not so fast—the Web isn't an "if you build it they will come" field of dreams.

You know your store is outstanding, but how do you let everyone else know? There are some obvious ways to promote your store on the Internet: submitting to search engines, finding quality links, setting up bounty programs, becoming part of an online mall, buying advertising (online and off), and being involved in newsgroups and mailing lists. In Chapter 10, we focused on how to get the most out of newsgroups; in Chapter 12 we'll give you some tips for advertising online and offline on a small budget. Here in Chapter 11 we will cover search engines, links, bounty programs, and malls and offer some traditional offline promotional and public relations tips.

This chapter focuses primarily on what you can do on the Web to promote your store without spending too much money or time. Creating an informational atmosphere (as discussed in Chapter 9) will give people a reason to repeatedly visit your store, but you have to get them there initially. That's what this chapter will help you do.

Search Engines

If you're on the Web and aren't sure where to find some information, what do you do? Go to a search engine, of course. And when you get that first list of ten hits, how often do you feeling like looking at the second ten? The following ten? Not often—and neither does anybody else. Therefore, it is of the utmost importance to be among the first ten sites listed by a particular search engine.

If you're interested in the nitty gritty of how search engines work, we strongly recommend reading *Getting Hits: The Definitive Guide to Promoting Your Website* by Don Sellers, published by Peachpit Press. Actually, we recommend that book for anyone with a Web site. Here, rather than get bogged down in the technicalities of how search engines work, we'll give you a little background and then get on to what really matters—how they can work for you.

Automatic Submission

There are a number of search engines to choose from—far more even than you're probably aware of or will ever use. If you don't want to take the time to submit your site individually to each search engine, there are a number of automatic submission sites that do the work for you. You fill out one form and the service does the rest. However, different search engines use different methods of ranking sites, and automatic submission does not allow you to tailor your submission for the quirks of each particular engine. Your automatic submission might get your site listed in the first ten by one engine and 150th by another.

Still, if you really don't have the time to submit to individual engines, automatic submission is a good alternative. Then, once your business is off the ground and you have a bit of time to catch your breath, you can re-submit to the engines with which you would like to improve your ranking. Make sure the particular engines understand you have already submitted automatically and you are updating your listing.

Submit-It
www.submit-it.com

Submit-It (Figure 11.1) is arguably the top automatic submission service on the Web. Submit-It helps you submit your site to more than 400 search engines, directories, announce sites, and award sites. Submit-It asks you to enter information once and automates the submissions process for you while still allowing you to choose the search engines and directories that fit your needs. It cuts the submission process from days to about an hour. The cost is $30 for one URL.

Submit-It additionally offers a number of paid services to help maximize and track your site's ranking. You can also get free information about the latest methods for driving traffic to your Web site.

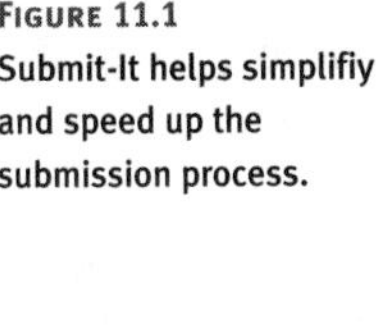

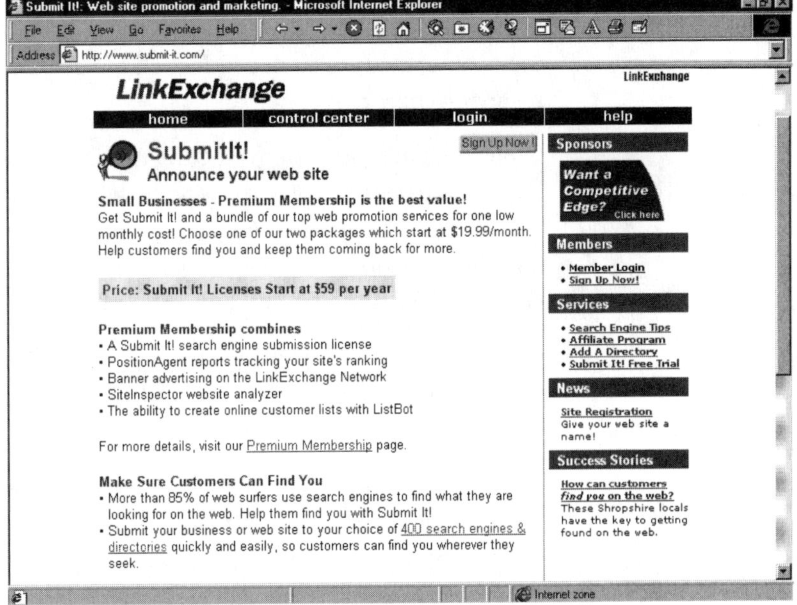

FIGURE 11.1
Submit-It helps simplifiy and speed up the submission process.

Individual Submission

Many search engines will find your site without your even submitting it. However, he who hesitates is lost. Go find the search engines on which you want to be listed rather than waiting for them to find you. Most of the major search engines provide you with an easy method of submitting through a link from their front pages to their submission pages.

As we have already mentioned, search engines work differently, so you need to tailor your submissions to each engine. While some search engines have "spiders" (information retrievers) that will dig through and index your entire site, others will index only the main page or one level deeper. Learn as much as possible about the particular search engine to which you are submitting before actually doing so. This chapter includes some basic information on some of the top search engines. The Web sites of the engines themselves provide much more information.

Maximizing Your Ranking

Search engines are changing constantly, and we'll emphasize again that they all have their own idiosyncrasies. If you are intent on getting your site ranked appropriately, pay particular attention to your submission. This doesn't guarantee anything, however. No matter how good the engine, they are all dependent on the searcher and which keywords he or she chooses.

Search engines aren't perfect, either. You might be the top source on the Web for a particular item and wind up with a poor ranking. This imperfection works both ways. You might just as easily wind up with a surprisingly high ranking. However, the smarter and harder you work, the better your chances of obtaining a high ranking.

Gaining a high ranking in one engine doesn't guarantee a high ranking in all of them, especially with a directory such as Yahoo, which relies on human actions and decisions.

There are a few things to think about that will apply to some search engines but not others: depth of search, meta tags, keywords, title, word repetition, word placement, text and page design, and number of external links.

Depth of Search

As we mentioned, some search engines send out spiders that dig through entire Web sites. Others dig a bit, but not into every page of a site. And others do no digging at all. Most search engines will let you know how much of your site you need to submit. If a search engine doesn't have a spider that will follow links throughout your site, you need to submit each page individually.

Meta Tags

Meta tags are pieces of information placed in the head of an HTML document. Although the information is not displayed by Web browsers, it can be found and recognized by some information retrievers. Not all search engines recognize meta tags.

The key to writing a good meta tag for your store is in optimizing the tags to get the best impact for your site. Don Sellers' book *Getting Hits* is a good resource for learning more about the peculiarities of each search engine. Another helpful resource is the Virtual Library Meta Tagging for Search Engines, located at www.stars.com/Search/Meta/Tag.html.

The Tag Structure

Two types of meta tags need to be considered in relation to search engines: description and keywords. A description meta tag allows you to include a brief description of your site that will appear when your site appears as the result of a search. If you fail to include a meta tag description, as many sites do, your search summary will be the first portion of text on your site, which might not be descriptive of your site at all.

Here is the basic structure:

<META NAME="KEYWORDS" CONTENT="KEYWORDS">

<META NAME="DESCRIPTION" CONTENT="DESCRIPTION">

And here is an example that might be used for a store like Tronix that sells computer and video games.

<META NAME="Keywords" CONTENT="Sony Sega Nintendo N64 Dreamcast games mail order Saturn Playstation imports video games">

<META NAME="Description" CONTENT="Tronix, a leading mail order company covering domestic and imported video games for playstation, saturn, nintendo 64, dreamcast and portables.">

That covers the basic structure of meta tags. You can skip writing them and learn to tailor them for some specific search engines on the Meta Tag Builder Site, which has a fill-in form that will build an HTML header all set with the optimal tag information. The Meta Tag Builder Site is located at vancouver-webpages.com/META/mk-metas.html.

The Web Developer's Virtual Library has some excellent information on Meta tagging for search engines located at www.wdvl.com/Location/Meta/Tag.html.

Keywords

Keywords are the words someone might use while doing a search for your site. Defining your site's keywords is essential but can be tricky. You need to come up with the words someone is most likely to use when looking for your site, which may or may not be the ones you would use yourself. Sellers suggests gathering a group of friends, colleagues, and potential site visitors and asking them to generate the keywords for your site. Think of any variation of those keywords, and once you have a list of as many as 30 keywords, have the group rank them in importance and descriptiveness. Use the top two or three words in your title, headings, text, and meta tags.

Title

Even without regard to search engines, your page's title should be as descriptive as possible. Most search engines display the title of the page in the results and rely heavily on the title words in their ranking of sites. Having an accurate, descriptive title for all pages—not just your home page—is essential.

Word Repetition

Word repetition used to be an easy way to increase your site's ranking. More recently, many search engines have actually begun penalizing sites with flagrantly unnecessary word repetition. Still, others use word repetition as a criterion for high ranking.

Word Placement

As we have mentioned, word selection in the title is essential. Also keep in mind that many search engines place a greater emphasis on words located near the beginning of the page than lower down, making this word selection very important also.

Text and Page Design

If you don't include any text on a page, the spiders won't be able to find it. Spiders also are unable to read text that is embedded in a graphic, so don't embed too much of your critical text in graphics.

Also, remember that some search engines don't recognize meta tags and instead take the early part of a page's text for the summary. Make sure that text will work well as a summary in a search result.

Number of External Links

Some search engines calculate the number of links to your site included on other sites and use that to determine your site's popularity. They then use popularity as part of their ranking process. The feeling is that the more popular a site is, the more links there will be to it. This makes it all the more important to get links to your site.

Monitoring Your Ranking

PositionAgent (**www.positionagent.com**) monitors your site's rankings in ten top search engines and provides weekly reports on your site's position. PositionAgent monitors AltaVista, Excite, Galaxy, HotBot, Infoseek, Lycos, Magellan, OpenText, WebCrawler, and Yahoo. The cost is $60 for five URLs and six months of reports.

Submitting to Specific Search Engines

Now that you have a general idea about what search engines look for, here are a few of the top search engines and some keys to submitting your site to them. Most of the sites have an icon for adding URLs and will step you through the process.

TIP▸ ***Many search engines and indexes like Yahoo (shopguide.yahoo.com) are actually setting up separate areas that index online merchants. As more of these specialty search engines pop up, make sure you target listings among them specifically.***

AltaVista
www.altavista.com

At AltaVista, click Add a Page and submit just the main page of your site. AltaVista says its crawler will follow links through the entire site, making your content findable usually within two days. AltaVista asks that you use meta tags to control the abstract served back with your page. Do not submit a description or keywords with your URL.

Even if you don't submit your site, AltaVista's crawler will most likely find it if there are external links to it.

Ask Jeeves
www.askjeeves.com

Ask Jeeves allows users to ask questions rather than enter keywords. Ask Jeeves uses language-processing technology to determine the meaning of the words in question, as well as the meaning of the grammar.

Human editors at Ask Jeeves consider but do not include all submissions. Ask Jeeves considers site performance (load time, ease of navigation, regularity of updates) and editorial criteria (thorough information). The site must also not require users to register to access the site.

DMOZ Open Directory Project
www.dmoz.org

The Open Directory Project relies on a large number of volunteer editors with the goal of providing a comprehensive Web directory. To get your site listed, find the appropriate category (Shopping), click Add URL, and submit your site's URL, title, and description.

Excite

www.excite.com

Excite uses artificial intelligence to discern your site's dominant theme. Check to see if your site has been found by Excite's spider and if not, click Add URL. In general, Excite doesn't honor meta tags other than descriptions. Using descriptive phrases near the top of your pages will help Excite's artificial intelligence rank your site correctly.

FAST Search

www.alltheweb.com

FAST Search is a relatively new search engine. Click Add a Site and enter your URL.

Google

www.google.com

To submit an URL to Google, click About Google and then Add to include your site. Simply enter your URL and include comments or keywords that describe the content of your page. Comments and keywords do not affect your ranking. Enter only your main URL, and Google's spider will do the rest. The process takes from one to four weeks.

GoTo.com

www.goto.com

GoTo.com is one directory that does allow you to guarantee a high ranking—assuming you can afford it. GoTo.com allows you to purchase placement within search esults, offering control over advertising placement, budget, and targeting.

Select the search terms that are relevant to your site and decide how much you are willing to pay on a per-click basis for those terms. The more you pay, the higher your ranking. To see how much other sites in your category have paid, search your category. The per-click cost is included in the search results.

HotBot

www.hotbot.com

To submit a site to HotBot, find the most appropriate category and click Add URL. Submit each page's URL once and limit submissions from the same domain to 50 in a 24-hour period. HotBot now uses human editors to maintain its directories. HotBot supports meta tags and focuses first on keywords in the title, followed by keywords in meta tags and frequency of keywords in the text.

Infoseek/Go Network

www.go.com

Click Add URL and enter your URL in the box provided. Allow one week or more for new pages or updates to appear. Infoseek does not accept automatic submissions, and you must submit each page of your site separately. To submit more than 50 pages, you must send them through email rather than be submitting directly on the site.

Infoseek says it chooses only the most relevant and valuable sites, and that an inappropriate site definition or spamming can lead to exclusion from the index. Infoseek Select sites are chosen from the index by Infoseek's editors based on editorial value, traffic, and the number of external links to the site.

Lycos

www.lycos.com

Click Add Your Site To Lycos and use the Site Finder to see if your page has already been registered. If not, enter the URL and your email address. Lycos says its spider will dig through your entire site and that you will show up on a Lycos search two to four weeks after submission. With Lycos, you should definitely use meta tags.

Lycos ranks sites based on keywords used in the title, in high-level headings, and in text near the top of the page. Page popularity also improves the ranking, while word repetition is penalized.

Netscape Netcenter

www.netscape.com

Netscape Netcenter allows you to register your Web site with 11 search engines for free. Netscape also offers other free Web site services. Visit Netscape's Web site and click Add Site for information and instructions.

Northern Light Search

www.northernlight.com

Northern Light combines information from premium material in one search. Results are organized into folders that help narrow searches. Click Register URL and fill in the required information. Submit only your main page, and Northern Light's crawler will index your entire site.

WebCrawler

www.webcrawler.com

WebCrawler indexes every word on your site up to one megabyte of text. You needn't submit keywords or categories. The keywords under which a page will be found in a WebCrawler search are the words on a page.

WebCrawler offers a few tips to help ensure your site a favorable index position. For example, using a uniquely descriptive title gives slightly more weight to titles than text or meta tags. Use short meta tags for keywords and a description/summary, but avoid repetition. Make sure the main page describes the site fully. Spamdexing (using keywords that don't match your site's content) could get your site eliminated from WebCrawler. Separately submit the URLs for the home page and the main subsidiary pages, but not for every document.

Yahoo

www.yahoo.com

Submissions to Yahoo (Figure 11.2) are controlled by people. Before submitting to Yahoo, you have to select a category and then narrow it down to subcategories. Once you have selected a specific category for your site, click the Add URL icon. If you have already submitted a site and want to make a change, select Change Form.

FIGURE 11.2
Submitting your site to Yahoo

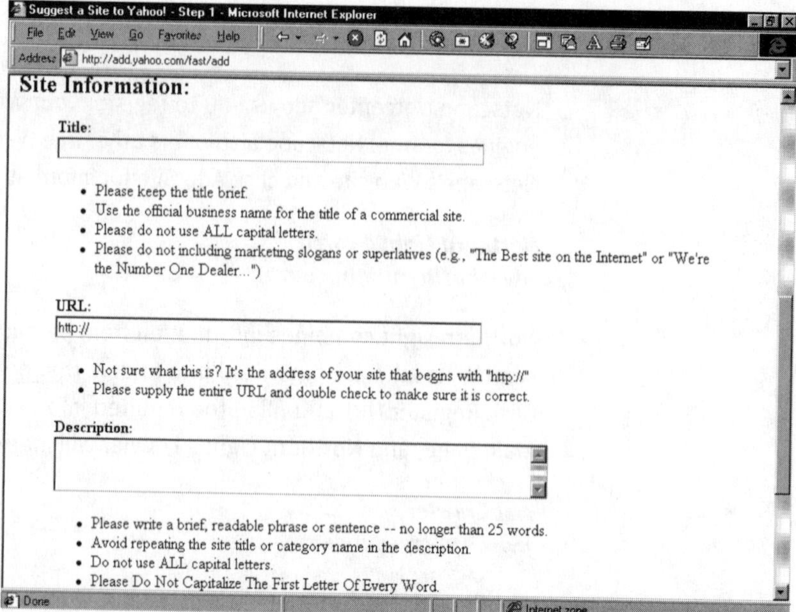

Yahoo suggests that before you begin the submission process, you read its information on how to suggest a site and its detailed explanation about how to find a category for your site. You should search Yahoo to confirm you are not already listed and confirm that you clicked Add URL at the appropriate category for your site.

You will then be asked to provide a title, URL, and brief description (25 words or less) of your site. Meta tags are ignored and Yahoo asks that you do not use phrases like "The best site on the Internet" in your description.

You then have the option to provide other category suggestions and time-sensitive information (if your site is going up or coming down on a particular date). Yahoo also asks for contact information.

More Information About Search Engines

In addition to *Getting Hits*, there are a few places you can learn more about search engines and how they operate. As search engines continue to evolve, it's a good idea to stay on top of developments by checking Search Engine Watch (**searchenginewatch.com**). You might also check out the book *Search Engines for the World Wide Web, 2nd Edition: Visual QuickStart Guide* by Alfred and Emily Glossbrenner (Peachpit Press).

Search Engine Watch includes a number of categories. The most useful (for storeowners) is the Search Engines Submission Tips. This guide explains how search engines find and rank Web pages with an emphasis on what Webmasters can do to improve how search engines list sites. The reviews, ratings, and tests on Search Engine Watch provide insight on how search engines perform in different areas and gives choices based on popularity and technical performance. The Search Engine Resources section is a collection of links to search engine-related sources.

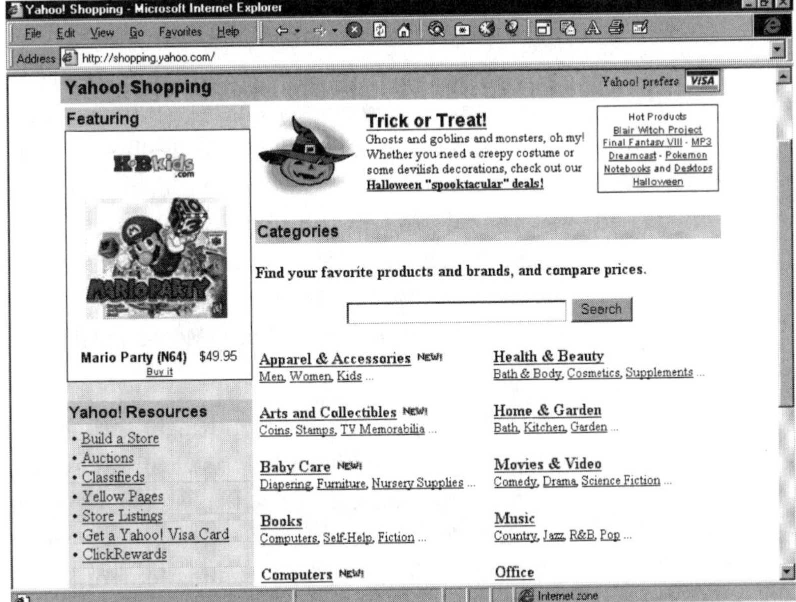

FIGURE 11.3
Many search engines and directories such as Yahoo direct potential shoppers toward Web stores.

Links

No matter how good your site is, not everyone will find it through one of the search engines. The inherent imperfection of search engines can lead potential customers to other sites. Don't despair. Search engines aren't the only way to draw customers to your site. Another common way for people to find your site is through a link on another site. But of course, people aren't just going to link their Web sites to yours for the heck of it. You can pursue links through exchanges and other incentives.

You can get links from other sites that are likely to be visited by your customers, topic-specific link pages and directories, award sites, or announce sites. You can shoot for a handful of well-researched, high-yield links, or you can try to link from every site under the sun. While a competing store is unlikely to link to your store (would you?), it isn't unheard of.

Widespread Links

The more links you have out there, the more likely someone will stumble across your site. As anyone who has done any Web surfing can tell you, it's amazing how quickly you can get from a site on one topic to another on a completely unrelated topic. It's like the "Six Degrees Of Kevin Bacon" game which claims that everyone in Hollywood is no more than six people away from having a relationship with the actor. (For example: John Travolta to Bacon. Travolta starred with Samuel L. Jackson in "Pulp Fiction." Jackson worked with Bruce Willis in "Die Hard With A Vengeance." Willis is married to Demi Moore. Moore and Bacon were both in "A Few Good Men.")

So it often goes with links. You might start at a site dedicated to classical music and within a few links wind up buying a new filter for your swimming pool. Trying to get links from a wide variety of sites operates on the idea that few people are so dull that they only have one topic of interest. Still, it's unlikely the proprietor of Ted's Fine Crystal will be interested in linking to Lucy's Death Metal Dungeon.

The broader the appeal of your store, the more likely you are to benefit from widespread linking. When we say broad, we don't necessarily mean your store has to be selling everything from dining room furniture to athletic shoes. It simply means you need to be selling something that a lot of people need. Clothes have an extremely broad appeal. Everybody wears them (unless they want to get locked up). Video games have a much more specific appeal. Be honest when evaluating your site's appeal.

Even stores selling a specific type of product can stray from that area when looking for likely links. For example, if you sell swimming pool–maintenance products, you can find potential customers all over the place—or at least wherever people with enough money to afford a pool might shop.

Assuming another site operator thinks it's worth her while, she'll link to your page if you link to hers. If you plan to go for a large number of links (and therefore offer a lot of links), you should organize them on a links page.

Staying Specific

Rather than shooting for links from every site that is remotely related to what you are selling, your time might be better spent looking for a few links that more likely to yield a better return. This takes a little more research and thought but is worth your while.

Even if you go for as many links as you can, you should still do enough research to guarantee that you have at least a few high-quality links. This section should help you do that. If you are to the point of running an online store and scouting out links, you are certainly aware of a number of sites to which you would like to be linked. Start here.

Contacting Similar Sites

As you move toward setting up your own store, you will probably spend some time looking at sites of similar interest. If you haven't already done so, bookmark the best sites you see. When you're up and running, contact those sites you would like to link with.

The best way to contact a prospective site is through email. If you can't find an email address on the site, you should find the Webmaster and slap him upside the head. Actually, we don't condone violence and slapping the Webmaster upside the head won't help you get a link anyway, so try "info@" or "webmaster@" or "postmaster@" followed by the domain name.

Use the word "link" in the subject line to differentiate your email from the rest. Keep your message brief. Tell the recipient what your site is all about, why you think a link would make sense, and give him the URL so he can check out your site for himself. Chances are he'll want a link from your site in return.

Link Exchanges

Link exchanges can be done on a barter system with similar sites. While looking for links, you'll almost certainly encounter a Webmaster from a more established site who will look down his nose and ask, "What's in it for me?" You should have an answer. Being linked to by any site is a good thing, but not everybody is quick to hand out a link. Stress the fact that your customers will be people who will also want to visit his site. Flattery might get you somewhere, too. Tell the Webmaster that, while you hope some of his visitors will link to your site and eventually become customers, you're sure they'll still return to his outstanding site. In other words, he'll gain some of your visitors and lose none of his own.

If you can't get him to link to your site, you may still want to link to his for the benefit of your customers, assuming the site contains some useful information. Although it's not legally required, you should get permission. Don't try to pass off an external link as a link to another part of your site unless you want to be known as a sneaky, conniving, little weasel.

Banner Exchange Services

LinkExchange (www.linkexchange.com) works as a free advertising exchange agent between sites. By joining LinkExchange (Figure 11.4) you display banner ads for other members, and they do the same for you. LinkExchange screens all member sites and does not allow those that display inappropriate content.

Members determine where they want their banner add to be shown by selecting one or two appropriate categories. A rating system and filtering technology help ensure that banners displayed on your site are appropriate for your audience and that your banner is displayed on sites that can help your site the most.

Surf Point is the LinkExchange directory. Simply categorize your site for inclusion. LinkExchange can offer the sevice for free because of the support of its Friends and Sponsors. Friends and Sponsors receive additional services for a fee.

Surf Point lists more than 100,000 sites, including several thousand shopping outlets.

Beseen's 1-for-1 Banner Exchange, called LookSmart Clicks (www.looksmartclicks.com), offers free targeted advertising for your site and detailed ad-effectiveness reporting. For every banner you show on your site, you receive a banner on another member's site. This differs from some banner exchanges that offer 2-for-1 exchanges, meaning your ad is shown once for every two ads you show on your site. The Smart Targeting feature automatically sends your ads where you get the best click-through. When you turn on Smart Targeting, ads are sent to a variety of segments. As certain segments bring more visits to your site, those segments become regular advertising stops for your banner.

BannerSwap (www.bannerswap.com) gives you one half credit for every ad shown on your site, meaning you must show two ads for your ad to be show once on another member's site. You receive an additional half credit each time someone clicks through an ad on your site.

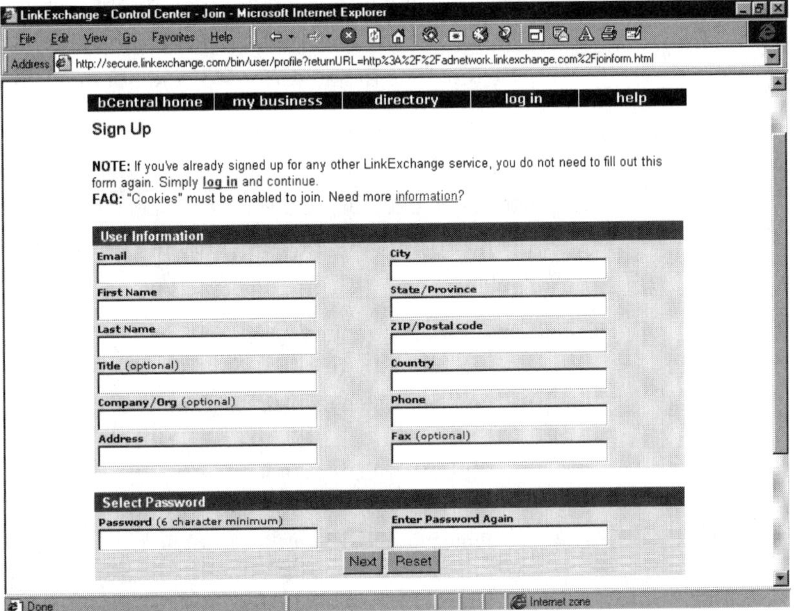
LinkExchange - Control Center - Join - Microsoft Internet Explorer

File Edit View Go Favorites Help

Address http://secure.linkexchange.com/bin/user/profile?returnURL=http%3A%2F%2Fadnetwork.linkexchange.com%2Fjoinform.html

bCentral home | my business | directory | log in | help

Sign Up

NOTE: If you've already signed up for any other LinkExchange service, you do not need to fill out this form again. Simply **log in** and continue.
FAQ: "Cookies" must be enabled to join. Need more information?

User Information

Email | City
First Name | State/Province
Last Name | ZIP/Postal code
Title (optional) | Country
Company/Org (optional) | Phone
Address | Fax (optional)

Select Password

Password (6 character minimum) | Enter Password Again

Next | Reset

Done | Internet zone

Figure 11.4
LinkExchange's sign-up form.

Friends and Acquaintances

As was the case with Tronix, you can look to friends, acquaintances, business associates, and even customers to link to your site. Chances are they'll be immediately receptive to your inquiry, and if you're having a hard time getting links, this is a good place to start.

Customer sites are usually good selections, assuming their sites and your store have the same topic. If you buy products from a small manufacturer or craftsperson, she'll probably be happy to send customers to your site, where they may well buy more of her product. The more of her product they buy from you, the more you'll buy from her.

Award Sites

Award sites can be beneficial in two ways. After you have exhausted the sites that you are familiar with, and before you go diving into a general search engine hoping to find something useful, check out a few award sites. Obviously, getting honored or obtaining a link from one of the award sites should be a boon for your business. However, only a fortunate few sites are so rewarded, and not many of them are online stores.

Even if your site isn't honored, though, award sites can guide you toward some of the outstanding sites in your field. Although inclusion on an award site doesn't guarantee a site to be spectacular, there is a better chance you will find high-quality links there than you will by using a general search engine.

Some top award sites are:

- Cool Site of the Day (**cool.infi.net**).
- TooCool (**toocool.com**).
- ProjectCool (**www.projectcool.com**).
- Netscape What's Cool (**www.netscape.com/netcenter/cool.html?cp=homo9cnw1**).

Announce Sites

Announce sites are directories of new Web sites. They are yet another way to get your store noticed. Keep in mind, these are only temporary listings, otherwise most of them would have to take the "New" out of their names.

Netscape's What's New

www.netscape.com/netcenter/new.html?cp=hom09cnew

Netscape's What's New includes the day's new Web sites (ranked on a scale of 1 to 10) and also offers The Best of What's New, where the top new sites are highlighted.

What's New Too

newtoo.manifest.com

What's New Too is a user-customizable announcement service that says it is updated daily and posts new sites within 36 hours of submission. What's New Too does not filter or limit the kinds of sites that are posted. Personal home pages, informational text files, and product announcements all are welcome.

Today's Sites lists and links to all sites added to the directory within the last 24 hours. The Custom form allows you to create a personalized Today's Sites page and get lists of new pages that fit your criteria each day. Users can also search the directory by date.

To submit a site, click the Add icon and provide your site's title, URL, and category; the name of your organization; your geographic location; a site description; and contact information.

Nerd World What's New

www.nerdworld.com/whatsnew.html

Nerd World's What's New lists sites by category, including Shopping. Nerd World suggests businesses include a company name, street address, city, state, ZIP code, phone number, and fax.

Link Pages and Directories

Link pages and directories—much like award sites—are not only good places to be linked from but also valuable searching grounds for potential links.

InfoSpace

www.infospace.com

InfoSpace is a leading directory and content aggregator on the Internet. InfoSpace includes an E-Shopping category that groups some of the world's biggest stores into a number of categories. Getting listed here certainly won't hurt your business.

InfoSpace also attracts potential customers to its site with content offerings such as Yellow Pages, White Pages, and city guides. There is also a Business Guide that helps people find your business Web site.

InfoSpace offers three options for ways to get listed, including one free option. Hot Sites, the first ones listed, are limited to just ten per category and cost $95 per month. Priority Sites are listed next and cost $99 a year. Free Sites are shown after the top two levels and include a brief description and a link to your site.

Webscout
www.webscout.com

Webscout asks you to select a category (Arts, Business & Investment, Computers, and so on) and then a subcategory. Each subcategory has 15 or 20 links with a short review of the site. You can also search the reviews for a particular subject.

Webscout's SuperSearch allows you to select a search engine from a floating window and search by keywords. You can also nominate a site for inclusion, but Webscout says it is "extremely selective," so be sure your site is in top shape before submitting.

Beaucoup
www.beaucoup.com

Beaucoup can help you find a search engine, directory, or index for your specific needs. Pick a category and you'll get a list of links to a number of topic-specific search engines or informational sites.

Beaucoup's Super Search allows users to query ten engines at once. As of this writing, the Shopping area was listed as "Coming Soon."

Bounty Programs

A bounty program is one of the better and more innovative ways to promote your store. As mentioned elsewhere in this book, Amazon.com's bounty program has over 10,000 member sites. That's a lot of links, and it is all done by people who actually seek out Amazon.

You can set up a bounty program as well, but before you rush out to start one, consider the needs you must fulfill in order to run a successful bounty program:

1. **Fulfillment.** You must be able to properly provide good fulfillment because people linking to your site as bounty members will quickly drop links to stores that provide bad service.

2. **Accounting.** You need to have a way to quickly account for sales by each bounty member. Amazon does this by having associate sites include a code in the URL that lets the Amazon.com server know specifically who sent the surfer over for the sale. Sales are then written to a database that at the end of the month adds up the total sales and writes out checks. Obviously this would require some good technical infrastructure on your part.

3. **Wide appeal.** You need to sell a product that will have a broad enough appeal that people will already be out and about talking about products you're selling. One reason Amazon's bounty program works so well is people on its sites are constantly discussing books. Now, your appeal doesn't have to be as wide as a bookstore's, but as a rule you shouldn't start a bounty program for things that aren't being discussed on Web pages very often.

In addition to those three key items, you need to promote your bounty program. Although customers will often start associate sites after visiting your store, you should be proactive in building your network of associate sites. Get up and surf! Find sites. Home pages and fan sites are some of the best that are dedicated to the same interests or products as your store. Send the Webmaster or site producer an email explaining your program and its benefits and let them know about how to join.

TIP ▸ ***The big sites on the Internet are actually forcing stores to pay up front in some cases or pay bigger than normal bounties for signing on to a particular bounty program. Depending on the site and its reach, this may be a necessary expense. Not every site will have this power, but don't be surprised to see this trend.***

What you want to accomplish with a bounty program is to first get people to recommend products you sell and then provide the link specifically for that product. The more links provided from one site the better. That means they're recommending more and more products for people to buy. You can accomplish your goal by educating your member sites.

For example, Amazon.com sends out a newsletter to members. You can also supply bounty members with other goodies, such as news on upcoming products (so they'll prepare links to them). You can even provide templates and graphics for their sites. In short, treat them as part of your sales team and shower them with information and tools that make it easier to be part of your program.

LinkShare
www.linkshare.com

LinkShare brings Web businesses together by providing tools, technology, and services. LinkShare's network, software, and business services provide the platform on which any type and any number of cross-selling, cross-referral relationships can be established and maintained. Affiliate partnerships through LinkShare can be structured to drive traffic, registrations, sales, or a combination of objectives.

Here's how the partnerships work: The affiliate puts links from the merchant on its site. These links market the merchant's goods or services on the affiliate's site. Visitors who click through are sent to a specified page of the merchant's site. If the visitor completes the action desired by the merchant (such as buying an item), the affiliate is compensated. LinkShare facilitates the partnership and tracks all elements of the transaction.

Be Free
www.befree.com

After you sign up with Be Free, an "implementation engineer" guides you through the process. For ongoing customer service, you are assigned a client development manager who answers your questions and helps you improve your affiliate sales channel.

Be Free also offers the following optional services:

- Affiliate management.
- Affiliate application review.
- Check writing.
- Ad trafficking.

Online Malls

Not surprisingly, there are hundreds of online malls. But because online stores all exist on a shopper's computer, a mall doesn't provide the same advantage of geographic convenience that a traditional mall does. However, it does give a merchant a chance to be included on a mall that is home to thousands of other stores. The real use for online malls is to provide smaller merchants a common portal that can provide an attraction to their individual stores or goods. For example, a user might not be attracted to your invidual custom clothing store, but he might find you by hearing about and then visiting customclothesmall.com. Being listed with other popular or similar stores might attract customers.

Advantages of Online Malls

The major advantage of an online mall is promotion. Many stores on the Internet have stand-alone sites and also join online malls. Some malls also comprise stores that use the same store-building or -hosting services (such as Amazon.com's zShops or Yahoo Store). Although these malls might send some some traffic to your site by offering huge directories or existing Web traffic, focused malls are usually the best option. Some malls also enable merchants to cross-sell products within the mall or to share shopping carts.

Successful Internet malls become destination sites. People turn to online malls for the same reason they turn to search engines—they can easily find what they are looking for. For example, someone might start an online mall called fishingstuff.com and, instead of selling everything on their own, they might sell "mall space" to hundreds of stores that sell fishing products. This could include boating equipment, fishing rods, lures, and so on. At the same time, a boating store that is registered with this mall could also exist as a standalone store.

There are also temporary malls that are built around holidays or special promotions, and regional malls.

Disadvantages of Online Malls

Many online malls have requirements such as rent or certain style guidelines you must follow. Premium malls such as AOL's Shopping Channel can be expensive to join. It is key to track sales and visits that are due to your presence on an online mall. If you aren't earning a return on your investment, stay away.

Unless you really think there is a compelling argument to join, avoid malls that demand your exclusivity. In promotional terms, malls are just another gateway to your store. Why would you choose just one and shut yourself off from other excellent mall opportunities?

Some Top Online Malls

Cyberspace malls, like traditional malls, are not created equal. Here are a few of the biggest you might want to look into.

iMall

www.imall.com

iMall (Figure 11.5) launched in January 1996 and has since signed an agreement to merge with Excite@Home. There are more than 1,000 stores located at iMall, and merchants choose from 12 categories in which to be included.

iMall provides merchant clients with order-tracking and -compilation services that can be sent to the merchant via email on a daily or weekly basis for final processing and expediting. iMall uses a secure server and the Cybercash system for online-transaction verification and processing.

For information on becoming an iMall merchant, click the iMall Merchant link, read the instructions, and fill out the form.

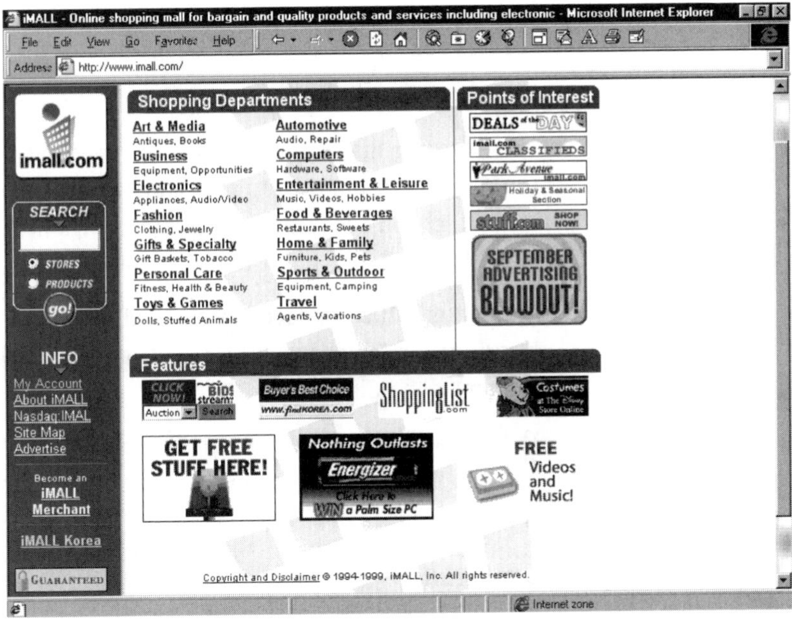

FIGURE 11.5
The iMall home page.

America Online Shopping

www.aol.com/shopping/

AOL Shopping is host to some well-known retailers such as J. Crew, Brooks Brothers, Eddie Bauer, 1-800-FLOWERS, The Sharper Image, and Starbucks. That's because inclusion here costs the kind of money that only established retailers can afford to spend. However, you should keep an eye on AOL's rates. If you ever have an enormous enough advertising budget (and we sincerely hope you do), AOL and its 10 million or so members is a nice market.

Amazon.com's zShop

www.amazon.com

A relatively new service, Amazon.com's zShop service lets you set up a store on Amazon.com itself. Amazon.com then drives traffic to your store and lets you use its 1-Click shopping service to sell your wares to the Web's top shopping service.

eBay and FairMarket

www.ebay.com

www.fairmarket.com

There are two major auction-oriented malls to consider—eBay and FairMarket. eBay is the top personal auction site on the Web. While eBay doesn't let you set up a specific store from a mall standpoint, it draws major traffic to individual items you might want to sell.

FairMarket's AuctionPlace is a customized auction solution created by a partnership between FairMarket, Microsoft, Excite@Home, and Ticketmaster Online-City Search.

The FairMarket Auction Network is a business-to-person and person-to-person alliance of auction sites that also includes auctions on Lycos, Tripod, XOOM.com, ZDNet, and more.

Other Malls

Most of the major portals (including MSN, Yahoo, Lycos, and Excite) offer malls as well. The major selling point is the traffic they can potentially draw to your store. Services like Excite and Yahoo, which offer online store-building, can offer two malls—one for merchants willing to pay top-dollar for extra services, and a catch-all mall for its store-hosting clients.

Working with Online and Offline Media

The amount of online media dedicated to the Web seems to grow every day. If you feel you have a truly unique or compelling Web store, you should consider putting together a press package and sending it out to some of the top Web-oriented online and offline magazines (Table 11.1). Even if you decide not to contact them, these can be excellent resources.

There will also be online and traditional magazines related to your specific industry. For example, if you sell rock- and ice-climbing gear, you should do whatever you can to get mentioned in magazines like *Outside*, *Men's Journal*, and similar media. This brings up another point: While online promotion is important, don't neglect traditional avenues of promotion. The simplest tip is to include your Web address on all pomotional materials, even if you get more business through a brick-and-mortar store. But there is more.

Tale 11.1 Online and Print Web-Oriented Media

InternetWeek (www.internetwk.com)
TechWeb (www.techweb.com)
Internet World (www.internetworld.com)
Internet.com (www.internet.com)
WebDeveloper.com (www.webdeveloper.com)
Inter@ctive Week (www.interactiveweek.com)
ZDNet E-Business (www.zdnet.com/enterprise/e-business/)
ZDNet (www.zdnet.com)
CommerceNet (www.commerce.net)
E Business Magazine (www.hp.com/Ebusiness/)
Wilson Internet (www.wilsonweb.com)

Public and Media Relations

A strong public relations campaign can be even more effective than an advertising campaign, and unless you decide to hire a PR firm, will cost far less. A positive story about your business has a stronger impact on potential customers than does paid advertising because people are more likely to believe a third-party endorsement than an advertisment.

However, you need to present reporters with a story that they feel will be interesting fo their readers. That requires some thought and effort. While a professional PR firm can cost hundreds or thousands of dollars per month with no guarantee of results, you can stay within your budget constraints by doing the work yourself.

Why my Store?

Before you begin pitching your store for coverage, you must decide what angle will interest a reporter. Does your store sell unique or rare items? Does it specialize in products that are currently garnering heavy media attention? Is there an interesting story (unprecedented growth, unconventional background) behind your business?

Contacting the Press

You shouldn't call a reporter or editor out of the blue and start spouting your ideas. Instead, learn a little about the publication (what kind of stories does it publish? has a similar story already been run recently?) and to whom you will direct your press release and media kit. If you can contact the relevant reporter directly, do so. If not, send your information to the specific section editor.

Here are a few tips for putting together and sending an inexpensive media kit.

- **Use company letterhead.** If you don't have any, get some. Include your company's name, logo (if you have one), mailing address, email address, phone number, fax number, and Web address. Also include the name of a contact person and a good time to call.

- **Include an honest description** of your site, what you sell, what special services or content you provide, how long you've been in business, how well your store is doing, and why it is of paramount importance to the readership. Reporters are interested in who, what, where, when, and why.

- **Don't use terms** like, "Hands down the best Web site of its kind." Don't use exclamation points. Be reserved yet confident. Read, re-read, and then have a friend who writes well edit your press release. No mistakes. No typos. No outlandish claims. When reporters or editors see a press release that screams like a used car salesman, they cringe. Then they throw it in the trash.

- **Now that you know not to be obnoxious**, sell your site. Everyone who reads your kit should say, "This sounds pretty cool" and check out your site.

- **Don't worry about mailing** out enormous press kits to every publication that might have an interest in your site. Chances are you are on a slim budget and won't be able to afford printing and mailing dozens of bulky, glossy press kits unless you know you are going to get a fantastic response. And you don't know that.

- **If possible, send the information to a specific person.** Of course you have to make sure you send it to the *right* specific person. If that information isn't readily available, a phone call should get the answer you need.

- **Don't send out media kits until your store is ready to be featured.** If a reporter decides to do a story and your Web store is in rough shape, the story will reflect that. Send your package so that it arrives early in the week, allowing you to make your followup contact later in the same week.

- **Follow up with a phone call** a couple of days after you think the package has arrived. Include in your letter an approximate time when the reporter can expect this call. It's easy to reject a letter. If an editor or reporter thinks your online store is unworthy of a mention in her magazine, make her tell you so.

- **If the answer is no,** don't respond angrily. It will immediately hurt your chances that the publication will do a story in the future. Ask the reporter what she looks for in a story idea and if she might consider doing a story in the future. Be patient but persistent.

- **If the answer is yes,** immediately offer help. Make the reporter's job easier by being cooperative and by answering interview questions in a thoughtful but concise manner. Don't be afraid to offer information you think is relevant to the story. And, after the story runs, a thank you note is always nice.

Never Underestimate Promotion

Can you imagine where Madonna would be without the power of promotion? She'd be little Madonna Ciccone, the singer down at the corner bar. Now, thanks to constant image changes, well-timed controversies, and a knack for getting her name in the news, she's one of the most famous people on the planet. No matter what you think of her musical ability, Madonna is a marketing genius. You should hope to do as much.

No matter how great your store is, it isn't going anywhere without a little promotion. Promoting your store correctly on the Internet can bring you countless visitors without ever spending a cent. The right search engine placement or the right link could help vault you past all your competitors. However, even expert promotion won't save a lousy store from an early death.

There's nothing like a little free advertising. However, you'll probably wind up spending money on advertising eventually. Now that we've showed you how to promote your store without spending any money, it's on to Chapter 12, where we'll show you how to get the most for your advertising dollar.

CHAPTER TWELVE

Advertising

Advertising will be a key element of your store's success. In fact, when some of the largest Web stores have gone public or gained additional financing, one of their primary reasons for doing so was so they could spend more money on advertising. Now most of the major online retailers advertise regularly on radio and television. With so much competition for Web traffic, advertising can be an essential means of spreading the word about your store.

How do you plan an advertising campaign that gets you the most return for your dollar? There are a number of options to consider, both on the Internet and in traditional media such as radio, television, newspapers, magazines, and direct mail. This chapter is intended to help you weigh all of your advertising options, both on and off the Internet. We'll cover when, where, and what to advertise.

Why, When, and What to Advertise?

Before you worry about *where* to place ads, you should decide *why*, *when*, and *what*. Here, an advertising agency, even a small one, can be helpful. But before you pick up the phone (and your checkbook) to get the expert advice of an ad agency, consider some of the following tips.

Why?

The biggest justification for advertising your store is not the premise of immediate sales. As you'll see a bit later in this chapter, it is difficult to guarantee an immediate return on your investment in online advertising (or any advertising medium for that matter). Most advertising does not immediately generate large new sales. Rather, what advertising can offer is the ability to capture new customers who over time will spend a lot of money and make the strategy pay off in the long run. In fact, most advertising done by stores on the Internet is to capture first-time customers and boost traffic, not to gain immediate payback.

Advertising is most beneficial for stores that expect to secure extensive repeat traffic. Advertising can also work well in the case of stores selling items with large profit margins, because they require fewer actual sales to make a return on the investment.

This doesn't mean you shouldn't advertise if your store isn't one that will generate a loyal customer base or if your margins are slim. However, it does mean that you should be more conservative in your spending in order to guarantee a good return on your advertising investment. This is why smaller store-owners and stores selling niche products must rely more on good word of mouth, public relations, community involvement, and techniques like swapping links and strong search engine placement—all the techniques we talked about in earlier chapters.

When?

As you prepare to launch an advertising campaign, you must also prepare for the added attention your store will receive as a result. One of the biggest blunders you can make is to advertise your store only to have new customers arrive at an unfinished site with a non-functioning order system and major items out of stock. In that case, you have simply advertised that your store is not worth patronizing.

So don't advertise too early. Build your store, get the kinks worked out, and until you are prepared to widen your campaign, gently test the advertising waters. Web stores shouldn't advertise until they are ready to handle the hoped-for influx of shoppers and their operations systems are able to deliver the kind of quality customer service that turns first-time buyers into repeat customers.

What?

What do you say about your site? The more comprehensive the site, the tougher this question is to answer. It may take a variety of messages to convey the feeling of your store. However, there are two critical messages to deliver: that your store offers advantages because it is on the Internet, and that your store is somehow different from, and better than, the competition.

The first message differentiates your store from competing retail locations to mail-order catalogs. To convey this message, you need to clearly demonstrate the advantages of online shopping. For example, that customers can place orders at any time without having to deal with pushy salespeople; that regular customers receive immediate notification of new product arrivals; that your site offers search capabilities that make accessing your unsurpassed selection very easy. Anything that shows the customer how smart it is to shop on the Web is worth mentioning.

Fogdog Sports has an effective television ad that emphasizes its motto, "Your anytime, anywhere sports store." A baseball player taking batting practice in an empty stadium in the middle of the night breaks his bat. A man in a dog costume (Fogdog we assume) suddenly appears and hands the player a new bat. Anytime, anywhere—even alone in a darkened stadium, the ad implies—you can shop at Fogdog.

Where the first message is directed at people who may not have considered shopping online, the second is aimed at attracting people who are already shopping online but may not have found your store. In this case, you must identify the advantages of shopping at your store rather than a similar one whether it is the fact that you have better prices, more shipping options, the best customer service, or something else special.

Also use advertising to establish your store's brand identity. This often involves nothing more than delivering a direct message containing your Web site address and a brief, memorable image of your store. For example, Amazon.com spends much of its time reminding millions of people of the Amazon.com URL. Before expanding its offerings beyond books, it also dubbed itself "Earth's Biggest Bookstore." Now Amazon.com runs frequent humorous radio advertisements touting its online auctions as it competes with other offerings such as eBay, boxLot, and Yahoo Auctions.

Where Should I Advertise?

Once you have a handful of solid advertising concepts, it is just as important to advertise in the right place. Just because your store is on the Internet, the Internet is not necessarily the best place or only place you'll want to advertise. While the Net is probably the first place you'll advertise, partly because of the lower cost, most successful Internet stores also place ads in trade magazines and in newspapers, as well as on television and radio. Two years ago television advertisements for Web stores were rare. Now most of the major online commerce sites, such as Amazon.com, Fogdog Sports, and eBay advertise on television and the radio, with more coming every day.

Online

Online stores will naturally find customers through online advertising. Customers can click on a banner ad and instantly be transported to a store or a page with an item ready to be bought. The majority of online company advertising takes place online. We'll cover exactly where to advertise online later in this chapter.

Online advertising is relatively simple and inexpensive, but even so, it is important to understand that spending all of your advertising money online is not wise. You should reserve a good portion of your budget for advertising through more traditional media.

Newspapers

Newspapers, being regional, help online stores advertise in a specific geographic location. Because newspaper readers tend to be more affluent, educated, and older, advertising in newspapers can also help you target a nice demographic niche. In addition, many newspapers have added regular sections dedicated to Internet and technology news and lifestyle. People also turn to newspapers to find the latest sales. All of these factors make newspaper advertising a solid choice.

Rather than focusing on large daily newspapers, small weekly, alternative, and university papers can provide a less expensive outlet, with readerships that fit into basic online user demographics. The best way to purchase ads for these newspaper outlets is through advertising networks that run your single ad across the country among their participating newspapers.

TIP ▸ ***Many college students have a certain amount of disposable income, computers, and fast and free Internet access via their university account. Most universities publish student newspapers that are generally funded by small ads that are placed by local business owners. According to statistics, the average college newspaper is read by 62 percent of the students in its market. Ad syndicates can help you place ads in these papers. This is often done at no cost to the advertiser since they are commissioned by college newspapers to represent them to advertisers. Some well-known college advertising syndicates are shown in Table 12.1.***

TABLE 12.1 COLLEGE NEWSPAPER ADVERTISING SYNDICATES

American Passage Media Corporation
100 West Harrison
Suite S-150
Seattle, WA 98119-4129
800-359-6676

Cass Communications
1800 Sherman Avenue, Suite 300
Evanston, IL 60201-3769
www.casscom.com/college/

AllCampus Media
26 Castillian Drive
Santa Barbara, CA 93117
805-968-8007
www.allcampus.com

Alternative newspapers have evolved tremendously since the counterculture publications of the 1960s. According to the Association of Alternative Newsweeklies, the combined circulation of alternative weeklies is 7.5 million, with an estimated weekly readership of 18.8 million. The AAN says nearly 80 percent of readers are between the ages of 18 and 49, the average household income is more than $50,000, and more than 70 percent have attended college.

The AAN has two ad networks—the Alternative Weekly Network (**www.awn.org**) and Ruxton Group (**www.ruxton.com**)—that can offer any combination of a regional or national ad buy.

More information on alternative newspapers is available from:

The Association of Alternative Newsweeklies
1600 L Street NW, Suite 316
Washington, DC 20036
www.aan.org
202-822-1955

You can obtain a membership roster, which includes addresses, telephone numbers, and staff information, as well as helpful circulation and demographic data from this organization.
Another source to contact is:

Alternative Press Center
P.O. Box 33109
Baltimore, MD 21218
www.altpress.org
410-243-2471

This organization produces the quarterly *Alternative Press Index*, a quarterly subject index to more than 250 alternative, and left-leaning periodicals, newspapers, and magazines.

Magazines

When advertising in magazines, concentrate on publications that offer readerships with a natural interest in your store's offerings. National magazines such as *Time* or *Newsweek* are a waste of time unless you happen to have established a major store such as Amazon.com.

TIP ▸ ***Many magazines have begun to research their readerships' tendency to be computer owners and online users. Before you consider buying magazine advertising, see if they have this information. If you sell gardening tools and only five percent of a particular gardening magazine's readers are online, advertising in that magazine is probably not worth the effort.***

Joe's Take: *Many monthly magazines cover the Internet—in fact, almost too many. Most of these magazines print a list of Web sites to visit in every issue. They may have a theme or feature article along with a list of Web sites that best cover the particular category. If you happen to have an outstanding Web site, you might find your store listed. Much to your surprise, you may gain a new group of customers who found your company in a magazine. It happened to me and was a pleasant surprise.*

Radio

Broadcast and cable television advertising are still the domain of the largest online stores. However, radio advertising can be a useful secondary advertising avenue. Radio can target an audience more precisely than television. More importantly, many people listen to the radio while at work where they actually have their only means of accessing the Internet. Amazon.com and CDNow.com are two prominent online retailers currently advertising on the radio. Table 12.2 shows some geographical areas that could provide the highest return on your radio advertising dollar.

Table 12.2 Top Internet-Using Metro Areas

By Absolute Numbers	By Population Percentage
1. New York	1. San Francisco
2. Los Angeles	2. Washington, DC
3. Washington, DC	3. Seattle
4. San Francisco	4. Boston
5. Chicago	5. New York
6. Boston	6. Chicago
7. Philadelphia	7. Philadelphia
8. Detroit	8. Dallas
9. Dallas	9. Los Angeles
10. Seattle	10. Detroit

Source: September 1997 "Local Information on the Net" by Scarborough Research, Arlen Communications Inc., and Find/SVP.

Cable TV

As Internet stores have begun advertising on television, cable has become a popular outlet, especially for small and medium-sized stores. Cable provides a better method of matching special-interest advertisements with related programming. For example, a sporting goods store could advertise on ESPN, while a record store might chose MTV.

Direct Mail

Direct mail, although often overlooked, is a great way to advertise a product or service. The catalog industry is the most obvious user of direct mail. Since the Web store industry is closer in style and workings to catalogs than it is to actual retail stores, direct mail can be a good advertising outlet.

Where Should I Advertise on the Internet?

Conventional wisdom says you should focus your advertising on search engines and on the top 20 Web sites. However, as the Web grows and audiences become more widespread, advertisers will move beyond the major areas and explore alternative sites. In many cases, niche sites will return the highest number of interested customers per impression.

Classified Advertising Sites

The Web is rapidly becoming a leading source of classified advertising from newspapers around the country. While classifieds are usually used to advertise used equipment and other items on the Web, it is also a good place to advertise in general. Not only can you advertise your store via a classified ad, you might consider buying banners that appear in various classified sections.

Excite Classifieds

classifieds.excite.com

Excite Classifieds (Figure 12.1) provides advertising across multiple categories through some of the Web's most visited sites. Formerly Classifieds2000, more than $500 million in goods and services it advertises weekly, and more than 2.1 million users access the listings database.

Customers select a category, then a subcategory, and narrow their search by brand, price range, and other options. This leads the customers to a list of items, with prices and a phone number. Customers then click on a desired item and receive a description. Categories include computers/ software, vehicles, general merchandise, and more. Each is broken down into numerous subcategories.

One buy places ads into a targeted Excite Classifieds category within six search engines (Excite, Infoseek, LookSmart, Netcenter, Webcrawler, and Snap!) as well as other sites like Bigfoot, GeoCities, NetGuide, iVillage, AT&T Worldnet, and ZDNet.

Excite Classifieds helps customers locate items based on preferences such as type, price range, and more.

Classified Warehouse

www.classifiedwarehouse.com

The Classified Warehouse allows users to search classified databases of hundreds of online and offline publications in North America. One buy allows the advertiser to place ads in these publications.

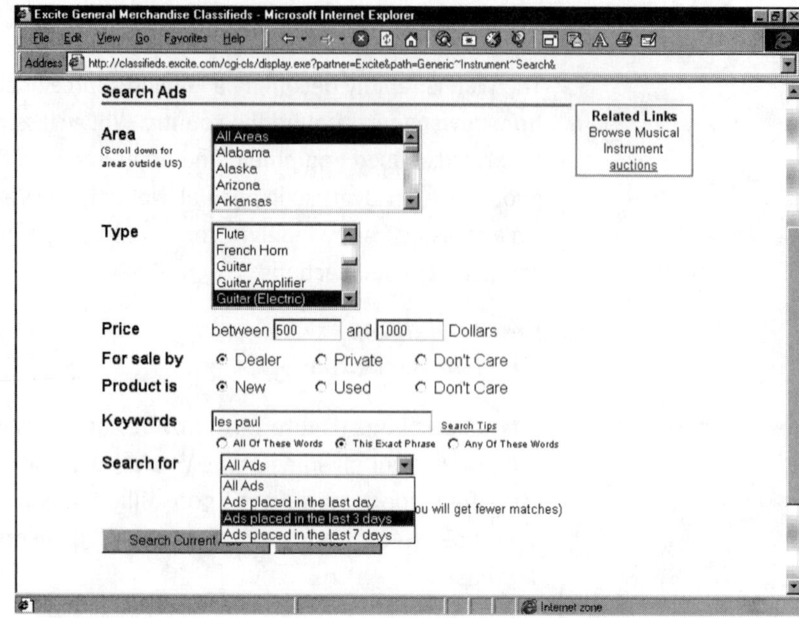

FIGURE 12.1
More than two million users look through Excite Classifieds every day.

AdQuest 3D Classifieds

www.adquest3d.com

AdQuest 3D Classifieds collects classified ads from hundreds of newspapers throughout the United States. AdQuest also provides Internet services, including Web site promotion, through links on AdQuest's site. The site has a list of member publications, most of which are small newspapers or advertisers. It breaks its classifieds into several categories such as merchandise, services, and automotive, each of which is further divided into subcategories. To place an ad, contact one of AdQuest's member publications directly, and your ad appears on the AdQuest site.

Advertising Networks

As advertising on the Internet expands, so too will the role of advertising networks. Information on a number of advertising networks can be found at Adbility.com (**www.adbility.com**). Part of the site is dedicated to advertising networks, brokers, and representatives, and in some cases includes evaluations and warnings about potential scams. The site also covers Pay-Per-Click Advertising Networks and Brokers, Affiliate Programs, Banner Exchange Services, and more.

DoubleClick

www.doubleclick.net

DoubleClick offers a number of Internet advertising solutions. The core of the DoubleClick Network Is DoubleClick Select, a collection of premium sites represented exclusively and available for custom ad buys and sponsorships. The network of sites is coupled with the company's DART targeting technology. Online reporting lets advertisers know how their campaign is performing and what types of users are seeing and clicking on their ads.

DoubleClick Local is a solution for regional and local businesses. It helps regional businesses advertise on national name-brand sites, while targeting and reaching only their local markets.

DoubleClick Shopping is a boutique shopping environment for online merchants that offers the reach of a portal.

DoubleClick International allows advertisers to reach users in more than 80 countries with one buy and one contact. Advertisers can also conduct campaigns in local markets and can target users in their own language.

AdKnowledge

www.adknowledge.com

The AdKnowledge System includes the Planner, a pre-buy and planning module that helps you make informed media decisions; Campaign Manager; SmartBanner, a technology that automates the targeting and serving of Web advertising campaigns; and Reporter, customized reports during and after campaigns.

In September 1999 it was announced that Engage Technologies, a provider of profile-driven Internet marketing solutions, had moved to acquire AdKnowledge, so watch this site for changes.

Adsmart Network

www.adsmart.net

Adsmart's network comprises more than 300 Web sites totaling more than 2 billion monthly impressions. The network includes brand-name sites in seven divisions: sports, business/finance, technology, travel, women, automobile, and NetFuerza (its Hispanic division). Targeted audience groups include small office/home office, young professionals, mothers, affluent customers, children, college students, music enthusiasts, and more.

Adsmart's technology offers targeting by content, keyword, geography, user profile, filters, and time and day of week.

@dventure
www.ad-venture.com

@dventure says it assures the ideal selection of advertising opportunities and accurate, real-time reports. The @dventure Network offers Run of Network and Site Specific buys and the opportunity to target by demographic, business size, and time of day.

24/7 Media
www.247media.com

The 24/7 Network accepts only sites with at least one million page views per month and a visible name brand and asks for exclusive representation.

The ContentZone is for smaller sites.

Adauction
www.adauction.com

Adauction is a business-to-business e-commerce service for buying and selling media—online, print, broadcast, and out-of-home. Sellers must have more than 100,000 unique users and 750,000 page views per month, as well as offer recognized brands.

Burst Media
www.burstmedia.com

Burst Media collects information about the content of its members' Web sites and the demographics of the sites' visitors with the goal of providing the best results for advertisers and members. On the basis of this data, it then directs advertisers toward sites on which they should consider advertising. Burst has had some rather high-end clients, but represents sites of various sizes. It helps manage more than 13 million advertising impressions per day in more than 400 purchase categories.

Link Ad Exchanges

As your store gains in popularity, you will correspond with other Web merchants and Web site operators, many of whom will offer to exchange advertising links. These simple links can lead to new customers. Although links from non-related sites can lead to new customers, you are more likely to gain customers when exchanging links with a site of similar interest. If you specialize in greeting cards, there is always a chance that a visitor to a comic book–related site will also be interested in greeting cards. However, a Web site that is dedicated to designing Christmas ornaments is more likely to send real customers your way.

The number of hits a particular site receives is another important factor to consider when exchanging links. It is better to have a link from an unrelated site that receives thousands of hits a day than one that is related to your site's offerings, but rarely visited.

Some Web sites will offer to link to your site for a small fee. You should certainly investigate the opportunity closely before making an agreement. Study the offering Web site. Does it provide information that will attract customers to your link? How many hits does the site receive? If the site has a hit counter, watch it for a week. Is it spinning like a traveling salesman's odometer, or does it remind you more of the little old lady from Pasadena? Does the site appear to be well maintained or is it just one of many offered free of charge by an ISP?

The more link exchanges you acquire, the better the chances you will win new customers. Don't be afraid to initiate link exchanges. You can easily find related sites by using a search engine and offer link exchanges to the sites that impress you the most. Sites that offer link exchanges might also be worth advertising on. However, consider that most sites using link exchanges are personal homepages with a fairly small amount of traffic. For more on link exchanges, see Chapter 11.

Advertising Directly on Small Sites

Depending on your store's focus, you might want to reach the audiences of narrow-interest sites. There are many excellent small sites that reach a significant number of people but have little or no advertising. On these sites, you can reach out to an interest audience for far less money than would be required to advertise on sites like Yahoo, c|Net, or HotBot.

Some neophyte Web sites looking to increase their exposure offer free banner advertising. If the Web site takes off, you'll already have had an advertising seed planted and will benefit from the deal in the long run. The hope of course is that you will see the benefit and maintain it at a cost later on when the site's audience has grown. Although Joe recommends looking for free direct banner ads, that isn't always feasible. Here are some things to remember when working with small sites:

- **Approach the site directly** and suggest that it post your ad. Your offer should include both a duration and a price—we suggest three months duration and a price of about $50 to 100 per 1,000 visitors. Be aware that site counters and logs can make results look more impressive than they really are. Make your offer a take-it-or-leave-it proposition.

- **Assuming you reach an agreement** on terms, supply the site with the banner(s) and links and track their compliance. Checking 10 or 15 sites every day can be time-consuming. To make this process easier, bookmark the sites and visit them periodically to see where your banner is positioned and how well the site is doing.

- **Check those logs to find out** which sites are sending visitors your way. Each visitor is worth between 50 cents and $2 in average sales. After you have an idea of how many visitors each site is sending you and what each site is averaging, you can try to renew your agreement at the rate that equals the number of site visits.

Advertising on small sites can be more effort than it's worth because many of those sites are maintained by part-time operators. Some disappear too quickly to be worthwhile advertising outlets. But many special interest-sites can be extremely useful—if you take the initiative and monitor your advertisements and their returns.

Advertising on Search Engines

Search engines are always among the most popular sites. Because they are the crossroads of the Internet, users often visit several times during one surfing session, and search engines collect major advertising revenue. Search engines, advertising networks, and some large content sites offer a variety of ways to purchase targeted ads, some of which are worth discussing here.

Keyword Purchasing

Advertising on search engines is effective not only because they are among the most viewed sites on the Internet but also because you can target potential customers by purchasing ads that will be displayed whenever a user enters a certain keyword. For example, a store selling baseball cards can purchase an ad that will display on that engine whenever someone enters a baseball-related keyword.

Cluster Groups

Often, one keyword isn't enough. A store-owner can purchase a suite of related keywords, commonly called cluster groups. For example, a gardening store could buy a cluster group of keywords related to gardening (gardening, planting, horticulture, and so on).

Domain Targeting

Domain targeting allows you purchase ads that are only shown to certain domain types. For example, if, like Tronix, you sell video games, you could purchase ads that target only .edu domains because of the high percentage of students, who make up a high percentage of video game players and frequently surf from .edu domains.

More Options

As Table 12.3 shows, there are increasing advertising options besides the above ones mentioned. As you get to know your customers, it should pay off to use that knowledge to further refine the targeting parameters of your ad campaign. Although it costs more to apply more targets to your ad buy, the increased rate of click-through should be worth it.

Table 12.3 Advertising options offered by DoubleClick Network

Target by Interest Category	Target by Organization Size or Revenue
Target by Search Keyword	Control Ad Frequency and Ad Banner Series
Target by Editorial Keyword	Target By Service Provider
Target by User's Geographic Location	Target By User's Operating System
Target by High Level Internet Domain Type	Browser Type
Target by Organization Type	Days and Hours to Display an Ad Banner
Target by Organization Name	

Search engines, ad networks, and large sites are amazing advertising tools given their sheer volume of users and the means by which they can target your ads. They are often the first place advertisers consider when they begin advertising. However, before you order any type of advertising, do the following:

- **Do everything you can** to get good positioning within a search engine's listings.
- **Make sure that you are capable of** making a good-sized purchase, because volume counts. If targeted precisely, $3,000 to $5,000 or more a month should provide good visibility. Stores that sell more commodity-style merchandise may need to spend more.
- **Familiarize yourself with all the options.** Ask the sales staff to walk you through them step-by-step.

Joe's Take: *If and when your budget allows, look into advertising with better-known companies that have major Web sites. Larger, well-established companies will of course have much higher advertising rates than average, independently owned Web sites. For example, I sell video games, but advertising with a major video game manufacturer such as Sega, Sony, or Nintendo is simply too expensive. I choose to advertise online with a popular video game magazine. The fee is more than that of an average Web site, but it is far lower than the same ad printed in the hard-copy version of the magazine.*

How Much Should I Advertise?

There are hundreds of books dedicated to advertising. Obviously we can't cover it all here, but one popular strategy involves a burst of advertising followed by quiet period and then a second burst. Research has shown that a highly visible advertisement made available over a concentrated time period not only gets the message across, people recall the advertisement long after it has stopped running.

TIP ▸ ***People see a lot of banner ads on the Internet. Buying a high frequency of ads in a short time frame will help you break through the clutter.***

Burst advertising works especially well for companies with limited advertising budgets. It also provides the opportunity to make a big splash and then mold that attention into customers during the quiet period.

How much advertising you do often depends on timing. For many stores, the majority of sales come at certain times, such as Christmas, back-to-school season, or a time specifically related to the market (fishing equipment in the spring, ski equipment after the first snowfall). By focusing your advertising budget on these time periods, you can target customers who are eager to buy.

Joe's Take: *Video games are popular Christmas gifts, so that is an obvious time for me to unleash some advertising. However, I also consider advertising based on new product arrivals. If you expect your store to have hit products throughout the year, consider advertising around the time of these major releases. Most customers won't wait until Christmas to buy the latest game, software, book, or music CD. If you have a hot item in stock, let everyone know.*

Banner Ads

Banner ads are the most popular form of advertising on the Internet. Although many advertising experts talk about moving "beyond the banner," it will be some time before that happens. Any advertiser on the Internet needs to be familiar with ad banner characteristics.

Creating Banner Ads

Once you know what, where, when, and how often to advertise, you must create a banner ad (Figure 12.2 top). The first Internet ads were simple banners that sat frozen at the top and/or bottom of a Web page. Animated GIF banners followed. As Web technology has improved, the options have increased. Now it is not uncommon to see banner-sized Java applets and interactive Shockwave ads. Other options include ads containing HTML forms with drop-down lists (Figure 12.2) or image maps that allow users to select a specific part of an ad to trigger a response. This style of ad can be effective for merchants who want to list all of their departments or some of their items in an advertisement.

Unless you possess the design skills necessary to create a good-looking advertisement, you can end up with an unattractive banner that wastes your advertising budget. So, once you have decided how you want your ad to perform, your wisest option is to hire a design firm familiar with Internet advertising creation.

FIGURE 12.2
A standard banner add (top) and a banner add with an embedded selection list (bottom).

Standard Ad Sizes

In 1996, two groups that work to develop Internet advertising standards—the Internet Advertising Bureau and CASIE (Coalition for Advertising Supported Information and Entertainment)—announced what they called voluntary model banner sizes (Table 12.4). These standard banner sizes are meant to give developers and advertisers a set of dimensions around which to design. The most common size is 468 by 60 pixels, which is used in about 75 percent of banner ads.

Although use of the size standards is voluntary, many sites accept ads only in these sizes.

TABLE 12.4 CASIE-APPROVED BANNER AD TYPE

SIZE (IN PIXELS)	TYPE
468x60	Full Banner
392x72	Full Banner with vertical navigation bar
234x60	Half banner
125x125	Square button
120x90	Button #1
120x60	Button #2
88x31	Micro Button
120x240	Vertical banner

Calculating a Return on Your Investment

We stated earlier in this chapter that the critical reason for stores to advertise is to gain new customers who hopefully become repeat customers. Now let's look at some straightforward calculations for gauging your return on your advertising investment. When you advertise on the Web, you can measure the actual return on an advertising investment because you can monitor the results of the ad campaign and measure the difference to determine whether your advertising campaign met expectations. Using the accepted averages of click-throughs and purchases, the resulting formula looks like this:

Number of Impressions * Average Click-Through Rate * Average Customer Turnover * Average Sale Net = Expected Return

- **Number of Impressions** is the amount of Web exposure you purchase.
- **Average Click-Through Rate** is the current average percentage of users who click on banners. Current statistics place this at an average of around 1 to 3.5 percent.
- **Average Customer Turnover** is the percentage of new visitors expected to become customers. The high end of this statistical range is 5 percent.
- **Average Sale Net** is the average net profit earned per customer order.

If your store earns an average of $5 per customer order, it is easy to develop an expected rate of return on an advertising buy of 200,000 impressions. For example:

200,000*.035*.05*$5=$1,750

According to the formula, you should expect approximately $1,750 in near-term new sales as a direct result of your advertising efforts. If your campaign cost $6,000 to $12,000, your effort didn't pay off, at least in the short run. However, if each of your new customers made several purchases over the course of the year, you might earn your money back. And if you improved your campaign and sold items at a somewhat higher profit, you could speed your return significantly. It could take a year or more of effective ads in conjunction with other efforts (promotional work, good customer service, and a compelling inventory) before you can build an active customer base through advertising. This is why most stores wait until they have achieved some success over a period of time before making large advertising buys.

Online advertising almost never offers an immediate return on investment; on the Internet it can take a while for your ads to settle in and provide the customer base you need. However, using the above formula can give you a rough idea of whether or not your advertising is effective.

If you spend significant amounts of money and don't receive a good return, you might need to adjust your strategy. But don't panic if after the first week of a six-week campaign, your results are negligible. In the early going, you may well spend more than you take in. However, if you see that you're gaining new customers, especially repeat customers, keep going—it could eventually pay off well.

TIP ▸ ***Studies show that people are getting better at tuning out banner ads. Good campaigns should have a number of different ads so that no one ad gets too stale (after two looks it can be curtains for an ad that failed to get a particular user to click). Part of this problem also concerns the targeting of the ad. Ads can be targeted very specifically. The more you define the target the more you pay, but it can be far more effective than advertising that goes to any and all takers.***

Do it, Mix it, and Maintain it

Cyberspace is already crowded, and it isn't going to get any easier to rise above the din. Not only are Web stores seeing more direct competitors, but the sheer volume of sites vying for attention makes it difficult to make an impact. Good promotion will only take many sites so far. That is where advertising comes into play.

Don't put all of your advertising eggs in one basket. Not everyone uses the same search engine (even though the most-used, Yahoo, is regularly used by an estimated 45 percent of the Web's population) and there are plenty of useful, non-Internet advertising media. Successful advertising campaigns are often intermedia in nature, combining ads on a variety of sites, search engines, and non-Internet print and broadcast sources to create a highly visible mix.

Once advertising pays off, don't desert it. Advertising isn't a quick-fix means of grabbing customers. It's something you should continue to use once it works. Advertising not only attracts new customers, it reminds previous customers of your presence.

In addition, it may take a year or more before someone clicks through on a banner. Sites that advertise should continue to advertise for long periods of time. Once they have created a successful mix, they should maintain it as an integral part of an overall business strategy.

Next up is Part IV, which includes everything you need to know about selling and shipping. We'll fill you in on taking credit cards, spotting and catching online thieves, electronic retailing, and shipping.

PART IV

Selling and Shipping

You've learned how to build a store and attract customers. Now for the next step: completing and processing sales of all kinds and fulfilling orders. Part IV covers international sales and helps you identify and avoid online thievery. It also shows you how to handle credit card orders and how to get orders from your hands into your customers' hands.

Part IV Table of Contents

CHAPTER THIRTEEN

International Sales

Making an international sale and shipping the package overseas involves a bit more work than completing a standard domestic order. However, the extra work will pay off handsomely in terms of an increased customer base. The Web makes your store a global entity the moment you launch. Even if you don't want international customers, unless you state that you don't accept international orders, you're going to get them.

Domestic customers have access to U.S. products through local stores, mail order catalogs, and of course online stores. Foreign customers who aren't planning a trip to the United States need access to American mail order houses. Ordering through a catalog involves finding the company's contact information, sending away for the catalog, waiting for the catalog to arrive, placing the order by phone or mail, and waiting for the order to arrive. Other overseas shoppers must rely on friends or family to purchase goods when they are visiting the United States.

But now international customers have immediate access to and direct contact with American retailers through online stores. They also have the shipping options laid out in front of them and don't have to worry about dealing with long distance phone calls and operators who barely understand their English.

This chapter steps you through the process of accepting and fulfilling an international order and shows you how important your overseas customers can be. The processing of international credit card orders is covered in more detail in Chapter 14.

Processing an International Order

Some aspects of processing an international order are the same as or identical to processing a domestic order, but it is a bit different. Although the process of completing the invoice is the same, shipping a package involves a few extra steps, which we take you through.

International Shipping

After your sale is processed, you need to include extra forms with foreign shipments. These documents are an absolute requirement from the big shipping companies such as FedEx, UPS, and Airborne Express.

Customs Form

One form required by every shipping company, including the United States Postal Service, is a customs form. The customs form required by the private couriers is contained in a clear plastic pouch attached to the outside of the package and contains a list of all merchandise enclosed, the value of each item, and the shipper's signature.

It used to be that merchants filled out international forms by hand. But with the couriers having converted to computerized shipping, international forms are generated for you. All packages containing merchandise pass through a customs house for inspection and collection of any dutiable taxes. But what if you neglect to include the required information, and the shipping company accepts the package without noticing the absence of this paperwork? The package will be held up in customs. Customs will inform your customer that the package cannot be released until an invoice stating the contents and their value is received.

When your customer informs you of the problem, you will have to fax or mail the missing information to the customs house. You should fax it—otherwise, your customer will probably end up waiting at least another week for the package.

TIP ▸ ***It is a good idea to email the package's tracking number to international customers who are using FedEx, UPS, Airborne, DHL, or Express Mail. Many times, the parcel will reach the destination country in the proper time but be held by customs for an extra day or so—particularly with larger packages. The packages are then delivered, in many cases, by a local courier working with the shipping company. To speed up the process, your international customers can find out exactly when their parcel arrived in their country and even get their package released more quickly with the tracking number on hand.***

Flat Packages

When sending flat letter packages (such as magazines and catalogs) through any of the private courier services, there is no need to fill out any customs forms. If you are required to include a customs form on a flat letter package, simply write "Documents, no commercial value" in the contents field or check off the corresponding box. Documents of no value are not taxable and can go through without being taxed.

Express Mail, Global Air Mail, and Standard Air Mail letter packages shipped through the post office still require a green form. Again, you can simply write "Documents, no commercial value" on the form.

The Airbill

When filling out an international airbill from a shipping courier, be sure the total value listed on your sales invoice corresponds with the amount on the airbill. If the package is lost or damaged it will be insured for the value listed on the airbill.

Express Mail packages from the post office are automatically covered up to $500, but Global and Standard Air Mail packages are uninsured. If you want to insure an item sent in this manner, you must fill out an additional form and pay an additional charge. You can simply transfer this charge to the customer unless you are feeling particularly philanthropic. Only Express Mail offers insured delivery to all countries.

Promoting Your Store Internationally

The Internet is a massive global community. Through newsgroups, email, and Internet Relay Chat (IRC), people from every nation are connected with one another. Once your domestic customers begin praising your business in the newsgroups or on the IRC, word of mouth reaches Internet users all over the world. A kind word can be seen as easily in Belgium as it is in New York.

You have several ways to make yourself known on an international level. Look for international Web sites related to what you sell. Just access a search engine and use names of countries or words like **international** in combination with the names of some of your products. For example, Tronix could use the words **Germany video games** to search for game-related sites based in Germany.

Once you have found a relevant site, you can email the Webmaster or whoever is responsible for the site and inquire about advertising or swapping links. Since people are more apt to hear about small companies from their own country and therefore visit those Web sites, this is an ideal way to promote your store in other countries. Assuming you advertise or link on a well-respected foreign site, you will gain immediate respect through your association with the site.

If you have enough money in your advertising budget, you can look around for some relevant foreign magazines and newspapers in which you might be able to advertise. You should be able to get some contact information from one of your foreign customers, a foreign Web site with which you have a relationship, or by searching the Web or domestic magazines.

As far as searching the Web, you can simply add the word **magazine** to the type of search we discussed when looking for Web sites. You should also check out some of the larger bookstores and magazine/news shops that might feature an international section.

When you do begin to gain international customers, be sure to ask them how they found out about your business. Many of Tronix's international customers found the site through newsgroups, links on smaller product-related "webzines," personal home pages, and major search engines. This will give you a better idea of how they are ending up on your doorstep and where you should focus your international promotional efforts.

JOE'S TAKE: *I've seen my international business grow in a pattern. I started out with a few customers from Germany and the Netherlands, and within a few months I noticed an increasing number of new customers from those two countries. Shortly thereafter, I received my first orders from Japan, Brazil, France, Canada, and Israel. Within a few weeks, I had many new clients from these same countries.*

TIP ▸ ***When supplying information about your Web site to the many search engines available on the Net, it is essential to include in your company description that you ship worldwide and specialize in exporting products. You should also try to become involved in newsgroups that not only deal with your particular type of store but also are dedicated to imported products or foreign countries.***

International Telecommunications

The majority of your international customers will use your online order form or standard email to place orders so they can save on the cost of expensive phone calls. International phone orders will be rare.

If you feel that it is important enough to your business, you can order international toll-free service, which is offered by both AT&T and MCI. You might want to offer this service only to your most loyal international customers.

With AT&T, the same toll-free number you use domestically can also be used internationally. Several options are available, described on the AT&T Web site (www.att.com), including AT&T Direct 800 Service, AT&T Toll-Free Service, and AT&T Universal Freephone Service.

MCI International Toll Free Service offers call routing, call termination, and network management services. For more information, visit the Web site (www.mci.com), contact your nearest MCI branch office, or call 1-800-988-9294.

Credit Card Orders

As with domestic orders, international credit card orders need to be verified. Credit card fraud is not just an American phenomenon, and verifying an international credit card can be a more time-consuming process than verifying a domestic card.

You should ask the customer to provide the phone number of the issuing bank. If the customer can't provide the number, you'll have to contact your credit card merchant service to obtain it. Because of the time differences across the globe, you may not immediately be able to speak with a bank representative for an international verification. You'll also have to spend money on a couple of international phone calls.

Be sure to set your requirements for international orders, spell them out on your Web site, and stick to them.

TIP ▸ ***One way to limit fraud is having all new international customers fax a photocopy of both sides of the credit card, along with a utility bill showing the billing address. You can use this rule for first-time orders over a specific amount, such as $100. Some international customers may feel that faxing their information defeats the purpose of using the Internet since they'll have to make a long-distance fax. Let them know that this is the policy for first-time orders and all future orders can be completed without faxing confirmation. You may lose a few customers who are required to meet these needs, but in the long run you will be less likely to get hit with a charge-back from your credit company. Charge-backs are tough to dispute, especially when you have accepted a fraudulent credit card order from overseas.***

Dealing with the Language Barrier

If you receive an international phone order, you may have to deal with a language barrier. A foreign customer who chooses to call will probably be able to speak at least some English. However, parts of the conversation, especially when it comes to foreign addresses, may be difficult to understand.

Politely ask them to spell out every letter in the address. Letters such as "S" and "F" or "M" and "N" can easily be misunderstood over the phone. Be sure to read back the entire name and address to your customer. If necessary, verify every letter using simple phrases such as "S as in sick,"
"F as in Fred," "M as in Mexico," "N as in nice."

Internationalizing Your Web Store

When international customers visit your Web site, they should immediately feel welcome and be made aware that you export products (assuming you choose to do so). Add a noticeable line of text stating that you ship around the world. You could even add an animated GIF of a spinning globe above or below the text line. But of course there's much more to creating a truly international Web site than that.

Translation

Many high-end Web sites offer specialized versions for people in various countries. Unlike the United States, where few speak a second language with much facility, in most other countries people speak at least two languages, if not three or four. And English is the most popular second language in most countries. According to an OTEC On-line Consumers Study (March 1997), English is cited as the first consultation language by 55 percent of all European Internet users. If you sell technical products, chances are good that your customers will speak English. In this case, you might want to simply create a foreign language summary page in order to be indexed in the countries you are targeting. Assuming you aren't fluent in the desired language or languages, you can either purchase a dictionary or hire someone to translate your page. The cost is generally less than 20 cents per word.

TIP ▸ ***There are a couple of places to find inexpensive translators—at local colleges and shopping on your Web site. As anyone who has attended college will tell you, college kids are always looking for a little extra money. Contact a local college's foreign language departments and ask if there are any students willing and able to give you a hand. You can also ask your international customers. Be sure that they know English well enough to do the job. If you find someone who can do the job, you can offer to either pay the person or give discounts or gift certificates to your store. However, if you are going to bother translating your site, make sure the translation is dead on. After the text has been translated, have it translated back into English to make sure it reads well. Otherwise, your foreign customers may read the text and come away feeling the same way you would if you found a site that greeted you with "This be my Web site. It are the most good on the Web if you are wanting the most coolest stuff."***

You might not be able to afford to translate your entire site or translate into more than one other language. If you decide to partially translate your Web site, you need to decide what languages you will include and what parts of your site will be offered in foreign languages. For example, if you sell photography equipment you might decide to offer part of your site only in Japanese and German given those cultures' affinity for photography.

Since many of you may choose not to internationalize your site immediately upon its launch, when you finally decide to do so you should target the countries from which you have the most customers. Unless your customer base dictates otherwise, the three most important additional languages for Web sites to offer are Japanese, German, and French.

TIP ▸ ***One company that offers a range of internationalization services is Access International (www.access-intl.net). A translation service worth investigating is JKW International (www.jkwintl.com).***

TIP ▸ ***Even if you can't afford to translate your entire Web site, you should plan to do so over time. Decide which pages are most crucial for your international customers and which foreign languages are most used by your customers and start there. Eventually, you will have a truly international Web site so you can take advantage of the global scope of the Internet. In the meantime, you should keep the English on your Web site simple for the benefit of those international customers who aren't fluent in English.***

Where to Focus Your Translation Efforts

Which pages should you have translated first? Good question. Ask your customers. Assuming you have gained some international customers prior to translating your site, ask them what parts of your site they have the most difficulty navigating due to the language barrier. Are there one or two pages that would make the entire shopping experience more enjoyable if they were offered in your foreign customers' native language? Your customers should be able to provide valuable insight and will be more than willing to help—after all, it is to their benefit. Generally, instructional pages such as Frequently Asked Questions, shipping pages, home pages, and indexes are good places to start. Additional content may take longer and be more expensive.

TIP ▸ ***One way to internationalize some of your content is to combine narrative efforts with simple ratings and grades that are universally understood. For example, if you write a positive review for a product, add a numerical grade (1 to 10 or 1 to 100) or a star rating.***

Integrating International Pages

Many sites offer links to the international version on the home page. However, it's also a good idea to offer links on other key pages, especially if you have only translated a few critical pages.

TIP ▸ ***A good reference book for those wanting to take their Web store to a global level is* Internet Resources and Services for International Business *by Lewis-Guodo Liu (published by Oryx Press, 1998, ISBN 1-57356-119-3).***

Is Translating Worth It?

In a word, yes. Because 84 percent of all Web pages are in English, there are a lot of potential customers out there suffering through English sites that they barely understand. If you can offer a site that is even partially translated into a few key languages and promote it in those countries, people may choose your site over your English-only competitors. A customer from Germany, France, or Japan is just as important as one from Kansas. In fact, foreign orders tend to be larger on average, and the customers can be extremely loyal.

International Hosting

Many of the larger international sites are learning the importance of the server location. Customers accessing your site from Germany or Japan may have a faster time doing so if the contents of your site are available on a local (in relation to them) Internet server. You can do this by "mirroring" your site on another server in a host country. Mirroring creates a localized version of your content and can make it much easier for international surfers to get to it.

If you find your international customers complaining about slow access to your site, consider putting up a mirror site with a foreign host. But also consider whether doing so is cost effective. If you only have a handful of overseas customers, it probably isn't worth the cost. But if a large percentage of your customers are from foreign countries, and you feel you may lose them because of slow access, a mirror site may be necessary.

As the Internet grows it will clog up and bog down at times. The farther away a customer is, the more difficulty he might have accessing your site quickly. This problem can also occur in fits and starts. Traffic might flow smoothly one week, only to grind to a near standstill the next. Listen to your customers. Go with a mirror site in the country where you have the most regular customers and where they repeatedly have the most difficulty accessing your site.

You can find international domain services by simply searching the Web using a search engine like HotBot or a directory such as Yahoo!. The international domain name registry NetNames (**netnames.co.uk**) handles overseas registrations in more than 200 countries. NetNames registers in every available top level domain in the world.

Finding a Web host in a foreign country is a matter of searching the Internet for **international Web hosting**. You might also query Webmasters of sites in the host country for a few good recommendations.

Most countries have their own top-level domain and each country has its own requirements that must be complied with to use their domain. The fees and regulations are subject to frequent change. It is a common stipulation that the registering organization must trade, and have a presence in, the country of the registration.

It isn't necessary to to have a foreign domain name to buy foreign mirror space; however, it can make your store appear more local in those markets.

Shipping Page

Divide your shipping page into domestic and international sections. You can have both layouts on one page with a link so that international customers don't have to wade through tables of domestic prices to get to the section in which they are interested. Or you could have separate shipping pages. If you decide to have a separate international shipping page, be sure to link to that page throughout your site.

When international customers fill out your order form, they're presented with a list of shipping options. Clearly specify which options are for international orders. Foreign customers who are unable to read English very well might simply choose FedEx Priority thinking that they will get their product overnight for a very low price, when in fact they are choosing a domestic service. The Tronix Order form clearly separates FedEx Priority from FedEx International Priority. Here are some tips for your international shipping page:

- **Customs.** Let your international customers know that they will be charged additional taxes by their customs house, which are separate from the charges that will be made by your company. Many foreign customers may be unaware of this, especially if they are ordering overseas for the first time. Unless you make them aware of customs charges, they may be upset by these extra charges and take their frustration out on you.

- **Do not internationalize prices.** Exchange rates fluctuate, so the price of a product on Monday might be inappropriate on Tuesday. Instead, maintain pricing in your home currency and let your customers do the conversion. You could offer a link to an online currency converter such as Olsen & Associates (www.oanda.com), which allows you to easily convert from one currency to another.

- **Voltage differences.** Be aware that certain appliances and electronic equipment may not function properly, or at all, depending on the type of standard or electrical current used by a particular country. Research your products for compatibility with foreign issues such as electrical voltage and television, VCR, and telephone standards. This information should be posted on your site so your international customers will be well informed before they make their purchase. If in fact you do sell products that need an adapter, you'd be wise to offer adapters for purchase on your site as well.

International Email Tips

Stay away from English slang words and complex or idiomatic expressions. Your customer in Spain is more likely to understand "Your shipment will arrive soon" than "It'll be there in a flash."

Simplify your language without talking down to your foreign customer. Domestically, you may want to sound professional by using sophisticated replies in email, but in this case, clever can mean daunting.

If an international customer becomes impatient waiting for an order to arrive (particularly nonexpress orders), explain how packages can sometimes be delayed passing through customs.

The most difficult decision for a first-time foreign customer is usually shipping. Many times, you'll get orders from foreign customers who choose an expensive means of shipping, which can turn out to cost more than the product itself. If you think the customer has made an uninformed shipping choice, feel free to point it out. In some cases, when a customer hears the price he might want to switch to a less expensive service simply because he didn't understand his initial choice.

If your foreign customer does not have a credit card, explain to her in email that she can make out a bank money order or wire transfer instead. Give her all the details she needs, such as the total cost of the item, plus the shipping charge, and be sure to mention that the currency is U.S. dollars.

TIP ▸ ***If you receive email in a foreign language, AltaVista has a translation service (Figure 13.1) located at http://babelfish.altavista.com. Simply paste the foreign text into the window and follow the steps to translate it to English. You can also translate your English message into a foreign language. However, computer translation can be rather rough.***

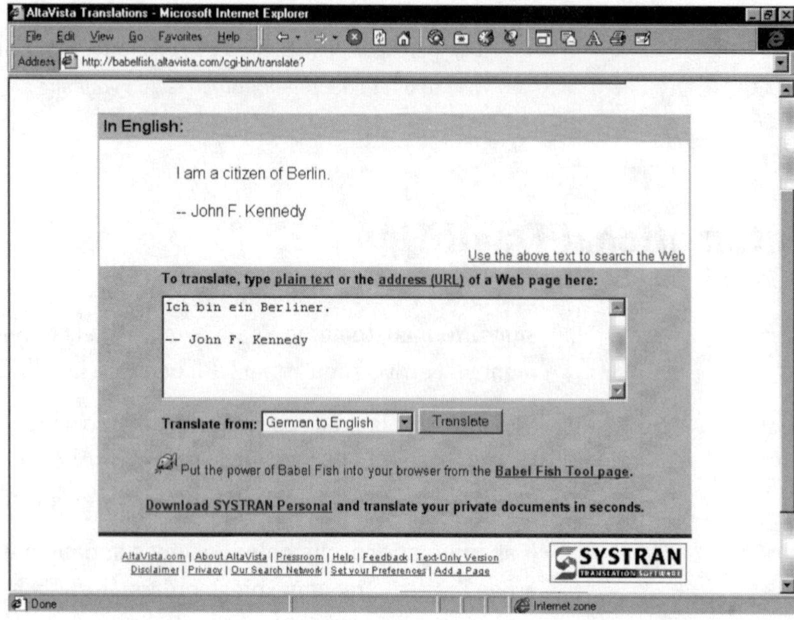

FIGURE 13.1
AltaVista's translation service in action.

International Access from Your Back Yard

Owning a Web store provides you with an opportunity to sell goods on a global level. Although someone from London would probably never walk into a store like Tronix to visit its small New York office across the Atlantic, that same person might well become a regular customer on the Web. Although international sales can involve some unique issues, don't shy away from them. Selling internationally is another way to increase your customer base. The more welcome you make your international customers feel, the better the chance that they (and their friends) will become regular visitors to your store. The better you promote your store to international customers, the more will visit.

Being a truly international store will require some additional work. While you might not be able to completely translate your site for a number of languages, you should make the extra effort to gradually transform your site. There is a whole world of customers out there.

CHAPTER FOURTEEN

Payment Acceptance and Processing

As an online store owner, the majority of your customers' orders will be paid for with credit cards, whether the customer calls with the information, faxes it, mails it to you, or enters it into your online order form. One advantage of shopping on the Web is the immediacy with which someone can have a product in her hands. Most people don't want to go through the process of getting a money order. They'd rather put the purchase on a credit card and get it over with.

Accepting credit cards improves your cash flow and reduces your costs. Without them, it can sometimes take 30, 45, or even 60 days after invoicing to receive payment from your commercial customers. By accepting credit cards, that time is reduced to two or three days. In addition to improving your cash flow, credit card acceptance eliminates the need to invoice your customers, thus reducing your administrative costs.

When you accept credit cards as payment, you avoid the cost of collection. Because you receive payment directly from the bank or, in the case of American Express, from the card company, you don't have to worry about possibly not getting paid.

However, a lot more goes into a credit card order than just punching in a number. Secure transfer of credit card information is an issue that has been addressed over the years. But to even accept credit cards, you must set up a merchant account with a merchant service provider or bank. This chapter helps you find and be accepted by a merchant service, discusses the major credit card companies, gives you an understanding of the major transaction technologies like Secure Sockets Layer (SSL) and Secure Electronic Transactions (SET), and covers the major transaction services on the Internet. In short, this chapter takes you through a credit card transaction from start to finish.

Setting Up a Merchant Account

We covered the basics of merchant accounts in Chapter 6, but the information is worth covering in more detail here. Setting up an account with a merchant service provider or a bank allows you to accept credit cards as a means of payment. Without a merchant account to accept credit cards, you'll only be able to accept CODs, money orders, or checks paid in advance.

Not accepting credit cards severely hampers your ability to do business. Most people ordering products over the Web want to use a credit card. As credit card transactions become more secure, that percentage will only increase. But as we mentioned in Chapter 6, enabling your store to accept credit cards is one of your biggest challenges. A merchant service provider will not accept you simply because you want to open a business and accept credit cards.

To find a merchant service company near you, refer to the Yellow Pages under "Credit Card & Other Credit Plans—Equipment & Supplies." A company representative will interview you about your business plan, and you will have to go through a credit check.

Before you meet with a merchant service provider, make sure you have your business set up, your bank account in order, a strong business plan, and a good argument for being accepted. Anything that shows you to be a capable and worthy reseller will help you.

However, you must understand that all Internet credit card transactions are placed in the highest-risk category (MOTO for mail order/telephone order or CNP for "card not present").

TIP ▸ ***Some merchant service providers are still a bit leery of working with strictly mail-order businesses, especially those on the Web. Although the explosion of e-commerce has made things easier, you should always look for an edge to secure your merchant account with a merchant services provider. We're not suggesting you lie, but if there is any chance your store will generate walk-in customers, emphasize that fact. In fact, if you can do something to generate a small amount of in-store traffic you'd be wise to do so, simply to help you get a merchant account in place. As e-commerce becomes more prevalent, it will become easier for Web stores to get the same treatment as traditional stores.***

What a Merchant Service Provider Looks For

Merchant service providers want minimal risk. They don't want to work with a store that has an unfocused or nonexistent business plan. They don't want to work with a business that will cease to exist in a couple of months. They don't want to work with a business that will be anything less than diligent about minimizing credit card fraud. And they don't want to work with a business that won't be able to pay its bills.

Merchant service providers, be they bankers or service provider firms, want to work with businesses that will succeed. You know your online store will be successful. Now it is up to you to convince them.

Building an Argument

As we said, you need to have your business set up with an employee identification number and a bank account before you go looking for the ability to accept credit cards. Your argument should include a well-defined, realistic business plan, and any supporting statistics about your industry and online retailing.

Statistics

Every research firm is predicting massive growth for the online retailing industry. You can check magazines (online and offline) such as Internet Week (www.internetwk.com), Internet World (www.internetworld.com), Internet.com (www.internet.com), or the Hewlett Packard's E Business Magazine (www.hp.com/Ebusiness/) to find articles about the current state and projected growth of Internet business. If you don't find what you're looking for there, go to the sources themselves—Jupiter Communications (www.jup.com), Forrester Research (www.forrester.com), or International Data Corporation (www.idc.com).

Find statistics that support the argument that online retailing is a stable, growing industry and present those statistics in an organized manner. You needn't offer every statistic supporting your case, but you would be wise to refer to more than one firm that has come to the same conclusion. That will keep the interviewer from wondering if every other research firm is predicting failure for online retailing. Crediting the firms will add weight to your argument. In fact, you might want to provide a copy of the article or the report from which the statistics were taken. You should also know a bit about the research firms you are using in case you are asked, "What's Jupiter Communications?" Although most people in the technology industry may know, there's no guarantee that a merchant service provider will.

As you research your decision about what to sell online, you will probably come across a number of statistics that point you to your selected industry (computer games, snowboards, etc.). Use those statistics to show the interviewer just how solid your industry is. Some industries will be an easy sell—computer software sounds more impressive than video games. Pointing out that video and computer games are part of a multibillion dollar industry should allay any concerns. Pointing out that the potential customers for a particular type of product are Internet users will further help your argument.

If you decided on your store's focus without researching the industry, now is the time to do so. Use your search skills on the Internet, check out an industry trade magazine, or go to the library (believe it or not, the Internet hasn't made them obsolete) to find the information you need.

Business Plan

Having a business plan is not only essential to the success of your business but will help you better explain your goals and projections to the interviewer. Your business plan needn't be a 20-page report, but it should cover your expenses, your sales and marketing plans, and your growth projections.

You should be able to back up your projections. Consulting with a similar store will help you. Your plan should be optimistic but realistic. Show the interviewer that you will begin making a profit immediately and that those profits will grow. However, don't claim that your store will be raking in $5 million a year just a couple of years down the road unless you have an extremely detailed plan showing how this will be accomplished.

You can open your business plan with a few paragraphs about what your business does, what makes it unique, what your goals are, and what needs to happen for you to reach those goals. The rest of your plan should include a detailed accounting of your costs (many of your start-up costs will be behind you) and your revenue. You should explain how you arrived at your projected revenue and show that your business will survive even if revenue falls short. You should conclude by reinforcing the growth potential of online retailing.

Even though online shopping is growing, a merchant service provider might still be a bit hesitant to jump on your bandwagon. Show a plan to include walk-in customers, even if you know there will be very few. Explain that the reason many consumers have been reluctant to shop online is the questionable privacy. Then provide a brief, nontechnical bit of information about the potential of Secure Electronic Transaction (discussed later this chapter) and existing security methods such as SSL and leave some literature. Don't dwell on the technical aspects of SET. Just explain how it will help online retailing grow.

Credit History

Although you probably will have been in business for just a short time when you approach a merchant service provider, any real numbers you can show will be to your advantage. If you've been in business for a month and are already selling well and paying your bills on time, this shows a business off to a good start and primed for an even better future. If you are off to a slow start, don't despair. Most businesses don't come flying out of the gate. Show that you are doing reasonably well for such a new business and emphasize how much business will improve when you can accept credit cards.

What a Merchant Service Provides

The most important thing a merchant service provides is access to credit card orders. If you are accepted, you will be able to lease a credit card processing terminal through the company for about $30 or $40 a month. Depending on your businesses needs, you can choose a point-of-sale terminal, computer software, or mainframe CPU-to-CPU connection for card processing. Once your have selected an option, processing an order is relatively easy.

Lowering Your Merchant Rates

Visa and MasterCard take a cut of between two and three percent of each sale and American Express takes even more. The merchant service provider or bank will give you the rates. As you begin to sell a higher volume, your rates will go down.

Your rates are also affected by the amount of fraudulent charges that are run through your store. In fact, too many fraudulent charges could lead to the revocation of your contract. Most credit card companies offer anti-fraud programs and advice that you should heed. For more on hindering fraud and online thieves, see Chapter 15.

Transaction-Related Terms

The following are some terms that you should understand when thinking about transaction processing.

Processor. A processor is a company that tracks all credit card transactions and prepares activity statements for merchants. The processor often underwrites risk or the amount the merchant agreed to process per month. If chargebacks occur, the funds are deducted from the merchant's account.

Chargeback. A chargeback occurs after a customer requests a full refund from his credit card company. Credit card companies have given consumers the right to charge back any product or service where their card was not presented for up to six months.

Discount rate. The discount rate is the rate charged per transaction by the acquiring bank for the privilege of accepting credit cards from the various credit card companies. This rate varies based on the type of business accepting credit cards. The higher the risk, the higher the rate.

Transaction fee. This fee offsets many of the charges for doing business between the processors that are handling transactions. Some banks charge higher rates for non-traditional processing of credit card orders.

Batch out or **capture.** A batch out or capture is when all of the days receipts have been reviewed by the merchant and have been submitted to the bank for settlement. When an approval is given, the money from the credit card is reserved. Funds are transferred after the batch out.

Rolling reserve. A rolling reserve account is maintained by the processor to protect against chargebacks. Some industries receive larger numbers of chargebacks from customers. Instead of the usual deposit account arrangement in which the processor keeps one month's receipts on deposit, three to seven percent of all receipts are held by the processor in a rolling reserve account and funds are paid over to the merchant on a daily basis commencing at the beginning of the seventh month. Any chargebacks or penalties are deducted from the funds maintained in this account.

Acquiring bank. An acquiring bank is an institution that may underwrite risk for merchant accounts but also sends money to the merchant's business checking account. After settlement, the money held by the credit card companies is transferred to the merchant's account at the acquiring bank.

Before You Enable Transactions

Before we list and describe some of the leading credit card transaction systems and services, here are some additional fundamental installation points.

- **No two services work exactly alike.** Thus we won't providing a step-by-step solution here. Authorize.net and a couple of the other services are very simple to install and often complete instructions on their Web sites.

- **High-end solutions** usually involve some scripts and some custom installation and configuration. If you need this kind of setup, you should make sure all parties involved with building your site's transaction system agrees on what to use. That means the hosting provider, the software vendor whose commerce server you use, the site developer, your bank, the actual transaction technology provider, and, of course, you.

- **Partners.** Many of the companies described below have reseller and integrator partners that you can work with to order and install the actual service. See their Web sites for more information or ask them about recommended help.

- **Hosted solutions.** If you choose a hosted solution for your transaction processing, ask them how seamless the service is. Some systems generate different headings on the URL bar on the browser or don't offer customizable templates. This can confuse customers. If you do go this route, and either the URL is different or there is some other indicator that you've outsourced your processing, you might place a word or two about this on the order page or elsewhere on your site to ease the security or privacy concerns of your customers.

- **Compare rates.** Also ask about the ability to process transactions outside the U.S. and about supported banks and cards. Every service will have different rates, they will not always interface with your bank, and they may not support all the various types of cards (especially Diners Club, JCB, and European cards).

Types of Payment and Acceptance

As a Web store, you can accept a number of payment types. In addition to traditional payment forms such as credit cards, checks, and money orders, customers may choose to pay through electronic cash or smart cards.

Electronic Cash

Electronic cash lets users send digital messages that act like currency to and from their accounts. Vendors can collect these messages and turn them back into a bank in return for their value. Unlike in credit card–based systems, users are not advanced credit, and the goal is to enable ways for "micro-transactions" to take place. So, whereas credit cards may handle payments of $10 to $20 or more, electronic cash systems will be focused on items that cost less. Electronic cash arrived with plenty of hype early in the life of the Internet. But the hype has died down as the first electronic cash companies fizzled and credit cards became the norm. Still, for low-cost transactions, e-cash provides the best future, and new forms may come the forefront in the next few years.

Smart Cards

Smart cards allow users to store either e-cash or digital verification information, which can be used to enable a transaction over the Web. Smart cards are not only for in-store transactions. Although smart cards can be used like debit cards for such transactions, they may also be used by customers who want to carry a portable digital certificate. This enables a user to transfer credit card and other e-cash information from whatever machine he or she is working at. Currently people who work at multiple machines must maintain separate certificates and/or electronic wallets. Smart cards are just now starting to be used in the United States, but in Europe stored cash cards have been popular for some time. Eventually smart card technology is expected to be a very important part of all electronic commerce.

Processing Options

A merchant can process credit card orders either through the Internet or by keying the information into a terminal. A processing terminal, which you can get through your merchant service provider, is usually available on a two-year lease for about $35 a month. That will also get you a printer that allows you to get copies of your transactional information at the end of the day.

Transactional Software

There are also a growing number of transactional software solutions available. The following are some of the companies, descriptions of their products, and contact information.

CyberCash

2100 Reston Parkway
Reston, VA 20191
Phone: 703-620-4200
Fax: 703-620-4215
www.cybercash.com
Email: info@cybercash.com

CyberCash's CashRegister software got off to a less than stellar start. It was difficult to install and took a lot of effort to integrate the system into a site or a commerce hosting solution. That all changed with CashRegister 3.0, which completely simplified the process. Now the majority of the applications that process and track credit card transactions are housed on CyberCash's own servers. All that is left for you to install are some simple software and scripts that help your site connect to CyberCash's servers and process your transactions.

To use CyberCash, find out if the company supports your merchant bank account. If it does, you need to open an account with CyberCash, which will issue you password and account information that will allow you to use its site and will enable your link for processing transactions.

Then you need to figure out what software and scripts to install on your server to be able to communicate with CyberCash and process a transaction. CyberCash has all of this software available for download on its site. It also has kits that are specifically tailored to several major commerce servers, as well as a general purpose kit. If your site is hosted by another company, you should consult with your Web host, which might already be a CyberCash reseller and can guide you through the set-up of the system.

CyberCash's system will deliver authorizations to your transactions and conduct fraud checks. Once a transaction is posted, you can use CyberCash's back-end system on its site to manage credits, clear transactions, and initiate captures after a product is shipped.

Authorize.net Corporation

3311 N. University Ave. Suite 200
Provo, UT 84604-4445 USA
Tel: 801-818-3311 ext.100
Fax: 801-818-3312
www.authorizenet.com
Email: webmaster@authorizenet.com

Authorize.net is one of the easier transaction systems to install and seems quite good for smaller stores. The company offers a series of products worth investigating.

AUTHORIZE.NET VIRTUAL TERMINAL

Virtual Terminal allows merchants who have Internet access to manually enter transactions on a secure page on Authorize.net's site. This offers a less expensive way to process transactions than buying or renting a card terminal. It is also faster than a standard dial-up card terminal.

If you have an account, simply log on securely to Authorize.net using any browser. After logging on to the system using your ID and password, you can access all the tools to input and manage a credit transaction over the Internet, including purchases, credits, returns, status, and activity reports.

AUTHORIZE.NET WEBLINK

Existing storefronts can be linked by a simple HTML code or via a shopping cart/storebuilder program that links with Authorize.net. Weblink takes information about the transaction from your server and then sends it securely to the Authorize.net transaction server. That server sends it to the card issuer's bank, returns a transaction page to the user, and sends both parties an email verification.

To link your site to the system, all you need to do is insert a few lines of HTML code provided by Authorize.net to establish the link. See www.authorizenet.com/pages/html.htm for details This system supports most shopping-cart and server solutions as well as home-brewed stores.

FRAUDSCREEN.NET

This new service from Authorize.net lets you check order information for potential fraud more thoroughly than a normal transaction authorization might. Merchants define risk thresholds and control several variables (such as, credit card address must match ship-to address). You can also apply these screens to certain levels of products (such as, screen extra hard for expensive items). The service works worldwide.

TIP ▸ ***Authorize.net has a sister company called Planet Payment that handles transaction payments for vendors operating on a worldwide basis with multiple currency needs and for those based outside of the U.S. Planet Payment can be found on the Web at www.planetpayment.com.***

CyberSource Corporation

550 S. Winchester Boulevard, Suite 301
San Jose, CA 95128-2545
Phone: 408-556-9100
Fax: 408-241-9270
www.cybersource.com

CyberSource provides two major packages, depending on your transaction needs. If you want to fully integrate a system into your custom solution and have complete control of your commerce servers, then its Cyber-Source Commerce Engine is worth looking into.

For small to medium-sized merchants, CyberSource offers a hosted solution called Easy Start Service. This system gives the merchant a customizable secure order form hosted on CyberSource's system and access via a single URL from your site. The service is only available in the U.S.

ClearCommerce

11500 Metric Boulevard, Suite 300
Austin, TX 78758
Phone: 512-832-0132
Fax: 512-832-901
www.clearcommerce.com

ClearCommerce has two major products for processing credit card transactions. Its Merchant Engine is a complete back-end solution that can be integrated into your site and provides fraud screening, payment processing, tax and shipping help, ESD downloading, and plenty of reports.

This solution is targeted more toward companies setting up larger-scale operations using dedicated or in-house services. ClearCommerce's Hosting Engine is for those companies that want to resell commerce services to other businesses.

iCOMS

One Indian Plaza
Nashua, NH 03060
Phone: 603-598-6500
Fax: 603-598-1226
www.icoms.com

iCOMS offers a number of transaction systems including a high-end solution known as SecureLink (see its Web site for complete details of this robust package). For small to medium-sized merchants, the SuperDOG (Super Digital Offer Generator) service is made to order.

The system provides a browser-based interface where you input information and use bits of HTML code that create special "buy" buttons. These buttons can be posted anywhere you want on your site, elsewhere on the Web, or even in email. Once customers click on SuperDOG-generated buy buttons, iCOMS MerchantTrax service takes over to securely capture and process the order.

iCOMS maintains a separate, secure database of these merchant-defined offers for each store. The customer receives an order form containing the selected product and iCOMS handles everything behind the buy button with MerchantTrax, its merchant-processing engine.

MerchantTrax supports four basic types of Digital Offers:

- **Physical Items.** For items requiring shipping (like books, clothing, furniture, food, cars, and so on).
- **Non-Physical Items.** For items that don't require shipping (like software, games, information, services, donations, and so on).

- **Subscription Items.** For items involving subscription payments (like access to content servers over a period of time, services, donations, and so on).

- **Coupon Items.** For offering discounts or incentives on items of the other three types as part of an electronic marketing program.

Globeset

1250 Capital of TX Hwy. S.
Building One, Suite 300
Austin, TX 78746
Phone: 512-427-5100
Fax: 512-427-5101
www.globeset.com

If you want to do SET-based transactions, Globeset is the leader. Globeset offers the following products:

- **ServerWallet.** This ensures simple installation and upgrades for the cardholder and enhanced security and comprehensive disaster-recovery capabilities for the issuer.

- **ServerPOS.** This is a payment server application designed to overcome deployment and management barriers and to ease secure electronic commerce.

- **Wallet.** The Wallet stores a buyer's account infomation and communicates with the merchant to complete an online sale using SET.

- **POS.** The Merchant Point-of-Sale connects the merchant to the buyer's electronic wallet and to the financial payment gateway.

- **CA.** The Certificate Authority (CA) issues and manages the digital identification certificates that authenticate the cardholders, merchants, and gateways in a SET transaction.

- **Gateway.** The Financial Processor Gateway connects cardholder and merchant systems to existing payment processing systems for SET transactions.

Additional Services

You can also try these additional processors:

OrderTrust (www.ordertrust.net) is primarily a higher-end service but offers some very interesting integration features and is used by a number of large-scale Web merchants.

Flexicom (www.flexicom.com) is another higher-end transaction service with a complete API and integration capabilities.

ECredit.com (www.ecredit.com) provides robust transaction services with a complete API and special capabilities for corporate and business-to-business transaction purchasing.

Credit Card Network, USA (www.creditnet.com) is similar to Authorize.net with a hosted order form and transaction solution.

Major Credit Cards

Not accepting a certain type of credit card can mean losing customers. Visa, MasterCard, and American Express are the most popular. Each credit card company has its own rules and benefits. Here's a bit about Visa, MasterCard, and American Express.

Visa

www.visa.com

There are more than 800 million Visa, Interlink, PLUS, and Visa Cash cards in the market, and they are accepted by more than 16 million merchants worldwide. Visa financial institutions typically pay merchants within 24 hours after deposit of sales drafts.

Visa has a number of risk-management programs and materials designed to help you decrease chargebacks, reduce fraud, and improve customer service. You can download the Visa Merchant Fraud Awareness Seminar and Training Script and get more information at www.visa.com/fb/merch/practice/main.html.

Visa Purchasing can help you make purchase information available electronically to companies to help them comply with tax regulations, reporting requirements, and expense reconciliation.

MasterCard

www.mastercard.com

MasterCard, Inc. has more than 700 million MasterCard, Maestro, Cirrus, and Mondex cards in circulation throughout the world.

With MasterCard transactions, you receive payment within 24 to 72 hours, improving your cash flow.

For more information, visit MasterCard's Merchant Center at www.mastercard.com/business/merchant/.

American Express

www.americanexpress.com

Accepting American Express cards is different than accepting Visa or MasterCard cards, because American Express is a company unto itself whereas Visa and MasterCard work with a collection of lending institutions. For information on accepting American Express, go to the Merchant Services area of its Web site at www.americanexpress.com/merchant/. You can also apply to accept American Express cards there.

Discover

www.discover.com

Discover is becoming more widely accepted, with more than 46 million cardholders and 3 million merchant and cash locations worldwide.

Discover has a merchant information center, which includes fraud prevention tips and seminars, operating regulations and more at www.novusnet.com/merchant/data/merch_default.htm.

Processing an Online Credit Card Order

Credit card orders can be processed with payment software, which does much of the work but lacks the human interaction that can make a merchant feel more in control of the transaction. Or the merchant can simply receive a credit card number, punch it in to a credit card processing machine, and wait for verification of the number. But that doesn't ensure that the card user is authorized (for more on that sticky subject, see Chapter 15).

In a totally electronic set-up, the online order form is secured using SSL technology which then transfers the customer's order information to a payment server. This server can be your own, a payment processor's, or your hosting company's. The payment server sends the information to a clearinghouse, which checks the information with the issuing institution. If the card information is authenticated, it is returned to the server, which logs the sale. It can also be set up to send an invoice and verification to the customer via a returned screen on the site or email.

That service processes the authorization, but the money isn't transferred into your account until you issue a capture command. The capture command is issued once the merchant has shipped the merchandise (many states require this by law). Once a capture process has been run, the payment processor will place the funds in your account.

For the most part, credit card processing software will be sold as part of your server choice or, in the cases of some of the vendors mentioned in this chapter, sold as a plug-in for other server software like Microsoft Site Server—Commerce Edition.

If you decide to process the transactions by hand, you will receive the information. Then you can determine whether the message is authentic and has all of the correct order information either by using a hand terminal or by entering the processing information into an online system on your premises. After receiving authorization, continue the transaction. If you receive a denial, alert the customer to the situation.

When processing the card manually, the electronic slip and card number are encrypted and sent to the merchant, who sends the information to the acquiring bank. The bank receives the encrypted information, decrypts the electronic slip, authenticates the cardholder certificate, and sends the card number out for authorization. The merchant receives the authorization response from the acquirer which, at the acquirer's option, may or may not contain the card number.

The merchant sends authorization status to the cardholder. If authorized, the merchant ships the goods or performs the requested services.

The merchant then enters a capture call via the terminal and receives payment from the merchant's financial institution.

Whether you use software or traditional processing methods is a matter of preference. While traditional processing affords you more hands-on involvement, it also requires more work. Software payment processing reduces the amount of work and the likelihood of data-entry mistakes, and it lowers transaction fees. But you increase the risk of fraud because you can't apply your keen eye to follow up all transactions.

In the end, automated processing is great for consumers and merchants as it speeds the entire payment process. If you want the best of both worlds, you can set your payment system to do automated transactions and then review all of the authorized transactions by hand (see Chapter 15).

Processing a Phone or Fax Order

If a customer calls to place an order, the first thing you'll do is collect credit card information—card type, card number, customer name as it appears on the card, expiration date, and issuing institution (Citibank, MBNA America, etc.). You should also ask whether the person you are talking to is the cardholder. Only the cardholder is authorized to use the card. If you suspect someone isn't the cardholder (or he's honest enough to admit he's not), you should deny the order and report the card information to the credit card company.

If the customer can't provide an issuing institution, deny the order and contact the card company. That information appears on the card, so if someone can't provide that information, it means the card is not in his possession. That could mean a thief got the card number, name, and expiration date but failed to get the name of the bank. You can also ask for the bank phone number to further verify the card.

After you have taken the information and the order, you can call your merchant service provider, provide the card information and it will pass it on to the issuing institution. You then call the issuing institution, give the card number and expiration date, and check the billing address it has with the one you have been provided by the customer. With American Express, you simply call the company (since it does not work with banks).

Once you have determined that the information you have received is legitimate, you can finish processing the order and ship the product. If something is wrong, you can either call the person back to ask for clarification or wait for her to get back in touch with you. If the person has made an honest mistake in reading a piece of information to you, she will most likely call back when she doesn't get an order confirmation. Only the most brazen thief will call back to ask, "Hey, where's my order?"

TIP▸ ***To take things a step further, you can ask for a business address to ensure that the customer is not a child using a parent's card.***

Chargebacks

If you don't verify the information, this is what might happen: a chargeback. Chargebacks occur when someone sneaks a fraudulent credit card past you, the cardholder reports the problem, and the credit card company asks for its money back. You not only lose the merchandise, but also the money you thought you had made from a sale.

Chargebacks are the reason you should do whatever possible to limit credit card fraud. For more on fraud, chargebacks, and how to avoid them, see Chapter 15.

International Orders

Processing international orders is a little trickier than processing domestic orders. If the customer can't provide the bank phone number on his order form, you'll have to contact your credit card merchant service to obtain it. Because of the time differences across the globe, you may not immediately be able to speak with a bank representative to confirm the authenticity of a credit card.

As we mentioned in Chapter 13, one way to limit international fraud is by having all new international customers fax a photocopy of both sides of the credit card, along with a utility bill showing the billing address.

You may lose a few customers by requiring them to meet these demands, but in the long run you will be less likely to get hit with a chargeback from your credit company.

TIP ▸ ***Make sure that any international sale is legal in that buyer's country. Not all products can be exported legally to all countries.***

Secure Electronic Transaction (SET)

Although Internet shopping has great potential, it will only begin to reach that potential when consumers are confident that online transactions are secure—that their credit card information can't be easily stolen by an unscrupulous hacker. There currently is no industry standard method of preventing fraud or theft of financial or personal information.

The development of Secure Electronic Transaction (SET) is leading toward a single standard for safeguarding credit card purchases over open networks such as the Internet. However, SET has run into some problems. There are still technical difficulties to be worked out, and as of late 1999, SET had not become the industry standard. Most merchants, companies, and software providers are still using SSL technology and not bothering with SET, which is harder to install and use. Still, the credit card providers are hoping that SET-based transactions will grow because they are more secure and thus reduce their costs. Thus it may be worthwhile to know more about the basics of SET transaction technology in case it gains in prominence.

The technology behind SET involves digital certificates—a way of verifying that a purchase is being made by a legitimate card holder. Digital certificates should help customers shop safely, thus driving Internet commerce closer to its potential.

SET is designed to utilize technology for authenticating the parties involved in payment card purchases on any type of online network, including the Internet. SET is being developed by card companies such as Visa, MasterCard, and American Express, and technology companies like Microsoft, IBM, Netscape, SAIC, GTE, RSA, Terisa Systems, and VeriSign. By using cryptographic techniques, SET will hopefully make cyberspace a safer place to conduct business and boost consumer confidence in electronic commerce.

Digital certificates will be used to authenticate all parties involved in a transaction. Not only will merchants know they are receiving a legitimate credit card from its actual owner, but customers will be made aware that they are sending their information to an actual merchant, not some crook with a Web site. The developers of SET hope it will eventually make online purchasing as comfortable as using a credit card at a traditional store. The SET specification is open and free to anyone who wishes to use it to develop SET-compliant software for buying and selling in cyberspace.

The growth in Internet usage, both real and expected, has drawn attention to the potential lack of privacy. In cyberspace, the potential for fraud and deception is far greater. How is a customer to be sure that a Web site is not just an elaborate front for thievery? And how is a merchant to know that the person typing in credit card information didn't come upon that information illegally? For electronic commerce to flourish on the Internet, all parties must be able to verify each other's identities.

Digital Certificates

Digital certificates are the key to secure transactions and give both sides of a transaction confidence, because they're based on the presence of a third party such as a credit card company, to verify information. For example, Visa or MasterCard provides digital certificates to the issuing institution, and the institution gives a digital certificate to the cardholder. Merchants also receive digital certificates.

When a transaction occurs, each party's SET-compliant software validates both merchant and cardholder before they exchange any information. The validation takes place by checking the digital certificates, which were issued by an authorized third party.

The technology behind digital certificates is encryption. A message can be converted or encrypted into code using a key, which changes the message into a collection of characters that make no sense to an uninvited interloper. In a very simple example of a code that would be very easy to crack, a number might be replaced by the corresponding letter beginning at the end of the alphabet. In this case, 03412 would become ZWVYX. To decode an encrypted message, the recipient needs to have the key that unlocks the code. Digital certificates use encryption codes that are extremely hard to crack.

The two most common forms of cryptography in use are secret-key encryption and public-key encryption. Public-key encryption is the key to safe electronic commerce.

Public-Key Encryption

In public-key encryption, each participant creates two unique keys—a public key which is available to all, and a private key is kept secret from all. The two keys work together. Whatever data one of the keys encrypts, only the other can decrypt. If you want to send a secure message to a particular recipient, you look up the recipient's public key and use that key to encrypt your message. The recipient then uses his private key to decrypt your message back to its original form. Even if the message is intercepted, the message can't be decoded without the private key.

Keys exist as series of electronic signals on personal computers or are transmitted as data over phone lines. The computer handles the encrypting and decrypting of messages. You don't have to do any of the work.

Underlying commerce software will be a layer of code that conforms to the new industry standard. This layer will use public-key encryption to ensure that messages containing card numbers and other information are strictly confidential.

Digital Signature

Through digital signatures, public-key encryption can also keep people from portraying others during online transactions. If you want to prove that you are, in fact, you, you can lock a message with your private key, and the recipient can then unlock it with your public key, showing that you are the only person who could've originally locked the message.

This "digital signature" links the message with the sender. Only you will be able to use your card account over the Internet.

Accept Credit Cards, But Be Careful

Not accepting credit cards is professional suicide. You have to do it. As Web retailing grows and online credit card transactions become more secure, the use of credit cards on the Web will continue to grow. You need to be prepared to grow along with it.

However, credit card fraud does exist. If you accept a fraudulent credit card, chances are good that you'll end up stuck with the bill. The more you do to eliminate credit card fraud, the less money you'll lose to online thieves. Chapter 15 focuses on how to spot and catch online thieves, including those using credit cards illegally.

CHAPTER FIFTEEN

Identifying and Preventing Crime

As the owner of a corner store has to deal with kids pocketing candy bars, so too will you be forced to confront potential thieves. Online thieves are different: Instead of sneaking out of your establishment with stuff in their pockets, these thieves will try to use stolen credit cards to purchase merchandise. Beyond that, though it's less likely, they might hack into your site and wreak havoc—the electronic version of graffiti or a brick through your window. They can cost you time and money unless you protect yourself against them.

Merchants lock up their shops when they leave for the day. Your online store will be open 24 hours a day, seven days a week, meaning you have to keep everything as secure as possible at all times. The shopping experience has become more secure and enjoyable for customers. And although increasing your customers' enjoyment must be your primary focus, you can do a number of things to make the lives of thieves and hackers miserable. That's what this chapter is about.

A Variety of Crime

Before you prevent a crime, you must know what you are trying to prevent. There are essentially three kinds of crimes a Web merchant must be aware of—those that are perpetuated electronically, those that are order-related, and those that are directed physically at your place of business. Some examples of these crimes are listed in Table 15.1.

Table 15.1 Web Store Crime

Electronic Crimes	Order-Related Crimes	Physical Crimes
Hacker attacks to steal goods	Customer attempts to use invalid/stolen credit card	Inventory theft or damage
Hacker attempts to "sniff" credit card or email information	Child attempts to use parent's credit card	Stolen credit card records
Hacker attempts to destroy or vandalize Web site	Customer claims items undelivered	Computer equipment theft or damage
Viruses		Vandalism

It is very difficult to completely eliminate the possibility of crime. However, there is plenty you can do to limit it and, more importantly, keep any crime that does occur from forcing you out of business.

Electronic crimes are those that occur when a bad "hacker" (yes, there are good hackers) or electronic intruder attempts to actually steal from you by illegally obtaining information from your site or from your Internet communications. There are a variety of ways they can do this. First and foremost, hackers can crack your site's security and rifle through your data attempting to steal software (a common problem for electronic software delivery) or credit card records.

Hackers also sometimes attempt to access a site and vandalize it by replacing files, deleting files, etc. They can also attempt to intercept and decode communications between you and your customers (a practice called *sniffing*) in search of valuable information. Fortunately, hackers attack less frequently than many people think. But since hacking a Web store can actually provide financial gain to the criminal rather than just a perverse good time, more hackers will likely engage in theft rather than simple mischief. Hackers who vandalize sites are far more likely to target large corporate, military, and government sites than small or medium-sized stores.

Preventing Electronic Crimes

Four important practices will help you prevent electronic crimes on your Web site. Follow basic Internet security practices; consult with either your ISP/Web hosting company or with a computer security expert about your site's security; utilize encryption whenever possible; and educate your customers about how they can protect themselves.

Following Basic Internet Security Practices

It is surprising how many Web site operators and Internet users fail to follow basic security practices. Some write down passwords on paper and hang them on the walls. Others repeatedly use the same simple password such as the name of a family member or a date of birth rather than choosing something unrelated to their personal life. Some hackers are even former employees who take advantage of easy-to-guess passwords.

Another problem occurs when a new employee is issued the same password as the person he replaced and the former employee supplies that information to a hacker. By avoiding these common mistakes you can close the most common intrusion routes.

Another common problem is failing to install and properly configure security systems (firewalls, up-to-date server software, and more) and not keeping backup information in the case of criminal deletions. Talk to your hosting provider, your server software vendor, and/or a computer security consultant about these issues. A book worth considering on the topic is *E-Commerce Security: Weak Links, Best Defenses* by Anup K. Ghosh, published by John Wiley & Sons.

Consulting with Experts

The best sources of introductory security are your technology partners. It only takes a day or so to make a few phone calls, read some manuals, or send some email inquiries to cover all the basics. What you need to find is any configuration-tweaking help or information on any specific problems that your partners have encountered.

If you plan to run any specialized software for your Web store, be sure to review any manuals or documentation for security issues, instructions, and tips. Be wary of using software about which you have little documentation or that doesn't have a solid company behind it. Poorly designed or secured programs can expose the user to hacker attacks. If you are unsure about the security of your software, contact the vendor. If you fail to get the necessary security information, you may become the victim of an easily avoidable intrusion.

If you are working with an ISP or Web hosting company, find out what basic security measures it has in place. ISPs generally have decent security and cover the basics well. Yet even the most professional ISP can be broken into. Listen to your ISP's security recommendations, know what they can do to help, and understand their procedures should your site be attacked.

If you decide to run your own site, you must install your own security measures. This can be a daunting task. A good Web consultant can guide you through the basics. There are also computer security firms that offer higher-end help. To find help, simply search Yahoo! or ask any friends or colleagues who have similar needs. Larger operations might also check into Andersen Consulting (**www.andersen.com**), a global management and technology consulting firm that is outstanding but probably exceeds the budget and the needs of smaller stores.

Finally, if you install a firewall or other security measures, those server software companies should provide some help and recommend consultants.

In most cases, implementing good store security involves knowing and installing all of the software security features available, having the names, phone numbers, and background of those who are responsible for protecting you from an attack (and helping you recover), and being educated about the security processes.

TIP ▸ ***If you run your own servers or use a dedicated server company, it is a good idea to do periodic security audits. A computer/Internet security expert will go over your entire system and look for holes in it, including password mistakes, poor script technology, and more. Request a complete checklist of items covered so you can see what was checked and changed. In many cases the auditor installs and upgrades components of your server and e-commerce software to versions that include the latest improvements on security issues.***

Utilizing Encryption Whenever Possible

Encryption is the key safeguard against many types of electronic crime and is a centerpiece of Internet stores. Encryption allows you to scramble information with a mathematical formula that is nearly impossible to decipher without the *key*. By using encryption to receive and transmit private and sensitive information, you can protect yourself against sniffers or other programs that intercept Internet communications. If your messages are encrypted, the programs can sniff all they want but a hacker won't be able to decrypt the stolen information.

Encryption is implemented by using technologies such as SSL (Secure Sockets Layer) and SHTML (Secure-HTML) with Web forms to protect their transmission to and from your server. Encryption can also be used in your email package through a technology called S/MIME (Secure/Multipurpose Internet Mail Extensions). Encryption is discussed in more detail later in this chapter.

Educating Your Customers

Securing your store involves your customers as well as yourself. Educating customers about Internet security involves three aspects: How they can protect themselves, the security measures you provide, and being involved in an audit program of your site's security practices.

Customers must first be educated about how they can best protect themselves, and you can do that easily with a Store Security FAQ on your Web site. This FAQ should include information about how customers can protect their credit card orders (e.g. "don't email your credit card information to us").

You should also inform customers of the security measures you provide to ensure their privacy. Customers want to know how you will protect any personal, credit card, or demographic information they have supplied.

Joe's Take: *One way to educate users about security is to include that information on the order form. Much of the attempted crime at my site involves kids trying to their parent's credit card, so I remind them (and others) what that means. The Tronix order form includes the following message:*

> *"Fraudulent transactions (which includes using a family member's/friend's credit card without a prearranged agreement with Tronix) will be reported to the appropriate credit card company for further action, as well as to the Internet service provider which hosts the account. If you don't want yourself and the card holder involved in legal difficulties, we suggest you back out now (this is one game you don't want to play). If you are authorized to use your parent's credit card, we need to confirm this by phone, and not email. Using a parent's credit card without his or her knowledge means* the actual cardholder will be held responsible *for your charges. When they receive their monthly credit card statement in the mail, we sure hope for your sake they gave you permission to make the purchase."*

You can also implement a WebTrust Examination (see nearby sidebar), which is a certified audit of your Web site's ability to meet "a defined criteria for standard business practices and controls over transaction integrity and information protection." If you meet the criteria, you can display a button and information that informs customers of your strong security practices.

TIP ▸ ***To understand more about Web security, read The World Wide Web Security FAQ at www.w3.org/Security/Faq/.***

Implementing Encryption

To properly implement encryption, you must accept orders on a server that is equipped for encryption. Many Web hosting companies have special servers to allow for secure order forms. Be sure to discuss with your hosting service how to place a form and script the right submission program to implement secure placement on the server.

If you don't use a hosting company, you must have the SSL and associated certificates on your own server. That requires getting an SSL-compliant server (most major servers are compliant) and applying to a certificate authority such as VeriSign or Nortel Entrust (see below for details) for the digital ID necessary for compliant browsers to register your site as valid. (If you use a Web hosting company, it should have digital ID for the server you use or technicians who can help you acquire a certificate of your own and install it.)

If you use a Web host, you should note in your Security FAQ why the digital certificate isn't your own. Essentially certificates reside on the server and are the responsibility of the server owner. Therefore the certificate for your site will be assigned to the host.

Obtaining WebTrust Certification

WebTrust is a service that was developed by the American Institute of Certified Public Accountants (AICPA) and the Canadian Institute of Chartered Accountants (CICA). Certified Accountant reviewers check your site and assess three critical principals:

- **Business Practices Disclosure.** The Web site owner discloses business practices for electronic commerce transactions and executes those transactions in accordance with its disclosed business practices.
- **Transactional Integrity.** The Web site owner maintains effective controls to ensure that customers' orders are fulfilled and billed as agreed to.
- **Information Protection.** The Web site owner maintains effective controls to ensure that private customer information is protected from uses not related to its business.

In order to begin the WebTrust process you must hire an approved accountant to implement the program. The specially trained CPA will go through your site and operations to see if they meet the developed standards. Once your site is certified, you are granted the right to obtain the WebTrust seal and place it on your site. Clicking on the seal will make the examination report and additional background on the program available to the customer.

Your site will be regularly revisited by the CPA to ensure continuing compliance. VeriSign uses its technology to authenticate the seal, allowing customers to find out if a seal is real, active, and still in good standing.

You can find out a lot more on the AICPA WebTrust site at http://www.aicpa.org/webtrust/index.htm. There are more details about the criteria you must meet and how to implement the program.

While there are a number of things you can do to reassure customers of your security efforts, the WebTrust program adds the legitimacy of a CPA audit and brand identity. Your customers' responses will likely be worth the time and effort.

Ordering a digital certificate isn't difficult. Simply visit the order page of any major certificate authority, choose the server certificate link, and follow the instructions. When you receive the certificate, it must be installed on the server. The process varies from server to server. Consult with your Web hosting company, the server software provider, and the certificate provider for more information.

The following are some major server certificate authorities.

- **VERISIGN** (www.verisign.com). Leading provider of Public Key Infrastructure (PKI) and digital certificate solutions.
- **ENTRUST** (www.entrust.com). Certificate authority spun off from communications giant Nortel.
- **THAWTE** (www.thawte.com). Another world-wide certificate authority with offices in South Africa and the United States.

After setting up your site with a digital certificate and a secure SSL server, you will need to develop a system to move information from the site to a form in which you can process it. The information also must be secure while it is in storage. Don't make the common mistake of emailing the secure form data back to yourself or of FTPing it off the server. Although the information has been moved to your server securely, emailing the information off the server or FTPing it down defeats the purpose of the secure form implementation. Sniffer systems can intercept the message in either case.

Instead, set up a secure directory on your Web site that is password protected. Then access the information in that Web directory via your SSL-enabled browser. You can also use a backend system that securely emails encrypted information to you. No matter which method you choose, remember to never allow retransmission of private data through unsecured means.

Email Encryption

Encrypting email is rather easy. Start by using an S/MIME compatible email client such as one of the major offerings from Eudora, Microsoft, or Netscape and installing a certificate that can be obtained from one of the certificate authorities listed a few paragraphs back. The resulting configuration process, no matter which email package you use, is also not complicated. While the process will vary from package to package, the instructions will certainly be available in the program's documentation or help file.

TIP ▸ ***Although the certificates do the same thing, you need separate certificates for your email and your server (if you are running your own server).***

To send encrypted email, your customers must also implement an encryption process. Although many will send credit card information through standard, unencrypted email, it is wise to offer them information about encrypted email. Certificates cost as little as $9.95 per year and are well worth the money when weighed against the potential loss.

TIP ▸ ***Include information in your Security FAQ about obtaining a digital certificate and using encrypted email.***

For information concerning encryption for specific email packages, check the help file, documentation, or Web site of your email package.

Joe's Take: *When an encrypted message is sent to a user, it still appears in her email box, which might not be particularly secure (if the computer is accessible to other people). Therefore you must be particularly careful about replying to email that contains credit card or other personal information. The worst thing you can do is send a message with a complete credit card number included. Anyone nearby the recipient's computer could simply copy the card number off the screen; not all Internet-related crime is high tech.*

Credit Card Fraud

Unless you do something or sell something to tick off a hacker, credit card fraud will be the most common thorn in your side. Whether it is someone who ripped off a credit card number or simply a kid using Mom's card to buy those CDs his parents refused to purchase, credit card fraud is an annoyance. If allowed to continue, it can be a financial disaster. Fortunately, it's also avoidable. It simply takes a little knowledge about what to look for and a lot of patience in verifying information to limit (and hopefully eliminate) fraud. When you realize that you not only lose merchandise but usually the money from the sale as well, it becomes worthwhile to do everything necessary to thwart online thieves.

Verifying Information

Some software packages automatically verify credit card information for you. However, since you may not have such a system, you need to know how to verify information yourself.

Your online order form should be set up so that a customer is forced to enter all necessary credit card information—card type (Visa, MasterCard, American Express, etc.), card number, customer name as it appears on the card, expiration date, and issuing institution (Citibank, MBNA America, etc.). If you take an order over the phone, you should also ask if you are talking to the cardholder. Never accept an order by anyone but the card's owner. And keep in mind that phone orders aren't totally secure either—especially those made on cordless or cell phones, which can be overheard on some kinds of shortwave radios.

Joe's Take: *American Express and other cards place four extra digits on their credit cards. These numbers don't show up on carbons nor are they read off the magnetic strip of the card. However, they are verifiable. These numbers are intended to make it more difficult to steal credit card numbers. By asking for these numbers in addition to the regular numbers, you can guard better against fraud. Check with your merchant services company and the credit card companies for more information.*

Don't process any order—online or by phone—that has incomplete information. If the order is placed online, the customer might have simply forgotten to enter a piece of information. You can either contact the customer about the missing information or wait for the customer to contact you. If a customer never contacts you again, you can be reasonably sure that the order was fraudulent. Why else would someone place an order and never call back when it failed to arrive? However, by holding the order and not contacting the customer, you run the risk of upsetting a customer who made an honest mistake.

TIP ▸ ***If you are using a credit card terminal, after you have taken the customer's information and order and a "Hold Card" order has not been issued, you can pass the information on to your merchant service provider. The merchant service provider will contact the issuing institution. To further verify that the customer is using a legitimate card, check the customer's billing address with the issuing institution.***

Once you have determined that the information you have received is legitimate, finish processing the order and ship the product. Remember that you needn't repeat this process every time a particular customer places an order. If you are a smaller store and become familiar with a customer who has established herself as trustworthy (two or three months of legitimate orders), you don't need to ask for the card information. You can simply keep that information on file and allow her to place orders and direct you to use the same information.

Joe's Take: *After two or three months, if someone is still using the same credit card information, you can usually trust that it is legitimate. Fraudulent credit card use doesn't last long because once the actual card holder gets a bill, he'll see the charges, contact the card company, and the card will be cancelled. For that reason, you'll also see more fraud early in the billing cycle. The card thief will want to get the most use possible out of the stolen information before the owner learns of the problem.*

Recognizing Suspicious Customer Behavior

Credit card thieves will often tip themselves off—if you know what to look for. Although none of these activities guarantees that the customer is trying to pull off credit card fraud, they are all warning signs to proceed with caution.

- **Watch for a customer** who makes large orders without regard to size, style, color, or price.

- **If an international customer** wants the fastest possible shipping option, keep an eye open. International shipping prices are so prohibitive that most legitimate overseas customers will take a less expensive option.

- **A first-time customer** who places a very large order and wants it shipped overnight should be treated with caution.

- **Free Email Accounts** (e.g. Yahoo!, Juno, Hotmail, Bigfoot) are commonly used as reply email accounts by people who might try to slip one by you. Be especially careful of orders which use these types of accounts until the user has established himself as being trustworthy.

- **Don't trust a customer** who won't allow you to call him and insists on either calling you or communicating through email.

- **If you get multiple orders** from the same person on the same day, the person will usually ask that you pack the items together to save on shipping costs. If the person doesn't ask that the order be packed together, there's a good chance it is a fraudulent order.

- **If a new customer wants an order** shipped to an address other than the card billing address, deny the request. Ship only to the billing address until the customer has established her trustworthiness.

- **A very common form** of credit card fraud is a child using a parent's card. If you get a large order for teen-oriented products, beware. Teenagers generally don't have credit cards and it may be a case of a youngster snatching a card out of dad's wallet and stocking up on those Sega games he couldn't get otherwise.

TIP ▸ ***Some higher-end merchants that process a heavy volume of transactions via the Internet should consider HNC Software's eFalcon (www.ehnc.com). eFalcon is a complete credit card fraud detection and case management solution for online merchants and service providers. The system checks credit card numbers against an enormous range of fraud rules that can indicate a fraudulent transaction. HNC is now also working with some of the major transaction vendors like CyberCash to integrate this software into those systems.***

Examples of Credit Card Fraud

The most common type of credit card fraud you will encounter depends largely on the type of store you run. In the case of Tronix, which has a relatively young clientele, the most common form of fraud is when children use their parents' credit cards. If you sell more adult-oriented products such as furniture, it is unlikely that you will face that form of fraud.

Joe's Take: *When Tronix first opened, I was very naive. On one occasion, a person from Kuwait made an order for $300. I didn't do any verification because it was Kuwait and I didn't think it would be worth the hassle. Sure enough, it was fraud.*

Although I rarely receive fraudulent orders from international customers, on another occasion a guy from Poland said he was from a magazine and ordered $2,000 worth of software. He gave me a story about how he could only be reached by fax—and I bought it. I sent him his order and I never heard from him again. To further complicate matters, the charge-back from the credit card company came while I was on vacation. You only have 12 days to respond to a charge-back before they pull the money from your account. By the time I got back, I only had two days to respond. That's when I became really vigilant about verifying credit card orders.

Stores that sell computer equipment, stereos, televisions, and so on are also likely targets for fraud simply because those items can be easily resold. The same goes for jewelry. In this case, the thieves use online ordering to avoid the hassle of breaking into a house and loading up a van.

How Credit Card Fraud Affects Your Costs

Allowing a stolen credit card to be used at your store is similar to getting arrested for drunken driving—you lose in a number of ways. First, you lose the merchandise (your license). Then, you lose the money (the fine). Finally, you pay higher merchant rates (car insurance rates). Yes, checking and rechecking credit card information can be a hassle, just like hailing a cab or sleeping on someone's floor. But it's worth it.

The worst aspect of accepting a fraudulent credit card order is that the credit card company will almost always side with the defrauded card holder because that's where it makes its money. If you think that's unfair, imagine if someone stole your card information, piled up a couple thousand dollars worth of merchandise, and your card company said, "Tough break, you have to pay us." You'd be canceling your account and taking your business elsewhere.

Even if a child uses a parent's credit card without authorization, the credit card company will usually rule against you. The only chance you have is if the shipments went to the billing address. Don't ever be foolish enough to send merchandise to a college dorm or an address other than the credit card billing address. While college students might be a solid percentage of your customers, they tend to use cards of their parents or their own which are assigned to their home address. What you must do in this case, if you accept the order, is simply send the order to the billing address.

JOE'S TAKE: *You might find people who try to soften you up with friendly emails before hitting you with a fraudulent order. I once had a guy submit a credit card order that completely checked out. He started with two games, then three, then five. He told me how much his kids were going to enjoy the games and told me a nice family story. One day I got a really big order from him, so I wrote back asking him how many kids he had and that I wanted to talk to him by phone. I called on a Saturday night and got an office. So I called back and quickly found out that it was a son using his father's credit card. We eventually set up a plan where I sold the (used) games at a discount and he got some of his money back.*

Merchant Education Programs

Credit card companies don't like fraud any more than you do. Although the card companies will usually get their money (out of your pocket), it's a time- and money-wasting process for them to deal with fraud. It is in their best interests to educate you about how to limit credit card fraud. And it is in your best interest to listen. Here's what Visa, MasterCard, and American Express provide for merchant education programs.

Visa

Visa offers a Merchant Education Program with materials written for merchants to provide information about Visa policies, procedures, programs, and services. Contact your Visa merchant bank for industry-specific and card-specific information.

Visa's Merchant Best Practices area (www.visa.com/fb/merch/practice/main.html) on its Web site is designed to help merchants avoid fraud and implement best practices.

MasterCard

MasterCard launched the Address Information Management Service (AIMs) to help combat credit card fraud, especially when an item is shipped someplace other than the billing address.

AIMs is a fraud control system that allows direct marketers to instantaneously check the identity of any address. By providing immediate, online access to real-time address inquiries, AIMs enables catalogers, airlines, concert ticket agents, book and CD clubs, and Web retailers to stop suspected fraudulent acts before they occur. For more information about how AIMs works, MasterCard suggests you contact your merchant bank or account service.

For more information, check out the MasterCard Web site's Merchant Center (www.mastercard.com/business/merchants/).

Internet Fraud Watch

The Internet Fraud Watch (www.fraud.org/internet/intset.htm) is intended to monitor, report, and prevent online fraud. The IFW assists local, state, and federal law enforcement agencies in gathering complaints about online fraud. The IFW also provides tips, articles, bulletins, and other information that merchants can use to avoid fraud.

American Express

American Express' Small Business Exchange Web site (www.americanexpress.com/smallbusiness/) includes an Expert Advice area. You can read the Tip of the Day, send a question to American Express or browse the previously answered questions in a number of categories.

For more information on limiting credit card fraud, visit http://www.americanexpress.com/smallbusiness/resources/tools/security/protect.shtml.

Cooperating with Competitors

Although retailing of any kind is competitive, dealing with credit card fraud is one instance in which online storeowners often work together. Despite the fact that you will be competing for the same pool of customers, no one wants a customer who is really a thief. It is a good policy to share information with other stores within your industry on bad credit card users. If you warn your competitors about potential thieves, they'll probably do the same for you. No one wants to get ripped off and no one wants to see anyone else get ripped off.

Joe's Take: *A competitor once sent me a message about a bad order he had received. About an hour later the same person tried to place an order at Tronix. Fortunately, since my competitor had shared the information, I was able to immediately deny his order. You'll find that within your industry, small storeowners are willing to share this type of information. It helps everyone and hurts no one—except the perpetrators.*

CyberSource

CyberSource (www.cybersource.com) and Visa announced in September, 1999 that they are developing and marketing an e-commerce fraud screening solution. The CyberSource Internet Fraud Screen measures the risk level of an order and returns a related risk score back to the merchant in real time. The product checks more than 150 different factors to calculate the risk of fraud associated with an online purchase. Web merchants can customize the program for specific shopping seasons or other deviations in expected customer behavior. After receiving the rating, merchants can decide whether to accept or reject the order. The process takes an average of five seconds.

For pricing information, visit CyberSource's Web site.

Physical Theft or Damage

Although it is probably the most uncommon form of crime that you will face, don't discount the impact that a physical crime can have on your store. Hopefully, you will never have to deal with a break-in or employee theft or damage. To minimize damage and prevent these types of crimes in the first place, consider the following tips:

- **Use password protection internally** as much as externally. Not everyone needs access to credit card information or to the Web site.
- **Screen potential employees carefully**, especially if they will be working with sensitive information.
- **Institute a vigorous backup system.** This should include daily backups of sensitive data including the Web site's files, customer records, inventory, and credit card transactions. Store copies both on and off site in a secure manner.
- **Have a catastrophe plan in place.** Everyone should know what to do in the aftermath of a site crash, attack, or in the case of site, inventory, or customer record theft.
- **Business insurance.** Purchase appropriate business insurance.

Although the security efforts of your business will focus on the Web side of operations, don't ignore the potential for real world theft.

Stop, Thief!

Most people don't steal. However, the ones who do can make life miserable for the rest of us. There's no need to be paranoid, but there is a great need to be careful. Unless you consistently verify credit card information and use the most secure transaction system available, you will be left open to fraud. The consequences of allowing fraudulent credit card use at your store pile atop one another. Not only do you lose merchandise, you also lose money and watch your merchant rates rise. In addition, other forms of crime can instigate disruptions that drive customers elsewhere.

Thwarting thieves requires a commitment to verifying credit card information and an eye for suspicious purchasing habits. It's also a good idea to follow the advice offered by the various credit card companies. They've seen every type of credit card scam imaginable and are more than willing to help you combat them.

This is kind of a downer of a chapter, we admit, but it is necessary. No one wants to lose their business because of a failure to combat thieves. And with a little effort and thought, no one should.

With all of this nasty talk behind us, it's on to something a bit more fun—electronically distributed software in the next chapter. You'll learn how technology now allows software to be delivered over the Internet rather than shipping out endless CDs, documents, or other hard goods.

CHAPTER SIXTEEN

Electronic Software Distribution

Electronic Software Distribution (ESD) is an alternative to the traditional distribution of software and other digital goods. Rather than physically mailing any type of software (whether it be music, computer programs, clip-art or even a book), online retailers can save time and money while providing timely customer service by distributing that software directly to consumers electronically.

This chapter will take you through the steps, benefits, and potential pitfalls of ESD. Although this chapter is certainly more useful for those who sell products (such as software) that can be transferred over the Internet, other merchants may find some of the information interesting as well. You may not sell software currently, but you never know when you might decide to add, for example, a piece of software on bike repair and maintenance to your online bike store. Or maybe you'll distribute electronic music or a book as part of your overall product mix. If that day arrives, you might want to employ ESD-type technology to help you distribute data profitably and securely.

Benefits of ESD

Everyone involved in software sales—including the customer—benefits from ESD.

Customers find ESD more convenient and timely. No longer does the customer have to pay shipping costs and wait for a CD to arrive before installing the software. Delivery is immediate. Nearly as important, in many forms ESD saves customers the agony of having to deal with that pesky CD shrink-wrap, sticker, and little metal thing.

ESD also makes subsequent upgrades easier. Software purchased via ESD can be easily upgraded over its life by the vendor or developer.

ESD also tends to include a try-before-you-buy component that allows users make a solid decision that they want the software, thus reducing returns.

If you not only sell software, music, or documents but also produce them, ESD offers lower delivery costs and a direct avenue to market for new products or upgrades. ESD is used by many of today's software companies to get their products to market. Rather than deal with the regular problems of the traditional retail channel, companies such as Borland, JScape, Sun, and RealAudio are setting up software-based stores right on their corporate Web sites.

For software merchants, ESD provides an even more extensive list of benefits. ESD allows merchants to eliminate physical inventory and its associated costs, risks, and headaches. The lack of associated inventory also allows the online merchant to offer a wider variety of products.

Selling software through ESD also allows the merchant to cut packaging time and get products to customers anywhere in the world immediately. A store offering ESD to its customers has an advantage over one that doesn't; what customer wouldn't prefer to receive software immediately and without shipping costs?

Although modem speeds currently hinder ESD's usefulness, when high bandwidth Internet access is widely available, ESD is expected to become the most dominant form of software delivery.

Types of ESD

There are several types of ESD. Each one has to do with the underlying piece of software that is being sold via download. For each major type of software there are actually specialized ESD tools and processes used to implement it. Current candidates for ESD are computer software, documents, graphics, audio, and video.

Computer Software

Any piece of computer software can be sold online and this is certainly the biggest part of the ESD revolution. In some ways computer software has been distributed electronically for quite some time. The concept of *shareware* and "try-before-you-buy" marketing of programs has been used by many developers for more than a decade. With shareware, the developer produces a piece of software that in some version is given away for free. Sometimes the free trial version lacks certain features or only works for a certain period of time before the customer must pay or lose use of the product. Other times customers are simply on the honor system. The developer often offers an enhanced version (and perhaps services, like free updates) to paying, registered customers.

It is important to understand that selling software through ESD may include shareware as a marketing concept. But the two items are entirely different. ESD may not involve the distribution of any free software. Formal ESD technology also tends to include features such as encrypted delivery and "digital wrappers" that enforce copyright compliance and protect against unauthorized use or piracy.

Software ESD also tends to include third-party reselling capability, whereas shareware registrations are done directly with the developer. Thus, shareware can be thought of best as a direct marketing method, whereas ESD is more akin to catalog or retail marketing, as it may involve a store like yours or the developer's own internal store.

Recipe for Software-Based ESD

1. Software publisher/developer prepares software master.

2. Developer partners with resellers, third-party clearinghouse, and ESD technology company.

3. Digital wrapper placed on product, vendors given software master.

4. Web retailer prepares site, accepts payments, and distributes software electronically.

5. Clearinghouse provides digital key to unlock wrapper.

6. Retailer provides follow-on transaction, installation, and sometimes product support.

Documents

It is sometimes easy to forget how often products sold either in business-to-business markets or to consumers consist of nothing more than documentation. Whether it is a computer book, a market research report, a legal document, yesterday's news, or the latest issue of the *New Yorker*, words and pictures of a printed page are products that can be distributed via ESD.

Most document-based ESD revolves around specialized document formats that render a document as a special file that, when viewed or printed, can actually reproduce the original layout, resolution, and complexity of the document. Two major technologies, Adobe Acrobat and Hummingbird's Common Ground, are used by most developers. Acrobat is the market leader.

A product called Softlock (**www.softlock.com**) can protect your documents from being routed around the world once someone buys a single copy. Softlock can be used in conjunction with Adobe Acrobat files to prevent piracy of the underlying Acrobat document.

Recipe for Document-Based ESD

1. Prepare all content for publication.

2. Render document in either Adobe Acrobat or Common Ground format.

3. Apply copy protection (e.g. use Softlock with Acrobat).

4. Produce an abstract, table of contents, or index for Web site informational listing.

5. Produce a commerce system that accepts payment and returns document (via email or password-protected site).

How Fatbrain and Others Sell Documents

Fatbrain (www.fatbrain.com) has started an interesting document publishing and store business in which it sells documents uploaded by authors on the site. Fatbrain does this using Adobe Acrobat documents secured with an encryption algorithim (Counterpane Software's Blowfish). The service, called eMatter, is a good example of a document-based ESD service.

Microsoft and others are also experimenting with interesting online document technologies, and at the forefront is the idea of *ebooks*—electronic devices no bigger than a simple paperback book. They use enhanced screens and type-rendering technologies to create simple lightweight electronic document readers. It is hoped that with these readers, consumers will download books, manuals, newspapers, and other documents for easy portable reading. Microsoft Reader (www.microsoft.com/reader/) supports copyright protection and e-commerce connections for electronic documents. Rocket eBook (www.rocketbook.com) by NovuMedia is an upstart electronic book product. The site's bookstore features books in its RocketEdition format, which includes various document protection schemes.

Graphics

Clip art, photographs, and other graphics are already big sellers online, and this will increase as better graphics-oriented ESD technology takes hold. The big issues with graphics are securing the graphic against copying and producing a way for it to support many different resolution styles. The first part, security, is handled by *watermarking* technology, which provides a constant copyright identifier with the image. No matter how often it is copied or changed, an artist or reseller will be able to identify improperly used product to help fight piracy. Leading the charge in digital watermarking is a company called Digimarc, which has a plug-in for Adobe Photoshop 4.0.

In terms of resolution, the issue is that graphical content is often sold for different purposes. For example, a piece of clip art might be used for a Web site one day and a major magazine cover the next. Each use has extremely different resolution needs. The Web image needn't be more than 72 dpi (low-resolution), whereas the version for the magazine cover must be in much higher resolution. Here, too, there is an emerging solution: FlashPix (**www.flashpix.com**), a format developed by Live Picture, Inc. (now a division of graphics software maker MGI) and backed by Microsoft, Hewlett-Packard, and Kodak. FlashPix allows several resolutions of the same picture to be stored together. Once transferred, the format only presents the image data relevant to the underlying needs of the display technology.

By combining the high-end technology of the Flashpix format with digital watermarking available from Digimarc, there is a clear way to distribute high-resolution imagery via Internet stores.

Recipe for Graphics-Based ESD

1. Prepare all graphical content by storing it in FlashPix format.
2. Add a digital watermark for each product using Digimarc's plug-in for Photoshop.
3. Produce a lower-res version for the Web site.
4. Produce a commerce system which accepts payment and returns image via email or password-protected site.

Audio

ESD-based audio distribution has taken several forms on the Internet. There are some specialized formats such as Liquid Audio (**www.liquidaudio.com**), AT&T's a2b music (**www.a2bmusic.com**), or Microsoft's new Windows Media Audio (**www.microsoft.com/windows/windowsmedia/**). Also worth learning about is MP3, the music format that has already swept the Internet for two years. MP3 is the highest quality with a standard quality rate setting of 128Kbps. Some sites opt to increase that to 160Kbps or 192Kbps to enhance the sound.

TIP ▸ ***To create MP3 files or any form of specialized audio, you must convert the original recording to the specialized format. This process, known as encoding, involves taking a raw .WAV or .AIFF file as digitized by your audio digitizing software, and converting it using encoding software. For MP3 files, many people use Xing Software's (www.xingtech.com) encoder or its AudioCatalyst, which encodes files directly from CD tracks. For RealAudio, you can use Real's digitizing software or the Real Producer encoding package, available directly at www.real.com. If you have large amount of audio to encode and can provide master CDs, vinyl, tapes, minidiscs, or raw audio files, visit Encoding.com (www.encoding.com), the leader in encoding services.***

The big difference between the types of audio formats is that Liquid Audio, a2b, Windows Media, and others are specialized formats that can protect copyright, whereas other formats, notably MP3, don't provide any form of copyright protection. College students in particular save money on music purchases by downloading songs in MP3 format for free from the Internet instead of going to the record store. This obviously has the recording industry worried about shrinking profits; some have sent out cease-and-desist orders to sites that make commercial releases available for free download; others are scrambling to find a way to use MP3 to its advantage. Many record labels have begun using MP3 as a promotional tool, allowing fans to download otherwise-unreleased material on the Web.

Using MP3 to pirate and illegally distribute music not only hurts the bottom line of the record companies but can also eat away at the artists' royalties. On the other hand, lesser known artists have begun using MP3 to distribute their music via the Internet and without the help of record labels. However, as of this writing, no artist has broken big via Internet-only distribution.

TIP ▸ ***The major record labels are joining together to develop a secure music technology based on an MP3-style format. Called the SDMI project (Secure Digital Music Initiative), it is still under development at the time of this writing. When it is released it may become the standard for secure, digitally distributed audio content.***

Copy protection doesn't necessarily preclude you from using an audio format. In fact one company, MP3lit.com, is using the open MP3 format to distribute audio books. Audible (www.audible.com), another major Web site, is also using the MP3 format, as well as RealAudio, to distribute audio books on the Web. As you can see, in this case the fact that the software could be easily copied doesn't necessarily mean it will hurt sales. It depends on your audience, pricing, type of product, and many other factors.

Of the three secure formats mentioned, Liquid Audio seems to be ahead of the pack at this point. Knowing how it works allows you to better understand some of the overall issues involved in audio ESD. The Liquid Audio system is composed of three major components:

- **Mastering** software, called Liquifier.
- **Server** software, called MusicServer.
- **Playback** software, called the Liquid MusicPlayer.

In addition, the company supports a digital watermarking solution from Solana Technology. Solana has developed a system known as Electronic DNA (E-DNA) which embeds (unbeknownst to the listener) copyright protection and secure tracking into the music. One key item of E-DNA and other ESD schemes is to embed a special customer number right into the music file before it's delivered. That way if someone copies it, they may actually be spreading it illegally over the Web to the point that the copying could be found and traced to the original source. Watermarking also ensures that an author of an audio file can brand MP3 files as being from the original source as opposed to a non-watermarked version that might have been illegally ripped from a CD.

TIP ▸ ***If you're going to use the open MP3 file spec, Liquid Audio offers a version of its technology, called Genuine Music Mark, that works with MP3 files.***

This sort of traceability makes it easy to go after people who illegally duplicate copyrighted audio files. Though it is not meant to catch individuals who make a copy for a friend, it is very good at preventing people from posting music publicly to the Internet. According to experts, there are more than 2,000 sites that are actively and illegally distributing music on the Internet.

The MusicServer software helps the merchant process the order, assemble it for delivery, and then send it down to the users' system, where it can be played back or written out to a CD. The server also works to record the song(s) sent and all the royalty information. The server manages the delivery of the content that, in the case of audio, can be of significant size.

On the other end, the MusicPlayer software allows users to preview titles and interact with the MusicServer to order the product, get it downloaded, and then play it back or record it.

RealAudio based ESD products are primarily focused on content that is used for informational purposes rather than for recording or high-end replication. Audible, Inc. leads in the RealAudio ESD space, providing a handy portable playback device for RealAudio content. Content is purchased from Audible and then downloaded directly for playback on their device, which holds almost two-hours of content.

After software, music content could become the next major market for ESD. You may have noticed that computer software is growing fast—file sizes for some applications may be even bigger than file sizes of digital versions of a record album. An album may be digitalized to as small as 40 or 50 MB, whereas a major software product like Microsoft Office can weigh in at 100 megabytes or more . Music sold directly on the Internet is already making some noise. Some companies are already saying that Internet music sales could exceed 1 billion dollars by 2002.

Recipe for Audio-Based ESD:

1. Record or obtain content for distribution.
2. Render content (MP3, Windows Media, RealAudio).
3. Apply copy protection by using a digital watermark or wrapping it in a secure format such as Liquid Audio, a2b, or SDMI.

4. Produce a low-quality version or small timed sample for Web site preview.

5. Produce a commerce system which accepts payment and returns sound via email or password-protected site.

6. Enable downloads.

Video

Broad-based video ESD is still quite a ways off. While some simple video clips may be sold via clip-services, it can be expected that video will remain out of ESD's reach for at least ten years. When that happens, the ESD process and solution will be somewhat similar to its audio cousin.

A Closer Look at ESD

ESD is not a terribly difficult process once you've put together the content, the formatting tools, copyright protection, and an underlying commerce system. However, this chapter would be incomplete if we didn't delve a little more deeply into the process.

Making ESD Work Securely

For ESD to be successful, secure delivery measures must be in place so that the product is delivered only to the intended recipient and only after the recipient has paid for the product.

One of the biggest worries about ESD concerns the accountability of the merchants who choose to use it. How does a developer know whether a merchant actually sold 500 copies of a certain ESD delivered album if all the merchant tracks are customer downloads? This is where ESD proponents have introduced a third party to the equation to ensure against counterfeit by merchants. Without third parties, it would be much more difficult to get vendors to move their distribution to ESD and thus the overall ESD revolution would be hindered.

A clearinghouse company restores the barrier to counterfeit reproduction. The clearinghouse acts as an independent means of auditing product distribution and sales. The software vendor also has a hand in controlling the validity of the software that is distributed.

If you want to provide ESD, you will be given a copy of the software master. ESD providers need the master because some systems rewrap the product every time to change the key codes and encryption process. Some also may distribute the ESD version and follow up with a mailed version for back-up purposes.

Before you can send a copy of that software to a customer via ESD, you must also have a secure version of the product that is packaged in a digital wrapper. That package cannot be unlocked and installed until customer payment is approved. The customer then receives a *key* to unlock the product. This key is a secret code that matches up with the software to uniquely unlock it once downloaded, so that it is operable.

The best way to ensure security is to have the master registered with the vendor. An independent clearinghouse then handles the distribution of the keys used to unlock the software. A key that is specific to the transaction ensures that the end user license agreement is registered, the vendor receives payment, and the publisher receives proper compensation.

The clearinghouse maintains a database of licensed users that contains customer transaction information. The software publisher assures customers that they receive software rights granted by the publisher and not by an intermediary. The vendor can also access the database when selling new software rights and returning or upgrading software to existing customers.

Clearinghouses are similar to digital certificate vendors mentioned in this book. They provide a means for everyone involved in the transaction to trust each other.

Stepping Through an ESD Transaction

Since you now have an understanding of the types of ESD and the role of clearinghouses, it is time to critically examine an ESD transaction.

A typical ESD transaction involves six steps:

1. The software publisher creates the software master

A software master is nothing more than the final original version of the software, be it a computer program, audio file, graphical image, or document.

2. The publisher or its manufacturing partner prepares the master for electronic distribution

The protected master is registered with selected partners and posted to appropriate Web sites. Preparation for electronic distribution can be done by the originator of the material. In some cases (primarily computer software), there are special vendors which help prepare the ESD version of the software. In the cases of art, audio, and documents, ESD usually involves the addition of a watermark that is a hidden attribute and can't be removed from the file. Once the final files are ready, the product is digitally wrapped or encrypted into a single file that requires a password or key to be applied to it before it will release itself for use.

For key-based orders, keys can be stored at a clearinghouse that then separately deliver that component to the user once a valid purchase is determined.

3. A customer orders the product

A customer will typically first access a degraded, timed, or preview version of underlying software before ordering the product. If the customer wants the product, she can then purchase the full version.

4. The retailer fulfills the order

Once a customer has placed an order, the merchant must provide him with several items. Many vendors first opt to present the End User License Agreement (EULA) to the user. (The EULA is the legal document that describes the terms under which the customer may properly use and transfer the software). The customer must accept it before the transaction can close. The merchant will also have to verify the credit card and undergo any other process needed to ensure that the software is being transferred to a reputable customer.

5. The retailer notifies the publisher and clearinghouse.

After authorization, the customer is given the key to download and install the product. Fulfillment usually involves delivering a secure password to a protected area of the retailer's site where the user can download the software. Many sites deliver the password and an authorization key via email first. Many keys are then embedded into the software as installed as a unique identification number so, as upgrades are ordered or customers request support, they can be identified as a legitimately obtained copy. Some may opt to simply deliver the full piece of software via email as well, depending on size.

6. Returns, re-installs, and post-purchase marketing

Returns are difficult in ESD in that, once downloaded and properly installed, it is difficult for a merchant to insist on the uninstallation of the software. In terms of corporate buyers, this is somewhat easier as adherence to proof-of-destruction notices by reputable customers can be effective.

However the honor system won't regularly work with individual consumers. Instead, ESD vendors must substitute strict return policies for such products. In this case, users could be allowed one return for every X number of orders. Multiple returns would be frowned upon. Overall, the hope is that a merchant can keep people from taking advantage of returns while leaving room to deal with loyal customers who make a small number of purchasing mistakes.

ESD Fraud and Other Concerns

When delivering software via ESD, make sure the software you sell is valid for sale outside of the country. The United States, for example, has strict rules against exporting software that provides certain levels of encryption and other security features. Serious fines and even jail time could result if someone overseas downloaded encruption software from you.

You might also have to deal with currency exchange, language issues, or local laws. For example, software depicting Nazi imagery is illegal in Germany. And while that might seem obvious, several years ago a WWII arcade game featured enemies with Nazi garb. It is difficult but very important to stay on top of such issues. You should make a concerted effort to keep from stumbling in the global marketplace.

As with traditional online sales (if there is such a thing), credit card fraud is the most common form of crime associated with ESD. And, as with traditional online sales, the merchant is usually liable.

Because unscrupulous online merchants (not you, of course) might not report the download transaction that was stolen through the use of an illegitimate credit card, the clearinghouse becomes more important as it looks over the shoulder of the merchant. The clearinghouse must work in cooperation with merchants not only to police them against high return rates, but also to assist them when legitimate returns or mistakes are made.

The other potential problem with ESD-based commerce is that goods are susceptible to hacker attack. Hackers can break through a site's protection and steal software. In fact, ESD vendors are prime targets for hackers. Hackers can also hurt merchants by cracking the digital wrapper that is used to protect the software. While this is more the responsibility of the ESD technology company that protects the software, it is something you need to be vigilant about.

Coordination Is Key

It is impossible to open up an ESD store immediately on the Internet unless you offer products that you make yourself. Due to the technology involved and the potential for piracy, many vendors and publishers of software are working slowly toward ESD. Not only must you construct a good ESD commerce site but you also need to work directly with the software publishers to make sure they approve you for ESD transactions. This might involve an audit of your site and company and a check to see that your site is properly configured for ESD transactions.

What this means is that if you want to implement ESD, you have to coordinate your efforts with the vendors and manufacturers. If not, you will never have the necessary stock. The software industry has rallied around several major vendors, all of which make digital wrapper products, and some, like Portland Software, that make server systems which also help. In terms of the music industry, Liquid Audio is absolutely in the lead, but others may soon join it. Most of the major record companies are taking it slow. RealAudio-based commerce is currently slow with most of it revolving around Audible, Inc. However that will only take off if its player does.

The document-based ESD market has been primarily left to individual companies; most book manufacturers remain uninterested. However, Adobe and its Acrobat product could begin to include some ESD features directly into Acrobat, making it even easier to begin selling documents over the Internet. Open Market has also begun to create specialized server software and back-end systems to facilitate large document-oriented Internet sales. This is important for companies with extensive archives such as newspapers, or which generate large sets of information such as research companies and textbook manufacturers.

For graphical content (like market leaders Corbis and Photodisc), most vendors are themselves the licensors or developers of the content.

ESD Is the Future

A large part of the future of e-commerce will be totally electronic in nature. So much of what people consume is deliverable over the Internet, given fast enough connection speeds. Once some of the remaining distribution and copy-protection problems are solved, it only requires the major producers to begin supporting ESD en masse. Once that leap of faith is made, expect this market to heat up considerably. Then stores will sell documents, music, digital stock art, and computer software as easily as they currently serve up graphics and text.

Being aware of the ESD universe and the basic framework of implementation places you ahead of the curve. As you explore ways to expand your store's offerings, you may want to consider the addition of digital goods and ESD.

ESD Terms

These are a few concepts that you might come across in setting up or electronic software distribution:

DIGITAL WRAPPERS. Digital wrappers provide a software shell aound the code of a pogram that prevents it from being fully usable without the proper key to unlock the software.

EULA. This acronym for End User License Agreement is simply the text that defines the terms of usage for the user. With ESD, you can create a screen that is displayed during ordering and includes the EULA and storing a code of the user's acceptance of it. This record can be used later to prove that the customer accepted the terms put forth during the sale. Some ESD solutions offer features to help with EULA implementations.

CLEARINGHOUSE. A clearinghouse ensues that all transactions are valid and makes them known to the software publisher and developer. They protect software developers from losing earned revenue.

PROOF OF DESTRUCTION. This is the virtual equivalent of a customer returning a product. If someone receives a product via ESD but decides not to keep it, the customer provides a Proof of Destruction form that guarantees the program's removal from the customer's hard drive.

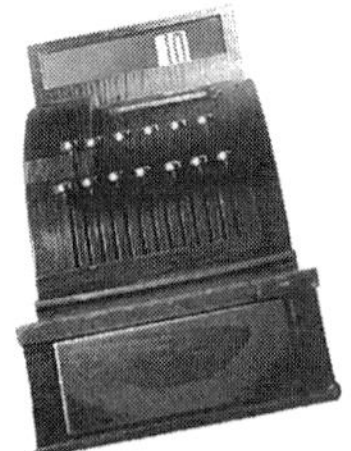

CHAPTER SEVENTEEN

Shipping

Online means mail order, and mail order means shipping. And, being an online store, you will have customers all over the world—some in very remote places. A significant number of them will be used to the immediate gratification of the Web, and that means being able to get them your goods as soon as possible. The speed with which you can deliver their orders can be critical to your business's success.

Shipping is one of the few things that links you physically with your customers. While pricing, promotion, communication, and order processing can be done virtually, the shipped package is what your customers will hold in their hands. The same level of speed, quality, and attention to detail you put into the Web-based portion of your store also needs to be applied to the shipping side.

You should understand that no single shipping option can cover you completely and provide maximum efficiency. The challenge is to stitch together the various services, software, Web sites, and your own store into a unified model that allows customers the best coverage, speed, and pricing options. Then you have to display this "shipping stew" on your site in a manner that is easy for your customers to understand.

A Web site with too many options or too few instructions is confusing to customers. When someone looks lost in a real store, the owner will notice and be able to physically respond. On the Web you won't. Customers will turn away without your even noticing as they find that you don't offer a particular option for delivery. All you will notice is lower sales.

All of these are reasons why something as mundane and physical as how you organize your shipping plan is incredibly important to your store. So get to know your solutions inside and out, use the Web as much as you can, and make sure your plan is clearly displayed to users. If you maintain that and utilize the software the shipping companies offer, your customers will get nicely packaged, on-time products, and you'll get repeat business. Many of the posts on newsgroups and much of the positive email Tronix has received from its customers concerns its attention to the details of shipping.

Setting Up a Shipping Account

A lot of account setup and management can be done via the Web. Setting up an account is especially simple online. The larger shipping companies have downloadable software on their Web sites, and you can also apply for an account by filling out a simple form online. To use the shipping software, you must have an account number.

Federal Express and Airborne Express have a representative contact you by phone, and once your account is set up, you'll be billed weekly. All three major private couriers will schedule a daily pick-up driver for your business. UPS requires a small weekly fee, whereas Federal Express and Airborne do not add any extra charges for this request (though you do pay for it with a higher per unit shipping charge). If your office is located near any of these major couriers, you can drop off your own packages and avoid the pressure of having the items ready for the driver—and perhaps save a small amount of money.

TIP ▸ ***When opening new accounts, every courier needs to know a time of pick-up. It's essential that you try to schedule your packages to be picked up as late as possible—preferably about 30 minutes before you close. This will give you the much-needed time to pack your boxes.***

All major couriers (except the U. S. Postal Service) want to know what kind of volume you intend on shipping per month or week. They may or may not offer a volume discount initially, but if you can eventually prove that you will move a decent amount of boxes per period, they'll work with you. At the beginning, you may be in a catch-22 situation. You'll need the discount to attract customers to your low-priced shipping, but the couriers want to see that you are moving volume before they offer that discount.

Here are some of the major shipping companies, some of their basic services, and how to set up an account. Joe has also offered up his special take on each one.

FedEx

www.fedex.com

FedEx is the leader in overnight shipping. FedEx Priority Overnight gets your package to most U.S. destinations by 10:30 A.M. the next business day. FedEx Standard Overnight gets a shipment to most U.S. cities by 3 P.M. the next business day and to most other U.S. destinations by 4:30 P.M. FedEx 2Day, the discount service, guarantees delivery by 4:30 P.M. the second business day to most U.S. destinations (up to 7 P.M. for many homes and residences). FedEx also has a freight service that handles packages from 151 to 1,500 pounds to most U.S. destinations. This service is available in overnight, 2Day and 3Day versions. Advanced registration is usually required.

Internationally, FedEx offers International Priority, which gets customs-cleared packages to more than 200 counties within one to three business days. Most major European destinations require two business days. FedEx International Economy offers a lower-cost solution for packages to Canada (two to three business days for delivery) and throughout the world (four to five business days).

Web and Software Features

FedEx offers several software packages for its customers. You can fill out the eBusiness Advisor form (www.fedex.com/us/software/advisor/) and receive a customized recommendation for the automation product(s) that best fit your business. FedEx offers its automated shipping software to businesses free of charge.

- **FedEx Ship 3.0** is the entry-level package available for download from the FedEx Web site. It lets you process shipments, track packages, create shipping labels, schedule pickups, and store frequently used addresses.
- **FedEx interNetShip** lets you process shipments directly on the Web site using any SSL-secure browser. You can ship a package and print Air Waybills on plain paper and save time with a personalized address.
- **FedEx PowerShip** is available for anyone shipping between 10 and 100 packages per day. PowerShip allows you to generate management reports

on shipping expenses and activity, helps you identify and correct process problems, send export data to customs officials electronically, and more. PowerShip Plus is for companies shipping more than 100 packages per day.

- **FedEx PowerShip PassPort** is for businesses shipping at least 100 domestic packages or 25 FedEx International Priority packages a day. PowerShip PassPort includes hardware, software, installation and maintenance instructions, and support to integrate with your existing computing environment.

Setting Up an Account

To open a FedEx account or sign up for a variety of services, go to www.fedex.com/us/registration/, click on the desired services, and follow the instructions.

Special Services

- **FedEx First Overnight** service guarantees delivery by 8 A.M. the next business day to nearly 5,000 U.S. ZIP codes for packages and boxes up to 150 pounds.

- **FedEx SameDay** service gets shipments up to 70 pounds to almost any U.S. destination the same day depending on availability. Call 1-800-Go-FEDEX for availability and booking.

Joe's Take: *FedEx services are nothing short of excellent, although their shipping rates are on the high side. When you begin to move a substantial amount of packages, you can work on getting a very good volume discount from your FedEx representative. FedEx offices are prevalent in major cities, with some operating as late as 9 P.M. If you plan on having late business hours, you can still get orders out in the early evening.*

TIP ▸ ***When you first set up shop, make sure you've checked the latest time for drop-offs and pick-ups for the local shipping companies. Times will vary from office to office and city to city. You never want to sprint to an office or a drop box only to find you missed the final drop-off deadline by five minutes.***

FedEx International shipments are always reliable, but keep in mind that its international rates are a bit expensive. Generally, if you start shipping across the globe to entities that rely on getting their products on time and without fail, they'll lean toward FedEx.

Airborne Express

www.airborne-express.com

Airborne offers traditional services including overnight (by 10:30 A.M.), afternoon (by 3 P.M.), and two-day service. Airborne also has international service to over 200 countries. It offers Sky Courier Next-Flight-Out International Service. It also has International Air Express Service, which provides door-to-door service within 24–96 hours, including customs clearance. The International Air Freight Service offers oversized and heavyweight freight shipping around the world, including customs clearance.

Web and Software Features

Airborne offers a number of software packages to help you better manage shipping products through its service.

- **LIGHTSHIP TRACKER** software provides basic tracking information and the ability to print shipping labels, estimate shipping charges, determine delivery times and schedule pickups. It is downloadable from the Web site at (**www.airborne.com/LightshipDownload/index.htm**) and runs on Windows 3.1, 95, 98, or NT.
- **WORLD DIRECTORY** helps you find any information pertaining to shipping to any of the more than 200 countries that Airborne serves.
- **LIBRA** system is a combination of tracking hardware and software that lets you weigh, rate and label every shipment. Libra also stores addresses, prints invoices and handles international forms and mailings as well.

Setting Up an Account

Airborne accounts can be opened by calling the toll-free number (1-800-AIRBORNE).

Special Services

Airborne has a custom warehousing and distribution solution it calls Airborne Logistics Services. There are several variants of this service, but the one that might be of interest to store owners is Stock Exchange. Same day service guarantees your shipment will be picked up within an hour of your call. Call 1-800-336-3344 to make arrangements.

Joe's Take: *Airborne has very competitive rates—usually cheaper than UPS or FedEx—but one disadvantage is the slightly complicated rate chart. For instance, Airborne offers an inexpensive next day afternoon service, but many less-accessible areas in the United States are not eligible. Therefore the shipper must constantly refer to a large Airborne manual to look up the state, city and ZIP code to see which areas are highlighted for this service. If an area you want to ship to is not eligible, the customer must pay a priority price (usually a few dollars more) just to get it there in the afternoon. During very busy periods, this extra bit of work slowed me down, and I didn't like keeping a customer on hold while I referenced their city to determine their rate. You can, of course, decide on one flat rate per pound and simply charge everyone the priority price to save time and headaches.*

DHL

www.dhl.com

DHL doesn't offer any second- or third-day delivery options; instead it only offers next day International Document Service and Worldwide Package Express (for dutiable, non-document goods of any size, weight, or value) and same day delivery.

Web and Software Features

Based on the volume you ship, you can set up shipping software that DHL calls Easy Ship. This lets you set up labels, track information, and fill out forms for fast and easy shipping within the DHL system.

Setting Up an Account

To set up an account with DHL, call 1-800-225-5345, and you will either receive a sales kit or be visited by an agent.

Joe's Take: *I've never used DHL because I'm relatively happy with what the other shippers provide for overseas service. DHL built a name for itself by being the company to use when shipping overnight overseas. However, now that FedEx, UPS and even the post office have beefed up their overseas operations, I—like many others—aren't as overwhelmed by their international prowess.*

U.S. Postal Service

www.usps.gov

Not surprisingly, the United States Postal Service offers a wide range of services. The USPS has even added delivery confirmation (for a charge of 35 cents) which includes a tracking number that allows you to check delivey status via phone or the Web. This does not insure the package.

The USPS offers the following:

- **Priority Mail** is a good choice if you are mailing small packages such as documents, contracts or small items such as, in the case of Tronix, CDs. Packages weighing two pounds or less cost just $3 to ship and arrive in 2–3 days. Rates for packages weighing up to five pounds do not vary by distance and there is a flat rate envelope available, for which you pay $3 no matter the weight.

- **Global Priority Mail** is available in two flat rate envelopes and ships to 31 countries.

- **Express Mail** offers guaranteed overnight delivery 365 days a year, morning delivery to 134 U.S. cities, automatic insurance, and delivery to post office boxes. However, each ZIP code has its own cutoff time in order for packages to arrive overnight. Most US ZIP codes will receive packages overnight even if the package is brought in or dropped off just before closing. However, there are many rural areas where the package must be dropped off in the early afternoon to ensure overnight delivery. Rates for packages weighing between two and 70 pounds are based on whole-pound increments no matter how far the packages are traveling. A flat rate envelope costs $15 for however much you can fit in it.

- **Express Mail International** offers many of the same features as Express Mail, although delivery usually takes two or three days. You can make overseas deliveries to military installations at domestic rates and international delivery to nearly 200 countries and territories. Prices start at $15.

TIP ▸ ***To request a free Business Information Kit, call 1-800-THE-USPS (843-8777) ext. 2049 or visit www.usps.gov.***

Web and Software Features

Global Package Link establishes a direct link between your business and the U.S. Postal Service, enabling the post office to handle most of the documentation for international shipments. This is a worthwhile feature for high-volume shippers.

Part of the Global Package Link is the Customs Pre-Advisory System (CPAS), which relieves you of paperwork and helps speed your packages through customs. CPAS enables customs agents to review the contents of your shipment prior to its arrival and decide if the parcel requires inspection. Although CPAS provides a declaration of contents, all shipments are subject to search at the discretion of customs agents.

Setting Up an Account

Setting up an Express Mail Corporate Account helps you avoid weighing packages, affixing stamps, and battling with postage meters. To set up an account, contact your nearest post office branch. To open an account, you must deposit $250 or your estimated Express Mail charges for four weeks, whichever is higher.

Once you have an account, enter your account number on the Express Mail label and drop off your package at any post office or Express Mail collection box. Each month you'll receive a statement detailing your mailing activity. You can pay for Express Mail with cash, a check or, in some cities, VISA, MasterCard, or Discover.

Special Services

- **Express Mail Custom-Designed Service** is tailored for your business's regularly scheduled, time-sensitive mailings and is available 24 hours a day, 365 days a year to meet your odd-hour mailing needs. You can have your shipments picked up or dropped off at any post office or airport mail facility offering Express Mail service. You can also have the package delivered directly to the addressee, have the addressee pick it up, or combine any of these options. Custom-Designed Service rates are determined by weight and delivery option and start at $9.45 for shipments weighing eight ounces or less.

- **Express Mail Drop Shipment** allows you to pick cities around the country and send any class of mail to those cities in overnight Express Mail sacks. The next morning the sacks are opened and the individual pieces are delivered according to their class.

- **Express Mail Reshipment** accelerates the arrival of incoming mail and can be useful for businesses that receive payments and fill orders by mail for their products.

- **Express Mail COD** lets you rush merchandise to customers who order by mail or phone and request fast delivery.

Joe's Take: *The U.S. Postal Service is generally a good choice and Priority Mail is a popular choice among Tronix customers. Keep in mind that, because of heightened security restrictions by the Federal Aviation Administration, any domestic mail other than Express Mail weighing 16 ounces or more and bearing stamps, or any international or military APO/FPO mail weighing 16 ounces or more, must be presented in person to a retail clerk at a post office or directly to a letter carrier. That means many of you must schedule pickups or make regular trips to the local post office.*

United Parcel Service

www.ups.com

As the largest shipping service, UPS offers a large number of services and is a very popular company, as evidenced by the broad effects its 1997 strike had on the shipping industry and UPS clients. The three basic services are GroundTrac, a reasonably priced two-day service known as "Blue Label," and overnight and early morning next-day shipping known as "Red Label." UPS also has a 3 Day Select service that guarantees delivery within three business days throughout mainland America.

TIP ▸ ***Depending on your account needs, you can schedule a daily stop by a UPS driver.***

UPS has begun aggressively building its international service. It offers Worldwide Express, which guarantees next-day delivery of packages to major cities in Mexico and Canada by 10:30 A.M., and to nearly 300 cities in the European Union by 10:30 A.M. the second business day. Saturday delivery to major cities in Canada is also available. Worldwide Express Plus can get packages to over 150 cities in 14 major European countries by 8:30 A.M. on the second business day.

The Worldwide Expedited service is cheaper and gets most shipments to Mexico and Canada in three days and to Europe and Asia in four days. For shipments to Canada, UPS offers Standard Service to Canada, which provides inexpensive service to every address in all ten provinces.

Web and Software Features

UPS has a number of software packages to help you better ship products, including a line of UPS Online software:

- **UPS Online Office** is free to every UPS account holder regardless of shipping volume. The package helps you process shipments, print address labels and pickup records, and track packages.
- **UPS Online Professional** requires a certain level of volume but offers increased options. You can generate detailed management reports, track multiple packages based on criteria, and receive major updates automatically.
- **UPS Online Tracking Software** is available for download right from the UPS homepage. This product lets you or your customers track packages directly from a PC.

Setting Up an Account

A UPS regional representative will usually come visit a first time account to set things up. Tronix has an agreement with UPS in which our shipping charges are deducted once a month from our business account.

UPS has a number of alternative payment plans, but anything automatic means one less bill to worry about at the end of the month. When business gets going, you'll thank yourself in the long run if you choose this option.

Special Services

Among UPS special services are Saturday delivery, COD service, and shipping insurance.

Joe's Take: *UPS GroundTrac is a great value for heavy items or for customers who aren't in a hurry to receive their order. Ground services go by truck, and therefore it can take as many as five days depending on how far the recipient is from the shipper. UPS provides you with a zone chart for your area that will estimate time of delivery. A good rule of thumb is to use UPS for any item over 12 pounds—or simply very large in size—that is a domestic order. Let your customer know that UPS GroundTrac may be the most cost-efficient. UPS GroundTrac automatically insures packages for up to $100. Each additional $100 will cost you about 50 cents more to insure. As far as international shipping is concerned, you can work out a deal where your UPS representative will apply special discounts to countries to which you frequently ship. This is a good reason to monitor where the bulk of your international business is coming from.*

Utilizing Each Courier's Strengths

Each shipping company has developed certain strengths. If you know precisely which ones are best for which situations and geographic areas, you can not only lower your overall costs but offer better customer service by providing the most flexibility and quickest service.

Post Office Domestic Priority Mail and Global Priority Mail are the two forms of shipping most often requested by Tronix customers. Domestic Priority Mail costs the customer only $3.20 for packages weighing two pounds or less, and only takes two to three days in transit, depending on the location. For each additional pound, it is an additional $1 to $1.50.

TIP ▸ ***Priority Mail is great for items of low value. The only major drawback to Priority Mail is the fact that there's no tracking number associated with the package—therefore you and your customer have no way of tracing a shipment if it's late or lost. The post office offers options like insurance and registered mail on Priority packages to keep your mind at ease. However, these additions involve extra charges, which put your shipment in the same cost bracket as the express couriers. Also, expect delays during the holidays and tax season. Priority mail is not a guaranteed delivery. Unlike express methods of shipping such as FedEx, UPS and Airborne Overnight and Second Business Day services, the post office will never guarantee a date of arrival on Priority Mail. You may want to remind your customer that Priority Mail can sometimes exceed the estimated time in transit, and if the package arrives later than expected, there's nothing that can be done in terms of a shipping refund to the customer.***

For small, international shipments, you can't beat Global Priority Mail from the post office. This shipping option is similar to U.S. Priority Mail, and the time in transit is anywhere from four to seven days. The post office will supply you with two types of mailers, which are good for magazines, books, CDs, jewelry and any other small, flat items. Both sized mailers have a low flat rate from $5 to $9, depending on the country you are shipping to. Tronix is able to ship up to six CD games in the larger Global mailer and, within a week, an international customer will receive his or her package without spending a fortune on shipping. Because these flat rate mailers are normally meant for documents, be sure to wrap your goods with a sheet of bubble wrap. Don't wrap it too thick—otherwise you won't be able to seal the envelope.

If your item is fragile or exceeds the size and shape of a Global mailer, then you can pack your order in a small box. The post office provides Global Priority stickers for boxed items; however, there is no longer a flat rate involved. Now you will need to refer to a Global rates chart which increases in price every half pound. The savings are still quite good compared to other major couriers. The maximum amount for any Global Package is four pounds and is good only for selected countries.

Like the other three couriers, the post office offers its own Express Mail shipping for U.S. and international customers. Express Mail shipments have their own tracking numbers, and the air bills couldn't be any easier to fill out. For U.S. customers, most Express Mail shipments arrive the next day, but you may want to check with your local post office about the city you are shipping to. Some cities require your package to be at the post office at selected cut-off times; otherwise the package will arrive on the second day. Be sure to make your customer aware of this.

TIP ▸ ***Separate your orders by courier. Work on the orders that need to be in at the earliest times first. In my case, it's the post office orders that require the most work, and have to be checked in first. If you are planning on using the post office for many of your shipments, be sure to call and check what time your local post office closes. The average closing time is 5:30 P.M., but many post offices in major cities have later hours.***

One major advantage of Express Mail is weekend service. If a U.S. customer places an order on Friday and wants it delivered on the weekend, FedEx, UPS and Airborne charge an additional $10 fee for Saturday delivery, whereas the post office does not have any additional charges. Besides saving the additional fee, many customers will be surprised to know that Express Mail shipments include Sunday delivery. If a package doesn't make it to a customer on Saturday, it will certainly get there on Sunday. This is also a great option if you plan to ship orders out on Saturdays.

International Express Mail is a good bargain. Most of Tronix's international customers prefer using this service to using the other couriers. It might take anywhere from two to four days for Express Mail packages to get to the international recipient, but the difference in price compared to other couriers is substantial. Many international customers visiting your Web site may need a little extra hand-holding when choosing their courier. If they want their order to arrive fast, without spending too much money, Express Mail is the first option recommended. Offering a little help like this also shows your individual concern for your customers' needs and will most likely guarantee you a return customer.

Admittedly, the only downfall with Express Mail is the reliability factor. Whereas FedEx, Airborne, and UPS International shipments are fairly expensive, they are generally accurate and arrive at the expected date, whereas the post office Express Mail shipments can experience delays. A lot of the delay has to do with how efficient a particular country's mail system is.

UPS and Airborne International Express shipments generally arrive in most major countries in two days. The shipper is required to include three copies of the original bill of sale for customs purposes. These copies should be placed together with the air bill in the supplied pouch, which is adhered to the outside of your box/envelope. FedEx and the post office supply their own customs form, so there's no need to print multiple copies of your customer's invoice for these couriers.

TIP ▸ ***Light items such as CDs, magazines and other small, flat goods, are great for shipping in FedEx, UPS, or Airborne mailers. These envelopes allow up to eight ounces, with overnight flat rates that are fairly inexpensive. The UPS letter package doesn't have an 8 ounce limit, but they are not as sturdy as boxes, so resist the temptation to overstuff them. Although these mailers are only intended for documents, you'd be surprised what can be shipped in a flat rate envelope. Once any small item is put into a box, the overnight price is automatically jacked up. So remember: if it is a flat, sturdy item weighing eight ounces or less, go for those mailers.***

Minimizing Your Shipping Rates

Courier rates are a private affair. Once you have obtained your personal discount rates for bulk shipments, you can decide on your own scale of shipping prices that can add a small profit to your orders. However, watch for the competition, especially well-established businesses that move mass quantities and already have frighteningly low rates.

In Tronix's line of business—primarily video and computer games—competition is intense. Tronix initially chose not to make any additional money on my shipping prices and that quickly attracted customers. If a customer has to spend a lot of money on shipping, then mail order may not be worthwhile, especially if the item is easily obtainable in their neighborhood.

TIP ▸ ***Mail-order houses that carry items which can be found in stores should always keep their shipping rates as low as possible.***

Originally, Tronix worked with a UPS and FedEx account and, when the number of orders began to increase, looked into working with Airborne Express, especially after hearing about their attractive rates. It quickly became obvious, however, that the savings would be minimal.

A representative will usually ask you which couriers you are currently using. You should tell the person the truth, while also mentioning that you would be willing to use their service over the others depending on their rate.

With this information, Airborne offered a substantial discount, and Tronix immediately added an Airborne basic rate chart to its Web site. Before long, there was a significant increase in overnight shipments and, more importantly, new customers. Using the same process above, FedEx eventually lowered its rates as well. Since it is hard to spread the business between the three couriers, each with a quota, Tronix uses FedEx and Airborne for express and second day services, and UPS for their inexpensive GroundTrac shipments.

TIP ▸ ***If there are a few mail order sites offering the same product, for the same price, a smart consumer will most likely drift toward the company offering the least expensive shipping and handling charges.***

Shipping Supplies: Easier to Get Than You Think

All couriers are more than happy to send your business free shipping supplies.

With the post office, you don't need to have a special account to order your supplies; you can call and get supplies shipped to your business any time you need them. The post office offers a variety of shipping materials such as Express, Priority, and Global Envelopes, rolls of Priority Mail tape, sturdy boxes for shipping garments, books and video tapes (to name a few items), and even pre-printed Express forms and self-adhesive Priority Mail labels with your business address. Materials other than pre-stamped packages or envelopes are free. In addition to packing materials, you will need a number of other things to make your shipping efficient.

Ordering Supplies

When ordering supplies, look at the range of items you'll be carrying and order boxes to accommodate each size (and even shape) of the item. Keep some boxes around that are at least two to three times larger than your largest item. You never know when you may have to ship two or three of the same large item to one customer. Larger boxes can also be cut down to make a smaller box, so they never go to waste.

If you're a small store-owner working alone most of the time, all of the shipping chores are in your hands. Boxing orders soon becomes an art form. Try to stay away from very thick cardboard boxes; they'll only add unnecessary weight to your order, thus increasing the customer's shipping rate. Remember that you want these people to order from you again.

TIP ▸ ***In addition to its standard box, UPS has two types of boxes which your UPS supplier never speaks of and are not even mentioned in any of the UPS guide books. Tronix's UPS daily pick-up driver mentioned this when he noticed we were shipping fairly small items (generally no bigger than a paperback book) and the standard UPS boxes were a bit too large. These generally unmentioned containers are called security boxes and are usually best used for small items in need of good protection. The collapsible boxes come in two sizes with easy, interlocking folds, creating a solid container for protecting any small, fragile item. UPS doesn't publicize these boxes because they do not bear the UPS logo and therefore can be used for shipping with other couriers. If you need them, don't be afraid to ask your UPS supply house. Tell them that you are shipping a lot of small, valuable items and the smallest box they offer is too big for your shipments.***

Packing Boxes

Pack most of your boxes with Styrofoam when needed; it weighs next to nothing and protects fragile items quite well. Seal your packages with thin brown packing tape—the kind with a shiny surface. This type of tape is very flexible and is thin enough to mold around box corners to protect your shipment and make it look more presentable.

Another excellent protective packing material is bubble wrap. It is great for wrapping any item, especially those needing extra padding. And who doesn't get a kick out of popping the stuff? It's almost an extra gift for your customer! A good place to order shipping supplies from is ULINE (on the Web at www.uline.com or by phone at 1-800-95-ULINE).

TIP ▸ ***Try to buy tape, bubble-wrap, Styrofoam and boxes in bulk. Many office supply mail-order houses offer discount pricing on all types of box sizes, rolls of tape, and other related material. This will save you money in the long run, rather than buying small quantities at your local supply store.***

Your Shipping Area

Have at least two shipping tables in your work quarters and keep them as clear as possible. You'll use one for working on orders, the other for complete orders. Many large office superstores sell these types of inexpensive tables, which come in various lengths. Try to fit the longest tables possible into your space. By keeping your shipping area clear you'll be able to pack boxes easily, and orders won't get confused. Eliminate unnecessary items—air bill forms, envelopes, paper clips, pens, music CDs—from your table. If you don't, when business begins to take off, your shipping table will become a nightmarish collage of office supplies, making it more difficult to find things when you need them. The more room on the table, the more comfortable and fast it will be to pack your boxes. If you work without a shipping table, you'll find the knees of your jeans wearing through in a hurry (and unfortunately the mid-'90s grunge look is out).

TIP ▸ ***Throw in goodies. Sometimes distributors will give out free catalogs or brochures on upcoming products. Make a habit of asking your distributors for any extra promo catalogs, advertisements, teasers, posters, or whatever they may have (which of course relates to your business). It's always a nice gesture to occasionally add a little something to your shipments, especially if it's something that may be of interest to the customer, which can be judged by what they're purchasing. On the other hand, remember that extra material can bog down your package. The next thing you know, you've charged the customer for a two- pound box, and now you are going to get charged for three pounds. Use your best judgement. If you can squeeze another ounce or two into your package before it jumps to the next weight, then go for it.***

One of the most essential tools for shipping—and one of the first things you'll want to buy—is a good scale. Tronix started with a basic scale for under $30 that had a ceiling of 50 pounds. With an average shipment in the one-pound range, we didn't need anything fancy. As the business grew, orders became bigger and the scale eventually wore down. There's nothing worse than an inaccurate weight reading that could result in overcharging the customer or shortchanging yourself. If you have the extra money, invest in a quality digital scale that will provide long-term, accurate read-outs.

Getting the Software You Need

As we mentioned, FedEx, UPS, and Airborne offer their own software for entering, tracking, and filing shipments. Once your account is set up, ask for the free software in case your representative neglects to offer it (reps are always on the move so when you pin one down, ask for the world if you can). FedEx, in particular, offers a package to their customers called Power Ship, which includes software, a laser printer, and a special terminal if you want to use it in place of your computer.

Power Ship allows you to automate all of your shipping, from keeping a customer database on file, to automatically printing out special bar-coded labels and the customer's address. You simply pop one on each box, and there's no need to write a thing. FedEx encourages their customers to use Power Ship, as both the business owner and the FedEx clerk who checks boxes are able to save time. Power Ship is free, with the equipment basically being loaned by FedEx to all types of businesses. But you do have to be in business for at least a year and have a steady record of volume shipping. Even 15 to 20 boxes per day should do the trick.

TIP ▸ ***The software offered by the major couriers is very convenient for shipping data entry. However, you should keep some of those old airbills around in case your shipping system goes down.***

Shipping Labels Made Simple

To make life simpler, make a return address template with your word processing software. Every few months, print out about 1,000 labels and simply peel and stick them on all of your UPS Ground or International Global Priority Mail shipments. Because you don't use pre-printed forms with these types of shipments, it saves time, rather than having to write your address on each box. Of course, you can also go to any stationery store and order a return address stamp and pad. But if you have a laser printer, designing your own return address logo is easy and it actually looks more appealing than a generic stamp. Plus, you have the advantage of changing your design any time you'd like.

Linking Shipping with Your Web Site

One thing you can do to make your Web site interesting is to add all the major shipping courier links to your Web site. Federal Express, Airborne Express, UPS, DHL, and the U.S. Postal Service all have their own informative Web sites, which include package tracking features and a wealth of information about their services. Customers who place orders through the express couriers can then click on these corresponding links and head over to the Web site. Customers can track their own packages and learn more about the shipping service they chose.

If your company doesn't have a toll-free number, customers won't want to keep calling you to check on their order. Online tracking saves them the long distance call and you the extra time and effort trying to find their package. Automating customer service onto your Web site is key to keeping your operations lean and mean. When designing your Web site, you can choose to add these links to any page you desire. You might want to copy and paste these links below your price lists, or have them on the bottom of every page along with your general links. Tronix felt it would make sense to keep all the shipping information together in one special shipping page (Figure 17.1).

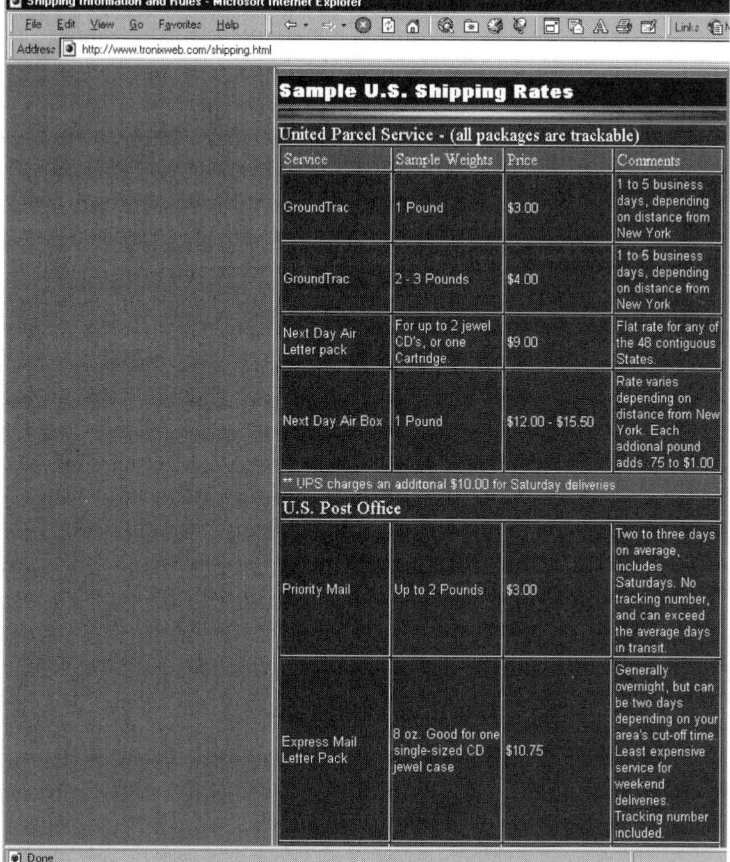

Shipping Information and Rules - Microsoft Internet Explorer

Address: http://www.tronixweb.com/shipping.html

Sample U.S. Shipping Rates

United Parcel Service - (all packages are trackable)			
Service	Sample Weights	Price	Comments
GroundTrac	1 Pound	$3.00	1 to 5 business days, depending on distance from New York
GroundTrac	2 - 3 Pounds	$4.00	1 to 5 business days, depending on distance from New York
Next Day Air Letter pack	For up to 2 jewel CD's, or one Cartridge.	$9.00	Flat rate for any of the 48 contiguous States.
Next Day Air Box	1 Pound	$12.00 - $15.50	Rate varies depending on distance from New York. Each addional pound adds .75 to $1.00
** UPS charges an additonal $10.00 for Saturday deliveries			
U.S. Post Office			
Priority Mail	Up to 2 Pounds	$3.00	Two to three days on average, includes Saturdays. No tracking number, and can exceed the average days in transit.
Express Mail Letter Pack	8 oz. Good for one single-sized CD jewel case	$10.75	Generally overnight, but can be two days depending on your area's cut-off time. Least expensive service for weekend deliveries. Tracking number included.

Done

FIGURE 17.1
Tronix's shipping page was designed to give customers a number of shipping options. Tronix no longer uses a shipping page because its shopping cart now generates shipping estimates.

Your Shipping Information Page

If you don't use a shopping cart that generates shipping estimates, one of the most important parts of your Web site will be your shipping information page. You'll want to have a page which will list your company's shipping policies, along with some sample, cross-reference shipping charts showing the name of the courier service, a sample of your prices with corresponding weights, and the time in transit. You may even want to have all of your general company information—which will include your ordering and shipping policies on one page—and a separate page for your rate tables.

If you plan on having a large table of rates for each courier, you may want to have a page dedicated to each service so you don't bog down the user's browser. It would be nearly impossible to post every weight and price for each courier, so it might be a good idea to list the rates for perhaps the first five pounds from each service.

If the type of products you sell have similar weights, you may want to show rates that would only reflect that range of weights. For example, if your line of business is dedicated to specific types of antique desktop clocks, and you know all of your clocks range from four to six pounds, set up a rate chart to reflect the most-used weights. You might want to show rates from four pounds to 12 pounds in case someone orders two of your heaviest clocks. Of course, there may be orders that exceed the weight of any information you have provided on your sample rate chart, in which case the customer can call or email you to inquire about that price.

Below your rate chart, it would be a good idea to add a linked message to your email in case customers need further price information on shipping or they need to know the weight of a specific item. If your line of business stocks only a small variety of items, you might even want to show the weight of each item right on your price list. Create your basic shipping chart using the table function in your HTML editor or a good word processor, which will allow you to easily create tables that can be converted into HTML format.

Pros and Cons of COD

You might choose to accept COD (Cash on Delivery) in your business. There are some advantages and disadvantages you should consider before deciding whether this payment option is right for you.

One advantage is that you will certainly have access to a larger customer base. Many people either don't have credit cards or don't want to use them every time they place an order. By having customers not use credit cards, you also keep the percentage of your sale that would be taken by the credit card company. You also don't have to worry about a fraudulent credit card order.

However, there are also a number of disadvantages. First of all, the customer is charged approximately an additional $10 by the courier for COD and a customer could change his or her mind while the order is in transit, thereby sticking you with the shipping charges as the order boomerangs back to you. Then you might need to ship that back to the distributor, incurring more charges and tying up capital.

The customer also has to be at home in order to pay the driver and, in some cases, it can take more than a week to get your payment. And, of course, that has to get deposited in your bank account and the check has to clear.

Joe's Take: *When I began to take CODs, I used UPS because I was under the assumption that UPS was the only company that took CODs. The problem I had with this, especially being a small company (with an equally small business bank account) was waiting for payment to arrive. So don't expect that money to be available in your account for at least two weeks. After doing COD exclusively with UPS, I found out that FedEx also accepts CODs and your payment is delivered by a FedEx driver on the next business day after delivery. Unfortunately, FedEx does not accept cash, so you'll have to remind your customer to have a money order ready for the FedEx driver. You can accept a personal check if that customer is a trustworthy regular customer.*

Mistakes Happen and That Means a Refund

In this imperfect world, there will no doubt be many times when you make a shipping mistake on a customer's order, especially when you are a one-person operation, having to take on every possible angle of a small business. Late, lost, or incorrect orders are probably the biggest reasons people are reluctant to use a mail-order service.

If you do happen to make mistake on a customer's shipping address, forget to check off the appropriate method of shipping, or send them an incorrect item or quantity, show your deep concern, apologize profusely, and offer the customer free shipping on the next order. If they paid to have the package shipped overnight, and it didn't get there because of a mistake made by your company, refund their shipping fee, as it will alleviate some of your customer's anger.

Most customers will understand the situation and they'll probably want to take advantage of the offer by placing another order. You may have lost some—or all—of your profit on this sale by refunding the current shipping fee and giving free shipping on the next order, but in the long run, you've probably gained a permanent customer and provided yourself some good word-of-mouth. Most reasonable people understand that mistakes can be made. As long as you work to correct them, you can turn a negative into a positive.

TIP ▸ ***Be incredibly careful when filling out your address labels. Always double-check all your information before you plaster that label onto your box. Check for spelling, ZIP codes, spaces, and capitalization—and by all means, make sure your handwriting is legible. You don't want packages sitting in a warehouse for an extra day—or worse, having your courier return boxes to your establishment because your "D" in Delancy Street looked like an "O".***

Joe's Take: *If you're using software provided by the courier, you can simply cut and paste all customer address information between the order form and the shipping form. Of course that means your ordering system and shipping software must reside on the same computer. This is one reason that Tronix uses FedEx Ship over FedEx PowerShip, which uses a separate computer provided by FedEx. Cutting and pasting data between forms helps eliminate errors, assuming the customer didn't enter incorrect information on the order form.*

As a Web-order business owner, you may become frustrated when packages shipped by your express couriers don't arrive at their destinations on time. This scenario is a common one for mail-order companies, so you're not alone. A customer calls and complains he or she paid for overnight shipping but the package never showed. You put them on hold while you retrieve the copy of their air bill. You dash for your database or point of sale program to double-check their address, and everything checks out fine. Now what?

Well, you can start by patting yourself on the back, knowing it wasn't anything you did wrong—it was obviously the fault of the courier. When this happens, ask the customer for a phone number where she can be reached immediately. Let the customer know that you'll call the courier to find out where the package is because the copy of the air bill's information is completely correct. After learning why the package is late and when it will arrive, remind the courier service operator that your company should receive full credit for the shipping (remember, you're getting billed for it, even though you've already charged the customer).

Now you can call your customer back, explain the situation, and offer a shipping refund. Sending email with a full explanation is also a good idea in case the customer is not there when you call back. You can either give the customer a credit to apply toward the next order or simply refund the shipping amount. Unless the package was late because of an act of God, your courier should refund your money, and you should refund your customer's.

TIP ▸ ***Keep your most recent, already processed FedEx, Airborne, UPS, or US Post Office Express Mail air bills handy. If a customer calls and requests his or her tracking number, or if a package is late, you can easily pull out the information without keeping the customer on hold. After a few days, you can file them away. Some of the more powerful shipping software will also help automate this process.***

Just In Case, Insure Shipments

Make certain that large ticket items are insured. Couriers generally have automatic insurance on your shipments, but they usually only cover the first $100. You should make it a habit to insure any orders over $300. When insuring a package, FedEx, UPS, and Airborne will have a specific area on the air bill to fill out the amount of insurance you want to declare for your shipment. You will then be charged a small percentage for every additional $100 beyond the first $100. Be sure to tell your customer that this will be added to their charges. They shouldn't mind, knowing that if their package is lost or damaged in transit, there will be a full, hassle-free refund or replacement. After your business grows and you can afford it, you can always include this insurance without charging the customer, because it's a small fee to pay and yet another option that can make a customer happy.

TIP ▸ ***Watch for addresses that contain a Post Office Box. FedEx, UPS, and Airborne will not deliver to these addresses—only the post office will. It's no fun to realize this after your local post office has closed for the day.***

JOE'S TAKE: *Unless you request "Signature Required" on the parcel, usually UPS will leave Ground packages and FedEx will do the same with Express Saver packages at the recipient's door. This is fine in most cases—however the package can be a target for theft in some neighborhoods. You can discuss this with your customer before shipping, especially if it is a large, noticeable package. Some will say that it is fine to have the package dropped on a porch or by their door while others will rather receive the package in person.*

Reinforcing the Shipping Link

As you prepare to launch your online store, it's to your advantage to set up all of your shipping accounts ahead of time—even if there is a service you don't plan to use immediately, it may be useful in the long run. You also want to know everything you can ahead of time because you never know when a particular shipper may offer the only way to get a product into the hands of a die-hard customer. For example, you should check with each courier about pick-up and drop-off times. In some large cities like New York, not all of the drop-off offices close at the same time. Knowing this ahead of time could be crucial to getting out an order at the last second—and it's this kind of attention to detail that will win you rave reviews by your customers on the Internet.

As this chapter stated at the outset, shipping is the physical link between you and your customers when everything else is so virtual. As the 1997 UPS strike showed, shipping is one of the most important aspects of many businesses, online stores included. Don't make the mistake of treating it as anything short of critical.

PART V

Maintaining and Growing Your Store

You have embarked on an evolutionary process. The stale store is the unsuccessful store. Part V shows you how to keep your store fresh, how to build loyal customers, and how to beat the competition. It also takes a look at some important issues in the emerging online legal landscape.

Part V Table of Contents

CHAPTER EIGHTEEN

Maintaining Your Store

You're up and running. Flying, we hope. However, you can't just let your site sit there. Operating an online store involves daily tasks that are easily scheduled and a number of larger, less frequent tasks. And of course there are those time-swallowing emergencies that you might as well count on. You never know when an order will get lost, you'll get scammed by someone using a fraudulent credit card, or a power failure will knock you out of work for a couple of hours. The more prepared you are for Murphy's Law, the better off you'll be.

This chapter gives you some tips on how to organize your day so you're not trying to pack 40 boxes an hour before they have to be out the door. You'll also get some tips on how to best deal with waves of email, when to redesign your site, how to handle invoicing, and how to organize your site's back end. Hopefully you'll reach peak efficiency. But remember, Pedro Martinez still works on his fastball. No matter how efficient you think you are, you can always get better.

Organizing Your Day

When you're running a small operation, the way to keep things running smoothly is by being organized. You can't show up in the morning without a plan and expect to be efficient. Everyone's schedule will vary, but the important thing is that you have one and stick reasonably close to it. Of course emergencies will force you to be flexible, but if you have a solid schedule, it will be far easier to deal with these unannounced problems. This is how Tronix schedules its day.

Checking Your Voice Messages and Faxes

The day usually begins with a check for any new voice mail messages that have arrived after business hours from the previous day (or over the weekend). If you have a fax, check your machine for orders or announcements from distributors.

Joe's Take: *I use a PIM (Personal Information Manager) program to deal with day-to-day tasks and contacts. The program I use is Lotus Organizer, which eliminates desk clutter and helps you avoid losing a message when you get sidetracked by ringing phones. Organizer is a great tool to have readily accessible. I leave Organizer running throughout the day for note taking. You can add your primary contacts (such as distributors, credit card merchants, and bank representatives) into Organizer's handy address book, with autodial features at the click of a mouse. If you're not a fan of Lotus Organizer, other PIM programs, including Starfish Software's Sidekick and Microsoft's Outlook, are also useful.*

Pull in Your Email, Extract Your Orders

After returning all of its business-related phone inquiries, Tronix begins pulling in the morning email, which takes 30 to 60 minutes. You should concentrate first on orders which have come through email or your online shopping cart. Check out the products requested by each customer and carefully look over all of the information they've submitted. Make sure they provided a phone number, the issuing bank of the credit card, the type of shipping desired, and all of the product information. As submitted orders are read, Tronix adds each of the requested items to a blank page in Organizer, creating a master list of items needed.

Orders vs. Inventory

Unless you are one of the fortunate few who have your order and inventory system tied together, now is the time to see which ordered products you have available on site and which you will have to order from suppliers.

Place Your Orders

Assuming there are orders for out-of-stock products, it's time to call your suppliers. You may have items in stock or may be selling products you have manufactured—if so, you won't have to worry about this.

When you call your suppliers, you need to find out exactly what they have in stock or when they will be getting restocked. If you work in a release-sensitive industry, you also need to ask what new products have arrived or will be arriving that day.

TIP ▸ ***Before finalizing your daily orders with distributors, check in with your customers. Is waiting an extra day for an out-of-stock order a problem? Why wasn't the credit card verifiable? Will the customer send a second email for additional items to be shipped with the first order? The later your distributor allows you to complete the ordering process, the more changes or additions you can make. Generally, distributors don't mind last-minute additions to your orders. Cancellations are another matter.***

Update Your Site

Daily updates to your site can become necessary unless your inventory doesn't change often. You will save yourself a lot of customer complaints by keeping your site and your list of products up to date.

Key items to update include new products, out of stock products, and price changes. Unless you offer a very wide range of products, these updates are usually minor and only require about 30 minutes to be added to your What's New page and your price lists.

Back to Email

With your site updated, you need to go back to your email and look specifically for orders placed by first-time customers. It's important to confirm that the credit card is valid. Once those orders are verified, you can begin responding by email to your customers to inform them of the status of their orders.

Process Your Invoices

Now you can begin processing sales for items that are readily available. If part of a current order is not expected in stock for a day or two, you can still process the order. You might wind up with a declined credit card and have time enough to cancel the order with your supplier. Orders expected to ship out that day should be separated from incomplete orders. You should also separate your daily outgoing orders by shipping type, since each method of shipping requires a different set of procedures.

Print Address Labels

If you are using UPS, Airborne, or FedEx online shipping software, you might want to process your address labels now since you will have to add any new customers to these individual databases. After your labels are printed, you can sort through any post office orders and begin filling out your domestic and international address labels.

If your point of sale program has such a feature, you can simply print those labels out. Tronix's day begins at 10 A.M. By 3 P.M., address labels have been printed and sorted by shipping type.

Pack and Ship

With your labels finished, you can begin putting together your boxes and packing any orders that involve readily available stock. Set those completed orders aside and prepare boxes and labels for any orders involving stock that is expected to arrive that day. Once that stock arrives, you can simply place the newly arrived items into the premade boxes or envelopes. Whether couriers pick up your shipments or you drop them off, allow yourself enough time to get every order out before deadlines. You don't want to have to email a customer and inform him that you didn't get his package out because you didn't have time. With experience, you will learn how to pace yourself. Orders will come in throughout the day. It's up to you to figure out how late you can accept an order and still get it shipped the same day.

TIP ▸ ***As discussed in Chapter 17, it is important to have a list of all your shipping outlets and their deadlines for shipments. You can either post this on a wall or have it easily accessible on your computer. That way if someone absolutely has to have something overnight, you can easily find the shipping company with the most convenient deadline.***

The Home Stretch

You've made your deadlines; all of your orders are out the door and on their way to your customers. You can breathe now. This is a good time to do a final email check and some general organizing around your office. If you have a scanner at work, you can start scanning in photos of new products. You can do minor Web work now or save it for later tonight at home.

Expect the Unexpected

You can have an entire day planned out beginning to end and even arrive to your office earlier than usual. But there's always the possibility of an unwelcome time destroyer:

- **Package didn't arrive.** You may have to spend time tracking down packages that did not arrive when or where they were supposed to.
- **Items missing.** You may have to call a supplier after realizing an item is missing from your order or you were overcharged on a specific item.
- **Bills bills bills.** You may have bills or taxes to pay.
- **Shipping overcharging.** You may need to call various shipping companies to find out why you were overcharged on a bill.
- **Charge-backs.** You may have to deal with the dreaded charge-back from a credit card company, which means you'll have to fetch the original invoices from the sale in question.

Joe's Take: *The best way to deal with shipping pick-ups is to arrange a time at which the various drivers will stop by daily. If you call whenever you need a pickup, be sure you know how late you can call each courier and still have your packages picked up that day. The later you can have your orders picked up, the better. This gives you time to fill all your orders without having to neglect all other operational aspects. However, if you are in the early stages of operation and only need to ship a few orders a day, you might want to arrange earlier pick-up times. Otherwise you might end up sitting around twiddling your thumbs until 8 P.M. waiting for your couriers to show up.*

Dealing With Email

Email is perhaps the most important tool for your business; it is the essential avenue of communication between you and your customers. You will use email everyday to follow up on orders, handle problems, sort out preorders, and answer general customer inquiries. As your store grows in popularity, the amount of email you receive can be nearly overwhelming.

If you can afford it, you should have a computer at home. Operating a small online business means you can't simply punch a clock at 5 P.M., go home, and put your feet up. Communicating with your customers from home, whether or not your home is your office space, is something you'll need to do nearly every day. As the email begins to pour in, you will find less time to answer all your email during business hours.

Joe's Take: *Once my business began to take off, I noticed I had very little time to ship out all of my orders after responding to all my email. Eventually I found myself completely stressed out late in the day as I tried to fulfill all the orders and answer the phone. By the end of the day, I was both wired and totally exhausted.*

At Home, Leave Mail on the Server

It is important to have 24-hour access both to your site's back end and your email. Many email programs offer the option of having your messages deleted from the server once you have downloaded them to the client. This option can allow you to easily access your messages from home without creating two separate pools of email. On your home computer, set your email client to not delete messages once downloaded. This way you can safely download and answer mail at home. When you arrive at work the following day, your work machine will download all those same messages again and then delete them off your mail server. That makes your work computer the master holder of all email but gives you the flexibility to answer and read new email from other locations. Once at work, you can simply delete or archive the messages you dealt with the previous night. It's the best way to have two locations accessing the same email account.

Prioritizing Email

Eventually you must prioritize your email. Orders come first. Customers expect to receive a quick response, which is the whole point of shopping on the Web. Whether or not the customer's order is in stock, you should let them know as soon as possible.

You will also receive a number of general inquiries, such as "When will you have the latest version of EZMoneyManager?" or "Do you ship to North Africa?" General questions can be answered during business hours if you have some spare time, but once the tide rolls in, you should forward these emails to your home. That gives you more time to fill orders during business hours and answer nonurgent email at your own pace in the comfort of your home.

TIP ▸ ***If you work out of an office, keep a copy all of your shipping information at home so you can answer general shipping rate questions after hours.***

You should check your email regularly throughout the day. If you have a phone line (or dedicated line) for Internet access, you can leave it running all day and have your email program check at regular intervals for incoming mail.

Filters

Email filters keep mail organized by applying a set of rules to all incoming mail. Filters look for keywords in the subject line, the body of text, and the sender's address. They trigger special events such as deleting, moving, or automatically responding to the message. You can design your online order form so that orders are sent to your email address with the word "order" in the subject line.

By having the filter check for the word *order* in the subject line, the incoming message can then be sent to a folder for orders. Separating orders from all other email eliminates the need to open every piece of email in search of orders.

However, not everyone will use your order form to place an order. Some customers may use email to submit an order. Regular customers might send a message saying something like "This is John Doe. Send me another one of those doggie beds using the same shipping, address, and credit card information as the last time." If John Doe's message has a subject line that reads "This is John Doe," the filter will not know to send it to the order folder. The message will simply be sorted with your regular messages in your incoming mailbox or main folder.

If the same message had a subject line reading "This is John Doe with a reorder," the filter would find the trigger word *order* in *reorder* and send it to the assigned folder. To limit the frequency of this problem, instruct your customers to use the word *order* in their email orders. Because some people will fail to do so, and therefore orders will slip past a filter, it's a good idea to occasionally check incoming email for orders.

Filters for Automatic Responses

Another useful filter is one that triggers an immediate automatic response to the sender. This type of filter can be used to acknowledge that an order has been received correctly, especially if the order is placed during non-business hours when you are not checking your email. For example, if a customer places an order on a Friday night and you aren't open on the weekend, the customer will at least be informed that the order reached its destination. A simple message stating that the order has been received and will be processed during business hours will do the job. This filter serves the same purpose during holidays or vacations.

Antispam Filters

Using a filter to check incoming email from a specific address can effectively eliminate messages from annoying individuals and spammers. You can use this filter to delete unwanted messages before they reach your mailbox.

Be careful with filters. Choosing a word that is too general can do more damage than good. For example, how can you eliminate endless solicitations urging you to "Earn More Money Now"? You could filter out any incoming messages containing the word *money*. That will work, but it will delete all messages with the word *money*. You could lose a potential customer who happened to us the word *money* in a message.

Organizing Mail with Folders

Any good email program allows you to set up folders to sort your mail. You can create folders for any type of email inquiry. For example, when a customer asks about an upcoming product, you can place the mail in a folder for inquiries about the particular item. When details become available, you can quickly go to that folder and forward the information to those people with messages in that folder. Your customers will be pleasantly surprised when the information becomes available and they are immediately updated.

Here are some other folders that Tronix has found useful:

- **Completed Orders**. After an order is processed, it is placed in this folder for future reference.
- **Unfinished/Undecided**. This is a folder for orders in limbo, such as those that need more information before processing or partially filled orders. If a customer fails to respond to a message that part of his order needs to be backordered, the order goes here. It's better to store the message in a dedicated folder rather than delete it.
- **Money Orders**. This is a good folder for people who are mailing payment. When their payment arrives, you can quickly notify them by going to this folder. You can also use this folder to notify customers when their wired money has arrived in your account.
- **Fraud Attempts**. The folder name says it all. Keep your fraudulent orders here. You can use this as a reference for all future orders and, if you have a relationship with other mail-order stores, you can forward and receive fraud alerts.

- **Web Additions**. This is where you can keep Web-related messages such as customer comments or questions about trading links.

TIP ▸ ***Construct a page of commonly used sentences and cut and paste them into your email messages as needed. You can copy messages such as "Thank you for your order. It will be shipped today." from this page and paste them into numerous emails rather than repeatedly typing the information.***

Redesigning Your Web Site

The speed at which the Web continues to evolve can make it difficult to keep pace. At one time, Web sites all looked relatively similar to one another, with the exception of font sizes and specific images. Today, a plethora of tools help Web designers envision almost anything and place it on a page.

Your site will always be under construction. All businesses have to change with the times, and your Web store is certainly no different. You can spend endless hours creating what you feel is a spectacular Web store, but one morning you will log on and think, "This looks stale." What was amazing six months ago has suddenly lost its kick. As you surf the Web, you come across features you've never seen before.

Start Surfing

When you feel your site is in need of an overhaul, start surfing. Search for sites or companies that are involved in Web development. Are there more advanced, sophisticated tools available than the ones you are using? Are there new Web add-ons available? The more you see, the better idea you'll have of what's available for you. Embrace change.

Take Your Time

If you plan to reconstruct your entire site, take your time and spread the work out so it doesn't affect your current site. Change the look of your site as often as you feel it is necessary. Tronix redesigns its Web site about every six to eight months.

You can begin rebuilding your site by making a copy of your current site and using it for remodeling by working on one page at a time. Retain the general information and simply work on the cosmetics. All links can remain intact and your entire site will run exactly as it did before, but with a fresh, new look. You don't necessarily have to do a major overhaul each time you redesign your site. Experimenting with different colors, font styles, and sizes and perhaps changing the structure of your price lists can breathe new life into your site.

Upgrading Technology

One thing to consider when retooling your site is upgrading the technology. As we've mentioned numerous times throughout this book, adding loads of automated commerce technology and other fancy site tricks can be a mistake because of the cost and because technology isn't always reliable. However, it is inevitable that better commerce tools will arrive, and Web technology will fall in price, making these additions worthwhile.

If you decide to add display and multimedia features, you should do so sparingly to test the reaction of customers. Rather than redoing your entire Web site using the superslick Flash product from Macromedia, add a single Flash object on a few pages and see how your customers respond. If your customers don't like it, or it causes their browsers to crash, you'll hear about it. Small tests will save you the pain of destroying your store with poor technology.

Regular Features

Daily, weekly, or monthly features keep your site fresh and give customers a reason to regularly visit your site. How often you add features depends on the size and type of business. Tronix receives new releases at least once or twice a week. Whenever you receive a new product, you can highlight it by posting photos and featuring the product throughout your site. The most important thing is to let your customers know about new products as soon as they arrive.

There are numerous types of regular features you should consider. For more about creating content, see Chapter 9.

Scheduling

Enhancing your site with feature articles, photos, and general graphical touches is best done at home or during nonbusiness hours when you have the time to really focus on the task at hand. The weekend can be a great time to fine tune your site by scanning images, making small visual changes, uploading screen shots, changing fonts, and adding fresh content.

Invoicing

A good invoicing system is an important tool for processing and tracking all of your sales. Several invoicing programs are available for Windows PCs and Macs. To get a feel for the type of invoicing program best suited for your business, you should search the Internet, using keywords such as **invoicing**, **business**, and **software**, for any shareware or free trial versions that you can tinker with before making a final decision. If you have experience with a good database program, you could use it to create a personalized invoicing program to handle your needs.

Most Point of Sale software provides good invoicing features. Printing your invoices on company stationery letterhead rather than a blank piece of paper can also help you reduce fraud.

Key Features

Any good order-processing program should be able to cover all types of sales. Whether you purchase a program or design one of your own, here are the key features that should be included:

Customer Information

- Billing address.
- Shipping address.
- Phone numbers (home, business, fax).
- Credit card field.

Sale Information

- Quantity field.
- Item field.
- Price field.
- Discount field.
- Tax field.
- Shipping field.

Additional Information

- Purchase order field.
- Net field.
- Payment type (check, money order, cash, credit card).
- Credit card number and expiration field.
- No charge field (for free items).
- Store policy.

Optional Information

- Special announcements/upcoming events.
- General notes (an area where you can type a personal note to a customer).
- Customer's email address.
- Issuing bank of the credit card.

Your invoices should display your company name, address, phone number, fax number, date of purchase, and your Web address. Having your Web address on your receipt is important in case a customer loses a browser bookmark to your site.

Whichever invoicing program you use, set it so it will print at least two copies of every invoice—one for your customer and one for your files. You can staple a copy of the customer's credit card slip to the invoice, unless you run a system automatically tied into a credit card terminal. In that case, the credit card approval code will appear on the invoice.

Your invoicing program should include customizable shipping and tax rates, a mailing list, and an easy-to-use inventory database. Some worth investigating are Invoice 98 (for small or home-based businesses) and Order Desk Pro (designed for businesses that take orders via the Internet, phone, or direct mail).

***Joe's Take:** I've seen programs that handled almost everything perfectly, but when it came to something simple like allowing the user to define her own shipping methods, it didn't work. Imagine a mail-order company using an invoicing program that only handles UPS. The more flexible your invoicing program is, the fewer dead ends you'll run into, and the more flexible your business will be.*

Inventory

Unfortunately most small online stores don't have the back-end ability to have live inventory status posted on the Web site, but that doesn't mean you shouldn't do your best to track inventory and sales. Most small online store software doesn't include any real inventory or long-term sales tracking. As we have mentioned, you should operate a good Point of Sale program behind the scenes.

Your Point of Sale program's inventory capabilities should efficiently store all of your items in an easy-to-find fashion. The program should allow for a large number of additions and making new entries should be simple. Most stores use a bar code reader or a labeling system that separates each item by a part number. For these types of systems, all items must be labeled for identification.

You might want to abbreviate your item names. For example, a Sony Analog Control Pad would be SACP. A business specializing in PC multimedia accessories might have an item called SBA64 for Sound Blaster Awe-64 or CLSBA64 for Creative Labs Sound Blaster Awe-64. By using abbreviated item names as part numbers, you can simply look at the name on the packaging and easily access the item during a sale.

You should also be able to enter miscellaneous items on the fly. For example, a customer may phone in an order before you have the time to enter your new releases. If you are in the middle of a sale and you have already taken most of your customer's information, it would be inconvenient to keep your customer waiting while you suspend the sale in order to enter a new item. Having a program that allows you to enter a new item during the sale will save time for you and your customers. Atrex 7 from Millenium Software (www.1000years.com) does allow for this.

Organizing Your Site's Back End

Using a good File Transfer Protocol (FTP) program allows you to keep your site organized by getting a visual representation of your file structure. Tronix uses a shareware program called CuteFTP. You can have your entire site in one main directory, but as your site grows you may want to separate specific files, such as graphics, into their own folders. Having separate folders eliminates the need to scan through dozens of files in search of the one file you need to update. You can keep all your HTML files in the main directory and all other file extensions out of sight.

When updating your files or adding new content, take note of any Web pages, screen shots, or other material to which you no longer link. Removing these unneeded files from the server will free up space and minimize clutter.

TIP ▸ ***Name your files logically for easy identity. For example, if you have a price list for gold earrings, a file name like goldear.html makes more sense than ge.html or golde.html. When it's time to locate that file for updating, you'll eliminate the need to load a number of files before finding the right one.***

Site Folders

Every site needs to be well organized on the back end. Your initial site design should have an organized directory system. In fact, your Web hosting company may already have some special requirements (such as where CGI scripts are stored).

Using folders is a good way to store various types of content. Graphics, audio files, video files, Photo-VR images, and so on should have their own folders. This system of organization allows you to quickly find whatever you are looking for. For example, if you need to address a graphical problem, you can simply go to the graphics folder. Because you might want to use particular elements on different pages, organizing by content type rather than by site area is the way to go.

You can also create folders that split HTML files into different folders for your site's key categories. This isn't necessary for sites with only a few pages. But if you've got a site with four or five sections and 30 or more pages, you'll want to build in some organization. If you have a variety of content types, you can create separate folders for reviews, features, news items, and so on.

Analyzing Store Traffic

Analyzing your store's traffic is a crucial maintenance activity. Unlike other Web sites, a Web store has two types of information to analyze: sales data and site traffic data. Even if you don't specifically analyze your sales, you will certainly know what sells well. Your Point of Sale program should be able to generate any number of useful sales reports and sales-history reports. However, you will need to turn to a site-traffic analysis program to track what people are doing on your site other than making purchases.

If you run a Web server, you can use one of the major site log or traffic analyzers. In some cases, with specialty store-hosting systems, you might not be able to do this. Check with the service to see what site traffic analysis they might offer. Since you may not run your own server, you'll need to rely on the hosting company's efforts. Although all Web hosts are different, most provide traffic analysis assistance. Some companies will send you a daily report via email. Other options include getting access to the specific raw data files (known as log files) or links to pages that are actual log reports, run by the hosting company, that summarize your site's activity.

The optimum traffic report is a solid log file which you can analyze yourself using a tool such as WebTrends. With WebTrends and products like it, you can run more reports and examine the site logs as you like. Figure 18.1 shows a sample report. Table 18.1 lists the reports you can generate with the basic version of WebTrends.

FIGURE 18.1
Two sample reports by WebTrends

Activity Level by Day of Week

This section shows the activity for each day of the week for the report period (i.e. if there are two Mondays in the report period, the value presented is the sum of all hits for both Mondays.) The Total Weekdays line indicates the number of hits occurring Monday through Friday of the report period. The Total Weekends line indicates the number of hits occurring Saturday and Sunday of the report period. Values in the table do not include erred hits.

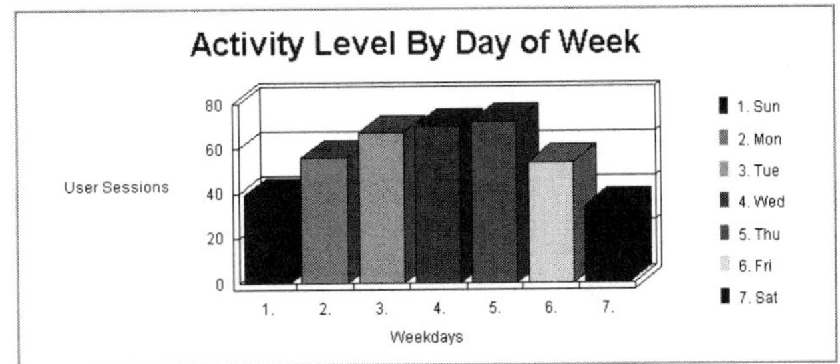

Activity Level by Day of the Week				
	Day	Hits	% of Total	User Sessions
1	Sun	327	10.13%	39
2	Mon	411	12.73%	56
3	Tue	492	15.24%	67
4	Wed	528	16.35%	70
5	Thu	712	22.05%	72
6	Fri	462	14.31%	54
7	Sat	296	9.16%	34
	Total Weekdays	2605	80.7%	319
	Total Weekend	623	19.29%	73

Single Access Pages

This section identifies the pages on your Web site that visitors access and exit without viewing any other page.

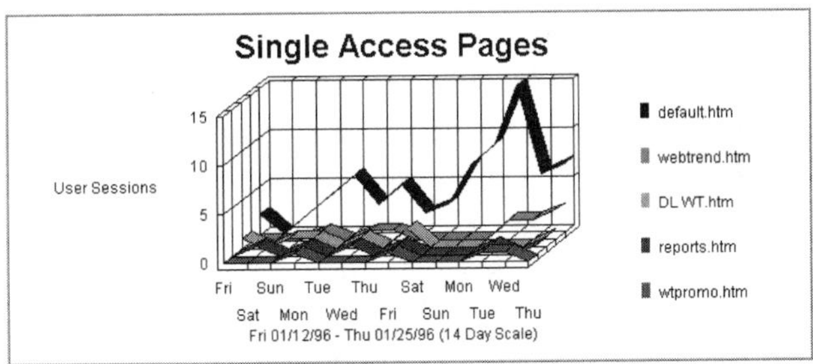

Single Access Pages			
	Pages	% of Total	User Sessions
1	**WebTrends Corporation** http://www.webtrends.com/default.htm	65.74%	71
2	**WebTrends** http://www.webtrends.com/webtrend.htm	9.25%	10
3	**302 Moved** http://www.webtrends.com/DL_WT.htm	6.48%	7
4	**302 Moved** http://www.webtrends.com/reports.htm	5.55%	6
5	**302 Moved** http://www.webtrends.com/wtpromo.htm	3.7%	4
6	**How can I order WebTrends?** http://www.webtrends.com/wtorder.htm	1.85%	2

Table 18.1 WebTrends reports

General Statistics	Client Errors
Most Requested Pages	Server Errors
Least Requested Pages	Most Downloaded File Types
Top Entry Pages	Organization Breakdown
Top Exit Pages	North American States and Provinces
Single Access Pages	Most Active Cities
Top Paths Through Site	Bandwidth
Advertising Views and Clicks	Most Accessed Directories
Advertising Views	Top Referring Sites
Advertisisng Clicks	Top Referring URLs
Most Downloaded Files	Top Search Engines
Most Active Organizations	Top Search Keywords
Most Active Countries	Most Used Browsers
Summary of Activity by Day	Netscape Browsers
Activity Level by Day of Week	Microsoft Explorer Browsers
Activity Level by Hour	Visiting Spiders
Technical Statistics	Most Used Platforms
Submitted Forms	Authenticated Users
Users	Web Server/Technical Infomation
Page Not Found (404) Errors	Browser Errors

One of the great things about the Web is that you can analyze every last click and page view to gain some insight on your next strategic move. However, the trick in analyzing your store's traffic is to keep it simple and not analyze every last element. Focus on learning what pages are most popular and when and from where users are arriving. Evaluate what searches and sites are sending you traffic and work to enhance that by including those keywords in your search engine tags. You can also consider purchasing advertising or recruiting affiliates at the sites that are pushing heavy traffic your way.

The most interesting information results when you combine sales results and Web site analysis results. For example, having sold 20 copies of a certain CD, if that item is housed on its own page, you can find out how many times that page was requested for you to reach those 20 sales.

Dividing the results will give you a percentage of buys per look. Also worth finding out are which countries are accessing your site the most, what browsers they use, and how long they stay on your site.

TIP ▸ ***One great thing about adding a search engine to your site is that you can track what items people search for. This will help you identify the items that people want but can't easily find.***

You should analyze your logs at least once a month—more often if you can manage it. You can also combine several monthly views to get a longer-term analysis.

Joe's Take: *One particularly interesting statistic is the Top Paths Through Site statistic, which will show you what paths customers are taking before placing an order.*

TIP ▸ ***Don't spend too much time microanalyzing every statistic; just make basic, solid decisions about your store. Eliminate poorly performing pages and give your customers more of what is popular. Statistics are meaningless unless you know how to use them.***

Backing Up

Backing up your site is critical. You may never need to use it, but having a backup is like having insurance. If you don't have it, that is exactly when something will go wrong. You should have at least two copies on your hard drive—one to alter as you try out new designs and a permanent backup. You should also save a couple of backups on removable media such as Zip disks.

Periodic Maintenance

Although you will perform a long list of tasks daily, there are also a number of things you will have to do less frequently. These chores are just as important and can be scheduled at intervals throughout the month or year.

- **Check your competitors' sites each month.** See what they're selling, how their prices are, what new features have been added to their Web sites, and so on. Keep up with the Joneses. Actually, keep ahead of the Joneses.

- **Check for dead links.** There are a number of programs that do this such as Theseus and Alert LinkRunner. You should also have a special email link for people who want to report dead links or other problems with your site.

- **Do minor Web upkeep weekly.** This includes changing price lists and fixing minor errors as necessary.

- **Do a major site redesign a few times a year.** This doesn't mean completely changing the look of your site, but changing fonts, adding features, and so on. You can experiment behind the scenes before actually presenting these changes publicly. The more you work on your design and HTML skills, the better you'll get. When redesigning your site, be careful about removing pages. If people were entering your site through a particular page and it suddenly disappears, they'll be told the page no longer exists. If you find it necessary to remove a page, use a redirect page, which automatically takes visitors from outdated pages to your home page. The search engine HotBot has a "Check links to this domain" feature that allows you to see who is linking to your site. You can also check your log file to see where people are coming in. Don't close your store's door by removing commonly linked pages.

- **Update your content.** A What's New page that never has anything new is sure to make customers uneasy.

- **Check the speed.** If you use a high-speed connection such as a cable modem, periodically access your site with a dial-up connection to see how fast it loads. Look for pages that are slow to load and do what you can to speed them up.

- **Check the search engines once a month to see where you're being listed.** Do what you can to improve your rating.

- **Ask for feedback.** When you have time, poll your regular customers about your store.

- **Stay on top of new technologies.** If something comes along that is both cost effective and enhances your site or ability to service your customers, investigate it.

If You Fail To Plan, You Plan To Fail

Yeah, yeah, you've heard it before. And no, we're not trying to sell you a retirement plan. But if you arrive at the office every day without a plan, you'll leave the office every night with a little less hair—you'll have yanked it out. There will be plenty of emergencies that force you to stray from your plan, but if you are disorganized, an unplanned disaster will be even more disruptive. By the time you have put out whatever fire you were dealing with, you might return to work only to find the rest of the day has burned down around you.

The more organized you are and the better you use the available technology to speed up your daily work, the better you'll feel at the end of the day and the more you'll look forward to going to work the next morning. Take advantage of the available technology that allows you to organize your operations.

Next up is Chapter 19, which will show you how to use online technology to best serve your customers and how to keep them coming back to your store for years to come.

CHAPTER NINETEEN

Building Loyal Customers Through Online Customer Service

Customer service is the backbone of all businesses: no customers, no business. Although a number of traditional customer service tenets (which you can find throughout this book) translate to Web business, several aspects of customer service are unique to the Internet. You can provide information to your customers without repeatedly answering the same questions. You can quickly respond to customer requests via email, and you can offer catalogs and updates on your products without the usual process of using the mail or buying advertising. And software solutions such as LivePerson (www.liveperson.com) can help you offer live customer service and sales solutions on the Web.

A loyal customer base can be the direct result of strong customer service. If you treat your customers well, don't insult their intelligence by being dishonest, and take advantage of the customer service advantages provided by the immediacy of the Internet, you'll eventually find the same people shopping repeatedly at your online store.

This chapter shows you how to get the most out of your email program and the best way to handle all kinds of customer messages. We'll run through some of the most popular email programs and also discuss how to deal with those pesky phones. Finally, Joe will provide the customer service keys that have helped Tronix survive and flourish.

Email Accounts and Customer Profiles

The key to providing good customer service is learning all the ins and outs of email. As discussed later in this chapter, utilizing advanced aspects of email products such as Outlook Express and Eudora is a good way to deal with email issues.

Another crucial element of customer service is learning more about your customers. Well-established stores do this by using personalization and profiling tools such as Net Perceptions, Microsoft Site Server Personalization, LikeMinds by Andromedia, or BroadVision's One-To-One products. However, these are expensive and intensive tools to use. If you are able to use them, you should. However, there are less expensive and less complicated ways to build loyal customer profiles and offer the personal attention that customers seek on the Web.

Laying Out an Email System

Most Web hosting accounts include email in the package. A standard hosting package should allow you to set up as many as five email accounts for your domain. In addition, you'll have your dial-up access email. Some more expensive packages will give you access to 10 or 20 email accounts, giving you the ability to set up different email departments to better handle user requests.

Here are five basic email accounts you should have (substitute your domain name for *mystore.com*):

- **WEBMASTER@MYSTORE.COM**. Use this at the bottom of every page to collect information from customers about Web site difficulties, broken links, and so on.
- **CUSTOMERSERVICE@MYSTORE.COM**. Always have an address directly related to customer service issues and responses.
- **ORDERS@MYSTORE.COM**. A separate email address for order inquiries will help you quickly sort incoming requests and mail that pertain to orders.
- **EDITOR@MYSTORE.COM**. Sites with a large amount of content and reviews might want to add a specific email address for editorial content.
- **LIST@MYSTORE.COM**. If you want to run an email mailing list, set up a specific email account for the service.

These email accounts give users a chance to send mail directly to an area where it can be easily dealt with. It also gives the appearance that you have a large staff of people dealing with email.

Answering Email

Answering email will be your most common daily task. No matter how slick your Web site is, the manner in which you answer email can make or break your business. There are two keys to answering email—prioritizing email and writing quality responses to your customers. In many cases it can boil down to two words: "Thank you."

Responses to email orders should begin or end with a thank you. Although your order form will trigger a "Thank you for shopping at..." page, adding direct contact with the customer is essential.

General inquiries are no different. If a customer is curious about a particular item and you don't have access to it, you should still thank him for his interest. You might even tell him where he can find the particular item. Although he'll be disappointed that you didn't have the item, your courtesy might encourage a return visit.

Numerous surveys have indicated that many companies don't return customer service email promptly or at all. A Web store that takes the time to answer email can quickly gain an advantage over those that don't.

Cancellations

There may be occasions when a requested item is unavailable for a few days. In this case you should ask your customer if she wants to wait for the item to arrive or to cancel her order. If she decides to cancel, be sure to reply and confirm the cancellation. There is a right way and a wrong way to respond to cancellations.

The right way:

> *Dear Customer,*
>
> *Your cancellation has been acknowledged. We are sorry we couldn't fulfill your request, but we thank you for your interest.*

The wrong way:

> *OK. Order canceled.*

The incorrect way of replying to a canceled order sounds juvenile, shows no personality, and gives the impression that the store owner didn't care about the order or the customer.

Be careful not to develop these kinds of bad habits. The Web can be a fast and furious way to do business when you're the store owner. Your customers probably aren't sending and receiving hundreds of emails a day and therefore will neither understand nor appreciate a terse response. It's easier to fire off a two-word reply, it's just not smart.

Even worse is not acknowledging a canceled order. This will not only upset the customer, but give the impression that the credit card is now held captive to a sale.

Time Waits for No One

During the infancy of your business, answering email is something you will look forward to. Detailed replies to email make customers feel they are being treated with a personal touch. But when business really heats up, you'll find yourself with much less time to respond to email. What was once a detailed reply concerning an out-of-stock item can easily become, "Sorry, we're out of stock." It's important not to neglect the art of email correspondence, no matter how busy you are.

Email should be answered in a timely manner. Unless you are closed when an order is placed, and that fact is posted on your Web site, replying to orders two days after they are made will not sit well with a customer. If for some reason your reply is late, be honest and let your customer know why. Be aware that email speed varies between servers. If a server is having technical problems, whether it is on your end or your customer's, email can arrive at its destination much later than scheduled.

Joe's Take: *I've had instances in which I received an email order or inquiry from a customer, and 30 minutes after that email arrived, a second message from the same customer came in, asking why he hadn't received a response. This usually means the person emailed you hours ago but a slow server kept the message from arriving promptly. You should make the customer aware of this, although people who are familiar with the Internet know email delivery doesn't always occur instantly.*

One way to make responding to email easier is to create some templates with a simple ASCII editor, such as Windows Notepad. If you receive a number of email messages with the same question, you can simply copy the answers from the template and paste them into your responses. These small templates can minimize typing, and the fact that it is a prewritten statement should give you more time to better word the response.

TIP ▸ ***An auto-responder is a good way to quickly reply to customers. This can keep your customers informed and relaxed knowing that their email has been received. Even if you don't provide an immediate answer to the customer's inquiry, it will let the customer know you're working on it.***

Here is an example of an auto-response:

Thank you for your interest in MyStore.

This is an auto-response to your message, which was sent out immeditely after we received your email. Please understand that email is not always instantaneous and it may have taken some time for us to receive your message. We are working to answer it as soon as possible.

If you require immediate service, please call us at [phone number]

Mystore.com is reachable by phone from 9:00 A.M. to 6:00 P.M. EST.

You may also want check the following sections of our Web site for the information you need:

1. *Our store FAQ (Frequently asked questions) is located at www.mystore.com/faq.html.*
2. *All new store information is located at www.mystore.com/whatsnews.html.*
3. *You can find reviews and product information at www.mystore.com/reviews.html.*

You can also join our mailing list for news and product announcements by sending a message with the word "subscribe" in it to list@mystore.com.

Thank you for your interest in MyStore. We will respond personally to your email as soon as possible.

General Inquiries

Not all email messages will be orders. In fact, the majority of your email will be inquiries. General inquiries are just as important as orders, so do not neglect them. Of course, there are exceptions to the rule, such as a question about how your logo was designed. These are the types of questions that you can answer at your leisure. They are also the types of questions you might want to add to your store's FAQ.

Back-Ups

Your email program should be set up to retain a copy of all outgoing mail. You never know when you'll need to retrieve an old message. For example, if a customer presents you with a problem with her order, you can prove that you warned the customer about potential problems by referring to your original message. You should also archive and back up old email (six months or older) on a Zip disk or tape backup.

Filtering for FAQs

An informative page of Frequently Asked Questions can deliver answers to the most popular questions about your business and minimize repetitious inquiries. You can also set up an auto-responding filter to send out a list of common questions (and answers) or general rules about your business. Have your filter search for a subject such as FAQ.

Mustang Software (www.mustang.com) is one of the leaders in email management. Mustang Message Center can help you manage high volume inbound and outbound email. Mustang Agent for Exchange/Outlook incorporates Mustang Agent into the Microsoft Exchange or Outlook environment. This package enables medium- to large-sized stores (that is, stores with a large number of customers and specific staff devoted to email customer support) to manage and easily answer customer service inquires in an expert manner. All emails are tracked and managers can look at customer service response times, productivity and more. If you have a sizable store with high volume incoming customer service email, it is worth looking into. Kana (www.kana.com) is another company focused on tools for email-based customer service.

Creating Email Mailing Lists

A mailing list is a great way to send information to your customers. It allows you to have contact with your customer, whether it is announcing an upcoming product, a special or sale promotion, a new arrival list with pricing, or even important information such as special hours or holiday closings. If your email program features good filter capabilities (such as those in Pegasus Mail and Eudora), you can easily set up a mailing list. By having your filter look for trigger words such as *mailing list*, you can have your customers' email addresses automatically sent to a specific folder for future mailings.

Once a mailing list begins to gain members, you can provide regular updates —daily, weekly, or as new products arrive. For a mailing list to be effective, your customers must be aware of its existence. You can do this in your signature or on your Web site.

Managing Mailing Lists

The more mailing lists you offer, the more work you will have to contend with. If you run a business containing multiple formats, you can split your mailing lists. For example, a business that specializes in computer software should have one mailing list for Macintosh customers and another for Windows users. A Mac user won't be interested in reading about "What's new on Windows" and vice versa.

A mailing list has to be maintained, so consider the long-term effects on your business and the amount of time you'll need to spend working on it. Can you handle more than one mailing list? Between conducting sales, shipping boxes, and working on your Web site, you may not have the time.

TIP ▸ ***Devote some time each week to cleaning up your mailing list. Email addresses can change like the weather. Customers might move to a new ISP or even cancel their accounts. When this happens, a message to that customer will simply bounce back with a "User Unknown" reply. The longer you let this go, the more unwanted "boomerang" messages you will receive. It's best to remove invalid email addressed from your mailing list after several bounce backs.***

Outsourcing Your Mailing Lists

One option is to outsource the project to a mailing list vendor. A mailing list vendor will maintain the list for you and provide robust archiving and monitoring of list activity. Mailing list vendors generally charge around $25 monthly for a list of approximately 50 people. The fee increases with the size of the mailing list. A mailing list with several thousand users might cost as much as $500 a month to operate, but the maintenance work alone on a list that size makes outsourcing the project worth the money.

Two good mail list outsourcing options are Skylist (www.skylist.net) and ListBot (www.listbot.com). ListBot offers a free version of its service and a Gold version that eliminates advertising associated with outgoing messages.

In most cases, lists will include an introductory level of messages that can be sent at any time. From there, charges increase depending on list growth. Top services will offer tools to manage the list, especially so you can purge list members, control the amount of subscribers, and eliminate bad email addresses.

TIP ▸ ***If you want to run your own mailing lists and have the technical knowledge to do so, the best software to use is Lyris, an email list server system from Lyris Software (www.lyris.com).***

Top Email Packages

As we've made clear throughout this book, email is a critical asset to your store, and selecting the right email package for your needs is extremely important. The things to look for in an email package are strong features for filtering, auto-responding, and accessing multiple mail accounts.

Here are some email packages you should consider.

Netscape Navigator

Netscape's email client is integrated with the Netscape Navigator browser, so alternating between Web browsing and email is convenient. Folders are easy to create, and the drag-and-drop capability makes it easy to place messages into any folders. However, there are no mailing list functions powerful enough to be useful for a small business.

Eudora Pro/Eudora Light

Eudora Pro and the freeware Eudora Light are Internet-based email packages. Eudora claims to be the most popular Internet email software with an estimated 10 million users. Eudora Pro includes built-in spell checking, user-definable message filtering, color-coded message labeling, and "hot link" Web page capabilities.

Eudora Pro's enhanced message filtering allows the user to use several filtering terms individually or together to sort messages into mailboxes, forward email to other locations, send automated replies, or alert users when important messages arrive. Standard message filtering (also available on Eudora Light) sorts messages into mailboxes and modifies subjects and priorities based on certain criteria.

Eudora Pro allows users to send mail to multiple accounts at once and lets the user incorporate various fonts, colors, layout options, and so on. Pro also has a customizable address book.

Some other features that Light shares with Pro include drag-and-drop support, nickname/address book support, and text searches within messages or headers.

Microsoft Outlook and Outlook Express

Outlook Express is a free product also available bundled with Internet Explorer. Outlook Express automatically detects and offers users the opportunity to import Eudora, Netscape, Exchange, and Windows Inbox mail messages and address books upon their first start-up. Users can create multiple hierarchical folders to email. Users can also read email and access newsgroups without having to switch windows or open new applications. You can create filters for each newsgroup to screen out postings that meet certain criteria. You can also sort their messages in a number of ways, including grouping messages by subject to keep related messages together for easy reference. Microsoft's Outlook manages email, calendars, contacts, tasks and to-do lists, and documents or files on the hard drive. Outlook is Microsoft's highest-end email productivity package. It may be overkill for some, but for those who want to manage email and other related information such as calendar and contact information, Outlook 98 or 2000 may be the best package for you. Outlook 2000 costs just over $100.

How to Handle Phone Calls

Although email seems to be becoming a preferred means of business communication, the telephone hasn't yet gone the way of the telegraph.

The way your business handles phone calls and the personality you project over the phone can be just as important as the manner in which you answer email. When you're on the phone you can't always hide the fact that you're sick, tired, or both.

Be Happy! (Even if You're Not)

Responding to a customer by email not only affords you the opportunity to respond at your leisure but allows you to think about what you want to say and change the message if you don't like the way it looks. Talking on the phone is a spontaneous situation. Assuming you can spell (or have a dictionary), handling email in a professional manner is relatively easy. Your phone conversations should be no less professional.

Most people have had both good and bad phone conversations with stores, mail order houses, technical support lines, even friends. When you call a store and the person on the other end gives you the impression he could not care less about your needs, do you quickly head to that store and spend a lot of money? Unlikely. Keep that in mind when you pick up the phone at your office.

However, we are sympathetic. You're only human, and when the phones are constantly ringing as you are trying to maintain the rest of your business, it's easy to lose your patience. If you feel you are about to answer the phone in a snappy, impolite manner, let it ring a couple of times and consider that the person on the other end is probably a customer. Answer politely, with a greeting ("Good afternoon, Tronix" rather than "Hello?"). Speak clearly and don't give the impression that you are in a rush (even if you are).

Crunch Time

As the clock winds nearer to pick-up time and the phones are still ringing, your life might appear to be spinning out of control. As you gain experience, you will be able to determine how late you can accept orders and still get the shipments in the mail that day. (This will depend on how many orders you are processing each day and whether you have any help packing the boxes.) For example, if your post office closes at 5:30 P.M. and your couriers arrive at 6 P.M., you might want to post a 4:30 P.M. deadline for orders to be shipped that day. This allows you to take a message and return any calls made after 4:30 P.M. after you have made your shipments. However, if you are not busy you might be able to fill orders placed after your deadline. Doing so will make your customer feel as if she is getting special treatment.

Joe's Take: *If you decide to take a message during crunch time, explain that your couriers are about to arrive and you want to be sure you get all of your shipments out on time. Don't ask the customer to call you back, especially if you don't have a toll-free number. Call her back as soon as possible. If you post your daily order deadline prominently on your Web site, you can cut down on phone orders made after that time. People who do call will at least be aware of the deadline and won't be disappointed if you can't fill their orders that day.*

May I Put You on Hold?

One of the most common (and annoying) situations customers have to deal with when ordering products by phone is sitting on hold for an inordinate amount of time. Putting someone on hold for a minute or two to see if you have what they want in stock or to check a tracking number from a shipment is fine. Otherwise, you're probably better off taking a phone number and calling the customer back as soon as you have the information he needs. In the age of automated phone systems, something as simple as taking a message and calling someone back can make your store seem more personable and caring.

If a customer inquires about a product you don't have, and you have to check with your supplier, tell the customer she can either wait on hold for a few minutes or you'll call them back. Some people don't mind waiting on hold as long as they know it's going to be a few minutes.

Two Calls at Once

Depending on your phone system, you might find yourself taking one order, only to have your other line start ringing. If you don't have voice mail (which you really should invest in) or a staff to answer additional lines, you're stuck. Ask the first customer if she minds waiting for a moment while you answer another call. Then you can answer the second call and tell the person you're in the middle of taking an order. Offer to put the second customer on hold or call him back. Then return to the first order.

How often you're forced to bounce back and forth between calls will be determined not only by your resources (voice mail, other employees, number of phone lines) but also by your store's popularity. Any customer who is repeatedly interrupted in midorder so you can take another call will quickly become annoyed with your service.

***Joe's Take:** International callers should not be left on hold for more than a very brief time. The quicker an international order is handled, the lower the customer's phone bill will be, and the happier the customer will be. The more you can avoid returning international calls, the happier you will be.*

Joe's Customer Service Tips

- Pay for return shipping when a customer must return a defective item.
- Stay on top of lost, late, or incorrect orders. Don't leave customers wondering when the situation will be fixed.
- Offer customers the best shipping option for their orders. Not having to pay unnecessarily high shipping costs will keep customers ordering online rather than shopping at a local store.
- Follow up on back-ordered items. Keep the customer apprised of his order's status so he doesn't worry that it has been lost or disregarded.
- Don't push items on customers that they don't want or need.
- Clean up mistakes quickly and completely. If you send an incorrect item, replace it immediately. If it was your mistake, don't force the customer to wait until you get the initial shipment back.
- Offer answers to ordered product questions if you can. If you are in the middle of crunch time and can't spare a moment, call back at your earliest convenience. If you don't have an answer, direct them to someone who will (for example, technical support or the manufacturer).
- Reply to all email in a timely fashion.
- Inform customers when preordered items arrive.
- If you don't have a product in stock, say so. Let the customer know when the product will be in and how quickly you can get it to her.
- Don't leave customers on hold for long periods of time. Offer to call back if you think it will take some time to provide an answer to their question.
- Keep your Web site well maintained. Fix broken links, spelling mistakes, and other miscues, especially when the problem is presented to you by a customer.

Encourage Other Means of Ordering

As you see, phone calls can be a bit of a hassle. At best, the order will be processed easily and without interruption and you will only lose a couple of minutes out of your day. At worst, you'll be frustrated by a crunch-time interruption, the customer will be annoyed when you put him on hold to answer another incoming call, and everyone will walk away from the transaction with a bitter taste in their mouths.

Do whatever you can to encourage people to order via your online order form or fax. Make it apparent that ordering in either of these manners is advantageous for the customer in that it eliminates phone charges and the possibility of being placed on hold. You don't need to relate what a pain in the butt that phone orders are for you.

Beyond Email or Phone Support

Customer service on the Web is first and foremost rooted in how you answer email, support customers through documentation on your site, and handle phone contact. However, the Web and new technologies are serving up many alternative customer service outlets that go beyond those basics. If your store grows or you see a unique opportunity, here are a couple of other high-end customer service practices that are gaining popularity on the Web:

- **Chat.** Companies are using chat rooms and servers such as those offered by eShare Technologies (**www.eshare.com**) or LivePerson (**www.liveperson.com**) to enable users to jump into a chat room and immediately ask questions, get answers, or deal with customer service problems.

- **Call back systems.** AT&T offers its Interactive Answers Service (**www.ipservices.att.com/wss/interactiveanswers/index.html**), which lets customers click a Web link, enter their phone number, and have a customer service representative call them directly. This is a good service to reach users who may be behind an office phone system that is blocked or to provide a way to offer phone calls to customers without opening your phones up to a flood of incoming calls.

Tracking Customers and Building One-On-One Relationships

A store's ultimate success relies on its gathering a list of regular customers who are committed to your store as if it were a club. Your customer service efforts need to be aimed at these people. That requires you to identify these customers, track them, and cultivate them.

Larger stores can do this by building sophisticated tracking systems into their sites as well as by using personalization tools that provide automated forms of personalization to store customers. However, smaller stores must substitute sweat equity in return for less money invested in technology for their sites.

Customer Database

You should build a database of everyone who orders from your store. Your Point of Sale (POS) ordering system software should do this. Atrex 7, from Millenium Software (www.1000years.com), is a Windows POS program that includes a customer database. A good entry system allows you to track each sale and retain information about the customer. This includes shipping information, phone number, address, and credit card information. More important, it allows you to print out a list of customers and how many times they've ordered from you so you can easily identify the key customers. For example, you can put a special filter on your email package to notify you of priority mail from top customers so you can prioritize email in their favor.

TIP ▸ ***Let regular customers identify themselves by providing things like mailing lists and holding credit card information on file. People who plan to be regular customers will almost always sign up for these offers. You can also take it a step further by turning your store into a buyers club, like retailing giant CUC does. In that case you offer customers a chance to get special offers, pricing, and service by paying a yearly club fee of $25 to 75.***

Personal Attention

Once you've got a handle on who your main customers are, and as you identify new ones, the key is to keep them coming back. There are a number ways you can accomplish this:

- **Offer them priority on new products**. Email your top customers ahead of arrivals and allow them to reserve purchases.
- **Keep their order information on file** and let them easily order products via email without having to reenter all their information.
- **Give them** a special toll-free number to use.
- **Offer them better** shipping terms and pricing.
- **Create a referral service for them.** For every customer they send you, give them a store credit. Your best customers are often your best spokespeople. Cultivate your ability to turn customers into supporters.
- **Create a private password-protected area** of your Web site with special content or invite them to join a mailing list reserved for your best customers.
- **Poll them occasionally** so they can have an impact on your store's content, service, and overall development.

Privacy

Another key to customer service is to sign on as a TRUSTe licensee. This new and popular service is a way to assure your users that you operate a site that adheres to welcomed principles regarding disclosure and use of personal information.

To join on as a TRUSTe licensee you must adhere to its principles.

Baseline Standards

- **The site must explain** and summarize its general information gathering practices.

- **The site must explain** up front what personally identifiable data is being gathered, what the information is used for, and with whom the information is being shared.

- **The site must disclose** whether users may opt out of having their information used by the site or third parties, whether they may delete or deactivate themselves from the site's database, and whether they may update or change their information once it is disclosed.

- **The site must display the trustmark** on its home page that discloses the site's overall privacy policy. (See the Sample Privacy Statement following this list.)

- **The site may not monitor personal** communications such as email or instant messages to third parties, except to the extent required by law or as necessary in the process of maintaining the site.

- **The site must adhere** to its stated privacy policies.

- **The site must adhere** to its stated privacy policies, even after the site discontinues from the TRUSTe program unless consent is obtained directly from the user.

- **The site agrees to cooperate** with all TRUSTe reviews and audits.

CASE STUDY

A Sample Privacy Statement Provided by TRUSTe

Company XYZ's Overall Privacy Statement

This Overall Privacy Statement verifies that Company XYZ is a member of the TRUSTe program and is in compliance with TRUSTe privacy principles. This statement discloses the privacy practices for the entire Web site.

TRUSTe is an independent, nonprofit initiative whose mission is to build users' trust and confidence in the Internet by promoting the principles of disclosure and informed consent. Because this site wants to demonstrate its commitment to your privacy, it has agreed to disclose its information practices and have its privacy practices reviewed and audited for compliance by TRUSTe. When you visit a Web site displaying the TRUSTe mark, you can expect to be notified of:

- What information this site gathers/tracks about you.
- What this site does with the information it gathers/tracks.
- With whom this site shares the information it gathers/tracks.
- This site's opt-out policy.
- This site's policy on correcting and updating personally identifiable information.

This site's policy on deleting or deactivating your name from our database.

Questions regarding this statement should be directed to Company XYZ's site coordinator or TRUSTe (www.truste.org) for clarification.

Information This Site Gathers/Tracks

Company XYZ is a Web site that allows users to buy Widgets. There is one Widget order form on the site that prompts users to give their name, credit card information, and postal address. This site also logs IP addresses.

Use of the Information This Site Gathers/Tracks

The information gathered on the Widget order form is used to process the order. Although Company XYZ logs IP addresses, we do not link them to any personally identifiable information. This means that users are anonymous. Our Web site logs IP addresses for system administration purposes.

Sharing of the Information This Site Gathers/Tracks

The postal address information gathered on the Widget order form is shared with Shippers Express. Shippers Express uses the postal address only to fulfill the transaction.

While navigating the Company XYZ Web site, you may find additional TRUSTe marks with links to privacy statements. These statements apply only to the page the mark is on and should not be construed as the Overall Privacy Statement.

Opt-Out Policy

If you would like to opt-out of being solicited by this site or third parties, please contact:

Webmaster
webmaster@companyxyz.com
1111 Company Way
Metropolis, CA 99999 USA

Correct/Update Policy

If you would like to correct and/or update your personally identifiable information, please contact:

Webmaster
Webmaster@companyxyz.com
555-1515

Delete/Deactivate Policy

This site does not offer a way to delete/deactivate your data.

How to Join TRUSTe

To receive the TRUSTe trustmark (Figure 19.1), you must send your signed legal agreement and payment.

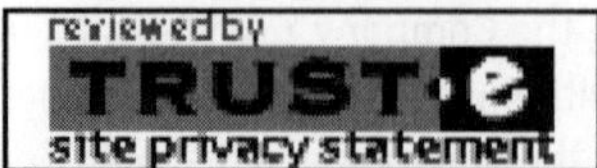

FIGURE 19.1
The TRUSTe trustmark.

You can print out an HTML version of the TRUSTe legal agreement or download a copy in Microsoft Word. In signing the agreement, you agreed to follow the TRUSTe standards and submit your site to the ongoing assurance process. An officer of your company must sign the agreement.

Once you've decided to become a TRUSTe licensee, go to the automated billing process to generate an invoice. TRUSTe will determine the cost of your license, based on your company's revenue and type of business.

After you've completed those steps, you're ready to complete the TRUSTe application process by submitting the following information:

- Two signed copies of the legal agreement.
- A copy of your invoice.
- Payment made out to TRUSTe.

Send the information to:

TRUSTe Application
4005 Miranda Ave., Suite 175
Palo Alto, CA 94304

Upon receipt of your application, an authorized TRUSTe representative will sign both legal agreements and return one to you for your records. A TRUSTe account representative will contact you, and you'll be given a confirmation number. This number will give you access to the For Licensees section of the TRUSTe Web site, where you'll build your privacy statements.

For a $10 million or less retail Web site, TRUSTe's yearly fee is $750.

Customer Service Is an Investment

Customer service is about being in contact with your customers as much as possible. This work is very time intensive. But if you lose one customer through poor customer service, you may lose many more as word spreads on the Internet.

Education is the best form of Internet customer service. The smarter you make your customers about how your business operates, the better. By convincing your customers to do things such as ordering online rather than over the phone, the less expensive your customer service efforts will be.

Customer service is an investment. If you correct one problem immediately, you can not only build a lifetime customer but, through that customer's recommendations, increase your customer base.

CHAPTER TWENTY

Fighting Off the Competition

You've done everything you can to attract customers to your store and provide them with an enjoyable shopping experience. Not only are your prices unbeatable, but you provide dedicated customer service, handle all complaints quickly and efficiently, and provide an unsurpassed selection of goods. Your Web site is attractive, easy to navigate, and a joy to visit. If they choose, customers can spend all afternoon bouncing around your site and checking out the new information before they even begin to shop. You tirelessly promote your store, you provide every shipping option known and your site always appears fresh because of your willingness to update its content and its look. You are organized and use the latest technology to maximize your efficiency. A minimal inventory minimizes your risk.

So what? Your competitors have most of the same things going for them.

Once you have built a sizable customer base, you'll have to fight to keep it. Competing on the Internet involves a number of unique aspects which we discuss here. We also show you how to track your competition effectively, how to compete both offensively and defensively, how to find your competitive niche, and how to keep in touch with the Web community. In this chapter, we prepare you for battle.

Unique Aspects of Internet Competition

Although a number of competitive aspects of online business are similar or even identical to traditional retailing, the Internet not only provides plenty of advantages for merchants but also a number of unique issues with which all store owners must wrestle. A Web store's worldwide reach and the fact that the Internet allows smaller outfits to compete directly with corporate giants are advantages for your business. Starting a small Web retail business is also generally less expensive than opening a traditional retail store. And once your store is off the ground, you can operate with a slim inventory. It is also much easier to track the competition and react accordingly. However, these are benefits that you share with your competitors. The businesses that best utilize the benefits of the Internet are the ones that survive and flourish.

There are also a number of issues that are uncommon for retail stores but important for Web stores to deal with effectively.

With so many competitors located just a few clicks away, the content of your Web site and your ability to promote your store is critical. The proximity of one Web store to all of its competitors also allows customers to more easily compare prices, selection, and service. Those customers can quickly take their business elsewhere if they don't like what you provide.

Worldwide Customer Access

Unlike traditional retail businesses, Web stores have access to potential customers all over the world. Your Vermont-based store, instead of competing with the store across town for a limited number of customers, might be battling with a California-based company for customers in Portugal. Smart online merchants use this to their advantage.

Access to a wide geographical range of customers won't do you any good unless you work to utilize that aspect of online commerce. As we have discussed, that involves promoting your store on the Internet through newsgroups and online forums, search engines, link exchanges and swaps, bounty programs, and banner advertising. It also includes advertising and promoting in traditional media as well as promoting your store and selling products on an international level. If you don't plan to take advantage of these online-specific business aspects, you might as well open a traditional store in the local mall.

For more on taking advantage of worldwide customer access, see Part III of this book.

David vs. Goliath

Money (when used wisely) can help any business on the Internet. However, if your small company on a tight budget presents the public with a professional-looking site, no one will know if there is one, 30, or 300 employees. Unlike traditional retail, one person with the right knowledge, creativity, and drive can appear as big as any corporation. You needn't open stores in every state in the nation. Your one Web site resides in every state in the nation—and in almost every nation in the world.

Depending on your market, there may be no huge corporations to compete with. Even if there are, don't throw up your hands and quit. It isn't like a superstore moving in next door and burying you. Find your niche and use it to your advantage. Remember: Bigger doesn't necessarily mean better, especially in online retailing. The big Web stores can outspend you on advertising, Web development, and inventory—but that doesn't make them smarter.

Lower Start-Up Costs, Minimal Inventory

One of the great things about operating an online store is the fact that start-up and inventory costs can be minimized. Rather than dumping thousands of dollars into inventory that might collect dust on a shelf, you can stock a few sure-fire big sellers and then add other items as they are ordered. As long as you know you can immediately procure the necessary items from your suppliers and quickly have them on their way to your customers, you needn't have the products sitting in your office. You can have them on your Web site (your virtual shelves) without assuming the risk of having bought them.

You also don't need to spend money on a snappy looking space. Assuming you don't have any walk-in customers, a cheap office is fine. You can also run your store on your own without having to hire salespeople.

For more on stocking your virtual shelves and minimizing your inventory, see Chapter 8.

Web Content

Your Web site's appearance and layout is obviously an important factor in the competitive world of online commerce. An attractive Web site that is functional and easy to navigate will attract customers and keep them. All other things being equal—prices, customer service, shipping options, selection—customers will flock to the site that is the most enjoyable to visit and the easiest to use. Conversely, a visually unappealing site that is illogically constructed will send potential customers scurrying for a more enjoyable shopping experience. Why would anyone feel comfortable submitting credit card information to a store that looks like it was slapped together by teenagers as an after-school project? The outside retail world can be more forgiving in this sense, as a shabby store with good pricing can still attract customers. (In fact, a ragged-looking store can be seen as having character and being free from corporate greed as long as it is clean and organized.)

Here are some tips for setting your Web store's content apart from the rest:

- **Stay on top of emerging technologies.** Every day it gets easier to add snappy graphics, design flourishes, and interactive technologies to your Web site. Don't get caught listening to 8-track tapes when the rest of the world has CDs.

- **Don't get carried away with emerging technologies.** Although it's nice to have a bell here and a whistle there, too many of them will scare the pants off your customers. Either that or it will bore the pants off them as they wait for the site to load.

- **Keep everything fresh.** When you grow tired of your site's content, assume your customers are equally bored. That goes for colors, fonts, graphics, news items, features, and so on. Change is good as long as it isn't distracting.
- **Make your site an informational destination**—not just a shopping destination. The more reasons there are to visit your site, the more people will visit. The more people that visit, the more you'll sell.
- **Make your site easy to navigate.** Your customers should be able to easily find whatever they want.

For more on creating content, check out Chapter 9.

The Enemy Next Door

Online shoppers have easy access to everything from cars to books without ever having to leave their desks. In the real world, customers can spend the day driving from store to store looking for the best price or the right item only to waste their savings on gas. Or they won't feel like wasting a Saturday shopping and settle on an item that might be more expensive and of lower quality than one available across town.

If a Web shopper wants to comparison shop, she is just a new URL away from a new store full of options. Rather than using a car, cab, bus, or subway, customers can bounce between stores with the click of a Forward or Back button.

Although the Web allows customers to easily hop from store to store, it also allows competitors to do so. Chances are your competition in California is making the quick trip to your store in Vermont. You would be crazy not to pay her regular return visits. Within seconds, you can access any online retailer on the Web. You can find out what your competitors are selling, their prices, their shipping rates, and the entire structure of their stores.

If you like certain aspects of a competitor's site, don't be afraid to incorporate the same ideas. Just look at Domino's, Little Caesar's, and Pizza Hut. When one comes out with a new idea (stuffed crust, double crust, whatever) the other two are sure to follow. However, copying proprietary JavaScript code or VB Script code is illegal, not to mention unethical, lazy, and plain old sleazy. The last thing you want to do is get a reputation as a code thief. That would fall under the category of bad public relations.

Joe's Take: *Shortly after I began using alternate-colored bars on my price lists to highlight new releases, I noticed two other mail order companies using the same technique with the same color combination! I felt like somebody had stolen my car then driven up to my house and said, "Hey, how do you like my new car!" There's a fine line between being influenced by other sites and stealing from them. Don't cross it.*

Tracking the Competition

Chances are when you set up your Web store, you'll think you have a truly unique concept. Then you'll start searching the Web and realize you're not alone. Well, at least you've found your competition. Not only should you visit these sites, you should bookmark the ones you find particularly interesting and visit them often. Assuming the owners of these stores have a clue, they'll be visiting you as well.

TIP ▸ ***Once you have found a search method that leads you to stores that are similar to yours, don't do it just once. Web commerce is growing at an alarming rate. You can be certain that the number of stores in your market will continue to grow. Check back every month or so for new competitors.***

Your potential customers are also your competitors' potential customers. Customers will compare sites and shop where they feel their wants and needs are best met. You want that store to be yours.

Comparison Shopping

It's critical to identify precisely where your store is stronger (or weaker) than your competitors' stores. Another store might have better pricing, but you might have lower shipping rates and more shipping options. Another store might have a later deadline for next-day delivery than your store, but not accept credit cards. You probably won't beat a competitor in every category—if you do, then they aren't really competitive.

For a side-by-side comparison of your store vs. a competing store, use the following chart in Table 20.1. Give yourself a checkmark if you feel you are better than your competitor in a certain area, and vice versa. If you feel the two stores are even, give both stores a check. The only way this exercise can work is if you are honest. Giving your store the edge in every category is not only probably delusional but can cause you to be complacent. If you can find a friend who will be honest and whose opinion you value, have her fill out the chart.

Table 20.1 Comparing Your Store's Features

		My Store	Store X
Availability	Representatives available via phone	☐	☐
	Longer store hours	☐	☐
Ordering	Better return policy	☐	☐
	Phone orders accepted	☐	☐
	Fax orders accepted	☐	☐
	International orders accepted	☐	☐
	Secure order form	☐	☐
	Payment options	☐	☐
Inventory	More items available	☐	☐
Shipping	Lower shipping costs	☐	☐
	More shipping options	☐	☐
	Better shipping deadlines	☐	☐
	Quality of packaging	☐	☐
Web site	Faster download	☐	☐
	Overall presentation	☐	☐
Web site content	Number, quality of product reviews	☐	☐
	Feature articles	☐	☐
	Informational content	☐	☐
	User-created content	☐	☐
	Discussion boards	☐	☐
	Chat rooms	☐	☐
Customer service	Direct customer service phone number	☐	☐
	Prompt email response	☐	☐
	Customer FAQ	☐	☐
	Privacy policy or TRUSTe participant	☐	☐
	Customer service chat	☐	☐
Promotion	Advertising	☐	☐
	Associate/bounty sites	☐	☐
	Email newsletter	☐	☐
	Newsgroup participation	☐	☐
Pricing	Average price discount	☐	☐
	More price options available	☐	☐

Following Your Customers

Usenet newsgroups are a great way to watch for customer comments. Take note of any headers that refer to purchases. A newsgroup topic that reads, "Where to buy..." or "I just purchased..." can lead you to information about your competitors. You might learn about a new store or find out which of your competitors are getting high marks (or low ones) from customers.

You can also track your competitors through your customers. If you feel comfortable doing so, ask some of your customers where else they have shopped or would consider shopping. If a new customer emails you asking if you can match or beat a price on a particular item, ask where he saw the price. Check the site and take a particularly close look at the shipping rates. Some online stores offer amazingly low prices but jack up the shipping charges. It's an easy switch; subtract most of the profit from an item and add it to your shipping rates.

TIP ▸ ***Picking up profits from low prices and high shipping rates might sound like a neat trick, but we don't recommend it. Most people will quickly figure out what's going on and just as quickly find someplace else to shop.***

Watch Your Competitors Watching You

Watch for any patterns that indicate how closely your competitors are following you. Is there are a store that seems to price its items exactly $1 less than yours? Do you see a store announcing the same new releases shortly after you do? Does a store respond to a new feature on your site by adding a similar one? If you see stores constantly making similar changes to keep up with you, that's a good sign. It means you are beating them to the punch and they are scrambling to keep up.

Joe's Take: *I have often seen competitors announce the arrival of new releases when they really didn't have the items available. We would get new product, announce it on our Web site, and within moments another store would announce the same information. When a customer calls to order the product, they tell the customer the item "just sold out but more will be arriving soon." Eventually customers catch on.*

Ten Keys to Tracking The Competition

Tracking the competition can be an overwhelming task. It is also one of the most important things you'll do. Keep the following in mind and you'll be in good shape:

- **Be a customer.** Either by yourself or via a friend, order something from a competitor and experience the service firsthand.
- **Subscribe to every email newsletter** or other service your competitors offer. Use an email address from a free email service if you want to conceal your identity.
- **Use search engines or search agents** like HotBot News (www.newsbot.com) or Deja.com (www.deja.com) to monitor Web articles or Usenet posts featuring your competitors.
- **Use the "search for links to this URL" feature** on HotBot or other search engines to gauge the popularity of a site.
- **Ask customers** what other stores they frequent and what they like about those stores.
- **Collect horror stories.** Ask customers why they no longer shop at a particular store to learn what makes your site attractive.
- **Check as many** update, sale, and home pages as possible every day.
- **If your competitors** offer discussion boards, monitor them for dissenting posts or customer service complaints.
- **Strike up conversations with your suppliers.** They might let something slip about one of your competitors.
- **At least once each quarter** evaluate your main competitors' sites from top to bottom. Identify what has been improved, changed, eliminated, etc.

TIP ▸ ***If you have more than one email account name, use your non-business alias to join the mailing lists of your competitors. This way you can keep up on what new products they are selling, where they are dropping prices, what new lines of products they are introducing, and so on, without their suspecting who you are.***

The Best Defense Is a Good Offense

As you prepare to launch your store, you should know what other similar stores are offering and be prepared to offer more. Open your cyber-doors with competitive, low prices even if it means sacrificing some early profit. You should also consider a Grand Opening special such as free Priority Mail shipping or a "buy one, get one half price" promotion. You might also include a small gift for your first 50 or 100 customers. No matter what you do to add a spark to your opening, make sure your first customers leave feeling they've discovered a great place to shop. This is how good word-of-mouth spreads. If your customers feel particularly excited about your store, they will quickly pass along a recommendation.

Look for your competition's weaknesses, and emphasize your strengths in that area. If one of your competitors only accepts CODs, emphasize on your site that you accept major credit cards. If others only use UPS, let it be known that you provide a wide variety of shipping options.

Defense Wins Championships

You won't always be able to beat your competitor to the punch. In these cases you need to be ready to launch a counterattack.

For example, an established competitor might receive a product before you. Instead of losing potential sales, counter with a lower price. If people become aware that you have better prices, they might be willing to wait an extra day to get their shipment.

Another store might try to secure as many pre-orders as it can by offering a discount to anyone who pre-pays for a hot, upcoming item. You can counter that by offering the same price with no obligation to pre-order.

Defending your territory means never giving your competitors an easy opening to pummel you. Here are some points that will help keep the wolves at bay:

- **Only a catastrophe** should bring down your Web site. You store should be on a quality hosting service with complete backup. If your site goes down, your customers go elsewhere.

- **Answer email as quickly as possible.** Do your best never to let an email sit unanswered for more than 48 hours. If you don't take an interest in your customers, they won't take an interest in your store.

- **Never sell email addresses** or other information about your customers to any other service without your customer's explicit permission. This is an easy way to annoy (and lose) customers.

- **Take orders securely over the Internet** using Secure Sockets Layer (SSL) and, when it is perfected and becomes the industry standard, Secure Electronic Transactions (SET). If you don't offer secure online transactions, you shouldn't offer any online transactions. If a customer has his credit card information stolen when dealing with your site, his next online purchase will be from one of your competitors.

- **Don't use hidden pricing techniques** such as inexpensive products and outrageously high shipping rates. If customers feel you are being dishonest, they will go to one of your competitors who is honest.

- **Never spam newsgroups** or customer email lists. The result will be a bad reputation.

- **Check content and other newsgroup postings** for validity, spelling, grammar, and other potential mistakes. If your content is unprofessional, customers will think your entire operation is unprofessional.

- **Make sure new items** and other inventory changes are posted as soon as possible. Don't let new items lag, especially in competitive consumer markets. If you have something, let people know. Otherwise, they'll find it somewhere else.

Finding a Competitive Niche

You can't be everything to everyone. Figure out what you do best and refine that area of expertise. Don't be afraid to break away from the standard online business formula and make your site different. Be honest rather than try to fool the customer. You might not be known for rock-bottom prices, but you can do well by offering the best customer service. Although everyone likes to save a few dollars, many people don't mind spending a bit more in return for excellent customer service.

As your store becomes established, you'll find your own corner of the Web. Some qualities your store could become known for include:

- The lowest prices.
- Unbeatable customer service.
- The largest selection.
- Fastest email responses.
- A well-designed site.
- A wide variety of shipping options.
- The most exciting sales.
- The best information and reviews.
- Flexible exchange polices.
- The first store with new releases.

Although you should do your best to provide all of the above, you probably won't be the best in every category. Whichever approach you take, stick with your plan and be the best at your specialty.

However, you may go after a certain niche only to find there is no way you can top a certain store. For example, you might design a beautiful Web site only to have a huge corporation with a ten-person Web development team come along and blow yours away. Be flexible. Don't trash your fine Web site, but don't sit around either. Shift your focus to another area and win there instead.

Better Business Bureau

The Better Business Bureau (www.bbb.org) acts as an intermediary to resolve disputes, facilitate communication, and provide information on ethical business practices. Better Business Bureau members are businesses and firms that meet standards, agree to follow the highest principles of business ethics and voluntary self-regulation, and have accepted an invitation to join. Becoming a Better Business Bureau member and remaining one in good standing indicates to customers that your business is ethical and follows the bureau's strict standard. The bureau's long, respected history of service gives consumers great confidence in member businesses. Conversely, unethical practices that are reported by the bureau can rightfully have a detrimental effect on your customers' confidence.

As a private, non-profit organization, the Better Business Bureau provides the following to businesses and consumers:

- **Business reports.** Information on a business's performance.
- **Dispute resolution.** Help in resolving a complaint against a company.
- **Consumer Information Clearinghouse.** Information on topics to assist consumers and businesses in purchasing decisions.
- **Business ethics promotion.** Promoting accurate advertising and selling practices.
- **Fighting fraud.** Alerting consumers and law enforcement agencies about scams and frauds.

The Better Business Bureau Web site provides instant access to the above information and more.

The BBBOnLine (www.bbbonline.org) program is designed specifically for the Internet marketplace. When a company displays a BBBOnLine seal, this secured seal provides a link to the company's Better Business Bureau reliability report, which reveals a company's past performance. Only companies that meet the bureau's standards have access to this seal. For more information about the BBBOnLine program, visit the Web site. To have someone contact you about the program or to apply for membership and the BBBOnLine Reliability Seal, fill out the form located at www.bbbonline.org/database/interest.html.

For more information or to apply for the BBBOnLine Privacy Seal, visit www.bbbonline.org/businesses/privacy/guide.html.

Keeping in Touch with the Web Community

Getting involved with the Internet community immediately elevates you above the pack of money-hungry retailers out to separate people from their money. Given a choice, people would rather give their business to merchants who share their interest in and passion for a subject. If you were shopping for rock-climbing gear, would you rather deal with an out-of-shape salesman who says, "I heard these boots are pretty good" or one who responds with a story about how a certain piece of equipment worked particularly well for her while climbing in cold, wet weather?

There's no better way to make your presence known than by joining Usenet newsgroups and participating in various IRC chat sessions. Participating on a non-commercial level shows you truly care about your work. Offering your expertise to others—whether by answering questions, giving advice, or providing useful information—can give you an edge on the competition. With your signature attached, you have made people aware of your business without intrusive advertising.

If you become an informative, active presence, you will be a welcomed guest rather than an ignored or contemptible intruder. On the IRC, it's best to participate using your business name, rather than a nickname. If another member recognizes the name of your business, it might spark a conversation that eventually leads to someone speaking highly of your store. However, it's best not to initiate commercial offerings.

For more on newsgroups, see Chapter 10.

Fight, Fight, Fight!

Competition: it's the American Way. Running any business should be fun, but it should also provide you with a way to make a living. If you aren't ready to compete, fight, scratch, and claw for customers, you probably shouldn't be in sales. And if you are ready to go to battle, you should go with a plan. We hope this chapter has instilled a bit of fighting spirit and has also reinforced some ideas for forming your own battle plan.

In athletics, some coaches say they worry only about their team's preparation and don't concern themselves with the opposition. In business, this is a mistake. Yes, your first concern should be with providing the best service possible. But there's no harm in taking a peek at the competition. Any professional basketball coach who says he doesn't pay particularly close attention to Tim Duncan when preparing his team to play the San Antonio Spurs is either lying or stupid. Don't let the online equivalent of Duncan sneak up and drop 60 points on you before you figure out what's going on.

The next chapter will present you with some legal issues to consider. With Internet law still developing, expect it to change rapidly and frequently. It is important to keep your eyes open and be aware of shifting legal winds. We'll provide you with some cases that provide a partial framework for Internet law.

CHAPTER TWENTY-ONE

Legal Issues

(This chapter was written by Peter S. Carlisle. Peter is an attorney in Portland, Maine, specializing in the representation of small businesses. His email address is peter@carlislesports.com)

The estimated number of Internet users in the U.S. and Canada as of July 1999 was approximately 110 million—more than double the number in June of 1997. While this volatile industry expands unfettered, the traditional means of governance for social and commercial interaction—the law—struggles to keep pace. Government legislation, the enactment of which is notoriously insensitive to the immediacy of social development and commercial innovation, and jurisprudence, a product of an even slower evolutionary process, must be applied to an industry that despite its ubiquity has only begun to define itself.

Introduction

Companies courageous enough to enter the fray of Internet commerce will assume the risks inherent in an industry where growth remains at least a step ahead of governance; at the same time, those companies will enjoy the potential for unparalleled growth.

The Internet dissolves traditional geographic barriers, increasing access and exposing a new crop of customers. Products and services can be advertised and sold in a geographic vacuum. But where do these transactions take place? Where are taxes due? What laws govern if there is a dispute relating to an Internet transaction? Naturally novel legal issues, such as those relating to jurisdiction and taxation, arise as business practices change. Unfortunately, given the rapid development of the Internet, it is difficult to predict how such issues will be resolved. Businesses participating in Internet commerce cannot refer to the law to conduct the typical actuarial analysis to weigh potential liabilities against potential gains. Until the law catches up with the expansion of the Internet, Internet commerce will require a roll of the dice.

Rest assured, the law will catch up. The development of the law will eventually correspond to the development of the Internet. Laws regulating static elements of commerce and society remain relatively static; laws governing developing industries must evolve accordingly. During the period of legal evolution, uncertainty is present. While that uncertainty cannot be eliminated, businesses can minimize the potential liabilities arising out of such uncertainty by gaining and maintaining awareness about how the laws governing Internet commerce are developing.

Jurisdiction

The most obvious legal issue that arises with the growth of the Internet is jurisdiction. In order for a court to entertain a lawsuit, it must have jurisdiction over the litigants and the claims; in other words, it must be appropriate for a particular court to decide a particular matter involving particular people. This issue arises in the context of Internet commerce where there is a dispute between people or businesses of different states. Is a customer in New York obligated to travel to Texas to defend himself against a Texas company suing him for breach of a sales agreement? Reciprocally, is a company in Texas forced to endure the costs of litigating in New York? The answers to these questions should affect the approach a business takes in conducting its business over the Internet.

Both state law and the U.S. Constitution limit a court's jurisdiction over a defendant from another state. In order for a court to exercise jurisdiction over a defendant, jurisdiction must be authorized by the state's long-arm statute (state long-arm statutes authorize courts to entertain lawsuits involving non-resident defendants) and satisfy the Due Process Clause of the U.S. Constitution.

The Due Process Clause requires that a defendant have "minimum contacts" with the state within which the suit is brought (the "forum state"). The presence of minimum contacts is determined through a three-part test: First, the defendant must be entitled to the protections of the forum state's laws by having purposefully conducted business in that state; second, the cause of action must arise out of activities related to the forum state; and third, the imposition of jurisdiction must "comport with traditional notions of fair play and substantial justice." (International Shoe Co. v. Washington, 326 U.S. 310 [1945]). These vague legal standards do not adequately resolve the uncertainties that have arisen in the context of Internet commerce. Nonetheless, it is important to review the handful of decisions that have confronted the challenging legal issues of Internet commerce.

In CompuServe, Inc. v. Patterson, 1996, the Sixth Circuit Court of Appeals found jurisdiction where the only contact between the parties was of an electronic nature. The court exercised jurisdiction over a Texan subscriber to CompuServe because he had entered into a "Shareware Registration Agreement" with CompuServe, an Ohio company through which he intended to sell his computer software. The court found significance in the fact that the defendant purposefully did business in Ohio—despite the fact that he never physically entered the state. The Court stated that CompuServe, in effect, "acted as Patterson's distributor, albeit electronically and not physically." A significant element to the CompuServe court's rationale was the existence of a contract.

Interestingly, two years before the CompuServe decision, in Press Kap, Inc. v. System One, a Florida state court found jurisdiction lacking over a New York company that had entered into a contract with a Florida-based company (and had actually accessed the Florida company's database). Press Kap, Inc.'s apparent irreconcilability with CompuServe illustrates the uncertainty in the judicial treatment of Internet commerce.

In McDonough v. Fallon McElligott, a case decided the same year as CompuServe, a federal court in California seemed to subscribe to the CompuServe court's requirement of a contract between the parties, holding that the creation of a Web site does not constitute the requisite "minimum contacts" to justify jurisdiction.

Despite the apparent importance of a contractual relationship, non-contractual activities such as advertising, which accounts for a large percentage of Internet activity, may also lead to the imposition of jurisdiction. In Inset Sys. Inc. v. Instruction Set, Inc., a Massachusetts company was subjected to personal jurisdiction for using a domain name inset.com when the plaintiff had a federal registration for "Inset." Despite the fact that it was never shown that the defendant made any sales in the forum state (Connecticut), jurisdiction was justified because the defendant company had "purposefully directed its advertising activities toward Connecticut, on a continuing basis." The 1996 Inset decision stands for the proposition that continual advertising can create sufficient contacts to justify the imposition of jurisdiction—despite the absence of a formal contractual relationship and a lack of sales.

In another 1996 case, Bensusan Restaurant Corp. v. King, a New York court adopted a more relaxed view on Internet advertising, holding that "[c]reating a site, like placing a product into the stream of commerce, may be felt nationwide—or even worldwide—but, without more, it is not an act purposefully directed toward the forum state." In Bensusan, the defendant advertised his business, but did not actually conduct sales.

In State of Minnesota v. Granite Gate Resorts Inc., Minnesota brought charges against the operators of a Web page that advertised a future online betting service. The Web site did not actually facilitate commerce, but rather provided information about the gambling service and created an opportunity to be put on a mailing list. The court characterized the defendant's actions in the following manner:

The defendants attempted to hide behind the Internet and claim that they had mailed nothing to Minnesota, sent nothing to Minnesota, and never advertised in Minnesota. This argument is not sound in the age of cyberspace. Once the defendants placed an advertisement on the Internet, that advertisement is available 24 hours a day, 7 days a week, 365 days a year to any Internet user (some of whom are Minnesotans) until the defendants take it off the Internet.

Despite the indirect nature of the solicitation (and the lack of formal agreements and sales), since the site provided consumers with phone numbers to call, the court held that the defendants had made "a direct marketing campaign to the State of Minnesota," and that "one who sets up his or her system...knows that anyone accessing his or her site will get that information, then the server ought to be held responsible for that information."

Similarly, the 1996 case of Maritz Inc. v. Cybergold Inc. held that the defendant's creation of a passive Web site triggered jurisdiction since the company's intent was clearly devoid of geographic restraint—despite the fact that the defendant had not made any sales.

In the 1997 case of Zippo Mfg. Co. v. Zippo Dot Com, Inc, the California court stated: "We are being asked to determine whether Dot Com's conducting of electronic commerce with Pennsylvania residents constitutes the purposeful availment of doing business in Pennsylvania." The court held that agreements with Internet service providers in a state, permitting that state's subscriber to access a company's news service, and advertising on its Web page in the state, were sufficient to establish jurisdiction. It should be noted that in Zippo, in addition to agreements, actual sales were shown.

In 1997, the same New York court that had decided Bensusan found an absence of personal jurisdiction where the defendant did not contract to sell or actually sell any goods or services to customers in the forum state. The court acknowledged but refused to follow the rationale of the Inset and Maritz decisions. In Hearst Corp. v. Goldberger, a New Jersey defendant had posted a Web site on the Internet that advertised future legal information under the name esqwire.com. Hearst Corp., owner of the trademark "Esquire" for magazines, sued in New York. The court declined to assert jurisdiction because the defendant's activities consisted solely of posting information, but no products or services were available for purchase by New York residents.

While the law of Internet jurisdiction remains confusing, these decisions constitute the existing jurisprudential framework for Web site businesses to consider when evaluating jurisdictional issues. These cases illustrate the unpredictable nature of the state of the law. Based on the standards articulated in these cases, it would be advisable for a Web site holder to be particularly careful when utilizing interactive capability on a site. The cases in which jurisdiction has been found have one thing in common: the Web sites allowed for the immediate retransmission of information back to the Web site; the mere posting of information on a home page is less likely to trigger jurisdiction.

Another consideration for a company that transacts business over the Internet is to limit Web site access from locales where they do not wish to be subject to jurisdiction. Indeed, businesses should not only gain an awareness of the potential costs of litigating in distant forums but also realize that the current state of the law may subject the company to the law of the state that is most favorable to the claim that plaintiff will assert.

Tax Issues

Similar to jurisdictional issues, tax implications relating to Internet - commerce are fraught with uncertainty. The dissolution of meaningful geographical boundaries raises questions as to where a taxable event occurs in a commercial transaction over the Internet. While it is difficult to determine with certainty how tax implications will be resolved, it is important for a company to be familiar with the pertinent issues.

Federal

In Congress, a bill entitled the Internet Tax Freedom Act was introduced in 1997. The Act set up a national three-year moratorium that prohibits the 30,000 U.S. tax jurisdictions from passing unfair sanctions on Net access, services, and sales, and grandfathered tax codes in effect before October 1, 1998.The Treasury Department published a Discussion Paper, which was a fact-gathering effort designed to resolve the uncertainty about taxation of online commerce. Interestingly, the Treasury Department has advocated a principle of neutrality that rejects the need for new or additional taxes on electronic transactions. It recommends that all income be treated equally, regardless of the means by which it entered commerce. As authority for its position, the Treasury Department notes that foreign businesses are not taxed for soliciting and filling orders from U.S. customers.

In the fall of 1998, the 19-member Advisory Commission on Electronic Commerce was created to study the effect of e-commerce on traditional retail businesses, and the ability of local, state and international officials to collect taxes on Internet sales. A final report from the commission is due in April 2000.

After some early and expected struggles, the commission released in October 1999 18 criteria for proposed taxation treatments of e-commerce. However, the outcome of the Internet Tax debate will not be clear until proposals are adopted. The proposals are expected to simplify the system of sales tax collection by Web businesses.

The commission represents a range of stakeholders from AT&T, America Online, an anti-taxation consumer group, and local and state lawmakers. To stay abreast of the workings of the commission, visit its Web site at www.ecommercecommission.org.

Meanwhile, Sen. John McCain (R-Arizona), the chairman of the Senate Commerce Committee and presidential candidate, introduced legislation in September 1999 to make the moratorium on Internet taxes permanent. McCain's bill would prohibit sales and use taxes on e-commerce transactions. The bill amends the Internet Tax Freedom Act.

Internationally, foreign companies typically pay taxes on income generated from the U.S. if the income is attributable to a "permanent establishment" located in the United States. Taxation of foreign companies is made possible by treaties with those foreign countries. Under the approach proposed by the Department of Treasury, a foreign corporation that advertised on a home page would probably avoid taxation. Issues that may arise in connection with international business include how a permanent establishment will be determined, and whether a foreign corporation's use of a United States server will lead to jurisdiction.

State

State taxation issues are similarly clouded. As a rule, a state must satisfy the nexus requirement under the due process and commerce clauses of the U.S. Constitution in order to tax an out-of-state business. The Commerce Clause, which would likely govern any Internet tax analysis, requires a "substantial nexus" and connection, for the imposition of taxes. In construing the meaning of "substantial nexus," the Supreme Court has relied upon the determination of physical presence. The Court has applied this test to the mail-order industry (which bears a strong resemblance to Internet commerce), where the only contact with the taxing state is by mail or "common carrier."

In the 1992 case of Quill v. North Dakota, the court held that simple contact with a common carrier does not constitute a sufficient nexus with the taxing state. The Court noted that the sufficiency of a nexus "may turn on the presence in the taxing state of a small sales force, plant or property." In fact, Quill has been interpreted as permitting taxation of a mail-order company that sent employees to install software and make repairs subject to a service agreement (Orvis Co. Inc. v. Tax Appeals Tribunal of the State of New York). Other courts have held that maintenance of offices, warehouses, equipment, and personnel in a state create a sufficient nexus.

The logical argument in favor of Internet commerce holds that Internet commerce and the mail-order business are analogous. The argument posits that the Internet operates like a common carrier such as a shipper or courier. Obviously, states will attempt to discount the analogous nature of these two industries in an effort to protect their tax bases.

Some state and local officials want to maintain their ability to tax Net services. The National Governors Association and the U.S. Conference of

Mayors are among the groups already working on a uniform state law package to deal with Internet taxation. The National Governor's Association is in favor of a flat tax system for e-commerce sales.

Intellectual Property

Many legal issues relating to the Internet deal with measures of protection for ideas and information a person or company may release into cyberspace. Traditionally, the appropriate protections for intellectual property were copyright, trademark, and patent. While these mechanisms are applicable to Internet commerce, some new protections have emerged with the growth of the Internet.

Copyright laws protect original works of authorship fixed in any tangible medium of expression. While notice is not required for copyright to exist (as copyright subsists automatically the moment a work is created and fixed in a tangible medium) notice is required for one to bring an action for copyright infringement. Notice typically includes the symbol of a circled ©, the name of the author, and the date.

Proof of copyright infringement requires the following elements: a copyright owned by the plaintiff; access by the defendant to the copyrighted material; and a substantial similarity between the copyrighted material and the defendant's material.

Copyright grants the following exclusive rights to the owner of the copyright: reproduction rights; derivation rights (or the right to prepare works derived from the copyrighted work); distribution rights relating to the copyrighted work; the right to perform the copyrighted work; and the right to publicly display the copyrighted work.

A trademark is a word or symbol that distinguishes a good from other goods; similarly, a service mark is a word or symbol that distinguishes the services of one from the services of another. Trade names are names used to identify a business or vocation. Trade names are not protected under federal law, but only under state law.

As Internet addresses become identifiable with the names of certain businesses, those addresses, or domain names, acquire value and demand protection. Just as traditional storefronts battle for the rights to use certain names and associate those names with their businesses, so too do Internet businesses. Domain names have become an important aspect of Internet commerce; consequently, administration and regulation of domain names assumes a heightened level of importance.

InterNIC, the entity that currently administers domain names, will register domain names on a first-come, first-served basis only if the applicant warrants that 1) the applicant has a right to use the name; 2) the applicant has a bona fide intention to use the domain name regularly; 3) the use does not infringe upon any third party's intellectual property right, including those mentioned above; 4) the applicant does not intend to use the domain name for any unlawful use; and 5) the applicant agrees to resolve disputes through arbitration.

The cost to register a domain name is $100 for two years and $50 a year for each additional year. To register for a domain name, the registrant selects its domain name and submits an application representing that the registration of the domain name does not interfere with or infringe upon the rights of any third party (to the best of the applicant's knowledge).

For businesses participating in Internet commerce, issues may arise where the use of a domain name conflicts with another's trademark. In such a case, the owner of the domain name can continue to use the domain name if the date he first used the name predates the trademark owner's first use of its trademark and/or the effective date of registration. The owner of a domain name may also enjoy continued use of the name if the owner provides Internic with a certified copy of its own trademark registration identical to the domain name showing that he is the actual owner of both the domain name and the trademark.

International Law

Any business planning to buy or sell its wares internationally must comply with all international import/export laws. Not only do individual countries each possess a distinct set of laws governing its particular commerce, but the United States regulates certain types of goods and services that companies may wish to export to these other countries.

Given the esoteric nature of international business law, it is essential for a business desiring to reach out to other countries to consult an expert in the field.

It may be said that it is easier to run afoul of international commercial law in a cyberspace setting than it is to violate the same laws through traditional means of trade, given the ease with which information is communicated. The established infrastructure of international trade governance at present is not equipped to regulate Internet commerce. Import/export issues have traditionally been identified by third parties that facilitate and broker international commerce. Shipping companies and customs agencies process such transactions through a well-established system that has evolved over the years to guard against potential violations.

With Internet commerce, transactions may be consummated between private individuals or entities without the need for any third party to facilitate the deal—international commerce may take place in an instant, in cyberspace. The convenience of Internet commerce may seem like an advantage at first blush, but when that third party is a company's only insurance that international commercial laws have been satisfied, potential liabilities quickly multiply.

While it is impractical to outline the many potentially applicable regulations that may affect businesses participating in international commerce, a brief sampling of some of the obscure concerns should suggest to businesses that a tolerable comfort level is possible only with the involvement of appropriate experts. For example, any company selling goods in France may only advertise those goods in French (is your Web site accessible in France?). Garments sold in Mexico must bear very specific labeling information (have you ever shipped a T-shirt south of the border?). Certain software, computers, and computer parts may not be exported from the U.S. to certain countries, as such exportation may threaten national security.

Just as our legal infrastructure is continually evolving, so too are the legal systems of other countries. The reconciliation of the laws of different countries and the facilitation of commerce between different countries are industries unto themselves, which should not be ignored by today's cyberspace companies. While the Internet may make it possible to bypass many of the traditional commercial procedures relating to international commerce, that fact offers no protection when a company is identified as having evaded international laws.

In addition to the complicated nature of international commerce, businesses must be aware of all laws and regulations governing their particular commodity—even when such business is consummated within the United States or even that company's home state. Food, alcohol, livestock, clothing, and nearly every other salable commodity is governed by a unique set of regulations when it leaves a state, travels along federal highways to another state, and enters the destination state. It is important for an Internet company to view its export business, both international and intranational, as if it were doing business through the traditional avenues of commerce. A business would be well advised to consult a lawyer with a specialty in its specific industry to ensure that compliance with all pertinent laws is achieved.

Miscellaneous Concerns

Miscellaneous concerns continually emerge with regard to Internet commerce. For instance, unauthorized sites may be found to infringe upon trademark rights. The James Dean Foundation in Indiana has sued a California fan for using James Dean's name. In CMG WorldWide Inc. v. America Legends, defendant Ronald Martinetti is being sued for the unauthorized commercial use of James Dean's name and likeness by selling memorabilia over the Internet. Given the number of unauthorized fan sites, and links to sites containing the names and likenesses of celebrities, this may be an important issue for many businesses.

Links to other sites may also be the cause of litigation. Linking a Web page to another page within another site may cause people to miss the logo and advertisements present on that other company's front page. Since links are an important element of any company's Web page, it is important to consider the ramifications of linking to certain sites.

Many companies doing business over the Internet utilize standardized written agreements to structure relationships with their customers; oftentimes, this relationship is established and defined through standard terms and conditions to which the customer agrees in the initial session by simply clicking a button. These agreements are sometimes referred to as "click-wrap" agreements. Because click-wrap agreements frequently go unread, there is some uncertainty as to whether an enforceable contract is formed through such a procedure. The click-wrap agreement is analogous to the "shrink-wrap" agreement used by software companies prior to the emergence of Internet commerce. Recently, in the case of ProCD Inc. v. Seidenberg, the Seventh Circuit held that shrink-wrap agreements are generally enforceable. The same rationale employed by the Seventh Circuit likely will be used to argue the enforceability of click-wrap agreements.

Conclusion

Although it is uncertain how the law will evolve with regard to Internet commerce, companies may maximize their protection by remaining adequately informed of recent developments and trends. Canvassing some of the more reliable sites that track legal issues affecting the Internet should go a long way in alleviating the uncertainty that accompanies Internet commerce.

Some of the more helpful sites on the Internet are listed below:

- Law News Network. www.lawnewsnetwork.com
- The Internet and Computer Law Association. grove.ufl.edu/~cmplaw/
- Internet Law & Policy Forum. www.ilpf.org
- Net Law News. www.mindspring.com/~moceyuna/
- Net Law U.S. www.netlaw.com/netlawus.htm
- Internet Tax Freedom Act. www.house.gov/chriscox/nettax/
- U.S. House of Representatives Office of the Law Revision Counsel. uscode.house.gov
- Weblaw Internet Law Services. www.weblaw.co.uk/internet.htm

PART VI

Store-Building Tips and Details

Most of this book covers your options in a way that is both specific but general enough that stores of all sizes and shapes can benefit. In Part VI we will cover some more specific options: building a store with Yahoo Store, taking advantage of the popularity of online auctions, creating a store from scratch, and, for those with larger budgets, advanced store-building options and features.

Part VI Table of Contents

CHAPTER TWENTY-TWO

All-In-One Store-Building: Yahoo Store and Other Offerings

The biggest change in e-commerce in 1999 has been the rapid growth of all-in-one store-building solutions. These are completely Web-based services that let you set up and run an online store simply by filling out forms and answering questions via the Web.

Yahoo Store is one of the all-in-one leaders. It is a combination authoring tool and hosting service. There is no software to install, and your site is built using Yahoo's point-and-click interface.

This chapter covers the features and resources offered by Yahoo Store and walks you through the process of taking a ten-day "test drive" of Yahoo Store. However, we won't bore you with every detail concerning every feature, all of which is available on the Yahoo Store Web pages. When specific information would be helpful, we will direct you to that Web page.

We also offer some information on some other easy-to-use store-building tools , including Amazon.com's recently announced zShops. zShops lets you set up your own shop on the number one e-commerce site in the world.

Introduction and Yahoo Store Features

Yahoo Store is used by merchants of all sizes but is particularly effective for small to medium-sized stores. The site is hosted by Yahoo, orders are accepted securely using SSL encryption, and orders can be retrieved securely from Yahoo's server or can be received via fax or processed online.

Making changes to your store requires simply logging in any time from any browser. The cost is $100 per month for stores that sell 50 items or less and $300 a month for stores selling up to 1,000 items. There is no startup fee and you can cancel your account at any time. You can either use a typical **www.yourstorename.com** URL (obviously you must pay to register the domain name) or one that follows the format of **store.yahoo.com/yourstorename/**.

Online Processing

Yahoo Store allows you to process orders online through a link to First Data. To take advantage of this, you must have a merchant account. If you don't have a merchant account, Yahoo Store merchants can choose to apply online with Bank One at **store.yahoo.com/vw/apply.html**.

With Yahoo Store, orders are authorized in real time and when you retrieve orders through your browser, you will see the authorization status at the bottom of the page.

For more on online processing, go to **store.yahoo.com/vw/merchant.html**.

The Regular Interface

Rather than using the Simple interface that allows you to quickly launch your Yahoo Store, you can turn to the Regular interface, which makes additional features available. Simply log in and choose the Regular interface. Clicking Edit will offer more fields and variables. Clicking on the red triangle that follows the edit buttons switches to the Advanced interface. The Advanced interface should be used by those with programming skills only, warns Yahoo. All protection against damaging your site is turned off and, Yahoo stresses, you can damage your site beyond repair.

Yahoo offers a number of features and options, most of which are covered below. For more detailed explanations, go to store.yahoo.com/vw/addfeattoyou.html.

Sale Prices

This option is available in the Price field when using the Regular interface. This allows you to display both the regular price and the sale price, which will be used by the ordering system.

Quantity Pricing

You can also offer quantity pricing—for example one of an item for $5, two for $8, three for $12, and so on. The ordering system automatically adjusts the unit price depending on the number ordered.

Orderable Items

Although the default is *Yes*, making items orderable, if you want to make an item unavailable due to its being out of stock or for another reason, change the Orderable field to *No*. The items page will not include an Order button.

Options

This feature allows you to add attributes to an item, such as size and color.

Monograms and Inscriptions

In the Options field, you can also add personalized options such as monograms or inscriptions.

Headlines

The title of an item page is the name of the item, by default. However, you can change this by entering the desired text in the Headline field. This allows you to add a more promotional title to an item page.

Layout Tool

Yahoo Store will automatically lay your sections out in two columns, with thumbnail images on the left and text on the right. The Layout tool (click on the Layout button) allows you to change that.

The Layout tool offers four properties—Put Contents, Alignment, Speed, and Columns. Put Contents lets you choose whether you want the current section's items to appear on their own pages or on the section page. Alignment allows you to align the elements of a page the way you want. Speed lets you choose between a graphics-heavy page that loads slowly or a leaner page that loads more quickly. Columns lets you select the number of columns that contain a page's elements.

Look Tool

Using the Regular interface, the Look tool allows you to customize your site's overall appearance further. (The Layout tool is for the individual page.)

You can change variables such as button font, button text color, display text color, display font, and more.

Accessories

Using the Regular interface, you can add a list of accessories to an item page: ski poles, boots, and bindings to go with skis, for example.

Your Logo

You can insert your logo into the button bar rather than the Home button provided by Yahoo Store. Simply upload an image.

Abstracts

You can use abstracts to add descriptive text for each link on your home page or in a section. This allows you to show a description of each section rather than just listing its contents.

Cross-Selling

You can set up your Yahoo Store to cross-sell automatically by grouping items together using the Families variable. When a customer orders an item that is part of a family, he will receive a message at the bottom of the shopping basket, asking if he is interested in the other products in the family.

Automatic Shipping and Tax

This is an option that many Web stores do not offer, however you can set up your store so that shipping and tax are automatically added to orders.

Advanced Features

Yahoo Store offers a number of advanced features such as uploading data files, uploading multiple images, special Yahoo Store tags, an RTML reference, and Publish1.

Uploading Data Files

This feature allows you to generate your Yahoo Store site from a database. Simply generate a text file in CSV (comma-separated values) and, using the Advanced interface, upload the file to Yahoo's server. For information on creating files in the required format and uploading those files, visit store.yahoo.com/vw/upload.html.

Uploading Multiple Images

Yahoo Store allows you to upload multiple images simultaneously. To do so, go to the Controls page in the Advanced interface and click on Multiple Image Upload. When you see the File Upload screen, select the appropriate ZIP file and click Send.

The name of each image file (minus the file-type extension) should be the ID of the object you want it to become the image for.

When the upload, which can take a decent amount of time depending on the size of the ZIP file, is finished, you will be returned to the Controls page. If the upload was successful, you will see a new image on the page of each object for which you uploaded an image. The size limit on the ZIP files is approximately 14 MB.

Special Yahoo Store Tags

Yahoo Store will be introducing a series of special tags for merchants to use with their store. You can use them anywhere in your site where you can use HTML. Yahoo tags are processed by Yahoo's software when your pages are generated and yield HTML that can be displayed by any browser.

For a list and description of these special tags, visit **store.yahoo.com/vw/specviawtag.html**.

RTML Reference

RTML is a language for describing Web sites that is designed for users with no programming experience. Every object has an RTML template that describes what its Web page should look like.

For more on RTML or to visit the RTML Reference, visit **store.yahoo.com/vw/rtml.html**.

Publish1

Publish1 allows you to republish an individual page without waiting for a regular Publish. It is for fixing minor errors such as typos in large sites.

You should not use Publish1 when you have done more to your site since the last Publish than change the item that you are using Publish1 for. For more on Publish1, visit **store.yahoo.com/vw/publish1.html**.

Merchant Resources

Beginning at the Yahoo Store page (**store.yahoo.com**), you can check out the merchant resources offered by Yahoo.

What's New

What's New offers information on the latest Yahoo Store features, such as the Login Merge, Yahoo Wallet and Express Checkout, and more. Each new item is described briefly and includes a short FAQ.

How To Sell Online

How To Sell Online includes numerous instructional columns covering topics such as "The Ten Secrets of Selling Online," "Choosing A Domain Name," "International Orders," and more. While we hope to have covered everything you need to know, you can never have too much knowledge. These columns are worth reading.

Monthly Newsletter

Yahoo offers a monthly newsletter that covers topics such as better customer communication, order tracking, Yahoo Shopping Search, and more.

Designer Directory

The Designer Directory offers a geographical list of links to Web designers who use Yahoo Store.

Helpful Links

Helpful Links offers just that—links to sites such as Yahoo Small Business, Yahoo News E-Commerce Headlines, Search Engine Watch, Online Privacy, and more.

Test Drive

Yahoo Store allows you to build a Web store in minutes using just a Web browser. To get started, go to store.yahoo.com. The Yahoo Store page (Figure 22.1) includes merchant resources and other information, which we have already covered. You can use the same Yahoo ID and password that people use for other Yahoo options and services, such as email.

If you don't already have a Yahoo ID and password, complete the signup process and log in using your ID and password.

Here you can optionally surf the Yahoo Store site for infomation and instruction. If you are ready to start building a Test Drive store, click on Create A Store.

Fill in the desired ID/address and full name for your store, click Create, and off you go (Figure 22.2).

FIGURE 22.1
The Yahoo Store home page.

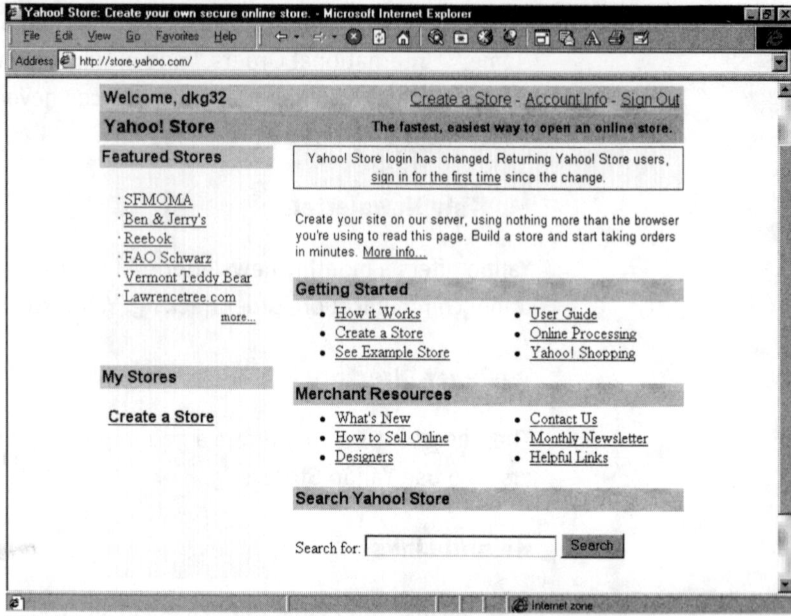

FIGURE 22.2
Creating a free trial account.

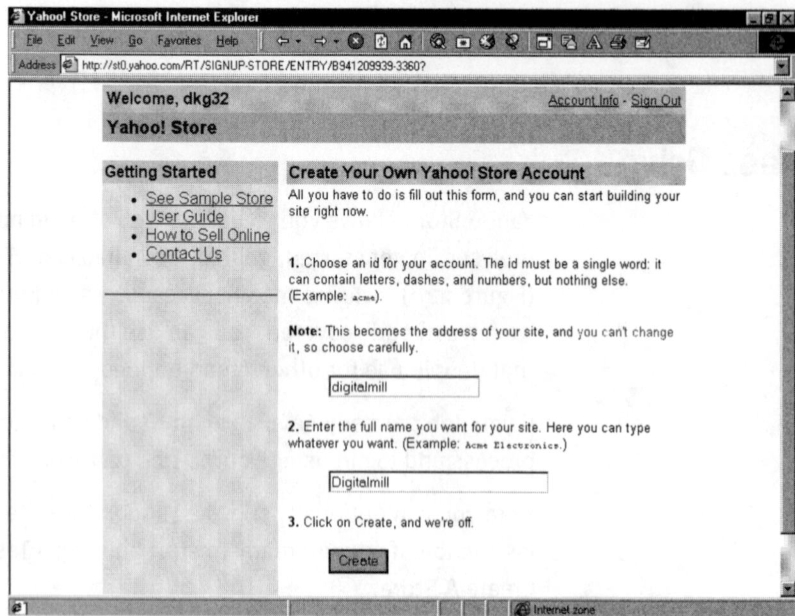

This creates a ten-day trial account which you are automatically logged into at this point. In the future, to edit your store you must go to **store.yahoo.com**, click on Edit to make changes to your store or Manager to retrieve orders, and enter your store name.

Your temporary account will allow you to do everything that a permanent account will, except that retrieved orders will be scrambled. Follow the instructions here to convert your temporary account to a working account. After accepting the terms of the Test Drive agreement, you can begin building your store.

Creating Your Account and Taking a Tour

Next up is a short Guided Tour that includes instructions on creating your store. This step-by-step process makes creating a store very easy.

The first page of the tour presents you with the front page of the store, including the name you have selected (Figure 22.3).

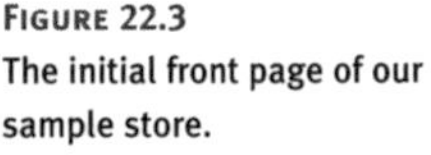

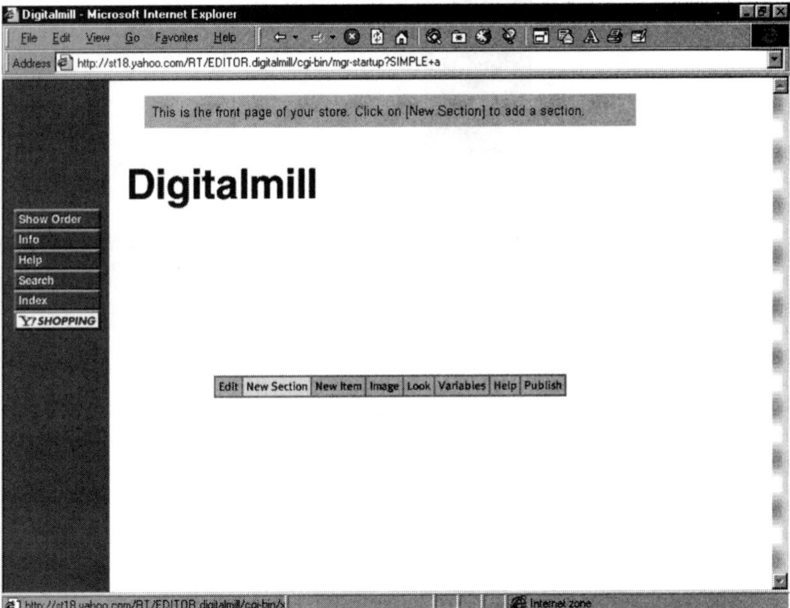

FIGURE 22.3
The initial front page of our sample store.

Click on New Section to create a new section, type the name of the section in the Name box, and click Update. This will give you a new section and will add the name of that section to the body of your home page and create a button on the left side of the page (Figure 22.4). To go to the section, click Up and then click on the button for the section.

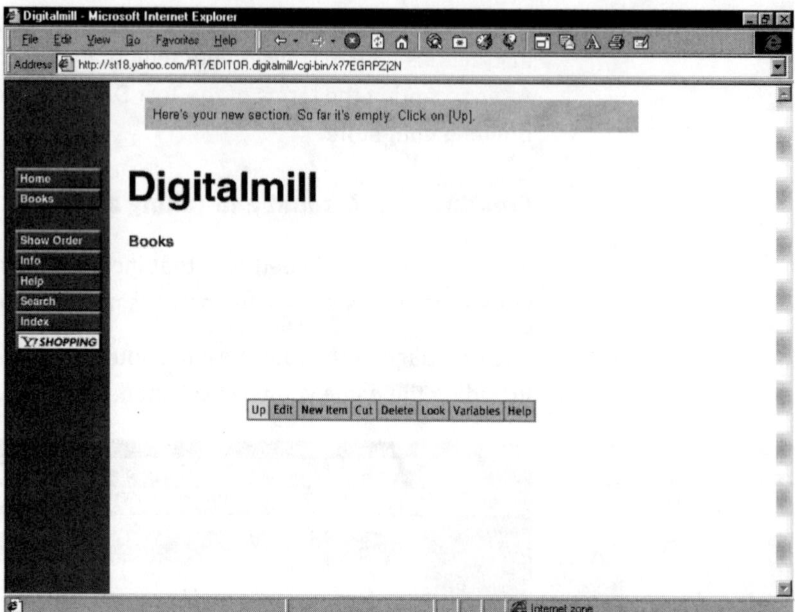

FIGURE 22.4
Adding a section to your site.

To add an item to the section, click New Item and fill in the desired information and click Update. This will place you on the page of the item. To see the section page and the item as it is displayed (Figure 22.5), click Up. Click New Item to add another item to the section.

Now your section has two items listed (Figure 22.6). Click on one and then click Edit to add some information.

The code field is where you should enter any product code and the caption field allows for a description. The result is shown in Figure 22.7.

Next the tour takes you to the uploading of an image by clicking on Image. If you don't have an image to upload or your browser doesn't show a browse button on this page, click Cancel. Otherwise, find the photo that you want to upload, select it, and click Send to upload.

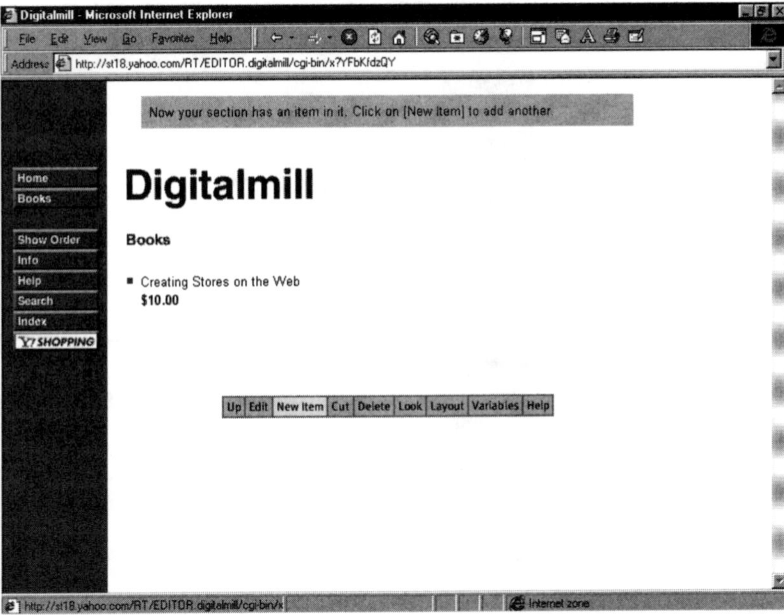

FIGURE 22.5
An item on your section page.

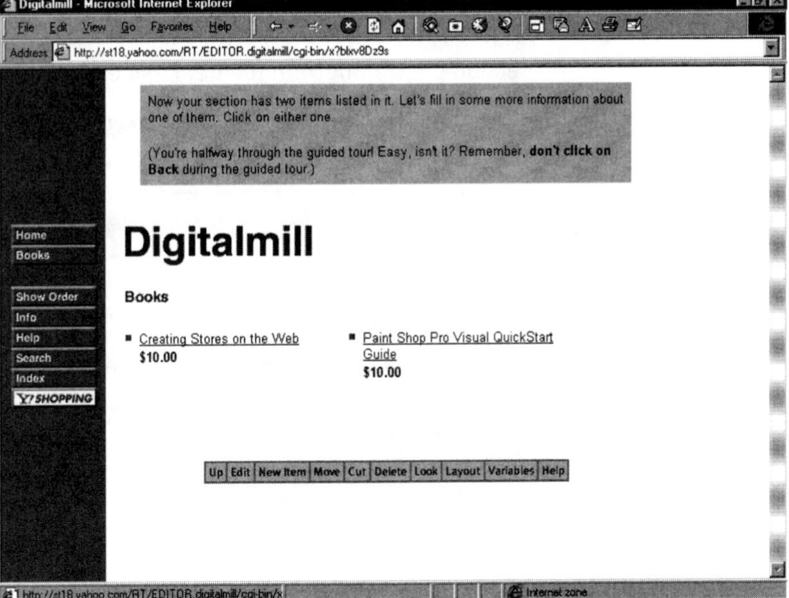

FIGURE 22.6
Your section is growing quickly.

FIGURE 22.7
Easily adding a description of your item.

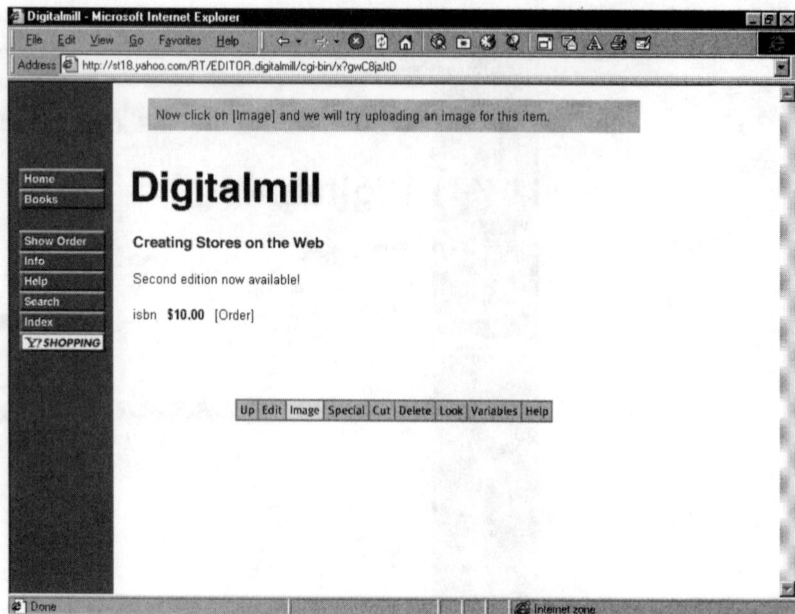

Ta-da! There it is—the item page, complete with accompanying graphic (Figure 22.8). A clickable thumbnail version will also be displayed on the section page along with the item name.

FIGURE 22.8
As easy as that, our item has a picture.

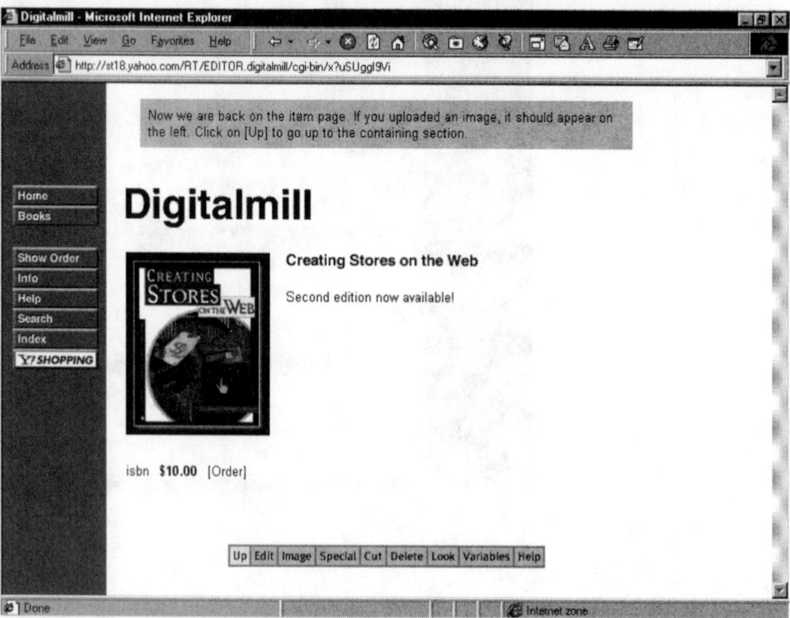

To feature this item on your front page, click Special. Back at the front page, click Edit to add some text. Type in the text and click Update.

Finally click on the Info button on the left side of the page to add infomation about your store and click Update. This will complete your company information page (Figure 22.9). Click on your company name to return to the home page and click Publish to complete the guided tour.

To visit your store, click on the link provided.

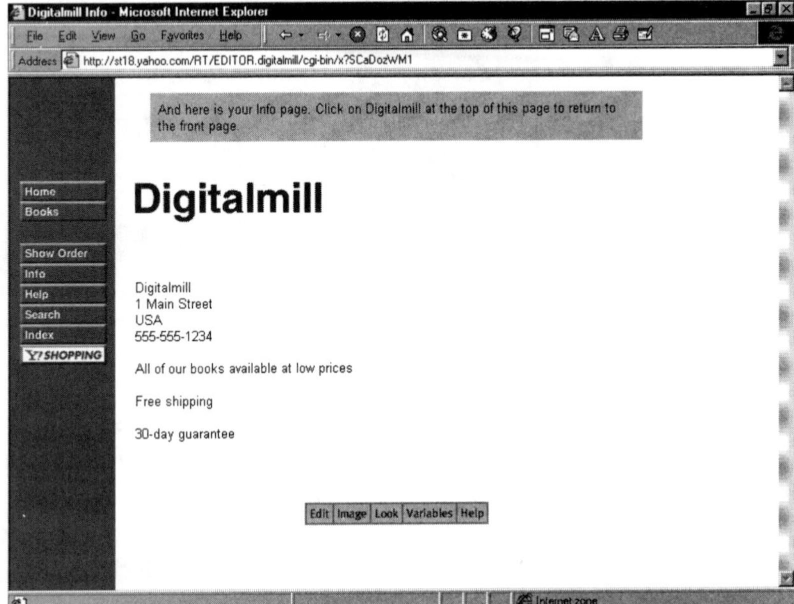

Figure 22.9 The company information page.

Continue Editing

The Guided Tour covers most of the basics needed to start building. As your store grows you will probably refer to the User's Guide until the simple interface becomes second nature. Being brave, we decided to immediately change the look of our store, because that option isn't covered in the guided tour. Start this process by clicking Look. Remember, you can always click Help if you are confused.

Changing the Look

Clicking Look allows you to play with fonts and color combinations such as Anglia, Arbeit, Tex, Tonic, and more. Since our test store sells computer books, we clicked on Hitech. The results are shown in Figure 22.10.

FIGURE 22.10
Our store's new Hitech look.

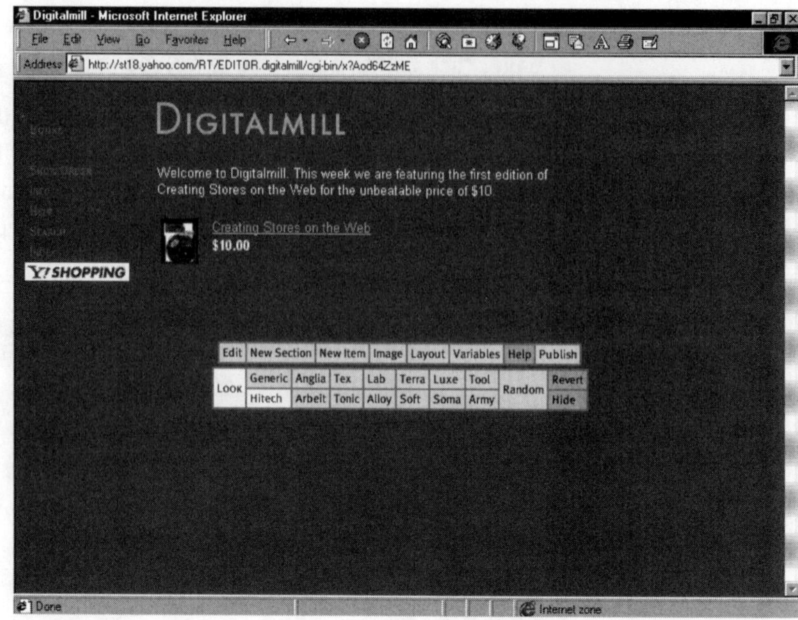

Changing the Layout

To change the layout, click Layout. This allows you to change the alignment (left or center), speed (fast or slow), and number of columns (one, two, or three). The current settings are highlighted. We changed them all to have a center-aligned, slower but more graphic-heavy site with one-column layout. The changes, which included a larger graphic of our featured product, can be seen in Figure 22.11.

Changing Some Variables

You can use the Variables button to add an email contact, a new image, minimum orders, new text, and contact infomation to the page on which you are working. Click Update to make the changes. Clicking Publish makes public the changes to look, layout, or variables.

To log out of the editing process, click on the Yahoo Shopping logo. To go back to editing, click on your store's name under My Store. Here you will be able to change the editing interface, process orders, change settings, check statistics, and more (Figure 22.12). Remember this is just a demo account that will expire in ten days. To activate your account, click on the link provided and follow the instructions.

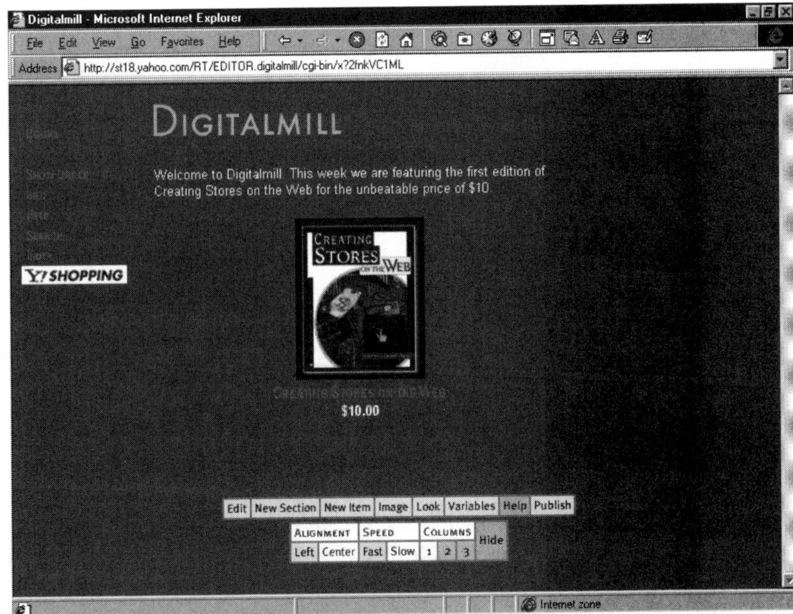

FIGURE 22.11
Our store's new layout.

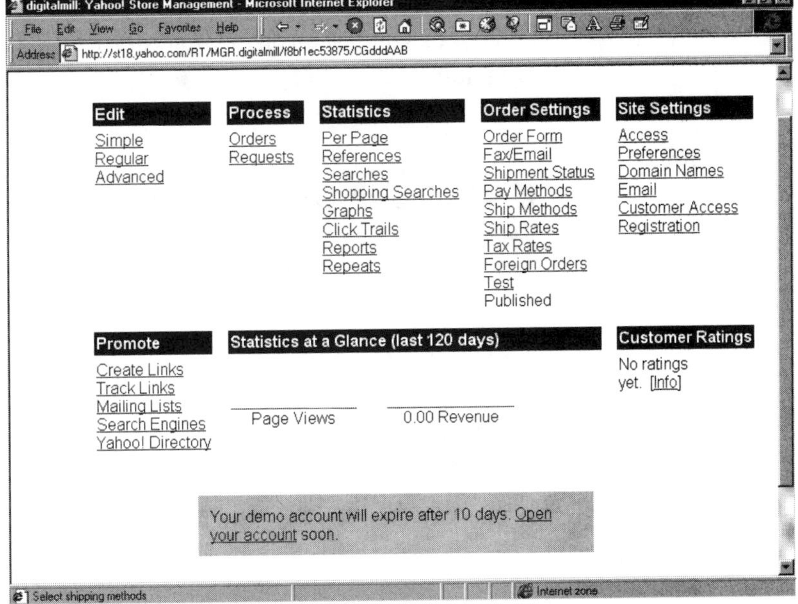

FIGURE 22.12
You have plenty of tools to change and manage your Yahoo Store.

We have covered the basics of Yahoo Store here. We suggest you take your own Guided Tour and take advantage of the Ten-day Test Drive to get accustomed to the interface and all the options offered by Yahoo Store. If you feel it works for you, activate your account—and welcome to the world of Web retailing.

Amazon.com zShops

zShops are Amazon.com's answer to store-building services. Although not as robust as some other services, it does have one huge advantage—large amounts of traffic. By building a zShop you gain access to the millions of customers who shop on the Web via Amazon.com.

With a zShop, you also gain access to Amazon.com's patented "1-Click" processing services, and your items are included in Amazon.com's universal product search, which is used by millions to find items for sale on Amazon.com and the Web.

zShops are essentially listed items for sale on Amazon.com (Figure 22.13). It is easy to set up shop on Amazon.com and take advantage of its amazing features.

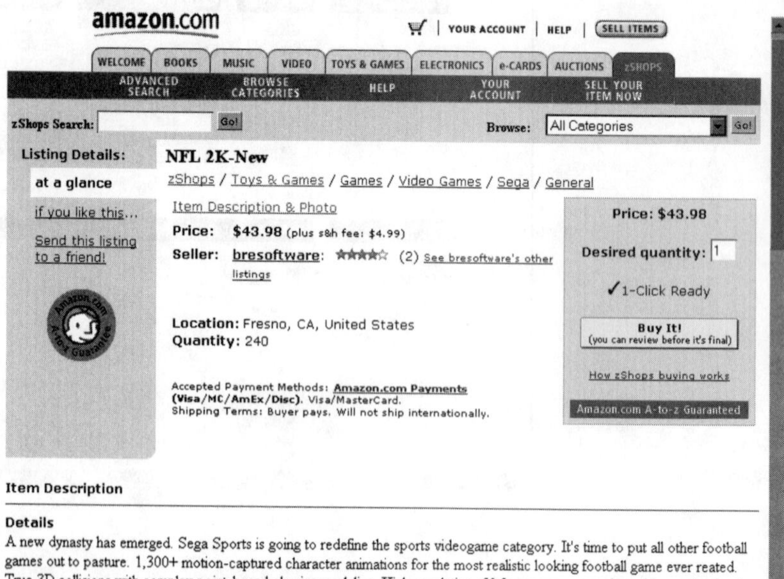

FIGURE 22.13
A zShop listing on Amazon.com

Start by Registering

To open a zShop, register as a zShop merchant with Amazon (Figure 22.14). This sign-up process is fairly simple, and if you're already an existing customer of Amazon you can sign in using your original customer email and password.

FIGURE 22.14
Registering as a zShop merchant.

Once you are registered to sell an item via zShop, you must fill out item lists for your store. You can do this an item at a time or, using the bulk uploader, you can upload many items at once, provided you've created a file with the proper format.

To enter in a new listing, click the Sell Items button at the top of the Amazon.com site, then click the Amazon.com zShops link. This brings you to the Auctions & zShops Sellers guide (Figure 22.15), a master index to all the forms, information, and pages related to selling an item on Amazon via Auctions or zShops. In many ways, the two services—Auctions and zShops—operate in similar ways, although items listed via zShops have fixed prices.

On the Auctions & zShops Seller's Guide, you will see a link under the "Listing Your Item" heading which reads "How to Create zShop Listings." Next to that is a "(List One Now!)" link. Click that link to create a zShop listing.

FIGURE 22.15
The main menu of zShop features and information.

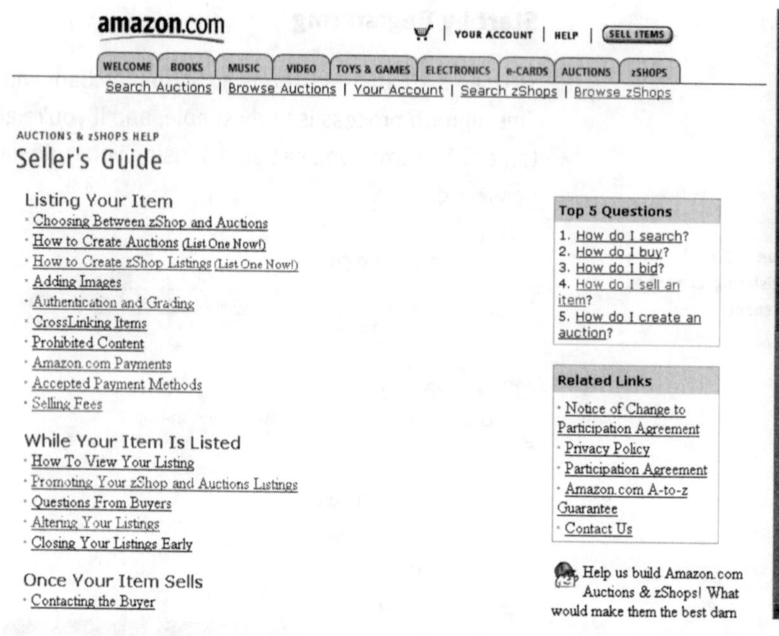

The Sell an Item form (Figure 22.16) contains fields for all the information about items you list for sale on zShops. The more information you provide, the better the chance someone will be interested. The form contains a name for the zShop Title, a description, and a field to upload a picture or provide a link to the picture.

TIP ▸ ***Third-party image hosting is popular with auction services. Because some auction listings and places like zShop only let you post one picture of your item, some enterprising services let you post multiple photos on the Web to which you can point shoppers. Some of these services are covered in Chapter 23.***

Next, you must tell Amazon more about how to locate your items for sale in their various product categories. Simply click the drop down lists associated with the relevant categories and further define it by making a selection. Some items may fit into multiple categories. For example, if you were selling a snowboarding jacket, you might click the clothing category, choose Clothing/Outdoor, then the Sports & Recreation category, and finally choose the Snowboarding item.

FIGURE 22.16
The Sell an Item form for editing a zShop listing.

Item Information

zShop Title:
Limit 80 characters

Describe your item:
Limit 4,000 characters (spaces count). Feel free to use basic HTML in your description.
Unsure about rights? See patent, copyright, and trademark Help.

Add a picture: (optional) ☐ Upload my image to be hosted at Amazon.com--It's FREE!!
Image tips and tricks
Click "browse" to locate your .jpg or .gif image file on your computer. (100K limit)
Or, if you are using a third party hosting service, just enter the URL where your image can be found

My image is located at URL:
Example: http://yoursite.com/image.gif

Price: (per item) $ U.S. Dollars

Quantity: # 1 Must be on-hand at time of purchase.

Shipping & Handling Fee: (optional) $ U.S. Dollars

Location, Location, Location! Choose Your Real Estate. Choose one category below that best matches your item. Buyers on the lookout for items like yours often browse in favorite categories--make it easy for them, and attract just the right people from more than 12 million Amazon.com customers.

Art & Antiques
Home & Garden
Books
Hot Topics
Clothing & Accessories
Movies & Video
Coins & Stamps
Music
Collectibles
Office & Business
Comics, Cards & Sci-Fi
Other Goods & Services
Computers & Software
Sports & Recreation
Electronics & Photography
Toys & Games
Food & Beverages
Gemstones & Jewelry

Listing Information

Relist once for free: ☐ Yes
(if item does not sell)

Selling Preferences

We'll remember your responses in this section to save you time adding other Auctions and zShop listings.

Accepted payment methods:
☑ Money order/Cashier's check
☑ Personal check
☐ C.O.D.
☐ Visa/MasterCard
☐ American Express

I will work with Online escrow: ☑ Yes
Details

Accepted shipping methods: ◉ Buyer pays shipping costs
How to calculate shipping costs. (Please specify a shipping & handling fee for each listing)
○ Seller pays shipping costs
☐ Will ship internationally

Country from which your item will be shipped: United States

ZIP or Postal Code from which your item will be shipped: Example: 90210

Customer Service & Shipping Policy:
Set expectations for shipping time and refunds to minimize confusion (optional).

These optional features will help your zShop listing be more eye-catching

Highlight your listing in Amazon.com zShops!
Get details

☐ Boldface title: $ 2.00
☐ Category feature sale: $ 14.95
☐ zShops Home Page: $ 99.95

Attract More Buyers with Amazon.com CrossLinks! Free Introductory Offer! Read more

◉ Pick keyword(s):
○ Pick up to 9 product ASINs & ISBNs (What are these?)

You'll have a chance to review your fees on the following page.

Preview your Listing

After choosing category locations, you can check Yes on the Relist Once For Free button if you want Amazon to relist your item if it doesn't sell. Amazon gives your item two weeks to sell or will clear it out unless you check this box.

TIP ▸ ***For $99.95, you can be featured on the Amazon.com zShop homepage, giving yourself further exposure. The item will be part of its featured listings for the day for this fee.***

With the Selling Preferences section, you check off the forms of payment you will accept for the item. You can also check whether you'll work with an escrow service (Amazon uses i-escrow.com). You also must set your shipping policy, which can be Buyer Pays or Seller Pays, and whether you will ship internationally. Also choose the origin point from which the merchandise will ship, including the ZIP/Postal code. You are also given a text box to enter your customer service and shipping policy for that item.

Optional Features

After filling out the basic information about a particular listing, you can choose other optional features (for a fee that is billed to the credit card you have associated with your shop). This includes boldfacing the title, listing it as a feature sale in its category, or having a complete zShops Home page. Check any of these features you'd like.

One very cool feature for zShop listings is creating Amazon.com Crosslinks. For an extra fee you can add keywords, ISBN (a special ID associated with all published books), and ASIN (Amazon Standard Indentification Number) numbers that are associated with your listing. Anytime a shopper on Amazon pulls up the associated items (e.g. a book on gardening whose ISBN you associate with your item), Amazon will promote a crosslink to your item listing. You can enter a number of keywords and up to nine separate ISBN or ASIN numbers.

Crosslinks work as soon as your listing goes live. Amazon cycles crosslinks so they don't show up every time someone views a particular item (especially if that item is crosslinked by a number of different zShops). Amazon doesn't show crosslinks for its top 500 books, CDs, and videos. Crosslinks also do not appear on items in the Toys & Games or Electronics stores. However, you can change your crosslinks as necessary. Amazon also asks that you use discretion when crosslinking to retail pages that may be viewed by children. Some products that are not specifically prohibited (knives or erotic material, for example), may not be crosslinked to Book, Music, and Video pages for children's items.

Payment Processing

Amazon has one of the best payment systems on the Web today. Called 1-Click, it's an easy way for people to store their payment information and rapidly purchase items by utilizing their 1-Click settings. As a zShop merchant, you can have Amazon process payments for your goods using their system—for a fee.

As a seller you must apply with Amazon to use the 1-Click system for purchases. To use 1-Click, Amazon charges 60 cents plus 4.75 percent of the transaction amount. To apply, you must fill out a five-step application and have a bank check handy so Amazon can deposit funds directly into your account once a payment is processed. It asks for some personal information, a mailing address, credit card number, and then checking account information for depositing funds. Amazon will also guarantee your transactions so you don't have to worry about any chargebacks from customers. They also provide a transaction summary for you to monitor payments and purchase history.

Once 1-Click is active, your listings will allow customers to purchase via that process.

TIP ▸ ***If you already can verify and authorize cards, you might decide to just take cards directly rather than use 1-Click. However, a lot of Amazon.com shoppers prefer to use 1-Click when shopping, so even if you can process cards directly you might still want to offer 1-Click as a means of payment.***

Advanced Features of zShops

Amazon offers a few features of interest to merchants who are selling a large number of items via zShops. These features, some of which cost extra money, include the following.

Pro Merchant Subscription

The Pro Merchant Subscription lets you get a reduced listings fee for bulk listings. After a set-up fee in the first month, Pro Merchants pay a subscription fee based on their running "balance" of zShop listings. Essentially you can list as many products as you want, but you only pay for whatever the most simultaneous lists you have are at any time that month. For example, if you list 1,000 items over the course of a month but never had more than 689 simulataneous listings, your fee is based on the smaller number. This is great if you sell a lot of items and have significant inventory fluctuation. The fee schedule for the Pro Merchant Subscription is between $29.99 and $99.99 depending on the number of listings you have. You can find a complete fee schedule on the site. Note that fees don't cover extra options such as bolded listings and home pages.

Pro Merchant Tools

Pro Merchants also get access to the Pro Merchant tool set. This includes tools for inventory management. Once you have registered for them, you can access the following features:

- **Sort zShop listings** by Opening Soon, Current, Closed, and Sold.
- **Track your inventory** by downloading Microsoft Excel spreadsheets with your zShops listing information.
- **Recycle old listings** into new batches using the Bulk Loading tool
- **Modify your listings.** Alter quantities of zShops items in a listing, alter images, update language.
- **Load zShop listings** up to seven days in advance of their availability.

The Bulk Loader

No one wants to create 1,000 zShop listings one form at a time. To help with this, Amazon has created the Bulk Uploader tool. If you can format your listings into a simple tab-delimited file that conforms to Amazon's specifications, you can upload hundreds or even thousands of individual zShop listings at once. This makes it easy to manage your store by updating a simple Excel spreadsheet or exporting properly from a good inventory or point-of-sale product, and then uploading that to Amazon.

To create a file for bulk uploading, you first create a template that includes the fields in which you will enter information. Amazon suggests doing so in Excel. More advanced advanced users can use a database and then output it properly to a tab-delimited file.

You are required to include the following fields:

- Item name.
- Item description.
- Category1: Amazon provides list of numeric codes that define each category.
- Price.

Then optionally you can include the following fields for further listing embellishment:

- Image URL.
- Shipping fee.
- SKU.
- Quantity.
- Boldface (y/n). Note: If you place a Y here you will pay a $2.00 fee per listing.
- Feature-in-category: Note: If you place a Y here you will pay a $14.95 fee per listing.
- Asin1-9: For using Amazon.com Crosslinks feature.

When you are done, if you use Excel, you can save it as a .TXT file (with the version that says Tab Delimited—*not* as a standard Excel file). From there you access the bulk loader (part of the Pro Merchant Tools) and then upload the file.

TIP▸ ***The complete tutorial and access to the bulk loader tool is at s1.amazon.com/exec/varzea/subst/selling/bulk/bulk-loading.html/. Amazon also has a simple service that will email you a predefined Excel template for using the bulk loading tool.***

The bulk loader tool does a good job of letting you quickly upload the basic information, but it is by no means complete. For example, you can't define multiple categories for products as you can with the Web-based listing form. You also can't provide a photo to upload (although you can provide a URL)—nor can you provide keyword crosslinks or customer service info. However, once your listings are uploaded, you can individually add these items via zShops Web-based form listings.

zShop or zzzShop?

Yahoo Store, Freemerchant, and Bigstep all offer more robust options for designing and developing an online store. In some ways, zShops are nothing more than glorified classified ads. However, no one else brings you the merchandising and customer power of Amazon, which makes this a compelling service. The question is how to use it most effectively, because listing ten items for sale via zShops does not a store make.

Amazon will probably add more features to its zShops program. Already more than 500,000 items have been listed for purchase via the program, so it is proving popular. What's more, its transaction system via 1-Click is as good as it gets with buyers and sellers getting amazing guarantees for using it. Only Amazon could bring this to bear on Web retailing.

In the end, zShops is probably a tool to use as part of your overall store-building efforts but is not the ultimate store-building tool.

Joe's Take: *Consider building a real online store first and then, using zShops, use the bulk uploader tool to list items for sale on Amazon as well. This is a nice secondary outlet for selling your inventory and getting access to Amazon's customers. With good customer service and promotion, it is likely that you can transfer customers who have experience with your zShop activity into visiting your more robust regular online store.*

Other Options

Yahoo Store and Amazon's zShops are solid solutions for many people, but they are not the only ones. Here are some details on some of the other options.

eCongo

www.econgo.com

eCongo allows you to set up an entire store for free. However, there are fees for features such as credit card processing, specialized merchant reports, and other value-added services. Still, you can set up a very well done catalog, complete with shopping cart and a hierarchical department→category→item scheme. You can also create a store FAQ, return policy page, set shipping policies, and more. The catalog scheme is fairly well done and, although it takes time to set everything up, you can do a great deal with eCongo. eCongo also provides a Web-based community for its merchants so they can trade advertising, share ideas, and network.

Catalog Building

The catalog builder aspect of the service (Figure 22.17) allows you to define departments, categories within departments, and fill out items. This includes uploaded photos that the service compiles into a browseable catalog on its service. Merchants can include an unlimited number of item descriptions and photos.

Advertising and Marketing

eCongo includes an integrated ad builder that merchants can use to create ads—and you can also trade advertisements with other eCongo merchants. eCongo also submits stores to popular Internet search engines. This is a basic level of submission and advertising.

Payment Processing

The free service eCongo includes the capability to let people choose to pay by check, COD, or provide credit card information over the phone.

Online credit card processing is provided for a fee via CardService International (a popular and highly regarded service discussed earlier in this book). eCongo has also partnered with Cybergold to offer a micro-payment solution. For more on Cybergold check out its site at www.cybergold.com.

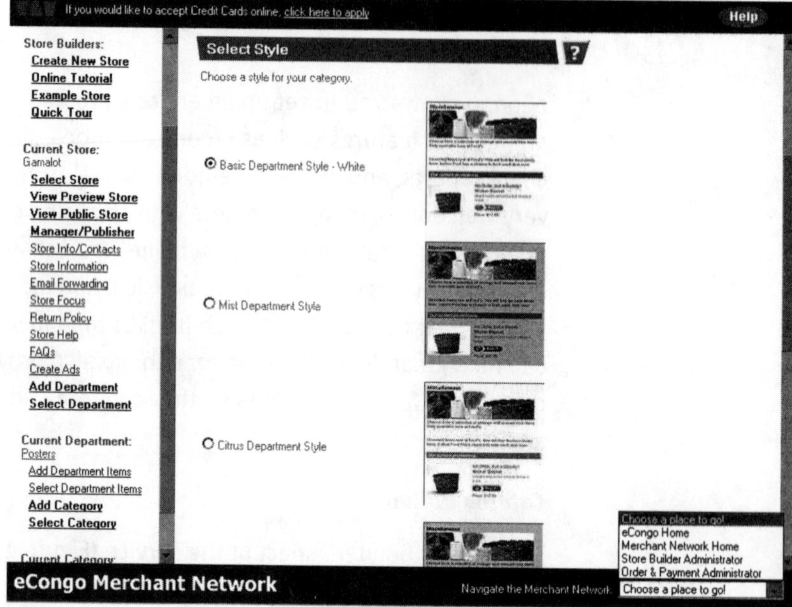

FIGURE 22.17
A sample screen for eCongo's catalog builder tool.

Customer Service and Fulfillment

eCongo lets you set up as many as seven customer service-oriented email aliases. Shoppers also receive purchase and shipping notification via email. Order status pages are also offered to customers.

Setting up your store takes about 30 minutes, plus an additional two or three minutes per item. All of it is forms-based, and there is an online tutorial and other help available. Overall, the service provides many of the basic needs for an online store. No store hosting solution is perfect, but eCongo is a pretty good place to get up and running fairly quickly, and at little cost. If you like the free service, upgrading to the more full-featured options—especially credit card processing—takes some additional work and money.

Freemerchant.com

www.freemerchant.com

Freemerchant.com offers you an easy-to-use catalog builder, but in return for letting you build and host a site on its service, Freemerchant sells advertising that appears on your page. Freemerchant also plans to provide value-added services to its member merchants as well. The site has a number of special features that make it very useful to certain types of store builders. Figure 22.18 shows the main menu screen for all of the Freemerchant.com features. Clicking on them takes you to a series of associate forms that helps you build your catalog, enable payments, promotions, eBay listings, and more.

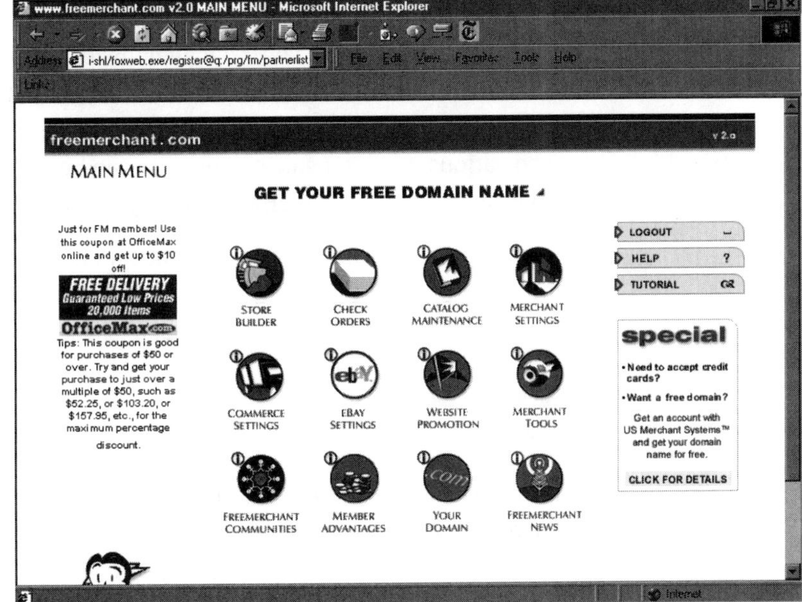

FIGURE 22.18
The Interface for Freemerchant.com, like most of the store-building services mentioned in this chapter, is a very simple icon and Web form-based system.

Catalog Building

With Freemerchant, you can choose from an overall store template and color scheme. Then you can add categories and items to a catalog. Items can be moved around at will, and each item can be uniquely edited and can have an accompanying image.

URLs are listed as yourstorename.safeshopper.com. You can also have a private URL such as www.mycompany.com once you purchase and point it to your freemerchant.com site.

Payments

Credit cards are not processed automatically at the start. You can retrieve credit card orders securely from your merchant backend or you can set up a merchant account with Authorize.net or Intellipay (www.intellipay.com). Once you do this, by giving freemerchant.com the login information, it will automatically set up the credit card authorization information as needed.

Special Features

Freemerchant.com has several ingenious features for store builders. One is the ability to integrate auction listings from eBay into your site. Once you've set up an eBay account you can tell Freemerchant about it, and various items for sale on your site can be ported for listing on eBay as well. Remember that eBay charges you for the listings.

Another cool feature of Freemerchant.com is that it can automatically output any of your invoices to you in a format that lets you export them quickly into Intuit Software's Quickbooks.

Bigstep.com

www.bigstep.com

Bigstep.com lets you put your business online, offering robust commerce and catalog services. The company also helps you create a business presence on the Web by letting you manage a total list of corporate pages like job listings, employee pages, surveys, FAQs, press releases, and maps.

Catalog Building

Bigstep.com's store-building tools are top-notch. After going through a rigorous set of templates to define the look and feel of every section of your catalog, you can then enter information about items, group them into categories, and upload pictures.

Shipping

You can create a complete set of rules pertaining to shipping rates on the various forms of UPS, FedEx, and U.S. Postal Service shipping services.

Payment Processing

To process credit cards, you can apply to CardService International for a merchant account and then integrate its processing services into your store.

Customer Service

There are no direct email contact features, but you can set up feedback forms for customer service information. The site also lets you set up an online customer database, and create groups of customers to whom you can send newsletters.

Reports, Marketing, and Advertising

There are no advertising services yet on Bigstep.com, but you can look at site reports and set up submission for search engine listings.

Vstore.com

www.vstore.com

Vstore.com is an interesting concept in online stores, essentially combining traditional store style, look, and feel with predesigned stores that you can set up. The catch is that these stores are all affiliate stores. Vstore and its supplying partners actually do the product fulfillment. Figure 22.19 shows a simple video game store that was developed in under 30 minutes using Vstore's system.

Catalog Building

The stores take no time at all to set up. Choose a type of product you want to sell—from books to CDs to sporting equipment or electronics. There are also theme stores that sell products from across several categories based on a specific theme such as Titanic, aviation, or Elvis. Once you choose a template, a store name (and URL), color scheme, and other visual attributes, you can publish the store. Stores have the URL of yourstore.vstore.com.

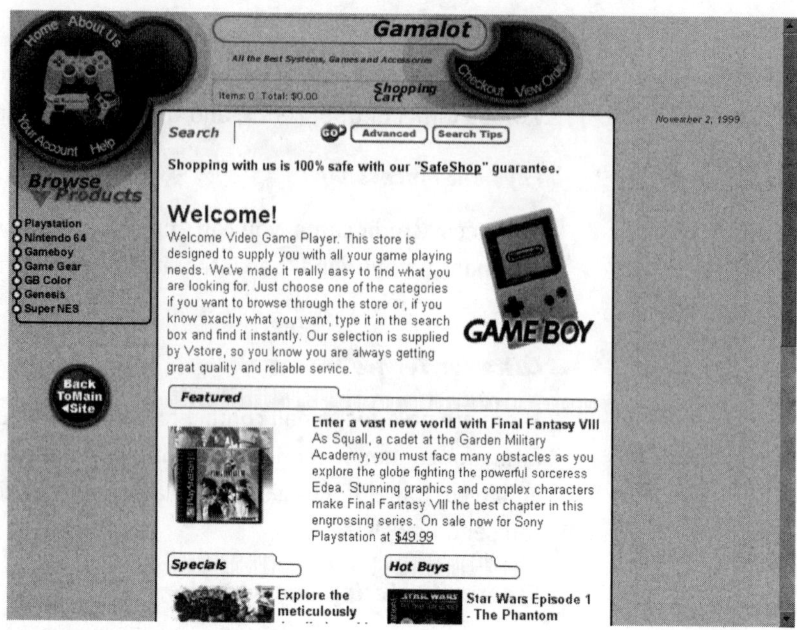

FIGURE 22.19
This Gamalot store was created on Vstore.com in less than 30 minutes.

Payment Processing

Users can shop the store, place items in a shopping cart, and then check out. Vstore.com processes the entire order, checks the card, and then sends out the order. Once the order clears, you receive a commission on the sale. Commissions vary, but there is a full reporting system on the site to track traffic, sales, and commissions.

Vstore.com is a good solution for people who want to set up a store of a certain affiliation type and see if profits appear. However, there is little you can do to change what the store sells and little opportunity to do any heavy duty merchandising. Essentially this solution is one that works well if you have a nice niche site about a specific topic and want to attach a simple store section to it.

But Wait, There's More

Space limits the number of store-building services that we can detail, so here is some more brief information about other services worth considering.

Excite Storebuilder

www.excite.com/storebuilder/

This service offers several levels of store-building tools from iStore Wizard to iStore Pro. It charges a fee based on number of products.

Merchant Planet

www.merchantplanet.com

At the time of this writing, Merchant Planet was renovating its service. This service from the LinkExchange division of Microsoft will be a full-fledged store-building service that will have the power of one of the best sites for small business behind it.

Buyroad.com

www.buyroad.com

As of this writing, this service had yet to launch, but was previewed at the 1999 Fall Internet World trade show and looked quite promising. It is expected to debut in the first quarter of 2000.

Finding the Best Store-Building Service for You

The services described in this chapter all do essentially the same thing—either for free or for a small monthly fee, they provide a complete set of Web-based tools to build, deploy, and manage an online store. However, before you dive into one of these solutions or one of the many that will likely launch after this book is published, consider the following issues:

Does the Service Support My Own Domain Name?

Should you ever want to change store services or the type of setup (e.g. your own server), and the only pointer to your store isn't a domain name you control, everything you've invested in promoting that Web address will be lost. Most services will let you use your own domain address either for free or an extra fee.

Does the Service Require Ads or Other Branding on Your Site?

Nothing in life is ever completely free. Some sites require you to have banner ads on your site; others require you to have buttons and other branding that points back to their services. In some cases, what you get for free service is worth allowing these elements. In other cases, you may decide that paying a fee to eliminate these items or finding a service that doesn't post ads on your site is a must.

Does the Site Offer Credit Card Processing?

For most of the free commerce and other store-hosting solutions, credit card processing is provided for additional fees. You may want to evaluate which services are used for processing payments and see if your current bank is compatible with that service before selecting it. Also check to see if the store-hosting service charges extra fees on top of the card processor's fees.

What Is Free and What Requires a Fee?

Many services offer a number of foundation services and catalog building items for free, but most services are looking to make additional money by offering value-added or enhanced services for a fee. Read the fine print to see what causes those fees to kick in. Some services charge fees if you list more than a certain amount of items in your catalog. Others charge fees for separate domain names, credit card processing, and more.

What Promotional Value Do They Offer?

Getting your store up on the Web is the easy part—getting customers to visit that store is much more difficult. Any special features that drive traffic and customers to your site is a major plus. Most store-building services submit your site to the major search engines—a minimal promotional feature. Others offer the ability to build email lists of customers, and some offer banner-swapping with stores on their network. Some of the portal-based services offer you the ability to have your store listed in their online malls. Most of the promotional work related to your store can be done without the help of the service, but check if they have any special promotional features that you might not get otherwise.

Look for Extra Special Features

Freemerchant offers integration with eBay and Quickbooks, Amazon.com offers access to it's 1-Click service, and Bigstep has robust site-building and customer management options. Every service will have those special features that might make it the best choice for you.

Take the time to test drive the service, talk to other merchants using it, and visit and play with the same stores to see if they look good and operate well. The all-in-one space is getting very popular on the Web, and there are a lot of services from which to choose. By taking the time to use the free and trial versions, you'll make the choice that works best for you.

You Now Have No Excuse!

If you haven't opened a store yet, you have little excuse to be sitting on the sidelines. Although the services included in this chapter still require a lot of work to build out, they are easy to use, and many offer all the necessary fundamental tools. Expect these services to become more user-friendly and advanced in the future.

Remember also that for all their features and free options, none of these store-building solutions guarantees success, and none will help you order the right inventory, offer the right wording for customer service replies, or pack boxes. There is still plenty of work for you to do.

Finally, you may want more flexibility than template-based store-building services offer. For those who want to be in total command of every detail but want to keep costs down, see Chapter 24, which details the "home-brewed" way to create your own small scale store, as Joe did with Tronix. In time, store-building services will probably become the predominant way for people to build their stores. However, there is still a lot to learn from a do-it-yourself solution.

Next up—auctions.

CHAPTER TWENTY-THREE

Creating Online Auction Stores

It's hard to find anything recently hotter than online auctions. From sites like eBay to auctions run on Yahoo, Amazon, Lycos, and Fairmarket.com, auctions are no doubt currently the biggest phenomenon within the world of e-commerce. In this chapter we cover all the major ways you can add auction elements to your online store endeavors and sell via online auction marketplaces. We also discuss some alternative services (such as escrow services) that can be critical additions to your online auction service.

What Are Online Auctions and Why Are They So Popular?

Online auctions use the power of computers and the Internet to create a dynamic market in which individuals bid on items. Keenan Vision, an e-commerce market consulting company, estimated that the volume of auction-based or market-priced Internet commerce transactions is now close to $4 billion annually. The company predicts that this amount will grow to more than $120 billion and nearly 30 percent of the market by the year 2002.

Auctions are popular on the Web for several different reasons, but primarily because the process of participating in an auction is fun and auctions usually focus on unique or rare items. Web auctions are also popular because the Web has made it easy for people to access auctions—previously rare, real-world events than most people had never attended. Finally, auctions are, in theory, designed to give sellers a good chance of getting a very bearable selling price for items that might lack a specific, fixed value. Bidders hope to find a few bargains in cases where the demand for an item is soft enough that, in their mind and perhaps in actuality, they pay below the potential final value of the item.

All of these aspects have combined to create a demand for online auctions and for the products sold via those auctions. That demand has created interest by many merchants to use auctions as a means of selling items from their Web stores.

Auctioning via a Service vs. Running an Auction Store

Most people have been introduced to the idea of online auctions through eBay (Figure 23.1)—or through other online auction sites such as Yahoo Auctions or Boxlot.com. However, although these sites allow you to list an item for auction, they do not allow you to open a store. As we stated in Chapter 1, selling an item on the Web is not the same as operating a store. With auctions, it is very easy to list an item on eBay and hope people buy it. Many stores—especially those that sell antiques or collectible items—operate on eBay and other auction sites. However, they are only selling items individually and do not exist as an entire site with their own policies and other information.

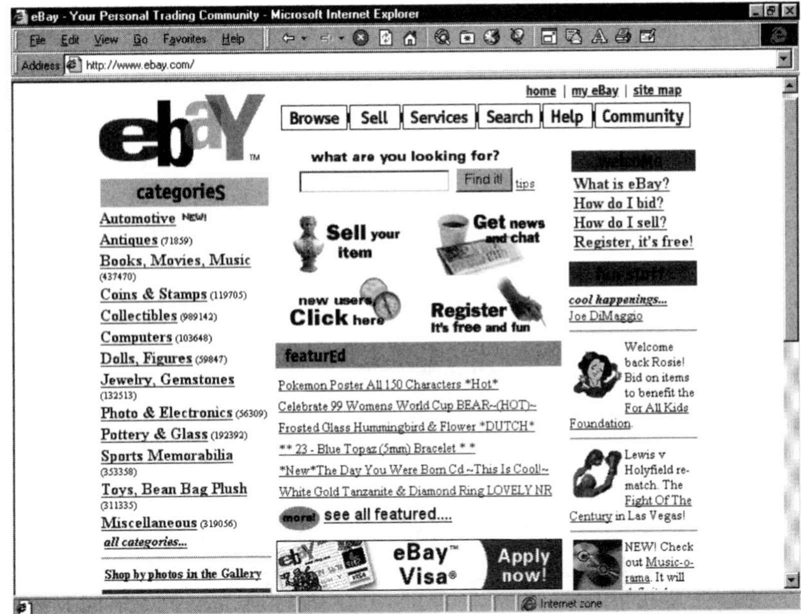

FIGURE 23.1
Online auction heavyweight eBay is the leader in the person-to-person auction business that has exploded on the Web.

However, with your own auction store, you create an entire site devoted to auctioning merchandise. You control the look and feel of the site and can complement that with standard Web store features such as FAQs, shipping policies, and more. Many combine traditional stores with auction components, allowing people the opportunity to shop for fixed-price merchandise and also bid on unique items that are up for auction.

Simple or Custom?

Your choice for running an auction store is fairly straightforward. If you only offer a few items for auction, setting up a static Web page with links to auctions running on sites such as eBay, Fairmarket, or Amazon.com is a fairly easy process. However, if you want to control the entire look and feel of your auctions, you'll need to install auction software or use an auction service that gives you more customizable options than does a service like eBay.

The major single-item online auction services are:

- eBay (www.ebay.com).
- FairMarket (www.fairmarket.com).

- Amazon Auctions (**auctions.amazon.com**).
- BoxLot (**www.boxlot.com**).
- Yahoo Auctions (**auctions.yahoo.com**).
- Excite! Auctions (**auctions.excite.com**).
- Lycos Auctions (**auction.lycos.com**).
- CNET Auctions (**auctions.cnet.com**).
- MSN Auctions (**auctions.msn.com**).

Hosted or Server?

There are two primary ways to build your own auction store. You can install specialized server software and run an auction site yourself, or you can use an auction hosting service that gives you customizable templates. This choice is similar to your traditional online store options, where you can use either a commerce server such as Microsoft Site Server or OpenMarket or use a hosting service such as Yahoo Store.

For most small-to-medium sized merchants, we strongly recommend using a hosting service rather than running and customizing an auction server yourself.

Running Your Own Server

If you decide to ignore our advice and run your own server instead of using a hosting service, there are several packages to choose from. The most notable is OpenSite's Auction (www.opensite.com), a complete standalone auction software package. Auction is available in many flavors for those in need of anything from a basic auction server to one that allows them to host multiple auctions for other people. OpenSite is widely recognized as being the one auction package most tailored toward the small to medium auction store operator. It also has high-end enterprise auction software but, unlike some of its competitors, it has a complete line of software for midsize to lower-end stores that is a breeze to operate. Table 23.1 lists the major auction server software companies. However, because of its focus and strong reviews, this chapter will focus on OpenSite.

TIP ▸ ***Microsoft's main commerce server, Site Server: Commerce Edition, features an optional auction module called the Auction Component, which lets you add online auction functionality to the Site Server system. The Auction Component enables sites to auction products, accept bids, and determine winners, using rules ranging from simple to sophisticated. Users can set reserve prices, minimum bids, start and end dates, bid increments, and resolve bid conflicts. The documentation for this optional downloadable add-on is available at: www.microsoft.com/siteserver/commerce/DeployAdmin/AuctionDoc.htm***

TABLE 23.1 OTHER MAJOR AUCTION SOFTWARE PRODUCTS

PRODUCT	COMPANY	SUMMARY
AuctionNet	Webvision	Focused on medium to large customers
LiveExchange	Moai	Focused on large corporate customers
BSI Auction 3.0	Beyond Software	Focused on small to medium customers
Auctioneer and Auction Master	Net Merchants	Focused on medium to large customers
Site Server Auction Component	Microsoft	Basic auction functionality; supports several auction types

OpenSite Auction Server

OpenSite offers a line of products and services for the online auction market. Its two most important for individual store builders are OpenSite Auction Professional and OpenSite Auction Corporate. These packages are installed on top of NT server, Sun Solaris, or Linux, and provide a fully functional auction server. OpenSite Auction Professional is the entry-level edition of OpenSite and costs $5,000. Corporate offers more flexibility in the types of auctions you can run, enables private auctions, and has other advanced features.

OpenSite also offers a version called OpenSite Auction Merchant, which you can use to establish an auction community. This version gives you the ability to set up and host multiple merchants who hold auctions on your site. It makes you an online mall operator of auctions. It also includes online store and banner advertising services.

OpenSite Auction is fully configurable and operable via its Web-based interface. This makes it easy to operate remotely and doesn't require you to have any extensive knowledge of the back end of your server system. With OpenSite Auction Professional, you set up specific pages—home, registration, contact, help, and more—and also set up specific category and item pages. You do all of this by entering information into Web-based forms and uploading various ancillary HTML pages and graphics. It's quite easy—one reviewer of the product actually set up his own auction site, Action Figure Auctions (www.actionfigureauctions.com), to help develop a store focused on collectible action figures (Figure 23.2).

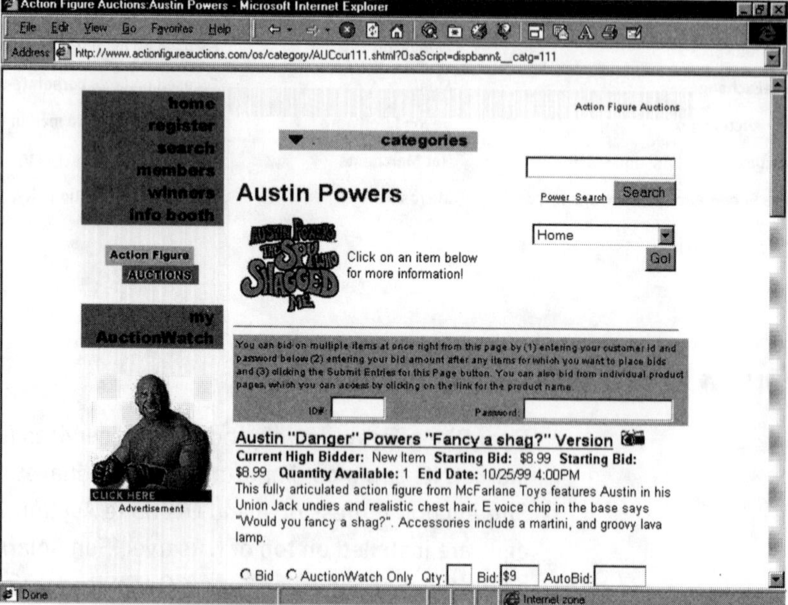

FIGURE 23.2
Action Figures Auctions was set up using OpenSite's Auction software.

You can also upload data to the server instead of manually entering it. The Corporate version can also interface with Oracle database and with the ISAPI for integration and extension with Microsoft's Internet Information Server. Other additional features of the Corporate version include support for reverse auctions, modified English auctions, sealed bids, private auctions, and consignment auctions. There is also an online storefront module for fixed-priced sales with the corporate version.

TIP ▸ ***Don't want to install the software or operate your own server? OpenSite works with major dedicated server companies that will rent you a server and install the version of OpenSite you want. Then you're off to the races.***

Using an Auction Hosting Service

Using an auction hosting service is slightly different than running your own server or having someone set up a dedicated auction server for you. In this capacity, an ISP or other Web hosting provider sets up a specialized version of OpenSite (or other auction system), and you rent space on that service. Unlike eBay or other auction services, these hosting services will give you simple templates you can customize and other options that give your auctions a more customizable, store-like construction.

If you would like a hosted service, OpenSite offers its Concierge Service where OpenSite will set up, customize, and host your auction. There is a flat set-up fee and a monthly service fee for maintaining and running the auction. The service allows you to test run an online auction store for a smaller investment than the $5,000 cost of Auction Professional. With the Concierge Service, the monthly fee is based on the number of auctions you run.

OpenSite also maintains a list of specialized hosting services that they can recommend to you. If you decide you need more power and flexibility, this makes it easy to upgrade to your own dedicated OpenSite server.

TIP ▸ ***OpenSite has also launched BidStream.com (Figure 23.3), an auction finding service that supports their auction software customers.***

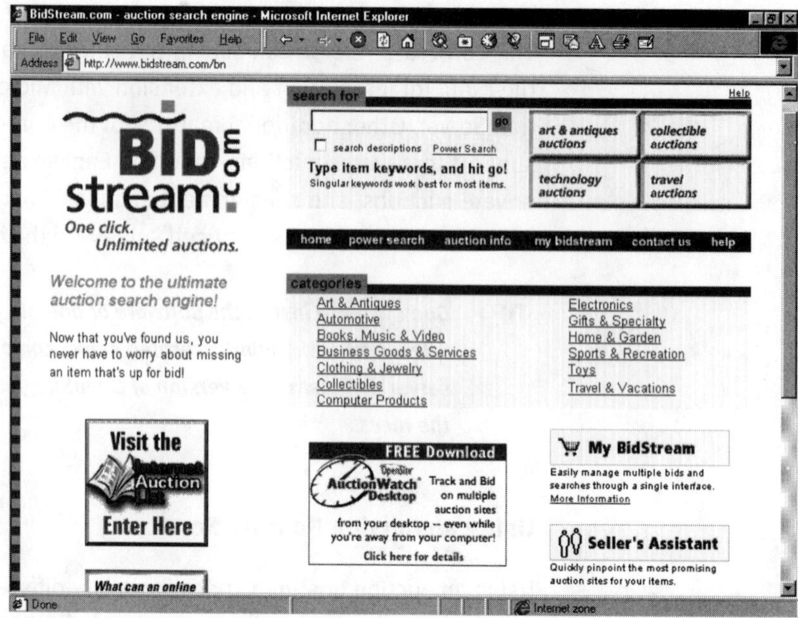

FIGURE 23.3
OpenSite runs its own auction-finding portal, Bidstream.com, to help its customers bring in curious online auction seekers.

Once You're Up You're Not Done

As with any Web store, once you've installed your auction system or contracted with an auction hosting service you are far from finished constructing your auction store. When it comes to online auctions, there is much more to add—especially those items unique to auctions.

First and foremost, you should make sure your auction store includes explanations of your terms of service and how you operate your auctions. Many people using Internet auctions are very new to auctions, so providing an FAQ about online auctions, complete with glossary (see the sidebar at the end of this chapter) is very important. You may also want to include information for, or contract with, some of the Web-based escrow services.

Often auctions are not about selling merchandise that is of a specific value, and thus inspection of the final purchase can be necessary. Escrow services allow people to bid on an item, pay the escrow service, and receive and inspect the merchandise. If the customer is happy with the item and accepts it, the escrow service pays the merchant. If the customer returns the item, the escrow service returns the money to the buyer.

If you offer an escrow service, be sure to outline what your rules are for using it. For example: who pays for shipping, are there special charges for using it, and is there a preferred escrow service that you work with.

There are a number of online escrow services worth investigating:

i-Escrow

www.iescrow.com

i-Escrow is a personal online transaction manager that allows users to complete purchases and sales at online resources such as classifieds, for-sale newsgroups, and Web auctions. The QuikTrack transaction manager provides point-and-click access to online selling and buying activity.

i-Escrow provides a safe, neutral environment to close sales and 24-hour access to the status of your iEscrow transactions. Payment goes from the buyer to i-Escrow. After shipment and buyer approval, the seller is paid by i-Escrow. i-Escrow accepts electronic payments (credit cards, wire transfers), checks, and money orders.

Fees, which are based on the cost of the transaction (Figure 23.4), are paid by either the buyer, the seller, or are split between both parties. The buyer is charged the entire fee (but not the cost of the merchandise) for any returned merchandise.

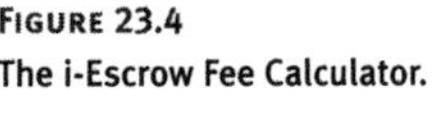

FIGURE 23.4
The i-Escrow Fee Calculator.

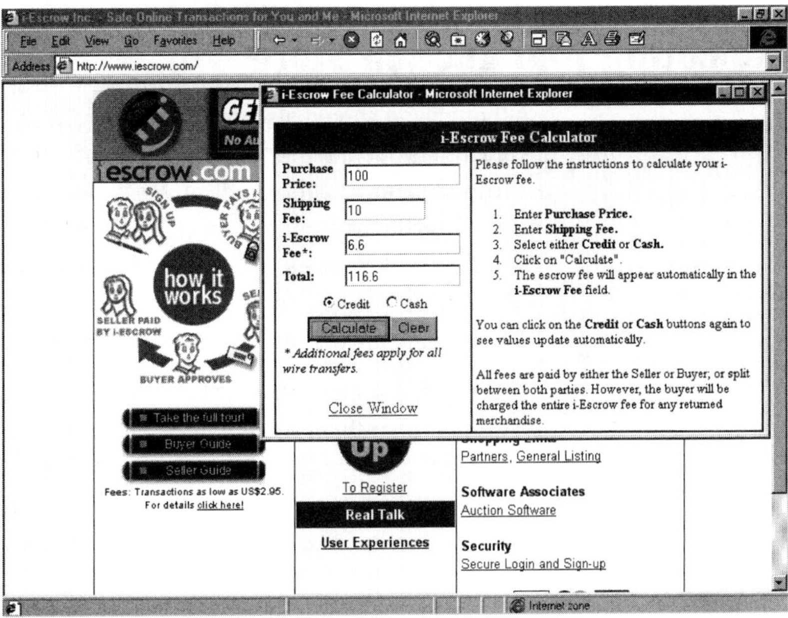

TradeSafe
www.tradesafe.com

TradeSafe invites the other party—either the buyer or the seller—to participate and receives information from the two parties. TradeSafe contacts both parties and issues the transaction via email. Within 24 hours after receiving the transaction number, the buyer sends payment to TradeSafe to be held in escrow. TradeSafe notifies the seller to ship the goods. Once the buyer accepts the goods, the buyer receives payment. Fees are based on the value of the transaction.

Billpoint
www.billpoint.com

Billpoint facilitates person-to-person credit card payments over the Internet for online trading communities such as auctions, classifieds, and community sites. You can sell via email, your Web site, or a classifieds or auction partner. Billpoint's account management reports and tools allow you to track the status of your pending and fulfilled orders.

For information about Billpoint's transaction fees, visit **www.billpoint.com/policies/fees.html**.

Promoting Your Auction Store

Although you should also do the standard Web store promotion as covered in this book, there are also some special services and sites that auction operators should utilize. Most of these services are either listings of auction sites or are specialized search engines that search auction sites and combine them with other listings from other sites. This allows people to compare auctions on similar goods and find items without jumping around to various auction sites.

If you run an auction store or have an auction component to your site, remember that there is a unique group of people who like the thrill and challenge of purchasing goods through auctions. Many of these people congregate in unique places on the Web and have their own favorite magazines and other news outlets to target. After you've gotten through the basics of listing with major search engines, trading links, and looking for other promotional opportunities, you should turn your attention toward the specific auction-oriented opportunities that exist.

Here is a list of the major sites to target and suggestions on how you can work with them:

BidStream.com
www.bidstream.com

BidStream's Seller's Assistant allows you to pinpoint the most promising auction sites for your items. Simply select a category or enter one or two keywords describing your item. You will receive a brief overview of relevant sites and you can click through on the ones you like to initiate your sale. You can also find out how many similar items are being sold on the suggested sites and obtain more detailed information on the items.

Bidder's Edge
www.biddersedge.com

Bidder's Edge is a free service for consumers that allows them to search across many auction sites simultaneously. You can't submit an item, but if your item is listed at one of the auctions that Bidder's Edge supports it is automatically listed on Bidder's Edge. The only exception is eBay, whose sellers must request a listing.

AuctionRover.com
www.auctionrover.com

AuctionRover provides Image Hosting and Hit Counters. Image Hosting allows you to store as many images as needed for free on AuctionRover's servers. Their smart counter records back-to-back visits by the same user only once.

AuctionBeagle
www.auctionbeagle.com

AuctionBeagle uses people to search for items at auctions on Amazon, eBay, Gold's, Up4Sale, and Yahoo.

Auction Patrol

www.auctionpatrol.com

Auction Patrol offers a number of free tools. "Norma" saves your often-used auction preferences and provides an URL to automatically create a new auction using your default preferences. "Sonny" generates HTML code to fit the desired look of your auction. "Jerry" handles the financial end of your auction and generates a list of fees you will be charged for listing at various auction sites. "Mr. Louis" allows you to use HTML and check your auction before going live.

Internet Auction List

www.internetauctionlist.com

The Internet Auction List (IAL) allows auction-related companies that have Web sites to place a free link in the category of their choice. To place a link in additional categories, there is a $50 charge per year for each additional category. For more information on placing a link with the IAL, go to www.internetauctionlist.com/UserList.idc.

AuctionWatch.com

www.auctionwatch.com

AuctionWatch.com aggregates auction-related information, posts daily editorial content, and provides services to sellers and buyers. Services include free image hosting, auction counters, a message center, and a categorized directory of auction sites.

bidXS

www.bidxs.com

bidXS's meta-search engine allows buyers to search auctions on eBay, Amazon, Yahoo, BidStream, and more than 500 other auction sites.

TIP ▸ ***Some of these sites may also offer banner advertising and other forms of paid listings. In addition, Yahoo and Newhoo.com offer separate auction site listings in their directories. You might also consider advertising in major auction magazines, on major auction sites, and in local newspaper auction listings.***

More Auction Tips: Getting People to Buy

Some auctions take a while to gather steam, and in some cases what you want is simply an acceptable price rather than the highest possible price. In these cases, auctioneers have developed a couple of useful ideas to entice buying and to get people to buy at a very good price for the seller. One idea is that the first bid wins. As a seller you accept the first bidder who meets a set price. Of course not everyone may accept that price, and instead bidding takes place and the high bidder is still short of the set price. Nonetheless, this combination of fixed price and auctions can entice people to snap up goods quickly at prices you're willing to accept.

Another idea is to draw in auction fans by using auction services. You can put a small portion of your auctionable merchandise up for bid on the various major auction sites. In your comments section of the item page, you can include the URL to your auction store's site. This will draw traffic from interested bidders to your site, some of whom will want to peruse your more extensive auctions listings.

Deadbeat Bidders and Other Forms of Auction Fraud

The problem with auctions is that sometimes people make bogus bids. It could be someone playing a prank or someone trying to scam you out of the item. This is only a small percentage, but like all forms of online fraud it only takes a few bad apples to spoil the barrel. How do you deal with a bidder who is bogus or won't pay?

First, you should vet all winning bids. Through email or phone contact, you can ensure that you're dealing with someone who wasn't entering bogus bids. If the winning bid was bogus, and if you have records of the next highest bidder, you can either move to the next highest bid or re-list the auction.

If the bidder was genuine but isn't paying, you have to either collect or cut them and move on. The trick with deadbeat bidders is not to waste too much time on them. At the same time, there is a difference between a deadbeat bidder and someone who might simply be trying to buy some time to get their cash together. It's up to you to gauge the difference.

To prevent deadbeats and bogus bids, many sites require users to log in and present some personal information before bidding. Special private auctions can also be run where you invite the bidders. This means you've vetted them beforehand (both of these options are available with Open-Site). You can also blacklist certain users if they are previous abusers of your auction site.

Another way to prevent deadbeats is to be very clear about payment terms and due dates. Don't be ambiguous and don't change your policy. If your policy is that payment must be received by certified check, money order, or major credit card within three days, don't back off. You should only consider making exceptions if a previously reliable customer needs an extra day. Be careful not to do this too often and create unbalanced auctions.

Always be on the lookout for high bids that are out of the range of your expected sale—this is a sure sign of someone playing around. Another scam is for someone to enter a low bid and then have someone else (or simply by logging in as a different user) enter a really high bid. Then when you can't contact or reach the first user, you fall back on the acceptable but not necessarily best bid of the second highest bid. This practice is known as *bid-screening* and is a trick to watch for. To protect yourself against this, hold the option to deny the next highest bid even if the first bid turns out to be bogus. Then re-list the item.

The unique nature of online auctions creates unique types of fraud. By being clear with your auction terms and being diligent to vet out winning bids and approved users for your site, you can reduce your exposure to auction fraud or deadbeat bidders.

Auctions: from Sideshow to Mainstream

The Internet has taken auctions from a sideshow where people drove to barns in the backwoods of Maine or took their limos down to Sotheby's on Park Avenue, to a full-fledge economic force. The basic ability of the Internet to gather large pools of customers, and for computer technology to create an automated auctioneer system, has created a strong e-commerce opportunity for merchants.

At the same time, auctions are not for everyone—the merchandise must be right, and you need a good group of bidders to gain the advantage of demand to drive up pricing. For many, the best model is a combination of the two basic commerce types. You can offer dynamic pricing via online auctions for unique goods that have an undetermined final value. And you can use traditional fixed pricing for more standard items.

Auction Terms and Phrases

You should be familiar with a number of terms and phrases as you dive into the world of online actions:

Absolute Auction. An auction in which the item up for sale is sold to the highest qualified bidder with no limiting conditions or minimum preset price. Also known as an auction without reserve.

American Auction. An auction in which a quantity of items are offered for sale at the same price. The highest bidders for the largest number of items in the group win the auction.

Auction Listing Agreement. A contract executed by the auctioneer and seller, authorizing the auctioneer to conduct the sale. Also known as listing agreement.

Auction Subject to Confirmation. An auction in which the seller has set a reserve or minimum price for his or her item. This price must be met before the item can be sold.

Auction With Reserve. An auction in which the seller has set a minimum price for the item and reserves the right to accept or decline any and all bids. The minimum acceptable price may or may not be disclosed.

Auction Without Reserve. An auction in which the property is sold to the highest qualified bidder with no limiting conditions or minimum price. Also known as an absolute auction.

Auto Extension. This option for sellers automatically extends the amount of time left to bid by five minutes if someone places a bid near the end of the auction.

Auto Resubmit. This option for sellers automatically resubmits your auction if your item is not sold when the auction closes. The auction reopens with the same information.

Bid Increments. Any new bid you place must be greater than the current high bid. The amount by which you must increase your bid depends on the current price of the item being auctioned.

Bid Retraction. The legitimate cancellation of a bid on an item by a buyer during an online auction.

Bid Screening/Shielding. Posting extremely high bids to protect the lower bid of an earlier bidder, usually in cooperation with the bidder who placed the shielding or screening bid.

Bid Siphoning. The practice of contacting bidders and offering to sell them the same item they are currently bidding on, thus drawing bidders away from the legitimate seller's auction.

Buy Price. The price at which the seller is willing to sell the listed item. The auction closes automatically when a bidder meets the buy price.

continued ···>

Auction Terms and Phrases ···> *continued*

Deadbeat Bidding. The failure to deliver payment on an item after securing the high bid in an online auction.

Dutch Auction. This is a descending price auction in which the bidding starts at a high price and is progressively lowered until a buyer claims an item.

Early Close. Sellers can choose to close their auctions early if they're satisfied with the current bid price.

English Auction. Allows sellers to secure the highest bid for an item. The auction begins with the lowest acceptable price and solicits successively higher bids until the auction is closed or the bidding stops.

Escrow Service. An escrow service can be employed to help you carry out a transaction once the winner of the auction is decided, ensuring the buyer and the seller that their transactions are secure and that the shipped items arrive safely and efficiently.

Full-quantity-only Bid. An auction or trading exchange in which bidders must bid for the entire quantity of inventory offered.

Insertion Fee. A fee paid by the seller to the auction site in order to list an item for auction. Usually a percentage of the opening bid or reserve price.

Maximum Bid. The highest price a buyer will pay for an item, submitted in confidence to an online auction site's automated bidding system to facilitate proxy bidding. The system's electronic "proxy" will automatically increase the buyer's bid to maintain the high bid. The proxy bidding system will stop when it has won the auction or reached the maximum bid.

Minimum Bid Auction. An auction in which the auctioneer will accept bids only at or above a predetermined price.

Minimum Opening Bid. The mandatory starting bid for a given auction.

No-Sale Fee. A fee paid by the seller if his or her item does not sell in a reserve auction.

NR. Short for "no reserve." This indicates in the item description line that the auction has no reserve price specified.

Parcel Bidding. Auction administrators accept bids on individual items within a lot.

Partial-quantity Bid. A bid in which a potential buyer is willing to accept less than the quantity originally bid for.

Private Auction. A group of bidders are given access to a particular auction that is not open for public bidding.

Proxy Bidding. To submit a confidential maximum bid to an online auction service's automated bidding system. The system's electronic "proxy" will automatically increase the buyer's bid to maintain the high bid. The proxy bidding system will stop when it has won the auction or reached the maximum bid.

Reserve Pricing. Administrators protect their investment and inventory by establishing a minimum price.

Reverse Auction. The reverse auction allows buyers to post items that they want to buy and sellers to offer the best price.

Sealed-bid Auctions. Bids and bidders are not disclosed until after the auction in this silent auction format. Buyers submit any number of bids for different quantities of goods until the auction closes.

Shilling. Fraudulent bidding by the seller (using an alternate registration) or an associate of the seller in order to inflate the price of an item.

Second or Lowest Price Option/ Vickery Option. In ascending price auctions, the second or lowest price options can be used to determine the winning price. Items are awarded to the highest bidders at either a price equal to the second-highest bid or the lowest winning bid.

Starting Price. All bidding for your item will start at this price. Bids below this amount will not be accepted.

Straight Auction. An auction in which there is no reserve and only one item is up for sale. This is the most common type of auction. The seller sets the opening bid and must respect the final price at the end of the auction.

Yankee Auction. An auction in which a seller lists multiples of an identical item. Unlike a Dutch Auction, in a Yankee auction each winning bidder pays his or her exact high bid.

CHAPTER TWENTY-FOUR

Home-Brewed Store-Building

Home-brewed store sites (Tronix is a fine example) are essentially personally built stores that don't use a store-building service or use a high-end commerce server. Instead, you build out your store in much the same way as a traditional Web site, and then, as dictated by budget and demand, you add an order form, use a shopping cart system, add credit card processing, and more. The result is a lot of flexibility in dictating how your store looks without spending the big bucks on a dedicated server and higher-end commerce server software.

In this chapter, we walk you through building a Web store using the home-brewed approach with which the Tronix site was built. We've decided to use ShopSite, a really good shopping cart solution available from OpenMarket and supported by a number of major Web hosting companies, such as Hiway.com. We recommend some other systems to use as well, since ShopSite might not be your personal preference. Joe uses ShopSite and recommends it highly.

The Three Approaches

There are three ways to create a store from the ground up, and each has its advantages and disadvantages.

No Frills, No Cart

The simplest way is to have a site with price lists and an order form that is secure but doesn't offer a shopping cart system. People fill out the form and send it in. This approach is very inexpensive and works well for stores with few products and relatively few orders. The disadvantage is that shopping is a bit tougher for customers. A shopping cart system makes it easy for them to click on what they want, continue shopping, and then eventually check out with the total price—including shipping, tax, and any other fees—already calculated for them. After finally finding a good shopping cart solution, Tronix's orders have increased at least partially due to the addition of a point-and-click system of browsing and adding to a cart. People no longer have to fill out an extensive order form and casual shoppers, first-timers especially, are more likely to shop at your store.

Packaged Approach

ShopSite and other shopping cart systems now usually include templates and services akin to what many of the hosted store-building solutions offer. In fact, ShopSite works similarly to the hosted solutions covered in Chapter 22. The problem is that you are locked into the publishing process these systems offer. Although they are great for many people, some storeowners want more ability to build out their store exactly as they want. That means that a packaged, home-brewed solution isn't necessarily as flexible.

Cart and Customize

For the home-brewed specialist, this is like having your cake and eating it too. By implementing just some of the features of a cart solution and combining that with a more custom-built site, you can have control over the look and feel without giving up the shopping cart system and its advantages. It's much more work and there are some limitations, such as less customization for the order form and shipping process (at least with ShopSite's current version). However, this combination has worked well for Tronix.

This process also works well for merchants who have built custom Web sites but may have forgone the shopping cart and automated checkout features, as Tronix did, due to unsatisfactory options.

This chapter focuses on this particular home-brewed approach more so than the packaged or no-frills approach.

Step 1: Get Hosting Service That Supports ShopSite

Since we are going to approach the home-brew store-building process by building a customized site and then setting up the shopping cart, one of the first things to do is to set up the store itself. However, the very first step is to select a service provider who will host the site and provide access to ShopSite's commerce services.

You can find a list of ShopSite providers by going to www.shopsite.com and clicking Purchasing ShopSite.

Once you select a provider, you need to open the account and initialize ShopSite services. This process will vary from provider to provider but overall it should be fairly straightforward—filling out account forms via the Web and perhaps placing a phone call to the provider for further assistance.

Once ShopSite is active you can begin developing your site.

Step 2: Build Out Your Product Information

ShopSite has two modes of operation: You can build pages using its template publishing system or you can generate the necessary links for products and embed them into custom pages you build yourself. In either case you need to first enter the product information for ShopSite's internal database system. This is a fairly simple process. Fill out a form (Figure 24.1) and then save the product to the ShopSite database.

FIGURE 24.1
ShopSite's Add a Product form.

ShopSite Wizard ?

welcome products pages appearance commerce publish

Add a Product

Use this page to add products to your store. Enter the data for a single product in the fields below. You must fill in the Name and Price fields. The other fields are optional.

Product Name:	Tomb Raider 4	(required)
Graphic:	none	Upload an Image
Price:	$39.99	(required)
Weight:	1 lb.	
SKU: *(stock code)*	PC00126	
Description: You can use HTML, but it isn't necessary.	Tomb Raider 4, CD-ROM, Windows PC.	

Save Changes Cancel

Once you've entered all of your product information, you can choose any product and generate a link to your ShopSite shopping cart. This feature is known as OrderAnywhere.

To do this, go to the Merchandising Section from the ShopSite main screen and then select the OrderAnywhere option, which brings up the OrderAnywhere Linker page (Figure 24.2).

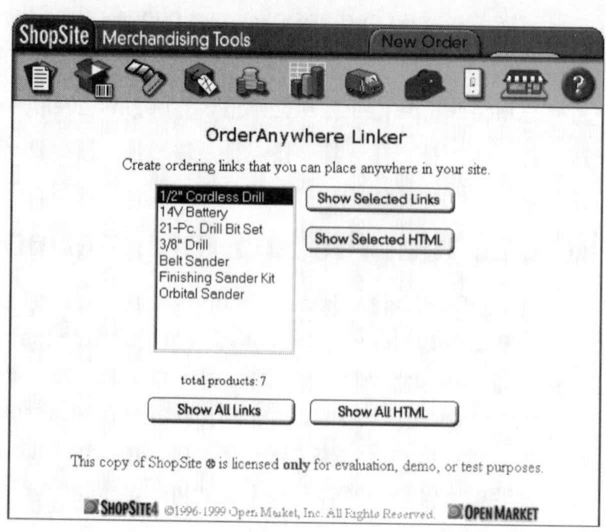

FIGURE 24.2
The OrderAnywhere Linker tool lets you generate HTML codes to embed in your custom pages so that they trigger the ShopSite shopping cart system.

To generate a link code, choose the product from the list on the left-hand side for which you want to create a link. Then choose to show selected links or show selected HTML. Selected Links generates an actual link (Figure 24.3). You can use this feature to drag and drop the links directly if you're using a product such as Microsoft FrontPage to design your site.

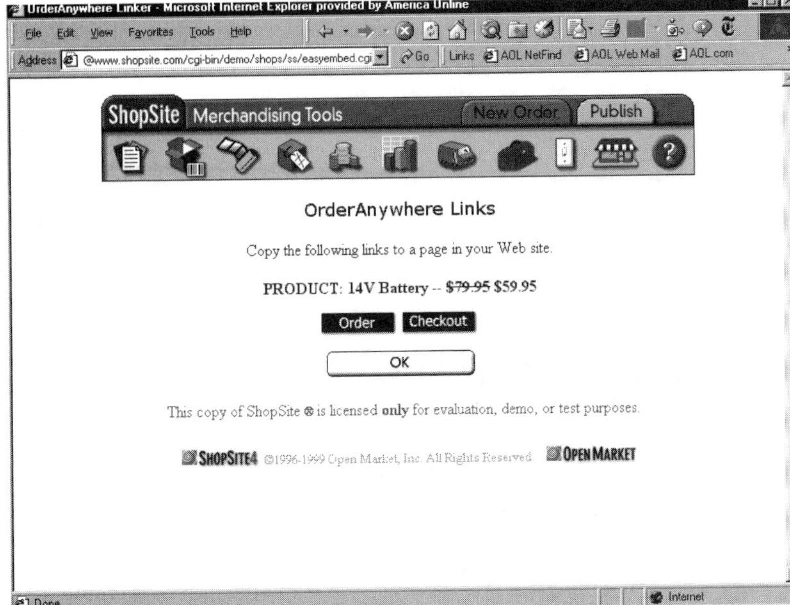

Figure 24.3
Use Show Selected Links to cut and paste links to a visual editor.

To generate the actual HTML code (which is preferred by those who edit Web pages at the code level using a tool such as HomeSite or BBEdit), select Show HTML and then highlight and copy the HTML code displayed (Figure 24.4). Paste that into your page's HTML code.

You can embed the link multiple times throughout your site. For example, a specific product's link might be embedded into a master list of prices, a sales page, the front page, and then a specific page containing more information about that product.

Assuming you've entered all your product information, move on to the process of building out the actual site. Then return to the Commerce Anywhere feature, generate the links you need, and get them onto the pages.

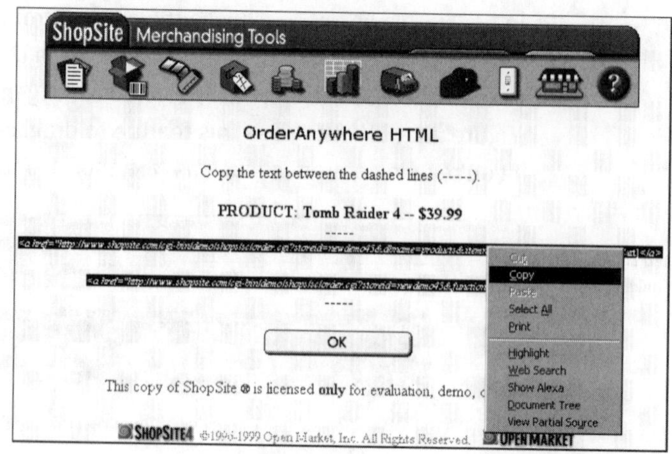

FIGURE 24.4
Use Show HTML to have ShopSite generate HTML code for your site.

Step 3: Build Your Custom Site

We can't teach you Web design here—and earlier in this book we covered store-building and sitebuilding issues. However, let's quickly recap some basics as they relate to this process of store-building.

The Basics

Every site should have pages covering basic store/Web site staples. These include a home page, company info, customer support, a store policy FAQ, ways to provide feedback, and links to other useful sites. These pages form the backbone of who you are and how you work. You should create a simple map on a piece of paper that helps you decide what types of pages you need and how they all fit together.

As part of this process you will need to design an overall look for your site. Most designers do this by designing a page that contains all of the items—and only the items—that will remain the same on every page of the site. This includes such page basics as the name/logo, buttons that point to the store's major departments, and page footer information that might include store address, additional links, email addresses, and copyright info. An overall design also includes basic choices of fonts, color scheme decisions, and any graphical elements. Some store owners might farm out the basic page look and feel to an accomplished designer and then, armed with that, do the individual pages and body design of each of those pages. As we've said—clean and simple is always better than fancy and cluttered.

Commerce Pages

After building out the basics, you need to build the pages that specifically list products for sale. There are two major ways to do this. One is to break your store into logical categories then create pages for those categories that contain the items for sale. In some cases, these might be nothing more than simple glorified price lists—more akin to classified ads. Tronix uses this format fairly well (Figure 24.5). It works especially well if you have a lot of products that are fairly simple to understand. In Tronix's case, most of its customers have already read reviews or seen previews of the games it sells. Thus a quick and easy list of products, prices, and some basic information is all that's needed.

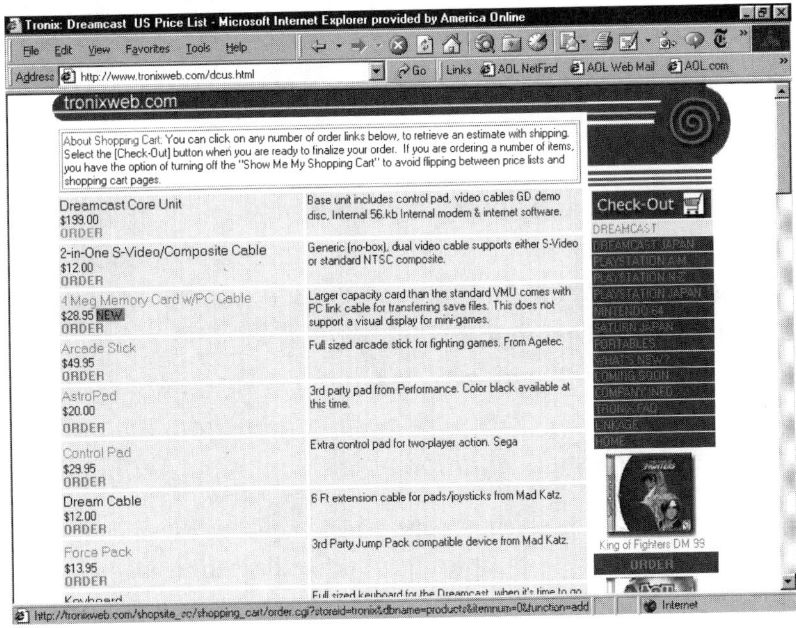

FIGURE 24.5
Simple price lists with ordering links works well as part of Tronix's store design.

For stores with products that need extra merchandising information, the other approach is to build additional pages that branch off from the department pages. In this regard, the department listings are more like an index to individual product pages than a final listing. Tronix does this as well. For products it has or wants to provide additional information for, there is another page specifically for that product. The product page is linked to and then links from the department price lists (Figure 24.6).

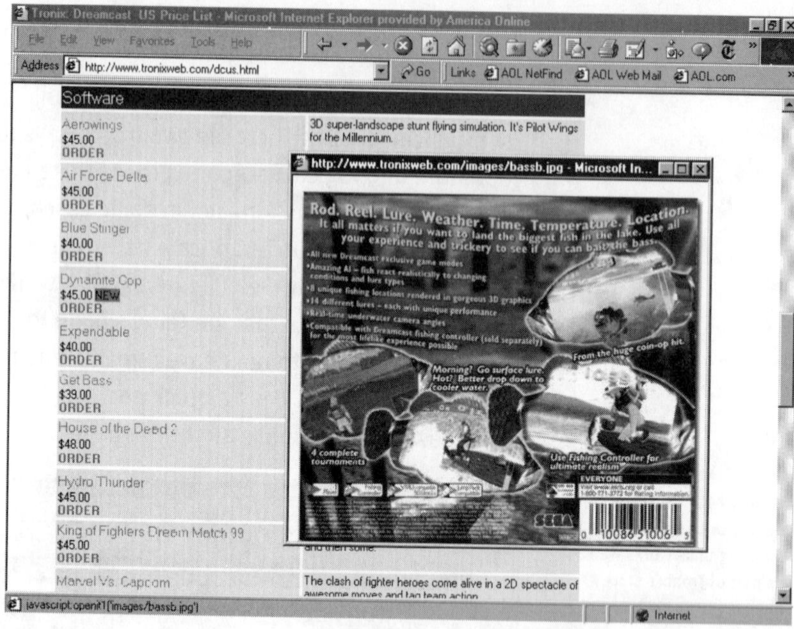

Figure 24.6
At Tronix, separate item pages pop up from links displayed on the main category price lists—which in Tronix's case show scans from the back of a particular game's packaging.

Joe's Take: *Not every product in your store necessarily needs its own page. I base separate product pages on whether I have good additional information or imagery or if it is a product with which my shoppers might not otherwise be familiar. Something else to remember is to provide a way for people to add a product to their cart from both the master index and from the extra product pages. I also like to make my product pages pop up separately from the price list window, by using the target="_Blank" addition to the common <A HREF=" "></A> link tag.*

Your product pages should be as uniform as possible and might contain other features such as links to compatible products and higher-end products of the same type, ratings, reviews.

Once you've built price list/category pages and, if needed, individual product pages, you will want to embed the shopping cart/ordering links into them.

Joe's Take: *I like ShopSite and the ability to just use this linking system with my custom pages. Many other shopping cart systems offer a similar feature. While the details are different, most work on the same principal. Design your own pages and then embed order or add-to-cart links to the pages that contain special code. This communicates with the shopping cart system in use on your server. The rest is automated by the Web host provider. Some systems require you to know the linking syntax yourself, whereas ShopSite, as demonstrated, has a simple wizard process that builds them for you.*

Building an Order Form

When you use ShopSite for your commerce system (and other similar products offer the same) you are more or less beholden to the product's checkout/order form system. Some sites may offer some customization abilities, but it's not the same as having complete customization.

To configure your order system as much as possible, ShopSite has an order system customization form (Figure 24.7). Here you can change colors for the screen and various bits of text displayed during different steps of the ordering process. All text typed in here can also include HTML code, so it is easy to embed other links and HTML code (For example, for an Affiliate Program) into the order screens. You can also add various surcharge settings, shipping instructions, and create a customized thank you screen and email receipt.

There are separate preferences screens to fill out for shipping and tax information. The tax screen lets you set up rates for your overall sales tax or one specific to people residing in your state or city. There are also a dozen or more fields to fill out additional localities on which you collect taxes.

For shipping you can provide rates for ground, second day air, and overnight shipping. You can also set up additional rates for other options, and configure the rates to scale up depending on weight of packages, number of items, or cost of the sale.

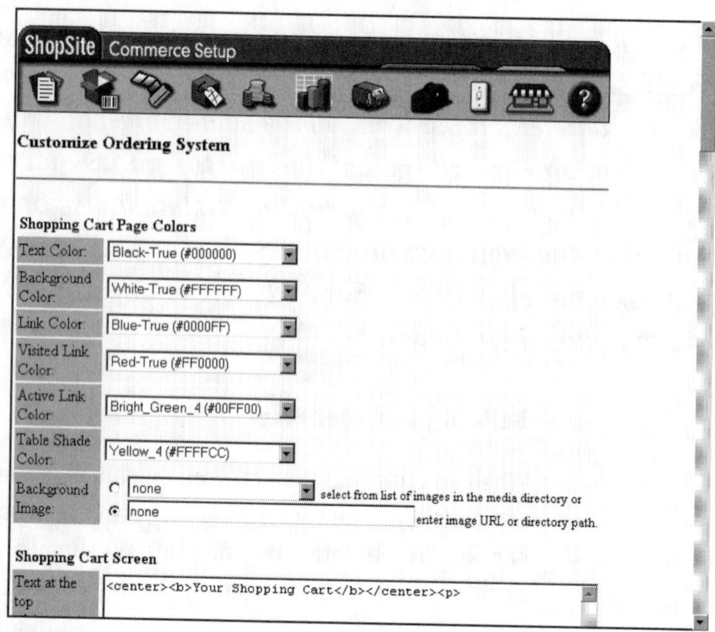

FIGURE 24.7
The Customize Ordering System form lets you better tailor the information shown on your order form and customize its look and feel.

***JOE'S TAKE:** ShopSite and other store-building products or shopping carts offer decent shipping preferences, but I still find myself short-changed most of the time. A key competitive point for small merchants like me is having a lot of different shipping options such as Saturday delivery, international shipping via DHL and Airborne Express. The time of day an order is placed can dictate which shipper we use, as some have later deadlines. Before you take the shopping cart plunge, consider how flexible the shipping options are. ShopSite is not bad, but I still had to narrow my options a bit. To get around these limitations, Tronix offers a process for customers to request special shipping and handling options via email.*

Custom Order Forms

Not every store will use ShopSite. Some will prefer a more no-frills system that doesn't use a fancy shopping cart or checkout process. If that's the case, then use the following information to aid you in building your order form and authorization system. Assuming you've built a site, listed products for sale, and now want to have a secure order form that lets people choose/type in products they want, quantities, and then submit critical order information—you need to figure out three things:

- How your host provider lets you process form information securely.
- What authorization method you'll use.
- How the authorization process can be included in the order process.

Processing Form Information Securely

This is the most critical item. Each Web hosting provider has a slightly different scheme for processing forms and for processing them using SSL encryption. However, they usually work in similar fashion.

You design your form as you would any other Web form. After designing the form, you embed in it certain information, provided by your Web hosting company, that tells its systems how to process the form, where to send/store the information, what page to pop up after completing it successfully, and so on. Most services use some form of Perl script to process forms, and they will have specific features for that service (including how to set up "thank you" forms, check it for required values, and so on). Before designing your own form, understand how your particular hosting service processes forms and how to design for it.

As far as SSL forms go, many providers require you to store that form in a special area of your site's back end, or even in a special section of their entire service. Then there is some additional HTML code you'll embed that invokes the protection for the data submitted by the user. The hosting service will then ensure that SSL encryption is turned on when that page is called up on their service. Information that is passed through that form will be readable or downloadable on the back end of their site (or, if they're really fancy, sent to you via encrypted email).

Remember, when doing SSL encryption using your host provider's system, the certificate that a user can view—and which you use to create the encryption for the data—is not directly licensed to you. It's the host provider's own certificate. In the grand scheme of things this is not a big deal—just understand that if your customers ask about this and want to know more about your security, they may view the certificate on their

Web browser and ask who the certificate holder really is. You will want to reply in a knowledgeable fashion. Additionally, if your provider forgets to update its certificate, people may be rudely greeted with an expiration notice. Although it is a lot of effort to have a server and set up your own certificates for SSL protection, for some stores it may be worth providing to ensure the highest level of confidence for their customers. However, most small stores should be content to use their hosting service's certificates but knowledgeable enough to reassure users who ask about it.

Armed with your Web host's information and help, refer to our order form design help in Chapter 22.

Authorization Method

The authorization process you link to in your order form will be determined by what your hosting provider can support or which you feel is easy enough to integrate into your custom form. The easiest processor to use is Authorize.net, because all you need to do is embed some extra HTML into the order form to trigger their service. You can find more information about Authorize.net's process in Chapter 14, which covers payments and processing, or on Authorize.net's Web page. Before you set up the authorization process, you'll need to apply and be accepted into that vendor's service. It will then provide you with some level of unique information that lets you tie into its system, which will include instructions, unique identifier information, and ways to pass information.

Including Authorization in the Order Process

With your payment processor sign-up complete, and information in hand, you must integrate the processor into your order form. Most hosting services offering some level of commerce support and may also have specific vendors with which they can provide easy integration. CyberCash is popular. This process usually requires some modification of a server script, which may require help from the hosting service or a contract programmer.

Implementing a custom order form is not too difficult. Your hosting provider will be responsible for the majority of the detail issues, and most work in a similar fashion as outlined by the steps presented. Once you've located all the needed information and made sure the hosting service and credit authorization service can work together, it's usually a matter of working with a programmer and the service to make the final installation.

Step 4: Build Credit Processing

It is easy to build in credit card authorization with ShopSite. Depending on the host provider, in the payments section of ShopSite you will be able to configure supported processors. It is wise to ask before signing with a provider what credit card processors they use and then check for compatibility with your merchant bank. Also, if you have signed on with one of these providers you'll have to potentially open an account with them first and then come back to the configuration screen (Figure 24.8) to enter any relevant information.

TIP ▸ ***Remember that all these services will authorize the transaction—however, as we've pointed out elsewhere in this book, you may still choose to further check the transactions before shipping and capturing the funds.***

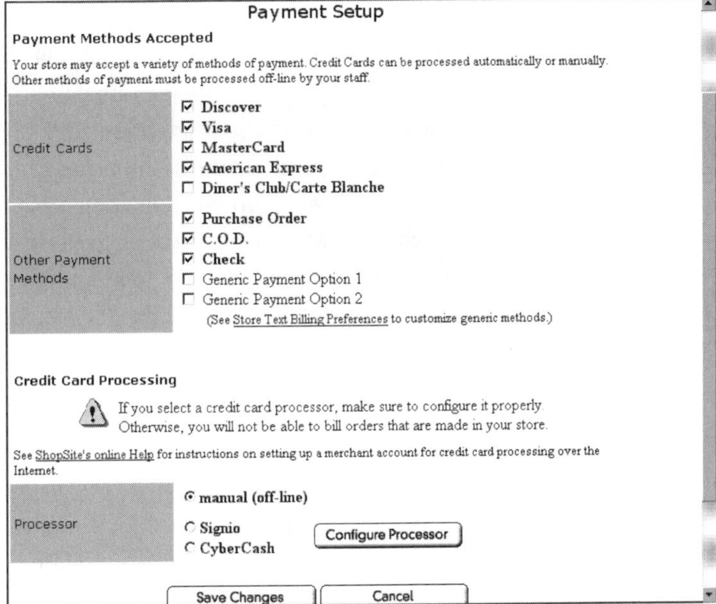

FIGURE 24.8
The Payment Setup section of ShopSite lists payment options to select. If your host provider offers easy integration with specific processors, they will be listed there for configuration as well.

Step 5: Additional Configuration Issues

ShopSite has a lot more power and features than what we have outlined so far. This chapter can't cover every detail of ShopSite, but there are some additional configuration issues to highlight. Some of these items may work in a similar fashion to those from other shopping cart solutions and may raise important issues in building your store online.

ShopSite offers a number of store preferences options (Figure 24.9), which are listed on the Preferences screen.

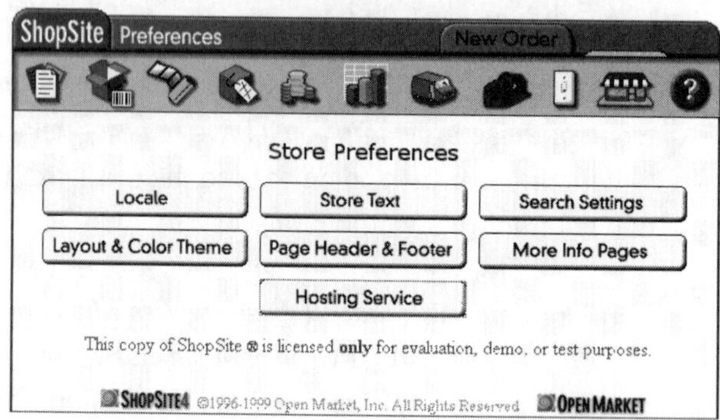

FIGURE 24.9 ShopSite's preferences options.

Locale

Locale handles where your store is physically located and what sort of languages, currency, and exchange rates are used. We recommend staying in U.S. dollars unless your situation works better with a different currency. The exchange rate setting isn't necessarily a good thing to use because this fluctuates too much in some cases—simply avoid it by not selecting an alternate currency. Let customers do this for themselves. You can help them by linking to a good currency exchange site such as finance.yahoo.com/m3?u. Or you can have customers send you an email asking for the exchange rate.

Store Text

This lets you set up text for special pages on your site. It is an important section because, for some checkout screens, you may want to embed special HTML code to activate various affiliate programs (see later).

TIP ▸ ***A good shopping cart system should let you add HTML level code or define a customizable "thank you" page. If not, some affiliate tracking systems such as Commission Junction (see later in this chapter) can't work with it.***

Search Settings

If you are using the entire ShopSite system, including its publishing features (rather than our more custom method, which uses OrderAnywhere links) you can configure a product search engine. Not every system offers this, and it isn't usable if you build a custom site.

TIP ▸ ***Want to add a search engine easily to you site? If you go the totally customized route, and can't use ShopSite's search engine, check out Atomz.com (www.atomz.com), an excellent search engine service that is very easy to install. If your site indexes less than 500 pages and you have less than 5,000 searches a month, the service is entirely free!***

Layout and Color Theme

If you are using ShopSite's custom page builder system for your store, you can use this preference section to detail how the store should appear to users. Choose different colors and layout templates.

Page Header and Footer

When using ShopSite's custom page builder system, this preference lets you embed text and code that will appear at the top and bottom of every ShopSite-generated page.

Hosting Service

The Hosting Service preferences control any specific issues about your store that relate to the hosting service you've chosen from ShopSite. Especially important on this screen (Figure 24.10) are the SSL Security Settings, which should be preconfigured by the host. The Store settings, which again are preconfigured by the hosting service upon sign-up, are also here. Finally the screen highlights the Hosting Service Configuration which details how the store is further set up to work.

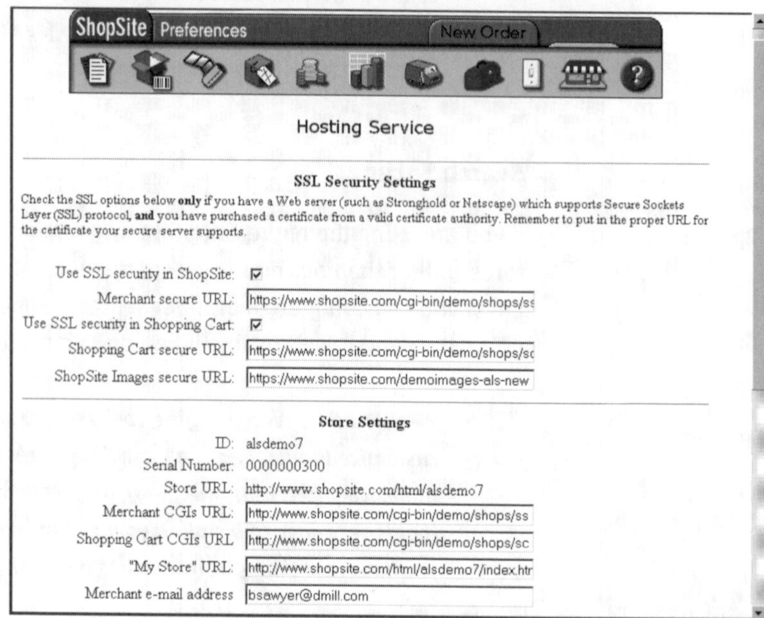

FIGURE 24.10
ShopSite's Hosting Service preferences.

Reports

ShopSite and other store-building services and shopping cart systems also include site report activity, including sales and order history and page view history. Many hosting sites will also include or use WebTrends, a popular site-tracking program.

On the Reports screen, you can also click a Configure button to further refine ShopSite's tracking reports. This lets you clear out sales counters, traffic counters, and various logs of activity on your site.

Merchandising Options

ShopSite and other cart programs and store-building services offer merchandising services which let you create discounts, cross-selling opportunities, and associate or affiliate tracking.

Discount Schedule

The discount schedule section of ShopSite lets you give customers a discount of a specific percentage based on their total order. For example, apply a 5 percent discount for all orders that are over $50 and a 10 percent discount for all orders over $80.

Associates

Several store-building software systems, ShopSite included, let you create affiliate or associate stores using their systems. To create or view associates you have with ShopSite, go to the Associates section of the Merchandising Options. A button there lets you add associates. When adding an associate, you give them a name, an email address, and then determine a commission which can be a percentage or flat rate. Then you must enter the URL where their click-throughs go. Then click the Create Link to Store button which generates the affiliate link to your store, which ShopSite uses to track commissions.

Joe's Take: *The ShopSite associate program lets you create simple affiliates for your store, but it doesn't do any sign-up for them, and it doesn't handle tracking and payments as well as a place like LinkShare or Commission Junction does. It and other similar features on other store systems are good for having a small amount of close associates, but if you want to build a much more robust and diverse set of affiliates and have a more turn-key system, consider the systems offered by LinkShare and Commission Junction.*

Custom Pages

The Custom Pages section of ShopSite lets you break out of its publishing system and upload any custom pages directly to the system. Of course, if you're using the OrderAnywhere feature, and our home-brewed approach, you needn't concern yourself as much with this section.

Banner Ads

This provides links to well-known banner advertising or banner exchange networks.

Search Engines

This provides links to well-known search engine submission systems.

OrderAnywhere

This section is a linchpin of the customized approach we've been detailing in this chapter. It lets you create custom shopping cart links for any page on your site, from any product listed in ShopSite's product database.

Order API

Good systems are always extendable in some way, and ShopSite is no different. The Order API preferences let you define a custom CGI script to run when a customer makes a purchase. This lets you extend the checkout process with your own custom programs. For example, the order might be checked against inventory to see if all the items are in stock or it might extend the user to a place where they can get software to download or return an e-ticket for a tour or trip. The ShopSite system has a complete API and instructions for programmers who might extend the checkout process for you. Talk to your host and the programmer you employ for this for more information.

Step 6: Publish and Manage

Once you've built your store it will be active. At that point you use your ShopSite backend to track orders, look at reports, and tweak any setting or generate new product links as needed. Orders are provided securely on the back end via a screen you can view. You can also download orders securely into a comma-delimited file that you can import into a Point-of-Sale program or spreadsheet. If you've integrated with a credit-card processing service, you'll get authorization information, too. However, you'll need to use that system's interface for capturing the money once you've shipped the product.

At this point you're on your own. ShopSite and other cart systems may offer additional features, and you may dream up new ways to build cool features into your site. However, the basics remain the same. Build a good site, provide a good ordering and checkout mechanism, keep on top of operations, and people will appreciate your store.

Do It Yourself Affiliate System and Stores

Earlier in the book we covered the concept of affiliate stores. An affiliate store or site is a Web site that recommends a product and a store as the place to purchase that product. When a user clicks on an affiliate link, he is taken to the store where he can purchase the products. You then track that purchase and, if it can be accounted to one of your affiliate sites, you pay them a percentage (or a fee) for the sale. The percentage or bounty can be whatever you feel like offering, although you and the affiliate agree contractually before hand what that is. Typically, the fees paid are in the between 5 to 15 percent of the overall sale. Some sites pay a one-time fee (for example, $50 for each new customer) while others pay a high percentage for first-time purchases and then a lower percentage for each subsequent sale. There are dozens of approaches to use—it's really up to you and your affiliates.

The hard part of an affiliate system is tracking it, making it easy to sign up for, and cutting the checks for affiliates. That is why affiliates have mostly been the domain of larger-scale stores that can afford the infrastructure to manage them, or those that can afford higher-priced services such as BeFree and Linkshare that can help sign up and manage affiliate programs. Fortunately for small- to medium-sized stores, a new service for creating your own affiliate program called Commission Junction is both affordable and easy to use.

Commission Junction: Step-by-Step

Commission Junction (www.cj.com) is a full-service commission management system. It will help you build your own custom affiliate system and allow you to sign up and manage affiliate sites. It can also help a bit in recruiting new affiliates to your store.

Commission Junction can help you create one of three types of affiliate programs:

- **Pay-per-click.** You pay a commission when an authorized affiliate refers a customer to your site and that customer enters your site.
- **Pay-per-lead.** You pay a commission when an authorized affiliate refers a customer to your site and that customer fills out a form or performs another action that potentially allows you to generate a new sale.
- **Pay-per-sale.** You pay a commission when an authorized affiliate refers a customer to your site, and that customer buys a product or service. Commission Junction can help track whether this occurs when the visitor is at your site or at a later time.

Affiliate Sign-Ups and Approvals

Commission Junction attracts large numbers of affiliates by offering a consolidated, easy-to-join revenue sharing network. As a merchant, your site is connected to a network of thousands of prescreened affiliates, and you have final say regarding which affiliates join your program.

Earn Money Back from Commission Junction

One of the cool features of Commission Junction is that as a merchant you can earn money back from affiliates you generate. Commission Junction tries to get new affiliates of any of its member merchants to potentially become affiliates of other merchants that use its service (with appropriate permissions from the user or member merchant to be contacted for such purposes). With its integrated two-tier program, you can receive $1 for each new affiliate you send to Commission Junction plus 5 percent of those affiliates' earnings. So, if an affiliate of yours signs on to become an affiliate of another store that uses Commission Junction and earns from that store $100, you get $5 in your account as a result. You also earn 5 cents for every valid click you send to CJ.com.

Costs

To join Commission Junction you must pay a one-time-fee of $795 (as of November 1999) and you must place in an escrow account $250, which will be used to start paying out affiliates of your store.

You then pay a fee to Commission Junction for each payout you make in your affiliate program. This fee (as of November 1999) is 20 percent of the payout rate. Thus for every $1 you pay an affiliate, you pay an additional 20 cents to Commission Junction. Which means that if you paid a 15 percent commission on every sale via an affiliate link, you'd actually be paying 18 percent since Commission Junction takes an additional 3 percent (20 percent of 15 percent is 3 percent). Commission Junction only charges on what you pay out—so, for example, you don't pay fees if your affiliate didn't earn its minimum required amount for a check and thus didn't actually get its money yet. All Commission Junction payouts to merchants and affiliates are in U.S. dollars.

TIP ▸ ***If you have trouble understanding this process or using its site, you can call Commission Junction at 800-761-1072 to speak with a salesperson.***

How It Tracks Affiliates

When a surfer clicks a merchant's link from an affiliate's site, he or she is sent to the merchant's site via a redirection from the Commission Junction system. To the surfer it appears as a direct link to the merchant. At this point, Commission Junction sets a cookie with the surfer. This helps it track the user through its system and on your site.

The system does different things depending on the type of affiliate program:

- **Pay-per-lead.** In this scheme the user will most likely fill out a form or perform some action on the merchant's site. After the user does this, the exit page for the process contains a unique ID that is sent back to Commission Junction's server. When the unique ID is received and Commission Junction reads the cookie, it stores the info in its database which is later used to compile a report.

- **Pay-per-sale.** A customer comes through to your site and makes a purchase and completes the ordering process. After she completes the order, the exit page contains a unique identification number that is sent to the Commission Junction server. When the unique ID is received, and Commission Junction reads the cookie, it stores the info in its database, which is later used to compile a report.

- **Pay-per-click.** The users info is stored instantly on clicking through to the page that contains a unique identification number which is sent to the Commission Junction server. When the unique ID is received, Commission Junction stores the click information in its database to use later when it runs reports for affiliate payouts.

Antifraud

All e-commerce has fraud pitfalls, and affiliate sales systems are no different. The last thing you need is an affiliate generating bogus leads, click-throughs, or sales. Commission Junction also doesn't want merchants shortchanging its affiliates and weakening its integrity. Aside from individual complaints and investigations, it has implemented several antifraud countermeasures.

- **A merchant is only responsible** for valid clicks, leads, or sales. A click, lead, or sale is valid when it is recorded in an active program between an approved affiliate partner and an active merchant.
- **Affiliate partners will only be credited** (at most) ten times every 24 hours (per unique IP address) for sending a click to each merchant's site.
- **Chargebacks** (where a sale is returned or never completed) can be credited. For frequent or questionable chargebacks, as long as merchants provide documented evidence, they will be credited (which means you should keep track of these things carefully).
- **Handling a chargeback** requires logging on to the Commission Junction Web site and generating a transaction report from a specific date range. You can then edit various sales or leads to indicate a chargeback. This includes duplicate sales, product returns, bad payment, or nonreceipt of payment. Once you select the type of activity, you can include additional notes (in case Commission Junction audits you because of abnormal chargeback activity).
- **Commission Junction** watches all its affiliates and merchants for questionable activity. If an affiliate for one merchant seems to be acting wrong, it notifies all of its merchants. It also notifies affiliates of merchant misconduct.

TIP ▸ ***Merchants suspecting fraud or wanting more info have a specific email contact at Commission Junction: fraud@cj.com.***

Signing Up Affiliates

Affiliate signup involves several initiatives. Commission Junction maintains a directory of its member merchants. You can also (and obviously should) set up a link for affiliates to sign up with Commission Junction directly from your site. Commission Junction provides you with a graphical button to link from your site to a form on its site that lets people sign up for your program on their server. You can also create a separate page with additional information on your program. This resides on your server, but it's recommended you detail out your affiliate system.

All affiliates must be approved before they are allowed into the system. You can set approvals to automatic or manually approve affiliates—it depends on how picky you want to be. Some sites might want to approve affiliates so they can control the quality of sites that are linking to them. Others might not mind a free-for-all approach. If you're going to sell items that appeal to kids, you might want to consider a more manual approval process. However, you can rest easy—adult sites, sites with adult-oriented links, and sites that promote hatred, racism, discrimination, or illegal activity are banned from the service. You can report any such suspected affiliate to Commission Junction.

With manual approval you will receive an email for all pending affiliate applications. You must then access your account and click Approve or Reject for each application.

TIP ▸ ***Commission Junction supports banner advertising for its affiliates and merchants. You can upload as many as five banners or buttons to its servers, which affiliates can use as part of their affiliate campaign for your store.***

Integrating Commission Junction into Your Site

Once you've registered, you need to make some changes to your site so Commission Junction can work. This mainly has to do with the order exit page or "thank you" page—your store generates a receipt and thanks the customer for their sale. Each type of affiliate program has a different set of rules.

The confirmation page must be able to display a unique order ID and, in the case of a pay-per-sale program, the dollar amount of the order. The order ID can be a number, a customer's name, email address, or other unique ID code that identifies each sale or lead. For a pay-per-sale model, the exit/thank you page must include final ordering information including the amount and/or products sold. For a pay-per-lead program, the thank you page can be basically anything confirming the information has been properly received.

You have three options on how you integrate Commission Junction's code into these pages. You can do it yourself, use a compatible shopping cart system, or have Commission Junction technicians do it for you. If you choose to do it yourself (which in some cases you have to do, as Commission Junction will not modify any compiled code and only handles minor changes for the necessary install such as Perl, ASP, or ColdFusion), you can find information for you or your programmers on its site.

TIP ▸ ***If you do it yourself or hire your own programmers, Commission Junction will provide your programmers one hour of telephone installation guidance. If the setup is not completed based on that hour of advice, you can have additional hours of help billed at a rate of $100/hour.***

If you want Commission Junction to modify your site, you must fax your hosting information (username, password, login process) and then wait for its answer. If it is not a major undertaking, it takes about one to two business days to modify your site, and then you're in business.

Commission Junction also has partnerships with leading shopping cart providers. Table 24.1 provides the most recent list (as of November 1999) that it supports. Check its site for the latest group.

Table 24.1 Commission Junction Shopping Cart Providers

Accesspoint Corporation	www.accesspoint.com
Americart	www.americart.com
Authorize.Net	www.authorize.net
Cart32	www.cart32.com
ComercePay	www.commercepay.com
CyberCash	www.cybercash.com
Hassan Consulting	www.irata.com
iBill	www.ibill.com
Intershop	www.intershop.com
IPOSS	iposs.creditnet.com
MerchantOnline	www.merchantonline.com
Miva	www.miva.com
Objectware	www.objectwareinc.com
Plug'nPay	www.plugnpay.com
ShopCart	www.shopcart.com
US WebSites	www.uswebsites.com
Virtualcart	www.virtualcart.com

TIP ▸ ***ShopSite doesn't have automatic integration with Commission Junction yet. By using the ShopSite API, though, Commission Junction or a programmer you hire should be able to write a simple Perl script that can generate the necessary codes.***

Managing Your System

Once you've set up your service, defined its payout, and begun recruiting sites, there is really little left to do except to continue building. A complete back end system lets you manage the account via any Web browser. Forms and reports exist to help you change payout rates (be sure to alert any affiliates before you do this), generate chargebacks, and make more deposits into your escrow account to pay affiliates.

Paying Out

As commissions occur, you will need to pay affiliates. Commission Junction handles this automatically, but you must have the funds in your escrow account to cover these amounts. Commission Junction will periodically notify you via email when additional funds are needed. Funds generated when Commission Junction pays you for signing affiliates up for other programs also go into this account. If you need to make a deposit or withdrawal, just log on to your account. For deposits you can use a credit card or US bank check. It takes one or two days to process the deposit.

TIP ▸ ***If your account balance is less than this threshold, your merchant program will be placed on hold, and no new affiliates will be signed up. Also, your links on affiliate sites will be removed. Keep that account in balance and don't provide huge payouts or percentages for your program if you can't afford to profit from them.***

You can only make a withdrawal when your account balance is greater than $25. Fill out a withdrawal form, and Commission Junction sends you a check on the 15th of the month.

Commission Junction issues payment automatically as part of its service. Each month it sends your affiliates a report detailing their earnings over the previous 30 days. If they have accumulated at least $25, they get a check. Your transaction and activity reports will detail withdrawals made on your account.

Easy as Pie?

When you run an affiliate program you're giving up a slice of each sale or lead to the site that brought it to you. This is an ingenious way to make the most of the Web's decentralized structure, which has spawned millions of sites, many of which are potential affiliates. However, before services like Commission Junction, it was tough to do it yourself. But as we've detailed here, now it's a snap. The hard part is making sure that in giving others a slice of your business, you leave a sizeable piece for yourself.

Large sites can afford to lose money on initial leads and customer sales; smaller stores need to be a bit more careful. If you run a lead generation payout scheme, make sure that the bounty for a new lead can be earned back either because the initial sale (once converted) will be worth more than the bounty or because initial customer leads earn out over a given period of repeat business. If you're running a percentage scheme, make sure that once someone takes 10 or 20 percent of the overall sale, there is still a profitable margin left for you. If executed properly, an affiliate campaign can be a huge boost to your business. However, if not done correctly you can quickly dig yourself a sizeable hole. It's all in knowing that each sale is going to be a profitable sale—whether it is an affiliate sale or not.

The Home-Brewed Affiliate Store

There is another form of home-brewed store-building—the affiliate store. With so many major retailers and online stores offering affiliate sales, it's entirely possible to create an online store that only works with affiliate links. With no inventory to handle and no shipping to do, you are essentially set up with a much lower cost to operate than if you did a complete online store with your own inventory and fulfillment operations. This is a great model for sites that are more content oriented and want to have a store that sells related items without actually being in the store business.

The disadvantage of this model is that many times customers want to order goods directly from the seller. You also don't earn as much on each sale and are beholden to the quality of service offered by the store with which you are working. In addition—and this is the biggest disadvantage to customers—if you're creating a store that links to multiple stores for products you recommend, customers might be forced to visit several stores. But with affiliate sales the customer often is focused on buying a single product or product type (for example, just books).

Keys to Building an Affiliate Store

There are two keys to building an affiliate store: having a compelling site that attracts visitors and recommending good products.

Your focus as an affiliate storeowner is almost exclusively the content, not the merchant services or order-fulfillment. You must build a specifically interested community of users who subsequently use your affiliate links to purchase products you've found for them. For example, Swynk.com (www.swynk.com), which has a large set of affiliated products for sale from Amazon.com and other stores, focuses on being one of the top informational sites about Microsoft's BackOffice and SQL Server products. The Swynk store focuses on recommending good books and products for its specific readers. You don't find links to Harry Potter books here.

To create an affiliate store is easy enough. Here are some tips that can help make it much more successful:

- **Focus on your content.** Generate articles that people want to read and services people want to use. Before you can have success as an affiliate you need traffic.
- **Focus on a specific topic,** one that people invest in (whether it is learning about the topic such as a how-to program, or as a hobby, such as astronomy) and don't deviate too much.
- **Always be careful what you recommend.** Focus on quality products that you know are good. Be the "Consumer Reports" of your topic and guide people to products they'll enjoy and like. That makes you a very valuable part of their shopping process.
- **Build your affiliate store like a regular store.** Make sure products and price lists are presented clearly and that you provide the proper links and background information on them.
- **Where possible, focus on top-tier stores** at which people are likely to have already made a purchase or feel good about.
- **Constantly be on the lookout for new stores** that offer products in which your site's visitors will be interested. At the same time, try to keep things as consolidated as possible using as few stores as needed to generate your product mix.
- **Always work on recommending new products.** A big key to the affiliate store's success is alerting rabid fans to new products before anyone else does.
- **Be sure to read each affiliate agreement** carefully to make sure you agree with terms, payouts, and schedules. Some programs forbid you from

linking to other competitors (a practice that is starting to relax but not stop), so read the fine print.

- **Watch your logs carefully.** If you can generate your own reports for clicks on your site, watch them carefully to track the relationship between click-throughs and payouts. Some systems have gone down in the past, costing the affiliate money. In some cases you may find bad links or stores that don't close the sale.

- **Merchandise.** Top ten lists, personal recommendations, and anything else that provides people with rankings or interesting recommendations generates click-throughs.

- **Be careful about crossing the line** between recommending, endorsing, and interweaving with your content. People like recommendations, and they don't mind endorsements, but don't run a glowing review of a product just to recommend it. Don't embed links to bad products just because they are topical.

Where to Next?

If you've headed down the path of building your own store from the ground up, you have two options where to go next. You can continue on your current path, building out your pages using the ShopSite system and your Web building tools. Or you might find it necessary to jump to the next level and move toward more of a dedicated server system, a database-driven site, and more extensive and advanced commerce building. This is where Chapter 25 takes you: the more advanced commerce servers and building processes that major Web retailers use.

CHAPTER TWENTY FIVE

Advanced Store-Building

If you have the desire and budget to build a top of the line Web store, using a hosted store or a small-scale shopping cart just won't cut it. If you are a major retailer or plan to have a large amount of traffic, products, or special features, you will need to take an advanced approach to store-building. This chapter specifically covers some of those issues that concern larger, more complex online stores and higher-end solutions.

Choosing a Server and an OS

The first choice to make when building with advanced tools and a large budget is your server and operating system. There are several high-end server products, including Open Market Transact, Microsoft Site Server Commerce Edition, IBM Net.Commerce, Intershop, and Broadvision. Oracle, Netscape, and a few other companies also make commerce servers, but the five we discuss are popular with many medium to larger scale stores. Table 25.1 provides some basic background on those five products.

Table 25.1 High-end Server Products

Open Market Transact	www.openmarket.com	Very high-end system that is used more to operate malls of sites and very high-end top trafficked sites.
Microsoft Site Server, Commerce Edition	www.microsoft.com/siteserver/	A staple commerce server for NT-oriented sites, at a good price.
IBM Net.Commerce	www.ibm.com	A well-reviewed server that is available for a number of platforms including IBM's popular AS/400 minicomputer line.
Intershop	www.intershop.com	Intershop is a top server from a European-based company. This commerce package is priced competitively and is used by many U.S. based companies, too.
Broadvision	www.broadvision.com	A strong commerce server priced between that of Open Market's Transact and lower-priced offerings from Microsoft and Intershop. Offers robust personalization services as part of its overall commerce package.

For an OS, Microsoft's Site Server is an NT-only product, whereas the others offer NT and various Unix versions. Some have criticized NT as not being a great OS for commerce applications, but that isn't necessarily true. Part of the knock on NT for commerce applications is that it doesn't scale well to a large amount of transactions. Also, the ASP (Active Server Pages) architecture, which Site Server uses to present dynamic pages that are based on elements pulled from databases, is a slow process. Again, it doesn't scale well. However, most commerce sites spread the traffic load across multiple machines (known as *load balancing*). By following the correct procedures and using advanced hardware correctly, Site Server/ASP-based stores can scale quite well. In fact 1-800-Flowers (www.1800flowers.com), one of the biggest sites on the Web, uses NT-based hardware. For more on this process, see Microsoft's white paper on the subject at http://technet.microsoft.com/cdonline/content/complete/internet/server/sitesrv/commerce/technote/comcomm.htm. The paper is aimed at ISPs and Web hosting providers, but it provides a lot of good technical information on building robust commerce services with Microsoft architecture.

Unix scales well. Unix is known for its industrial-strength ability to handle large loads of processing traffic. Many large-scale sites use Web servers running some version of Unix—especially Sun hardware running the Solaris OS, and Pentium-based systems running free derivative Unix operating systems such as FreeBSD and Linux. The drawback with Unix is that the hardware needed to run a commercial Unix OS can be expensive (unless you use cheaper Intel-based hardware and Linux), and the engineers and talent needed to run and manage a Unix-based system can be much more expensive than more prevalent NT-focused talent. And even though Unix can scale extremely well, with even one well-honed Unix system handling a large load of traffic and transactions, you will still need multiple machines to help balance traffic and provide redundancy.

Your OS and server choice should be based on what you feel most comfortable using. That could come from recommendations by your store-building staff, outsourcer, and site hosting provider. If these people are Unix fans or favor a commerce server that works best on Unix, you might be convinced to pick that OS. In short—don't make an OS choice based on reviews or head-to-head comparisons. Base it on what your people feel is best for them. Talented people who are comfortable with their choices and educated about building stores with that setup will offer you the best store and the best ability to manage it.

Database Choice and Plan

Most higher-end stores (most Web sites for that matter) are based on databases that hold critical information about products for sale, product photos, pricing, size, and so on. Databases may also store critical customer information or be plugged into distributor databases for further supply-chain coordination. That means that you will need a database system running that holds and serves critical information into your commerce system. The system publishes this information as users request items.

The choice of your database is one that you should make in a similar manner to your OS and commerce server choice. Most top-of-the-line database systems—whether they are Microsoft SQL Server, Oracle 8, Sybase, or IBM's DB2—are well-designed systems. This means that your site's staff and the consultants who build and help manage the site should play a key role in the decision. Some commerce systems also work better with certain databases because the developers of those systems provided better tools and documentation that help with the integration. For example, Site Server, Commerce Edition and Microsoft's own SQL Server 7 are well tuned for each other. IBM's Net.Commerce and DB2 are another strong pair. All the major servers should offer ways to integrate with the major database systems available, but usually they will favor a certain combination.

A final issue concerning database choice is compatibility with other systems your company is using. Having compatibility between your database and your internal systems is even more important than your server software/OS compatibility.

Other Key Decisions

Large-scale stores aren't finished with a server, OS, and database choice—there are more architectural issues to consider. Other aspects are the basic hardware choices that will run the system and the load-balancing and other equipment that supports the site. When making your hardware choice, defer to your site hosting provider and maintenance staff. You should also consider products that can speed site responsiveness. When it comes to PC-oriented hardware, look for higher-end systems that contain Intel Xeon processors. Xeon's built-in expanded cache has been shown to dramatically speed site responsiveness, especially sites based on ASP architecture (such as Site Server), and it is shown to dramatically speed database information retrieval.

Another key hardware feature are top-end servers that provide additional monitoring functions in their design. These features can help engineers monitoring your site identify machines with hardware problems that are slowing down your site's responsiveness or ability to function properly.

If you are going to buy top-of-the-line hardware, look for products that let your site operators monitor hardware issues such as machine temperature, hard-drive speeds, and more to ensure hardware operates at peak performance.

Hosting Provisions

You will also need to make decisions about how you will host an advanced site. The difference between an advanced solution and most beginner-to-intermediate level approaches is that your high-level store is much more like a custom-built application than a simple Web site or a turnkey store design. An advanced store may include several critical software components in addition to the commerce server itself. It may also include multiple types of hardware and servers, specialized devices such as routers that can balance incoming traffic, and devices that speed SSL processes.

Thus, the requirements of a more advanced store are a site-hosting setup that has the ability to handle the custom setup and management of higher-end commerce designs. Advanced commerce hosting is really advanced application hosting, and only a handful of firms can provide this level of service, which comes at a premium cost.

Here are some questions to answer when looking for a hosting provider for an advanced store. Does the vendor:

- **Have the ability** to quickly add new servers to help deal with extra traffic during key buying periods?
- **Have support staff** familiar with your server systems and software choices?
- **Provide secure facilities** and strong security features for its customers' systems?
- **Have 24-hour support staff,** including OS and commerce oriented engineers on site?
- **Operate a 24-hour** staffed network monitoring center?
- **Offer multiple operation centers** around the world so you can build a distributed network of servers for fast responses to a global customer base?

- **Specialize in helping to maintain and optimize** large database server systems that are part of cutting edge Web sites?
- **Host other** top-tier retailing sites?

The most critical service your hosting provider will offer is keeping your store online and monitored for uptime and speed. For advanced stores that might number as many as a dozen Web servers and include servers for personalization, database, and commerce transaction processing, this can be a tough job that includes 24-hour round the clock network operations.

Personalization

Most small site owners can't offer personalization tools—instead, they need to use their individual ability to recommend products and cross-sales to their customers. However, larger-scale sites with large budgets can purchase personalization tools to automate this process. Personalization software such as Andromedia's LikeMinds and Net Perceptions is not a trivial investment. The leading package by far, Net Perceptions, is a $50,000 product that requires its own system, installation, and integration work. To get the most out of it you must continuously analyze the collected data. Studies show that good personalization and recommendation software can increase sales by as much as five percent, which can be a significant gain.

Another form of personalization involves a customer database that holds direct personal settings for particular customers. Repeat customers will appreciate the ability to store their credit card information on file, set options like email updates to receive, and maintain shipping address and other personalized information. There are two options to consider for this type of direct personalization. Most companies use a straightforward customer database that is designed to hold and manage the information that the site uses. However, some companies use LDAP (Lightweight Directory Access Protocol) systems, which is what Microsoft's Personalization Server is based on. LDAP is essentially a specialized database scheme focused on storing information about users. If you use Microsoft's Site Server system, your development staff should consider using this technology to store and retrieve user information for your customer database.

Personalization systems like Net Perceptions work via a process known as collaborative filtering. Collaborative filtering is a process whereby a computer records to a database all the choices of every user. Then, by comparing the results of all the users who made a similar choice, it searches to see if those users made any other similar choices. For example, if 100 people who purchased a book by Anne Rice also purchased a book by Stephen King 80% of the time, then every time someone purchased an Anne Rice book you could instruct your store system to display titles by Stephen King.

Installing Net Perceptions is a several-day process. It involves setting up both the software that records and manages the datawarehouse and setting up the software that lets your site, through any number of programming and scripting languages, interact with that information to generate personalized recommendations for given shoppers. Be aware that a good personalization system will need a few days or weeks of traffic before it can generate enough data to make stable recommendations. It also generates a huge amount of data that has to be stored and managed. The more information it gets, the better. Be prepared to have extensive information in your personalization database.

Integrating Shipping Results into the System

For advanced stores, shipping integration can be a great addition. Customers can automatically receive their confirmation and tracking information from you, and you can provide shipping status directly to them (for example, "your order shipped today from our Kansas City warehouse via UPS at 2P.M.") through your own site.

TIP ▸ **Ops and Fulfillment** ***magazine is a key read for people who run catalog and Web retailing sites that have advanced fulfillment needs. Check it out at http://www.opsandfulfillment.com/.***

Both FedEx and UPS provide integration tools for advanced store-builders to build scripts and specialized Web services (see sidebar, next page). Some companies are taking this a step further by turning to advanced logistics software from TanData.

TanData offers a specific package called Progistics Merchant geared toward multiple carrier relationships. The software lets you create robust shipping solutions for your store that let shoppers pick a speed of delivery (and TanData's software will let you match that with the best available option) or let the shopper pick from a list of carriers. In each case, the system will return real rates to shoppers and charge rates based on whatever negotiated rates you have with your various shippers. The system can also return carrier-approved tracking numbers as hyperlinks to let the shoppers track their own packages.

The system runs on top of TanData's Progistics CS product suite. At the core of the Progistics CS suite are programmable objects that you place within your store's server system. These components, which can be programmed via Java, CGI, C++ and other languages, let you check shipper ratings, routing capabilities, shipping, tracking numbers, and do other shipping-related tasks such as automatically printing carrier labels and other supporting documentation. If you interface with your shipper's own systems, the system can generate some of the more common carrier electronic communications such as EDI requests.

TanData continuously updates all the shipping rules and data that is contained in its software as shippers debut new rate structures and make changes to their business rules. The software also lets you input custom rules and pricing data and can work with systems that have multiple warehouses and shipping centers. The product ships with interface documentation for Microsoft, Oracle, and Intershop.

TanData has set up a couple of sample e-commerce stores to demo some of the features of Progistics Merchant. Access a Microsoft Site Server demo store at microsoft.tandata.com or an Intershop version at intershop.tandata.com.

TIP ▸ ***You will need a "valid" credit card number if you want to make a simulated purchase on these sample stores. A valid but inactive number that will pass check digit and format tests is 4111 1111 1111 1111.***

Integrating Shipping Results into Commerce Systems

FedEx and UPS both offer software options for integrating shipping. As noted in Chapter 17, both companies offer tools for small merchants online. These companies also offer much more advanced systems and online tools.

UPS has advanced services and online tools for higher-end store-builders. Its Online Professional package (www.ups.com/bussol/solutions/professional.html) offers advanced services to qualified shippers. The company also offers downloadable tools for integrating package tracking into your site. Advanced store-builders might want to use UPS's logistical services division and or its Professional Services group, located on the Web at www.ups-psi.com. UPS even has software and technicians that can help you integrate your back-end systems into its shipping systems.

FedEx offers numerous eBusiness tools (www.fedex.com/us/software/). FedEx's automation solutions include Shipping Tools, Business Building Tools, and Supply Chain Management Tools. Select software developers can take advantage of the Global Developer Program, which offers free tools designed to help build FedEx's automated functions into your company's systems.

Advanced Tax Technology

So far in the U.S., sales taxes on the Web has been a fairly moot point. The Internet tax moratorium has made it simple to focus on collecting sales tax only in states where you have an operational facility. However, this may not be the case forever, and, when operating in other countries, there may be VAT and other types of taxes to consider. To solve complex tax issues, advanced merchants can turn to Taxware, a creator of software that automatically analyzes every transaction passed through to it and calculates all applicable taxes. The software can also generate tax reports and interface with other accounting systems you may have.

Internet Taxware is a combination of programmable server objects that integrate with a database system maintained by Taxware that constantly updates the system with the latest tax issues. After inputting nexus information about your store (that is, defining the various geographical areas in which you do business), the system offers the ability to submit through Perl/CGI, Java, and other Web programming languages the information concerning a transaction. The system will report back the taxes to collect and add to the sale. Taxware can also verify address to ZIP code information to ensure that it's applying the correct tax information.

Advanced Customer Service Options

Customer service on the Web is a big issue. The responsiveness to customer service by many retailers on the Web is abysmal. For small stores, the best customer service involves staying on top of incoming email and just working hard to keep customers happy. Larger stores, with a presumed larger amount of customers and more money, have some additional items available for their customer service options.

First and foremost they can consider using some of the higher-end email customer service software.

Another option is to hire a calling center that specializes in customer service handled via email. Companies such as Envisionet (www.envnet.com), which handles email customer service for eToys and several others, can recruit and train a bank of customer service professionals for your store needs. Some of these centers can also make customer service representatives available via phone and chat as well.

To find companies that do outsourced customer service, check out the major call center magazines and Web sites (Table 25.2).

Table 25.2 Call Center Magazines and Web Sites

CallCenterOps	www.callcenterops.com
TMCnet	www.ccsmag.com
CC News	www.ccnews.com
IT Support News	www.servicenews.com
TeleProfessional Magazine	www.teleprofessional.com

Advertising and Promotional Options

As with everything else in this chapter, we assume you have the kind of budget that makes some of the more advanced options available to your store. In the area of promotions and advertising, there are of course more advanced (and more expensive) options to consider than we covered previously in this book.

When it comes to site promotion, your main advanced option is to hire a seasoned PR firm that can help secure reviews, interviews, and news stories about your store. However, there are other options beyond scaling up to a high-end PR firm. I-traffic (www.itraffic.com) is a firm that specializes in building customers for Web sites through a variety of traditional media and online PR tactics. The firm is used by a number of high-end merchants including Beyond.com.

NetCreations (www.netcreations.com) specializes in opt-in email direct marketing. Using its databases of email addresses (called PostMaster Direct), the firm can pinpoint messages and inviting email to customers who have previously asked to be contacted for specific offerings (as opposed to *spam*, which is unsolicited). This could include offerings from your store. Yahoo! also offers similar permission marketing, having bought permission marketing firm Yoyodyne.

Another high-end option is to enable frequent buyer points and other bonus offerings to encourage customers to surf and do other things (especially purchase) on your site. ClickRewards (www.clickrewards.com) lets you offer redeemable points that work together with more than 50 other merchants. Customers can redeem points for merchandise and frequent flyer miles. Another similar program (but one with fewer merchants at the time of this writing) is MyPoints (www.mypoints.com).

Coupon-based promotions are also gaining popularity online. Established merchants mail out coupons to people who have subscribed to their mailing lists or purchased in the past. They do this by maintaining a database that records the customer's most recent purchase and then sending a coupon to those customers who may not have purchased since a specific date, or to customers who have been loyal purchasers.

Advanced Merchandising Options

When it comes to advanced merchandising, the name of the game is providing unique applications that help users shop and make choices. You will recall from Chapter 4 that the process of shopping generally is as follows:

- Seek out the largest possible selection of options.
- Screen products down to top selections.
- Deeply evaluate final possibilities.
- Make final choice.

Advanced merchandising tools are programs and services that help people accelerate the four-part process. It is important to develop services—actual programs that run on your site that give people the tools to shop better. These can include tools that let people compare products, or that let people input desired characteristic ranges (color choice, price range, weight, and so on) and offer results that fit the stated profile.

Other merchandising tools help people overcome the inability to physically evaluate the product. Amazon.com and other stores overcome this online issue by providing tools for people to post reviews for products, including voter ratings and narrative reviews. Offering this is a fairly straightforward process. A database system stores the reviews and programmable scripts, displays them on the product page, or compiles all the votes into summary tallies. Of course, you have to manage this and police it for abuse once it is launched.

Another advanced merchandising service helps you tie products together or provide upselling opportunities. For example you might instruct the server to offer a series of products at a discounted price whenever a customer's order exceeds $100.

You can also make it easier to tie together recommendations on products based on your own knowledge vs. a collaborative filtering process. For example, building a simple way for store managers to tell the server to display a specific shirt that goes well with a pair of pants. Some servers such as BroadVision help you automate this process and others may require custom scripts to be developed to make it possible.

There are thousands of merchandising services and ideas you can translate to the Web. The best way to enable the development of such services is as follows:

- **Build merchandising** that enhances the advantages of online shopping.
- **Evaluate your server choice for flexibility** to develop custom applications and scripts that can make it easy to build robust shopping services.
- **The more individual fields** in your product database, the more types of merchandising tools you can provide for people to sort and manipulate that data.

- **After providing basic tools** to sort through products, to compare products, and to recommend products, move on to merchandising tools that enable people to overcome the physical deficiency of Web stores. This is best done through providing user reviews, comments, and other third-party communication tools for shoppers.

Toward the Fully Integrated Store

The best online stores are the ones that can fully integrate all company systems into the front-end Web site. This way inventory on the site reflects inventory in the warehouse, invoices are generated and sent to accounting, shipping receives its orders, and, if you have EDI messaging for various segments, those messages are also generated and shipped. It can be a daunting process—and be sure to consider that many top online stores for traditional retailers are still not operating in a fully integrated manner with the rest of the store's back end systems, or with other vendor or distributor databases.

Depending on your situation, you either have existing back-end systems or you don't. If you do, integrating your Web store with back-end systems is straightforward in that the coordination is an internal issue to be dealt with. If the systems for inventory that you want to integrate are outside your realm, then you'll have to coordinate with distributors to see if they have systems you can hook into. The advantage of this is that once you've hooked into their systems, you gain the advantage of their information database and the ability to have orders pass automatically through to the distributor level. This enhances the chance to offer items quickly to customers.

At this time in the e-commerce game, not many distributors make their catalogs available simply because they don't have them in a form that is easily shared for Web stores. Over time, expect this problem to lessen. Look for opportunities to combine in-house inventory with distributor-based inventory to offer a wider selection of goods to your users.

Here Comes XML

HTML is a great system to publish written content on the Web, but it does little to help publish content that might actually be more than a written paragraph about a product. Wouldn't it be cool if every piece of descriptive data about a product could be easily tagged as such? For example, you could tag information about a product such as its size, weight, the address of the manufacturer, and more so that the Web browser or another Web application actually knew what this textual information really was. That's what XML enables. XML (Extensible Markup Language) is a framework to embed text information between tags that actually describes what the information really is. HTML only describes what data should look like on a Web page. XML is known as a metadata language—it is data that describes other data.

XML is important to e-commerce because entire industries are coming up with XML frameworks (sometimes known as *schemas*) that are used to describe useful business data within that industry. By creating applications that recognize and can act on this industry specific XML framework, you can enable even more robust stores. For example, an XML framework known as the Open Catalog Format helps companies publish catalogs of items on the Web. These catalogs, which are used mostly for business-to-business, supply procurement, use XML to describe all sorts of extra information about products listed on a page (such as what other items to crosssell with that item), or what the price is for the object so it can be translated into different currencies.

For the most part, XML is a young technology, and the tools and server support for it, such as Microsoft's BizTalk technology (see sidebar), are just coming into play. In addition, the frameworks for different industries are still being worked out and, in some cases, there may be competing proposals to consider.

Most store-builders may never really work directly with XML; instead they may simply use software that makes use of XML to provide more features and better services. Overall, XML is expected to be a critical component for e-commerce and online store-building. In some emerging select cases, you might use it now, but for the most part you should simply begin exploring its possibilities and looking for products and XML frameworks that the specific product areas and industries in which you retail might be using.

Microsoft BizTalk

With XML gaining as a key e-commerce technology, and Microsoft looking to make it easier to integrate frontline e-commerce Web sites with back-end systems, along comes BizTalk. BizTalk is to e-commerce as HTML is to Web publishing—a platform-neutral system to enable the publishing of e-commerce services on the Web.

Right now, though platform-neutral, BizTalk is still very much a Microsoft-focused technology. Partners of Microsoft are supporting it and Microsoft has published the framework for others to adopt, but BizTalk isn't a standard adopted by the Web community as a whole like HTML. BizTalk as a major new e-commerce tool for advanced store-building does warrant further investigation for top-tier store-builders, especially those who use Microsoft's Site Server and other server tools.

The BizTalk system is an Extensible Markup Language (XML) derivative that makes it easier to integrate e-commerce services that might run across different operating systems, different languages, and different software programs, both internally within a company and with outside vendors and partners.

At its core, BizTalk provides a way for different programs and systems to exchange business information. In this sense it is similar to EDI. EDI, although widely used, is still difficult to implement and is often too expensive for smaller vendors. With BizTalk, Microsoft looks to provide the promise of electronic business messaging with an easier to use system similar to other Web languages.

For the most part, BizTalk helps with the integration of your back end-systems that can assist with frontline store development by providing better services to shoppers. This includes more detailed inventory status and the ability to compare products and track current order status.

Developers wanting to work with BizTalk should check out www.biztalk.org. There you will find information about the technology, XML schemas, and the BizTalk jumpstart kit. This kit, which requires Windows NT, IIS, Visual Studio, and some other Microsoft technologies, includes sample code and Web tools that will help you begin investigating how to use BizTalk-enabled technologies to build e-commerce applications.

Summary

You don't have to be a huge company to make use of advanced store-building tactics and products. Even a site with as little as $1 million in annual sales can start to take advantage of services such as PostMaster Direct or can operate its own commerce server such as SiteServer or

Intershop and integrate elements such as TanData Progistics Merchant into their systems. At the same time, new products and services are dropping in price as vendors try to broaden their advanced services to a wider group of merchants. Although you might not have hundreds of thousands of dollars or more to invest in every top-tier option, you should familiarize yourself with the top products today. When you can afford them, or when they drop in price, you will be already armed with the knowledge of where to get those tools and services and what sorts of ideas and technologies separate the mom and pop stores from the BigWebRetailer.coms of the world.

Index

B

C

D

E

F

G

H

I

J

K

L

M

N

O

P

Q

R

S

T

U

V

W

X

Y

Z